*Discovering the Women in Slavery*

# Discovering the

EDITED BY PATRICIA MORTON

The University of Georgia Press : Athens & London

# Women in Slavery

*EMANCIPATING PERSPECTIVES*

*ON THE AMERICAN PAST*

© 1996 by the University of Georgia Press
Athens, Georgia 30602
All rights reserved
Designed by Kathi L. Dailey
Set in PostScript Bulmer by
Tseng Information Systems, Inc.

The paper in this book meets the guidelines for permanence
and durability of the Committee on Production Guidelines
for Book Longevity of the Council on Library Resources.

Printed in the United States of America

00  99  98  97  96      C      5   4   3   2   1

00  99  98            P      5   4   3   2

Library of Congress Cataloging in Publication Data

Discovering the women in slavery : emancipating perspectives
on the American past / edited by Patricia Morton.
p.      cm.
Includes bibliographical references.
ISBN 0-8203-1756-x (alk. paper). — ISBN 0-8203-1757-8
(pbk. : alk. paper)
1. Women slaves — United States — History.    2. Slavery —
United States — History.    3. Women abolitionists — United States —
History.    4. Women — Southern States — History.    5. Afro-American
women — Southern States — History.    I. Morton, Patricia.
E443.D57    1996
975'.00496073 — dc20          95-14154

British Library Cataloging in Publication Data available

*For David, Denise, Neil, and Christi*

# CONTENTS

# ACKNOWLEDGMENTS

*T*HIS BOOK provides a new slavery studies collection that is specifically devoted to the placing of women in American slavery history. Yet while in this sense "new," this book is profoundly indebted to the years of research, dedication, and wealth of studies provided by scholars that now make such a collection both possible and perhaps necessary — and at the least, potentially useful. Indeed, while although even up to the relatively recent past American historiography has still largely portrayed American slavery history as if women's experiences and roles could be subsumed under those of men, by the closing decade of the twentieth century — and especially in concert with the explosion of attention to southern women's history — a host of studies have now brought and are bringing a rich new attention to gender and to how women experienced and shaped slavery history as women.

In this context it seems time to provide a woman-focused collection that brings specific attention to this exciting field of inquiry by presenting studies that both contribute to and illuminate the emancipating new perspectives on American slavery history that are engendered by "discovering the women in slavery."

I am very grateful to those who have provided support and advice to this project, including our Press, its former director, Malcolm Call; managing editor, Kelly Caudle; and copy editor, Elaine Otto. Catherine Clinton deserves special thanks for her warm and useful encouragement.

Above all, I am deeply indebted to the scholars who contributed their rich research, talents, and dedication to this volume. Moreover, these authors have brought a wonderfully shared cooperation with this compiler and editor's goal of making such scholarship accessible and meaningful to a wide audience. Thus, it has truly been an immense pleasure to work with them in what is clearly a shared labor of love.

Finally, my very special personal thanks to my family and especially to David, whose support has been constant, warm, and vital throughout this project as for all that I undertake.

*Discovering the Women in Slavery*

PATRICIA MORTON

# Introduction

SALLY MCMILLEN has written, "For too long, the history of slavery has focused solely on the male experience." As she has also pointed out in her book *Southern Women,* by today "the history of southern women has come into its own."[1] And it is a key goal of *Discovering the Women in Slavery* to illuminate the significance of linking these two fields of inquiry.

By presenting studies that examine slavery and women's histories together, this collection hopes to contribute to the placing of women's history in slavery history. This is both to emphasize the rich contributions of southern women's history to discovering the women in the Old South's "peculiar institution" and to focus more attention on the slavery experiences of women outside of the American South. And this is to emphasize the emancipating new perspectives on the past that are engendered by the exploration of slavery and women's histories together.

The essays presented in this collection examine a variety of women, over time and place, class and race. By showing *how* these women can be discovered—by pointing to the available sources in reader-friendly ways—these studies promote the accessibility of this field of inquiry. Thus, they complement this collection's ability to speak meaningfully to a wide audience. Indeed, this collection is designed to speak not only to scholars but equally to students and general readers who may have little familiarity with slavery history, let alone with the slavery histories of women. For these reasons, this introduction is deliberately historiographical, although it cannot possibly be and is not intended to be comprehensive. What this introduction is intended to do is to contextualize some of the major issues that are raised by placing women in slavery history.

This is to begin by examining what Peter Parish's important synthesis, *Slavery: History and Historians* (1989), has presented as "the modern golden age of the historiography of slavery" and by emphasizing this historiography's continuing and influential exclusion of women. By the "golden age" Parish has pointed to the slavery studies that "came to a climax with the publication of the major studies of John Blassingame, Robert Fogel and Stanley Engerman, Eugene Genovese, Herbert Gutman, and Lawrence Levine during the 1970s." Indeed, these are major historians of what have been known as the "new slavery studies," which as Parish has noted constructed "major reinterpretations of the institution of slavery, and particularly of slave life . . . which have had and will certainly continue to have a pervasive and constructive influence on our understanding of the subject." Certainly this historiography has influenced the endeavor to discover the women in slavery. It also deserves attention from a perspective that asks, in effect, "but where were the women?" [2]

The new slavery studies constituted a major challenge to the dominance in American slavery historiography of U. B. Phillips. This early-twentieth-century southern historian's influential work reflected his beliefs in inherent black racial inferiority. Characterizing southern slavery as an economically unprofitable system for the masters, he portrayed it as a benevolent racial institution that provided for the well-being as well as control of an inherently backward race.[3]

While African American historians had long struggled to present a countervision of black American history, during the immediate post–World War II decades the rejection of Phillips's vision of slavery was newly embraced by white historians who sought to remove racist stereotypes from the told story of the past. Their endeavor was in concert both with the era's civil rights movement and with the new social history's interest in discovering the ordinary people of the past. In this context an expanding number of postwar white as well as black historians turned to discover the experience of the, by 1860, at least four million African Americans who were enslaved, led by Kenneth Stampp's reinterpretation in *The Peculiar Institution* of slavery as a profitable economic system for the masters but a harsh, cruel, and damaging institution for the slaves.[4]

Stanley Elkins's *Slavery* (1959) also emphasized the system's damage by arguing that the South's "Sambo" stereotype reflected the reality that the slave was so damaged by this fundamentally totalitarian institution that he was "infantilized," as one who had internalized the master's views of his inferiority as a permanent "boy." But this book stimulated immense debate and opposition. To seem to support a stereotype that so demeaned the masculinity of black men was especially unacceptable in the context of the contemporary emphasis on a historically assertive African American *manliness.* In this context, the Elkins thesis came under intense attack as forwarding a racist, "emasculating . . . and effeminate image of the Black male."[5]

It would not be until several decades later that someone would ask, "Where were the women . . . in Elkins's theory?" As Deborah Gray White pointed out in her study of slave women, *Ar'n't I a Woman?* (1985), Elkins's book and his thesis were strikingly male-focused. Enslaved women figured very fleetingly and only to show that the slave family was mother-dominated — that is, in the words of contemporary scholars, "matriarchal." Indeed, Elkins was by no means alone in arguing that slavery had left the black family in ruins as a mother-dominated, matriarchal institution that rendered the slave man powerless and emasculated even in his own home. However, it was Elkins's *Slavery* that became a major catalyst for the debate that followed during the 1960s and '70s, as a host of historians set out to restore historical black manhood to health.[6]

Among African American historians, John Blassingame led the challenges to the Elkins thesis in his book *The Slave Community* (1972). This study and many others emphasized the ingenuity and courage with which blacks survived slavery's damage by creating a self-empowering and rich community and cultural life. These revisionist studies especially challenged the conventional portrayal of the ruined slave family as mother-dominated and matriarchal. However, they often seemed to redefine slave health by reconstructing the slave man as the head of the household and community. Thus, as White has pointed out, Blassingame showed "how slave men gained status in the family and slave community, but he did not do the same for women."[7]

Eugene Genovese brought another set of challenges to the Elkins thesis by presenting the peculiar institution as based upon a paternalistic, familylike relationship between the master and slave. In this view, within the southern white family the father's rule as the patriarchal head of the family was fundamentally legitimated by his responsibilities to provide for and protect his dependents, who in slaveholding households included not only his wife and children but also his slaves. Hence, with the duties of his dependents to obey him came their reciprocal rights. Genovese argued that in this context the enslaved were able to carve out spaces in which to shape their own self-empowering institutions and community life.

This "paternalist thesis," however, has inspired considerable controversy.

By interpreting the enslaved as significantly accepting the masters' view of the plantation as a kind of family, this thesis has argued that the master's rule was not fundamentally based upon physical force but rather upon the slave's acceptance of its moral legitimacy. Thus, it has seemed to Robert Harris, for example, that Genovese's worldview still saw slavery "through the slavemasters' lens" and attempted "to strip Ulrich B. Phillips's idea of paternalism from its racism."[8]

Perhaps equally controversial has been Genovese's worldview of southern slave society as a whole. In this view the South's peculiar institution was above all a system of class rule that reflected and maintained the power of the "slaveocracy." By this interpretation, the paternalistic ideology and ethos of the planter elite spread throughout the Old South as a value system supporting the society's hierarchical social order because it emphasized the importance of familylike relationships. Slavery thus created a special, non-bourgeois southern civilization, which distinctively stood against the value system associated with northern society's move toward capitalism, individualism, and market relationships. However, many others have disagreed. For example, James Oakes has argued that Old South society was characterized by its many small slaveholders and middle classes, whose behavior and values point at most to a southern variant of American capitalism.[9]

Yet perhaps most controversial of all the 1970s slavery studies was Robert Fogel and Stanley Engerman's *Time on the Cross* (1974). As J. William Harris has observed, this contributed to "the rise of the 'new economic history'—the application of economic theory and statistical techniques to the study of the past." Their application of quantitative methodology to slavery history also stimulated substantial debate, especially because they presented what they called the "new history" as vastly superior to the "old." By the "old" they pointed to the traditional historical interest in qualitative, literary sources. Arguing that such sources are by nature subjective, biased, and unreliable, they emphasized the importance of numerical and quantifiable data to creating a new scientific history that discovers the truth. In response, such historians as Kenneth Stampp pointed out that "history is not an exact science. . . . Ultimately the . . . data, both numerical and literary, must be subjectively interpreted by the historian, for historical facts do not speak for themselves."[10]

Controversies also raged over Fogel and Engerman's portrayal of slavery as a profitable economic institution that demonstrated the efficiency and productivity of slave labor. In their view, because the master's outlook was fundamentally capitalist, in accordance with his rational economic interests in maximizing labor force productivity, he provided good physical care to the enslaved and positive incentives to hard workers. Hence the slave workforce developed the strong work ethic that made the system so efficient and profitable. However, critics objected that in this interpretation the enslaved seemed to emerge as beneficiaries of the slave system. And as Harris has observed, this "portrayal seemed to show slavery as an even more benign system than the one portrayed by Phillips."[11]

It is important to note, however, that *Time on the Cross* was actually in concert with a slavery historiography that continued to leave the lives and perspectives of women largely opaque. Indeed, the "golden age" studies all marginalized women. This was in concert with their largely shared interpretation of the slave family as father-led—a vision from which the slave family and community often reemerged in a strikingly patriarchal light. Fogel and Engerman's book fully supported this interpretation, at a time when it seemed essential, in Genovese's words, to slay "the legends of the matriarchy, the emasculated . . . male, and the fatherless children," by reconstructing the slave family as "a two-parent, male-centered household."[12]

In this context, although Herbert Gutman was a leading critic of *Time on the Cross,* as Deborah White has pointed out, even his important book, *The Black Family in Slavery and Freedom, 1750–1925,* "made so much of the role of slave men . . . that women's roles were reduced to insignificance and largely ignored. Thus, the emphasis of recent literature on slavery has been on negating Samboism. The male slave's 'masculinity' was restored by putting black women in their proper 'feminine' place." In this context, Jacquelyn Dowd Hall's characterization of the slave studies of the 1960s seems equally applicable to those of the '70s: "The revisionist historians of the 1960s collapsed the categories of race and gender, using the struggle for 'manhood' as the central metaphor for their valorization of African-American culture." Moreover, just as these studies marginalized slave women, so also they rarely mentioned slaveholding women at all. In short, this was a historiography that portrayed slavery fundamentally as if it were a man's world.[13]

*Yet as Peter Kolchin* has pointed out in his synthesis, *American Slavery* (1993), this historiography did "revise radically our understanding of American slavery," especially by discovering the enslaved "as subjects in their own right rather than as objects of white treatment." Indeed, this scholarship "abandoned the victimization model in favor of an emphasis on the slaves' resiliency and autonomy."[14]

Peter Parish has also pointed out that these new slavery studies were "comprehensive, panoramic, or synoptic in their approach." And his praise of these studies has included some important reservations. In his words, in "attempting to treat the subject at large," they tended "to flatten out differences and variations (whether of time or space, or social context or individual personality)."[15]

It becomes clear that this was not a historiography that encouraged attention to pieces that did not fit into its worldviews of slavery as a monolithic entity. Yet as Parish has observed, slavery was replete with "contradictions and paradoxes . . . [as] a growing, changing, mobile, flexible, and variable institution." And as he has warned, "There can be no greater mistake than to regard slavery as monolithic. . . . Slavery was a system of many systems, with numerous exceptions to every rule." Kolchin's synthesis has also emphasized that "antebellum slavery was a heterogeneous institution" and that "human variation belied the rigidity of the system."[16]

Parish has characterized the scholarship of the 1980s as bringing significant challenges to that of the 1970s: "If the seventies were the decade of the grand synoptic overview of the South's 'peculiar institution,' the eighties have been the decade of the in-depth study. . . . [T]he telescope has given way to the microscope." As he has observed, such scholarship has brought a rich new attention to "variations" and to "particular aspects of slavery." Pointing, for example, to studies of urban slaves and of the South's free persons of color, Parish has emphasized the importance of such attention to "the edges of slavery" to raising new questions, for example, "about . . . the rigid structure normally associated with Southern slavery." Yet his own *Slavery* has seemingly failed to notice that what underpinned the special contributions of many 1980s studies to these new ways of exploring slavery history was their close attention to gender and women.[17]

In fact, Parish's comprehensive synthesis was surprisingly noninclusive even of the major 1980s studies of women and slavery that were presented by historians such as Catherine Clinton and Elizabeth Fox-Genovese.[18] Moreover, although southern women's historiography has expanded during the 1990s at a remarkable rate, even Peter Kolchin's useful new synthesis, *American Slavery,* has brought little attention to its contributions to slavery history.[19]

In this context it is important to note that even during the 1970s some historians were pointing to the distinctive slavery experiences and roles of women. Gerda Lerner, for example, provided a pioneering collection of documents and commentary on the history of African American women. And Anne Firor Scott's *Southern Lady* brought a new attention to white slaveholding women.[20]

Scott's book argued that the "Lady" image portraying pampered and "delicate, frivolous, submissive women" was a myth shaped by slavery: "Because they owned slaves and thus maintained a traditional landowning aristocracy, southerners tenaciously held on to the patriarchal family structure. . . . Women, along with children and slaves, were expected to recognize their . . . subordinate place. . . . Any tendency on the part of any of the members of the system to assert themselves against the master threatened the whole, and therefore slavery itself." Thus, this book interpreted slavery and patriarchy as two sides of the same coin.[21]

*The Southern Lady* also argued that the mistress exerted a softening influence on slavery in accordance with her empathy for enslaved women and her often private opposition to slavery. Thus, Scott pointed to the Civil War as a liberating development: "Defeat . . . undermined the patriarchy. Slavery, which had provided the original need for the idea, was gone."[22]

While Scott's interpretations have by no means gone without challenge, her work has been an inspiration for the tremendous expansion of southern women's history during the following decades. Moreover, as Catherine Clinton pointed out in *The Plantation Mistress* (1982), it was time for historians to bring attention to southern women, in light of the "New Englandization" of women's studies.[23]

During the 1960s and 1970s American women's history remained focused on the experience of northeastern, middle-class women, which was often interpreted as a story of "progress" toward sisterhood and women's rights. In contrast, during the 1980s historians such as Clinton argued that it should not be assumed that this dominant story could be applied to the women of the slave South. And Clinton's *Plantation Mistress* pointed to their experience as distinctively shaped by slavery and patriarchy together: "In a biracial slave society where 'racial purity' was a defining characteristic of the master class, total control of the reproductive females was of paramount concern for elite males. Patriarchy was the bedrock upon which the slave society was founded, and slavery exaggerated the pattern of subjugation that patriarchy had established." While this book thus argued that enslaved women and mistresses were together victims of slavery, it also called for a new attention to the "sexual dynamics of slavery."[24]

As Clinton has emphasized, southern slavery was not "simply a system of labor extraction." It was also a system "of sexual and social control" of women and slaves together and a means of production that required the slave labor force to reproduce itself. Pointing to the damaging interventions of masters in the sexual and family lives of slaves as well as the system's licensing of sexual assault upon enslaved women, Clinton's work has challenged interpretations portraying the peculiar institution as based upon paternalism and/or a code of honor.[25]

Paula Giddings has also emphasized that the sexual exploitation of slave women was central to American slavery as a racial institution in which the status of offspring was defined by the status and race of the mother. Even if a black woman's children were fathered by a free white man, if she was a slave, her offspring also were slaves. Thus, "white men could impregnate a Black woman with impunity, and she alone could give birth to a slave. Blacks constituted a permanent labor force and metaphor that were perpetuated through the Black woman's womb." Such historians have drawn attention to the sexual history of slavery. In Clinton's words, "It is essential to place gender and sexuality in the foreground of our portrait of the Old South in order to sharpen our focus on some important areas of exploitation and suffering . . . [and] to understand the critical dynamics of slavery as social system."[26]

Together with the new attention to sex, southern women's historiography has especially brought to slavery history a close new attention to gender as, like race and class, a major tool of analysis. In the words of Elizabeth Fox-Genovese, unlike *sex,* "gender is a social, not a biological, category. . . . Gender relations constitute the foundation of any society and lie at the core of any individual's sense of self. . . . Societies have also tended to promote distinct roles for women and men." Hence "gender constitutes an indispensable category of analysis because it imposes the recognition that to be a woman or a man is to participate in a set of social relations in a specific way."[27]

Fox-Genovese has argued that slavery was a major influence on the gender identities of southern women. Under slavery, southern society remained largely agrarian and rural and the household remained the primary unit of both production and social life, so that southern women had little access to other than familial roles and relationships. Thus in contrast to northern women's expanding individualism and emphasis on the special identity and rights of women, southern women's gender identities remained especially defined by their familial and communal ties. Fox-Genovese's thesis brings southern women's history to the support of the thesis portraying the Old South as a distinctive civilization.[28]

This historian's study *Within the Plantation Household* illustrates another key characteristic of southern women's historiography: its attention to both black and white women together and their relationships with one another. On this basis Fox-Genovese has challenged views that mistresses softened the harshness of slavery. Instead, they "lived—and knew they lived—as privileged members of a ruling class," and they were fundamentally "elitist and racist." Hence, while within the household, slaveholders and enslaved women "shared a world of physical and emotional intimacy," this was a "world of mutual antagonism . . . that frequently erupted in violence, cruelty, and even murder." Finding no support from the mistress, slave women also had no legal protection against sexual assault and no support "for their personal relations as daughters, wives, and mothers." In thus emphasizing the damage of slavery to the gender identities and relations of the enslaved, this historian has eloquently argued that ultimately the slave woman confronted the master's power "in the ultimate loneliness—the absolute opposition of power and submission, of one will to another. In that extreme case, gender counted for little."[29]

In contrast, however, Suzanne Lebsock has pointed to slaveholding women as often forming close bonds with slave women, in concert with a women's culture of personalism that promoted affection for individual slaves and signified that women were "a subversive influence" on slavery. Lebsock's study of free and enslaved women in Petersburg, Virginia, argues that like their northern counterparts, antebellum southern white women were creating a woman-defined value system and culture.[30]

Moreover, Lebsock's portrayal points to a slave society that left at least urban, free black women with enough autonomy to shape their own lives and to define their own identity as women. In this view, the large number of free women of color who remained unmarried reflected the *choices* of women who wished to remain free from patriarchal control. Yet in contrast, Michael Johnson and James Roark have pointed to the sexual imbalance of the South's urban black populations as leaving "eligible marriage partners . . . in short supply."[31]

While the gendered attention thus brought to the "edges" of slavery has shaped new debates, the "centers" of slavery history have also become all the more controversial. For example, while Jane Turner Censer's *North Carolina Planters and Their Children* (1984) brought close attention to women and the family to her analysis of the planter elite, what she found was not any distinctive patriarchal oppression of women. What she found was substantial female autonomy in marriages expressive of romantic love and the sentimentalization of domesticity. Thus, she argued that the slaveholding elite embraced a value system that was not fundamentally different from that of the northern bourgeoisie.[32]

Yet during the 1980s it was especially Deborah Gray White who provided a sustained new attention to enslaved women. Her book *Ar'n't I a Woman?* constituted a significant reinterpretation of the experience of the enslaved, which emphasized that "black males and females did not experience slavery the same way. . . . [W]ithin the institution of racial slavery there were two systems, one for women, the other for men."[33]

White challenged the prevailing portrayal of the slave family as male-led by arguing that this institution was typically matrifocal and that in the slave community relations between the sexes were fundamentally egalitarian. Moreover, her work argued that slave women constructed a supportive female network that underpinned their strong group identity and individual self-esteem. Jacqueline Jones has also maintained that slave women had a strong gender identity. In her view, however, this was shaped especially from their family ties and relationships with men. In contrast, White's interpretation has pointed to slave women as creating a separate world of their own making.[34]

Read together, what emerges from such studies is an expanding sense of women as experiencing slavery as not one but a multitude of worlds. Moreover, during the 1990s the unfolding discovery of the women in southern slavery has pointed all the more to variations, differences, and diversity, in accordance with gender, class, and race and also with time and place. For example, Joan E. Cashin's book *A Family Venture* has pointed to migration to the southwestern frontier as a process that isolated white women from eastern kin and stripped slaves of the protection of paternalism. Thus, the frontier experience emerges in her work as intensifying the harshness and violence of slavery and patriarchy.[35]

Victoria E. Bynum's study of North Carolina women who deviated from and challenged the dominant gender conventions illustrates the expanding interest in examining class as well as regional differences in the histories of southern women. Her *Unruly Women* has focused attention on the struggles of impoverished and marginalized women, as well as on the slave South's intersecting systems of social and sexual control.[36]

Stephanie McCurry's examination of yeoman women has also addressed the question of the relationship of the largely nonslaveholding yeoman class to slavery. While the Old South's yeoman farmers have often been interpreted as the society's democratic majority, McCurry argues that the shared gender definition of *men as masters* of the household created a patriarchal alliance of southern white males. In this context, yeoman women served, in effect, as the slaves of the yeoman farm. Thus, McCurry points to the yeomanry's support of slavery as reflecting their "commitment to hierarchical social relations . . . and slavery . . . in their own households."[37]

Understanding of the divided worlds of white and black southern women has been expanded by those who have joined Catherine Clinton in examining the sexual dynamics of slavery. For example, the work of both Joel Williamson and Nell Irvin Painter brings psychoanalytic theory to explore the relationships between sexual experience and identity. And Darlene Clark Hine points to the cultural results of black women's struggles against slavery's institutionalization of sexual assault upon their identities as well as their bodies.[38]

While several studies have illuminated the dominant racist stereotypes of the slave woman as either a "Mammy" or a sexually licentious "Jezebel," Darlene Clark Hine argues that these women developed "a cult of secrecy, a culture of dissemblance, to protect the sanctity of the inner aspects of their lives." Her attention to the "self-imposed invisibility" of African American women also points to the difficulties and challenges of discovering and reclaiming their history.[39]

Today it is clear that the challenges posed by the endeavor to reconstruct an inclusive southern women's history are addressed by the will and the talent of a host of scholars. Moreover, this scholarship is increasingly accessible. Together with a wealth of new monographs, excellent series have been or are being published: for example, *Black Women in United States History,* edited by Darlene Clark Hine et al., and Carol Bleser's series "Women's Diaries and Letters of the Nineteenth-Century South." And while Sally

McMillen's *Southern Women* has provided a useful synthesis, a new slavery anthology finally has been provided that pays some attention to women: J. William Harris's *Society and Culture in the Slave South*.[40]

Also promoting the accessibility of southern women's history are the several collections that have by now been published. These provide useful guides both to the subjects that are being explored and to the methodologies underpinning the close new attention to the "sensitive areas of personal lives" and the "dynamics of interpersonal relations." Indeed, this is a field that transcends the historiographical distinctions once drawn between private and public—political—life. Instead, private life and personal and familial relations become rich new windows on the larger society. This is a field characterized by a methodological eclecticism that equally values both quantitative and numerical sources, as well as qualitative literary sources in which women wrote directly as women. Moreover, because so many women could not write at all, the reclamation of their histories often requires sensitive and creative reading between the lines of any and all sources that can be found. And as the editors of *The Web of Southern Social Relations* (1985) have observed, "The best analysis draws from all of these approaches."[41]

What also becomes very evident in such collections is the integrally combined analysis and empathy that is brought to reclaiming the history of southern women—and thus brought to slavery history. For example, as editor of *In Joy and in Sorrow: Women, Family, and Marriage in the Victorian South* (1991), Carol Bleser writes that this book's central theme is "not only that slavery crippled the lives of slaves, free blacks, and the poor whites before the Civil War, but that the institution damaged the lives of the husbands, wives, and children of the Old South's planter elite, supposedly the principal beneficiaries of the peculiar institution." Slavery and its legacies were "the poison affecting Southern family life . . . wrecking the private lives of men and women . . . for generations." In short, this is a scholarship that both humanizes slavery history and also demonstrates that slavery and women's histories can only be fully understood together.[42]

Just as, in the words of the editors of *Southern Women: Histories and Identities* (1992), "the histories and identities of antebellum southern women were preeminently shaped by slavery," so also slavery history cannot be fully understood without attention to the experiences and roles of women. Similarly, that the collapse of slavery in the Civil War can only be partially understood without attention to women becomes clear in George Rable's monograph, *Civil Wars: Women and the Crisis of Southern Nationalism,* and in Catherine Clinton and Nina Silber's important collection *Divided Houses: Gender and the Civil War* (1992).[43]

It is now clear that the American Civil War can no longer be understood as simply a military conflict amongst men. As LeeAnn Whites has said, it was "a crisis in gender." That northern antislavery feminists cast the South's peculiar institution as a major assault on the family and the virtue and rights of women promoted the sexualization of a conflict perceived by many southern white men as a test of their manhood—as equated with power over both women and slaves. Moreover, Drew Gilpin Faust has argued that because men away at war could not protect and provide for their women, southern white women increasingly challenged patriarchy and the Confederacy together, promoting the desertion of husbands and sons from the Confederate army. Thus, Faust has daringly suggested that "it may well have been because of its women that the South lost the Civil War."[44]

All of the above discussion, however, is only to point to some of the landmark studies of this historiography in a way that, it is hoped, may contextualize the major themes and questions addressed by the studies presented in this collection, while also demonstrating the rich contributions brought by women's history to slavery history. These are contributions that build upon and expand the themes of the "golden age" historiography. Yet, by bringing gendered and woman-focused lenses to the worldviews constructed by that historiography, these are perspectives that also deconstruct such vast and synoptic portrayals. For example, to views portraying southern slavery as based upon a paternalistic, familylike relationship between master and slave, they bring a close new attention to relationships between mistresses and slave women and between mistresses and masters and, equally significantly, to sexual relations between masters and slave women. And to worldviews portraying the enslaved as creating their own self-empowering institutions and culture, they bring a close attention to how self-empowerment was defined and constructed by slave women as well as by slave men.

In short, it becomes clear that placing women in slavery history brings new perspectives to the past. These are perspectives that both emancipate women's history from slavery's silencing of women's voices and also emancipate American slavery history from the stifling exclusion of half of the population, in a way that frees us all to raise and examine a host of new questions. Thus, it becomes possible to explore what once seemed to be a monolithic institution as instead, in Peter Parish's words, "a growing, changing, mobile, flexible, and variable institution" and "a system of many systems."[45]

In a sense discovering the women in slavery is to replace the telescope with the microscope. Yet the microscope can engender creative new ways of perceiving the macrocosm of slavery by exploring the microcosms within. As Drew Gilpin Faust has noted, for example, "on a microcosmic level, the daily interactions of particular women slaveholders with specific slaves yield a striking vision of the master-slave relationship." Indeed, this is a process of exploration that, by discovering women both as individuals and as members of groups, rediscovers the slavery universe from within by reconstructing its worlds of women.[46]

Melton McLaurin's *Celia* may especially exemplify how this exploration is forwarded by the case study approach that calls attention to individual and particular experience as a way of penetrating the peculiar institution from within. Reclaiming the story of a young slave woman who was hanged for killing her sexually abusive master, McLaurin has shaped Celia's story into a "case study of . . . the moral dilemmas" posed to Southerners by slavery's denial of the humanity of the enslaved: "Her case starkly reveals the relationships of race, gender, and power . . . [and] the manner in which the law was employed to assuage the moral anxiety slavery produced."[47]

Seemingly in contrast is the methodological construct that begins not with the individual but with the experiences of a group. Yet the group study can provide an equally exciting way of penetrating slavery from within. For example, in examining enslaved women and men as members of Louisiana plantation households from 1819 to 1864, Ann Patton Malone's *Sweet Chariot* has shown that while these slaves attempted to construct two-parented nuclear families, the substantial number of households that, over time, were headed by single mother parents were seen by the enslaved themselves as normal and valued family types. Hence in reinterpreting the slave family by discovering the diversity, flexibility, and adaptability of the slave household as a major pillar of slave survival, Malone discovers a society in which diversity and variation were not so much the exception as the norm.[48]

*The studies that* are presented by *Discovering the Women in Slavery* are organized into a case study section and a group study section, in spite of the fact that essays so rich could be organized in a number of ways. Indeed, these studies are significantly representative of the contributions brought by women's history to slavery history, both in the topics and themes they address and expand and in the new questions they raise from gender- and woman-focused perspectives. The exciting methodological eclecticism of this field is also fully exemplified in these essays, ranging from their attention to qualitative sources such as letters, novels, oral history, and court case records—and even to racist local history—to their attention to quantitative or quantifiable sources such as census data and parish records. In this context the case study/group study structure has been chosen simply because together these essays may illustrate and illuminate the major methodological constructs constituted by these different and yet complementary ways of penetrating the universe of slavery.

The first section of this book presents the case study contributions as "Making a Case for Women and Slavery." These studies demonstrate the importance of discovering the inner worlds of women to exploring slavery history from the inside out. The second section, "Worlds of Women and Slavery," calls attention to how group studies reveal and interpret women's worlds of the universe of slavery. Within each of these sections these essays are organized in terms of theme and approach to emphasize the exciting and innovative perspectives that they bring to both slavery and women's histories. And this is to emphasize that what characterizes and unifies these contributions is their deliberate exploration of women and slavery together.

The case study section of this book begins with Virginia Bynum's reconstruction of Rachel Knight as a former slave woman who played a significant role in Mississippian rebellion against the South's Confederacy. As Bynum has found, Rachel's story was profoundly mistold by the local "history" and racist folklore that stigmatized her as the "miscegenous" lover of this rebellion's white male leader. Yet Rachel's mistold story may well argue that the racist taboo against miscegenation was fundamentally against those interracial sexual relationships that, because based on love and desire rather than on force, inherently challenged the integrally related sexual and racial controls of slavery and racism. Certainly Bynum's reclaiming of Rachel's history shows that even such racist sources can be utilized as historical evidence. Indeed, her creative deconstruction of these sources eloquently brings Rachel alive as "the captor, not the prisoner" of her legend. This case study makes a compelling case for the possibility and necessity of discovering the historical agency of even those women most silenced by slavery and racism, thus bringing their stories to penetrate the integrally connected racial and sexual dynamics of slavery.

Carolyn Powell's study of Mira makes an equally eloquent case for the necessity and possibility of breaking the silence about the violent underpinnings of slavery's sexual history. Her essay reconstructs the story of Mira as a slave woman who experienced horrendous sexual abuse and ultimately died at the hands of her master, as a case that demonstrates the sexual violence embedded in slavery. Moreover, both in penetrating the communal silence that allowed the murder of this slave woman and in asking why this master was hanged for her murder, Powell's study illuminates the moral dilemmas and contradictions posed by slavery to southern white society's professed codes of paternalism and honor.

Yet it is crucial to remember that white society included women as well as men. And John Inscoe's study of Mary Bell encourages us to ask to what extent their perspectives on slavery differed; that is, to what extent did gender count? Mary Bell was a somewhat unusual mistress in that, by her own initiative and choice in her husband's absence at war, she became a slaveholder during the Civil War. Thus, it is all the more important to understand the reasons for her choice. Inscoe's findings point to the importance of socioeconomic and class motivations among women as well as men. Mary's case was typical, however, in the sense that like many Confederate women she was left to manage her slaves alone. This study makes a strong case for examining how these women managed, in order to address the question of how Confederate mistresses dealt with their wartime role of maintaining slave control and of whether this was an empowering role.

Wilma King's essay describes their problems with slave control before as well as during the Civil War, by bringing close attention to the daily interactions between Tryphena Blanche Holder Fox and her slave women. Moreover, she argues that the southern "Lady" ideal itself intrinsically shaped embattled relationships between slaveholding and enslaved women. As a northern-born woman of working-class background who married a southern slaveholding man, Tryphena strove especially hard to live up to the Lady ideal, which signified to her that the mistress must always be in firm control of her "maids." This study makes a strong case for focusing on woman-to-woman relations within the household to reveal the conflictuous dynamics of control and resistance that underpinned slavery's day-to-day realities.

What emerges from these case studies are the contradictions and tensions of slavery, as well as a sense of how immensely southern white and black women were divided by class, race, and racialized constructions of gender. In this context it becomes all the more ironic and tragic that northern antislavery white feminists emphasized the inherent sisterhood of all women and that, as Margaret Kellow's case study of Lydia Maria Child shows, they also constructed and supported racialized and stereotypical constructions of black womanhood. In the context of their essentialist constructions of the moral superiority of "true womanhood," Child's emphasis on the equality of women as individuals was distinctive. Yet as Kellow shows, this leading abolitionist-feminist's portrayals of slave women as either helpless victims of white male sexual lust and/or as paragons of female sexual and moral virtue ironically reflected and shaped the same stereotypical conceptualizations of black womanhood that Child challenged with respect to white womanhood. Thus, Child emerges as a case that demonstrates the importance of bringing attention both to the North's feminist-abolitionists' influence in sexualizing the conflict over slavery and to the immense contradictions that underpinned this group's own perceptions and constructions of enslaved and black womanhood.

Kellow's case study thus helps to bridge the seeming gap between case and group studies in a way that illuminates the potential complementarity of these different approaches to the past. Indeed, while the *group studies* section of this collection points to the commonalities and universalities of women's experiences of slavery history, like the case study approach these group studies equally encourage our attention to historical particularities. Thus, while the group study section examines women as members of groups, each of the groups thus discovered reveals both the particularities and the diversity of women's worlds of slavery.

In this context, the group study section is led off by David Sheinin's essay on Connecticut and New England slave women. He emphasizes the importance of discovering an inclusive slavery history. By bringing particular attention to the continuing historiographical invisibility of Connecticut's enslaved women, Sheinin explains why New England slave women have wrongly remained so undiscovered. While American women's history has been overly "New Englandized," Sheinin's essay argues that perhaps slavery history has not been sufficiently New Englandized.

Closely examining the exclusion of Connecticut slave women from the state's historiography, Sheinin analyzes the barriers to their discovery as including the double invisibility of gender and race, as well as the regionalist myths portraying Connecticut and New England as leading the struggle against slavery. The same self-serving regional perspectives that emphasized

Yankee racial progressivism also cast slavery as the South's "peculiar institution." Moreover, Sheinin argues that ironically today's historians may continue to portray American slavery as a peculiarly southern plantation institution. This is a point well taken. And this collection is intended to encourage that much more attention be brought to the experience of early American and nonplantation slave women.

Indeed, Kimberly Hanger's study of New Orleans free and enslaved women of color reminds us that women were experiencing enslavement throughout the colonial era, long before slavery became the South's "peculiar institution." Her attention to the Spanish period of Louisiana history also makes an important case for examining the experience of women in a culture in which race was not defined in terms of black and white. Her essay argues that a society that manifested complex distinctions of color provided many more avenues to freedom than were available in an Old South dominated by Anglo-American culture. And as she points out, free women of color in early New Orleans were often able to accumulate considerable property and to protect their property and rights. Yet, in pointing to the intersecting worlds of free and enslaved women of color, this essay also clarifies that the property held by free women often included enslaved women. Thus, Hanger's findings warn against bringing judgmental, presentist perspectives to a group who had to struggle hard for their tenuous socioeconomic status. In several ways, this study complements Michael Johnson and James Roark's examination of antebellum free black Southerners in their book *Black Masters.*[49]

Bringing New Orleans's women forward in time into the antebellum South, Virginia Meacham Gould's study makes a strong case for analyzing how the urban environment shaped the experience of nonplantation slave women. Her findings point to a context that, in promoting skilled female labor and the practice of hiring out slaves, allowed this group of women to create "a cohesive community away from the supervision of their masters and mistresses." Yet this study points out that while their world was more autonomous than that of plantation women, with their gains came costs that were especially damaging to their ability to form a stable family life.

Cynthia Lynn Lyerly's essay then encourages attention to a quite different way of discovering the worlds of slave women. By examining the religious experience of early black Methodist women, she makes a significantly pathbreaking case for the importance of exploring women's spiritual culture. While most studies of slave religiosity have tended to portray this as if it were gender neutral, Lyerly's analysis argues that their gender shaped the religious perspectives of slave women. Asking why they embraced a patriarchal church and faith, she points to their shaping of this into an institution that provided secular as well as sacred supports for their worth and rights as women, especially as mothers. Thus, this essay points to women's spiritual culture as providing a rich new way of rediscovering slavery from the inside out.

In seeming contrast, Patricia Hunt makes a strong case for examining material culture as a new window on the worlds of women and slavery. Yet like Lyerly and many of the contributors to this collection, Hunt also points to the struggle of even the most oppressed women for historical agency. Her study argues that although the South's plantation slave women were generally provided with uniform fabrics and clothing, they creatively converted these into expressions of their personal tastes. This historian's visual evidence also enriches her innovative use of clothing and self-adornment as historical artifacts testifying to the struggles of African American women to express their feminine self-identity both under and after slavery.

As Peter Kolchin has pointed out, by the outbreak of the Civil War, "about one-quarter of Southern slaves lived on very small holdings of 1 to 9, one half lived on middle-range holdings of 10 to 49, and one-quarter lived on large estates of 50 or more slaves."[50] Thus, it becomes clear that there was no typical plantation slave woman. In this context, Marie Jenkins Schwartz's study brings an important attention to comparing the experiences of slave women as mothers on units of various sizes. Her findings argue that both on the plantation and farm slave women were able to shape their own world of motherhood. While for the master, profit and paternalism constituted competing motivations, these women found in this competition ways of carving out a space for some autonomy in their mothering of their infants. Thus, while this study testifies to the importance assigned to good parenting by slaves, it also makes an innovative case for examining slave motherhood as a way of understanding slavery as *both* an economic and a paternalistic institution.

Read together, these group studies point to the striking diversity of enslaved women's worlds. They may also point to slavery as variegated and open enough that these women were able to carve some self-empowerment out of both the system's variations and contradictions. Yet Hélène Lecaudey reminds us that while by no means merely powerless victims, these women shared a world of extreme sexual vulnerability. Moreover, she argues that their vulnerability can be discovered in their own memories, that is, in the ex-slave narratives recorded by the New Deal's Works Progress Administration interviewers. Lecaudey maintains that the voices of ex-slave women can be garnered from these oral history sources by careful textual analysis that brings close attention to the dynamics of gender and race in the interviews. She finds that ex-slave women's own voices can thus be discovered as rich testimonials of collective memories passed down from mother to daughter, from woman to woman—memories that illuminate the dark, sexual side of slavery history.

Thus, it is important to readdress the question of how the Old South's slaveholding women lived with an institution that so assaulted enslaved womanhood. And as McLaurin's case study of Celia emphasizes, it is important to examine the moral anxiety and dilemmas that were produced by the peculiar institution. In this context, Marli Weiner's group study makes an eloquent case for expanding this attention by examining the moral dilemmas underpinning the world of elite white women and plantation mistresses.

In comparison with portrayals of these women as a privileged group who appreciated that their class privileges were based upon slavery, Weiner's findings argue that their moral dilemmas were for them often painfully compounded by their class. As elite and literate women they were the targets of propaganda about how southern ladies should behave. Thus, they were besieged by the gender ideology prescribing that as the "gentler sex" and as the counterparts of paternalist masters, they should treat the enslaved with maternal protectiveness and benevolence. And by bringing close attention to how and why their actual behavior contradicted this ideology of womanhood, Weiner's study engenders a new window on the moral contradictions of slavery.

On the other hand, Lauren Ann Kattner's essay encourages us to remember that most slaveholding women were not elite plantation mistresses. Moreover, this study makes a pathbreaking case for examining the influence of ethnicity and ethnic heritage on the experience of southern white women. Focusing on German American women, Kattner argues that as a group these women brought distinctive attitudes to slavery. She maintains that in accordance with the German traditions of servitude and the republican ideals of the German revolutions, many German-American women viewed and treated their slave women fundamentally as servants rather than as slaves. Thus, in this view these slaveholding and enslaved women were able to share a workaday world that did not render their day-to-day interactions inherently incompatible and conflictuous.

In contrast to Kattner's argument, however, read together, most of the essays comprising this collection argue that to place women in slavery history demonstrates that slavery was inherently conflicted. On the other hand, like Kattner's study, together these contributions argue that to discover the worlds of women and slavery is above all to discover a remarkable diversity. And in this context perhaps a key question that emerges is how to explain the existence of such diversity in the midst of an institution that needed to promote the homogeneity and conformity of all to its dictates and needs. Thus, readers are especially encouraged to consider this question for themselves.

It is my own view that perhaps a central underlying theme that emerges in this collection is that slavery engendered conflict and diversity together. This is to suggest first that this collection's contributions illuminate what Peter Parish has described as the institution's "multifaceted character and . . . inner tensions and contradictions" and also argue that these tensions and contradictions were especially experienced by the black and white women who were simultaneously pushed together by the slave system into the household and driven apart into separate and antagonistic worlds. Moreover, as Drew Gilpin Faust has pointed out, their conflicts may provide especially rich windows into the power relations and politics of slavery, because "the very domesticity of slavery in the Old South, its imbeddedness in the social relations of the plantation or yeoman household, made those households central to the most public, most political aspects of regional life."[51]

Yet as many of the studies presented by this collection demonstrate, women also struggled to shape their own worlds outside of the household context. And Peter Parish has pointed to another way of explaining the diverse worlds—in his words, "compartments"—that were created by slavery. In this view, "whites and blacks, masters and slaves learned to live with slavery by learning to live a lie. They divided their lives into compartments, . . . evaded rather than confronted some of the inherent contradictions of slave society, and blurred the harsh lines of the system by bargain and compromise."[52]

Yet *Discovering the Women in Slavery* does not point to the worlds of women as constructed out of living a lie. These studies may point, instead, to women's confrontations with slavery's contradictions and lies, as underpinning their struggles to construct worlds that expressed their own diverse perspectives, needs, and identities. And in this context perhaps what emerges as one of slavery's greatest tragedies is that these same struggles have so often been expressed as conflicts of woman against woman.

## NOTES

1. Sally McMillen, *Southern Women: Black and White in the Old South* (Arlington Heights, Ill.: Harlan Davidson, 1992), 3, 2.

2. Peter J. Parish, *Slavery: History and Historians* (New York: Harper and Row, 1989), x, 6, 9. Because the monographs of the "golden age" of slavery studies remained noninclusive of women, so also did the influential collections of slavery studies that were available to teachers and students. For an example of a contemporary slavery anthology that, although providing regularly updated editions, still left women virtually invisible, see Allen Weinstein, Frank Otto Gatell, and David Sarasohn, eds., *American Negro Slavery: A Modern Reader,* 3d ed. (New York: Oxford University Press, 1979).

3. Ulrich Bonnell Phillips, *American Negro Slavery: A Survey of the Supply, Employment and Control of Negro Labor as Determined by the Plantation Regime* (1918; reprint, Baton Rouge: Louisiana State University Press, 1987).

4. See, for example, W. E. B. Du Bois, *The Gift of Black Folk: The Negroes in the Making of America* (Boston: Stratford, 1924), and *Black Reconstruction in America: An Essay toward a History of the Past Which Black Folk Played in the Attempt to Reconstruct Democracy in America, 1860–1880* (1935; reprint, New York: Russell and Russell, 1956); John Hope Franklin, *From Slavery to Freedom* (1956; reprint, New York: Knopf, 1964); Kenneth Stampp, *The Peculiar Institution* (New York: Vintage Books, 1956).

5. Stanley M. Elkins, *Slavery: A Problem in American Institutional and Intellectual Life* (1959; reprint, Chicago: University of Chicago Press, 1968); Roy Simon Bryce-Laporte, "Slaves as Inmates, Slaves as Men," in *The Debate over Slavery: Stanley Elkins and His Critics,* ed. Ann J. Lane (Urbana: University of Illinois Press, 1971), 274.

6. Deborah Gray White, *Ar'n't I a Woman? Female Slaves in the Plantation South* (New York: W. W. Norton, 1985), 20–21. By today a host of scholars have challenged the "Black Matriarchy" mythology. For discussion of the origins and development of this especially damaging interpretation of the black family and black womanhood, see, for example, Patricia Morton, *Disfigured Images: The Historical Assault on Afro-American Women* (Westport, Conn.: Greenwood Press, 1991).

7. John Blassingame, *Slave Testimony* (Baton Rouge: Louisiana State University Press, 1977), and *The Slave Community* (1972; reprint, New York: Oxford University Press, 1979). See also Sterling Stuckey, "Through the Prism of Folklore: The Black Ethos in Slavery," in *Black and White in American Culture,* ed. Jules Chametzky and Sidney Kaplan (New York: Viking Press, 1971), 172–91; Lawrence W. Levine, *Black Cul-*

*ture and Black Consciousness: Afro-American Folk Thought from Slavery to Freedom* (New York: Oxford University Press, 1977); and Albert J. Raboteau, *Slave Religion: The "Invisible Institution" in the Antebellum South* (New York: Oxford University Press, 1978). White, *Ar'n't I a Woman?* 21.

8. Eugene Genovese's views have been presented in a host of publications. However, they may be especially discovered in his book *The World the Slaveholders Made* (New York: Vintage/Random House, 1971), and in his *Roll, Jordan, Roll: The World the Slaves Made* (New York: Vintage/Random House, 1976). Robert Harris, "Coming of Age: The Transformation of Afro-American Historiography," *Journal of Negro History* 67 (1982): 120. See also James Anderson, "Aunt Jemima in Dialectics: Genovese on Slave Culture," *Journal of Negro History* 61 (1976).

9. James Oakes, *The Ruling Race: A History of American Slaveholders* (New York: Knopf, 1982). See also Edward Pessen, "How Different from Each Other Were the Antebellum North and South?" in *American Historical Review* 85 (1980): 1119-48.

10. Robert Fogel and Stanley Engerman, *Time on the Cross: The Economics of American Negro Slavery*, 2 vols. (Boston: Little, Brown, 1974); J. William Harris, *Society and Culture in the Slave South* (London: Routledge, Chapman, and Hall, 1992), 3; Kenneth Stampp, "Introduction: A Humanistic Perspective," in *Reckoning with Slavery: A Critical Study in the Quantitative History of American Negro Slavery,* ed. Paul A. David, Herbert G. Gutman, Richard Sutch, Peter Temin, and Gavin Wright (New York: Oxford University Press, 1976), 1.

11. Harris, *Society and Culture,* 4.

12. Genovese, *Roll, Jordan, Roll,* 450, 493.

13. Herbert G. Gutman, *Slavery and the Numbers Game: A Critique of* Time on the Cross (Urbana: University of Illinois Press, 1975); Gutman, *The Black Family in Slavery and Freedom, 1750-1925* (New York: Random House, 1977); White, *Ar'n't I a Woman?* 21-22; Jacquelyn Dowd Hall, "Partial Truths: Writing Southern Women's History," in *Southern Women: Histories and Identities,* ed. Virginia Bernhard, Betty Brandon, Elizabeth Fox-Genovese, and Theda Perdue (Columbia: University of Missouri Press, 1992), 14.

14. Peter Kolchin, *American Slavery, 1619-1877* (New York: Hill and Wang, 1993), 136, 137.

15. Parish, *Slavery,* x, 97.

16. Ibid., 3, 4, 5, 6; Kolchin, *American Slavery,* 62, 99.

17. Parish, *Slavery,* 97-98 and chap. 7, "Slavery and Southern White Society," 124-48.

18. Ibid., x, 9; see 91-92 for brief reference to Deborah Gray White's *Ar'n't I a Woman?* Excluded from attention are, for example, Catherine Clinton, *The Plantation Mistress: Woman's World in the Old South* (New York: Pantheon Books, 1982); Suzanne Lebsock, *The Free Women of Petersburg: Status and Culture in a Southern Town, 1784-*

*1860* (New York: W. W. Norton, 1985); Minrose C. Gwin, *Black and White Women of the Old South: The Peculiar Sisterhood in American Literature* (Knoxville: University of Tennessee Press, 1985); and Elizabeth Fox-Genovese, *Within the Plantation Household: Black and White Women of the Old South* (Chapel Hill: University of North Carolina Press, 1988).

C. Vann Woodward and Elisabeth Muhlenfeld, *The Private Mary Chesnut: The Unpublished Civil War Diaries* (New York: Oxford University Press, 1984), is mentioned in Parish's synthesis as a well-known source "presenting white views of slavery and Southern society," 187.

19. Kolchin, *American Slavery*, 123-24, 140. Kolchin's bibliography does include two brief sections on women's history, one pointing to a few sources on enslaved women and the other to some studies of white women, 275, 283.

20. Gerda Lerner, ed., *Black Women in White America* (New York: Vintage Books, 1973); Anne Firor Scott, *The Southern Lady: From Pedestal to Politics, 1830–1930* (Chicago: University of Chicago Press, 1970).

21. Scott, *Southern Lady*, 36, 16-17.

22. Ibid., 50-51, 96. See also Anne Firor Scott, "Woman's Perspective on the Patriarchy in the 1850s," *Journal of American History* 61 (1974): 52-64.

23. Clinton, *Plantation Mistress*, xv.

24. Ibid., 6, 188, and chap. 11, "The Sexual Dynamics of Slavery," 199-231.

25. Catherine Clinton, " 'Southern Dishonor': Flesh, Blood, Race, and Bondage," in *In Joy and in Sorrow: Women, Family and Marriage in the Victorian South, 1830–1900,* ed. Carol Bleser (New York: Oxford University Press, 1991), 53, 54, 57; Bertram Wyatt-Brown, *Southern Honor: Ethics and Behavior in the Old South* (New York: Oxford University Press, 1982).

26. Paula Giddings, *When and Where I Enter: The Impact of Black Women on Race and Sex in America* (New York: William Morrow, 1984), 39; Catherine Clinton, "Caught in the Web of the Big House: Women and Slavery," in *The Web of Southern Social Relations: Women, Family, and Education,* ed. Walter J. Fraser Jr., R. Frank Saunders Jr., and Jon L. Wakelyn (Athens: University of Georgia Press, 1985), 32.

27. Fox-Genovese, *Plantation Household*, 29, 49, 39.

28. Ibid.; see also Fox-Genovese, "Family and Female Identity in the Antebellum South: Sarah Gayle and Her Family," in Bleser, *In Joy and in Sorrow*, 15-31.

29. Fox-Genovese, *Plantation Household*, 35, 47-48, 326-27, 29, 333.

30. Suzanne Lebsock, *Free Women of Petersburg*, 138, 234.

31. Ibid., esp. 89-90; James L. Roark and Michael P. Johnson, "Strategies of Survival: Free Negro Families and the Problem of Slavery," in Bleser, *In Joy and in Sorrow*, esp. 91-92.

32. Jane Turner Censer, *North Carolina Planters and Their Children, 1800–1860* (Baton Rouge: Louisiana State University Press, 1984). Also illuminating affection and

female autonomy in southern white family relations are, for example, Daniel Blake Smith, *Inside the Great House: Planter Family Life in Eighteenth-Century Chesapeake Society* (Ithaca: Cornell University Press, 1980); and Steven M. Stowe, *Intimacy and Power in the Old South: Ritual in the Lives of the Planters* (Baltimore: Johns Hopkins University Press, 1987). For studies emphasizing the patriarchal nature of the white southern family see, for example, Orville Burton, *In My Father's House Are Many Mansions: Family and Community in Edgefield, South Carolina* (Chapel Hill: University of North Carolina Press, 1985), and Jean Friedman, *The Enclosed Garden: Women and Community in the Evangelical South, 1830–1900* (Chapel Hill: University of North Carolina Press, 1985).

33. White, *Ar'n't I a Woman?* 62.

34. Jacqueline Jones, *Labor of Love, Labor of Sorrow: Black Women, Work, and the Family from Slavery to the Present* (New York: Basic Books, 1985).

35. Joan E. Cashin, *A Family Venture: Men and Women on the Southern Frontier* (New York: Oxford University Press, 1991).

36. Victoria E. Bynum, *Unruly Women: The Politics of Social and Sexual Control in the Old South* (Chapel Hill: University of North Carolina Press, 1992).

37. Stephanie McCurry, "The Politics of Yeoman Households in South Carolina," in *Divided Houses: Gender and the Civil War,* ed. Catherine Clinton and Nina Silber (New York: Oxford University Press, 1992), 36–37. While yeoman women have otherwise received little attention as yet, see, for example, Keith L. Bryant, "The Role and Status of the Female Yeomanry in the Antebellum South: The Literary View," in *Southern Quarterly* 18 (winter 1980): 73–88, and D. Harland Hagler, "The Ideal Woman in the Antebellum South: Lady or Farmwife?" *Journal of Southern History* 46 (August 1980): 405–18.

38. For example, Clinton, "Caught in the Web of the Big House"; Joel Williamson, *A Rage for Order: Black-White Relations in the American South since Emancipation* (New York: Oxford University Press, 1986); Nell Irvin Painter, "Of *Lily,* Linda Brent, and Freud: A Non-Exceptionalist Approach to Race, Class, and Gender in the Slave South," *Georgia Historical Quarterly* 76 (summer 1992): 241–59; and Darlene Clark Hine, "Rape and the Inner Lives of Southern Black Women: Thoughts on the Culture of Dissemblance," in Bernhard et al., *Southern Women,* 177–89.

39. See, for example, White, *Ar'n't I a Woman?* 28–29; and Cheryl Thurber, "The Development of the Mammy Image and Mythology," in Bernhard et al., *Southern Women,* 87–108.

Clark Hine, "Rape," 182–83.

40. For a useful introduction to such sources and series, see Catherine Clinton, "In Search of Southern Women's History: The Current State of Academic Publishing," *Georgia Historical Quarterly* 76 (summer 1992): 420–27. See also this special issue of the *Georgia Historical Quarterly* on "The Diversity of Southern Gender and Race: Women in Georgia and the South" for a useful collection of articles and reviews. A thought-provoking historiographical discussion is provided by Jacquelyn Dowd Hall, "Partial

Truths: Writing Southern Women's History," in Bernhard et al., *Southern Women,* 11–29.

41. Fraser, Saunders, and Wakelyn, *Web of Southern Social Relations,* xii.

42. Bleser, *In Joy and in Sorrow,* xii. See also Paul Finkelman, ed., *Women and the Family in a Slave Society* (New York: Garland, 1989).

43. Bernhard et al., *Southern Women,* 5; George C. Rable, *Civil Wars: Women and the Crisis of Southern Nationalism* (Urbana: University of Illinois Press, 1989).

44. LeeAnn Whites, "The Civil War as a Crisis in Gender," in Clinton and Silber, *Divided Houses,* 3–21; Drew Gilpin Faust, "Altars of Sacrifice: Confederate Women and the Narratives of War," *Journal of American History* 76 (March 1990): 199.

45. Parish, *Slavery,* 4, 5.

46. Drew Gilpin Faust, " 'Trying to Do a Man's Business': Slavery, Violence, and Gender in the American Civil War," *Gender and History* 4 (summer 1992): 198.

47. Melton A. McLaurin, *Celia, a Slave* (Athens: University of Georgia Press, 1991), x, ix, xii.

48. Ann Patton Malone, *Sweet Chariot: Slave Family and Household Structure in Nineteenth-Century Louisiana* (Chapel Hill: University of North Carolina Press, 1992), 271.

49. Michael P. Johnson and James L. Roark, *Black Masters: A Free Family of Color in the Old South* (New York: W. W. Norton, 1984). These historians have pointed to the increasingly tenuous status of free blacks in the antebellum South, a biracial slave society that sought either to exterminate or to enslave them.

50. Kolchin, *American Slavery,* 101.

51. Parish, *Slavery,* 6; Drew Gilpin Faust, " 'Trying to Do a Man's Business,' " 198.

52. Parish, *Slavery,* 1, 2, 3.

# *1* *Making a Case for Women and Slavery*

VICTORIA E. BYNUM

# Misshapen Identity

## MEMORY, FOLKLORE, AND THE

## LEGEND OF RACHEL KNIGHT

I N DECEMBER 1948, the Jones County Circuit Court of Ellisville, Mississippi, debated the identity of Rachel Knight, a woman who had been dead for fifty-nine years. At stake was the fate of her twenty-four-year-old great-grandson, Davis Knight, who was on trial for the crime of miscegenation. Davis, in physical appearance a white man, had married Junie Lee Spradley, a white woman, on April 18, 1946. Whether Davis was white or black, and therefore innocent or guilty of marrying across the color line, hinged on the racial identity of a distant ancestor whom he had never met, but who still excited the memories of the older citizens of Jones, Jasper, and Covington Counties in southeastern Mississippi.[1]

For four days in the Ellisville courthouse, Davis Knight's neighbors and relatives argued whether Rachel Knight was a Creole, an Indian, or "just an old Negro." Of special interest to the court was Rachel's relationship to Newton Knight, the legendary leader of Mississippi's most notorious band of deserters during the Civil War. In 1948, however, the state of Mississippi expressed no interest in Newton Knight's Civil War exploits, only in the intermarriages of his daughter Mollie and son Mat with Rachel's son Jeff and daughter Fannie. These marriages, contracted around 1878, began the mixed-race community of "white Negroes" into which Davis Knight was born; thus, both Newton Knight and Rachel Knight were his ancestors.[2]

Several witnesses testified at Davis Knight's trial that Newton Knight, his wife Serena, and their children, Mollie and Mat, were of the "pure white race." Indeed, the state's major witness at the trial was Newton and Serena's "pure white" son Tom, who had published a sympathetic account of his

29

father's Civil War activities two years earlier. The witnesses hotly debated, however, Rachel's racial identity and her relationship to the white Knight family.[3]

Long before and after their deaths, Rachel and Newton Knight captured the attention of southern Mississippians. Gossipmongers speculated that Rachel, the former slave of Newton's grandfather, had been more than simply Newton's accomplice in his actions against the Confederacy, that the two had been lovers and had produced mixed-race children.[4] After all, Rachel shared Newton's surname, property, and, in death, his private cemetery.

In the increasingly segregated postbellum South, such intimacy aroused suspicions of forbidden sexual behavior. Indeed, Jacquelyn Dowd Hall argues that by the 1920s the public's obsession with interracial sexual relations amounted to a well-entrenched "folk pornography" that underwrote violent systems of racial and sexual domination. Between 1890 and 1920, white southern literature—especially newspapers—commonly portrayed interracial sexual relations as the result of sex-crazed black "fiends" ravishing innocent virginal blondes, rather than white men raping black women or blacks and whites participating in consensual sexual relations.[5]

For defeated white Confederates who began their return to power during Reconstruction, the alleged lust of black men for white women provided a further pretext to impose racial segregation and restrict the political and social rights of African Americans.[6] Most whites were too horrified by tales of racial violence and lust to question their veracity, and most blacks did not dare to challenge the source of such stories.

Those Southerners who dared campaign for laws against lynching, however, understood that the "protection" white lynch mobs provided white women against ravishment by black men served a larger purpose. Such was the case of black feminist Ida Wells Barnett and her white counterpart, Jessie Daniel Ames. They recognized that lynch mob protection controlled African Americans through terror and white women through enforced helplessness.[7]

In 1922, in the midst of rigid racial segregation, Newton Knight died. Despite Mississippi's five decades of pro-Confederate, white supremacy campaigns, he died an unrepentant foe of "Johnny Reb," surrounded, as he had been since 1880, by his mixed-race kin. In his obituary, the *Ellisville Progressive* lamented that he had "ruined his life and future by marrying a negro woman," although no proof of such a marriage existed.[8]

By the time Newton died, Rachel had been dead for thirty-three years. Then, in 1948, twenty-six years after Newton's death, the marriage of Davis Knight and Junie Lee Spradley revived the old rumors and scandals that had long plagued the numerous branches of the Knight family. The jury of the Jones County Circuit Court decided that Davis Knight's descent from Rachel Knight did indeed make him a Negro, and it accordingly convicted him of miscegenation. The judge sentenced him to five years imprisonment in the state penitentiary.[9]

In November 1949, however, the Mississippi Supreme Court reversed the lower court's decision, ruling that it had failed "to prove beyond all reasonable doubt that the defendant had one-eighth or more negro blood." Since Mississippi law held that one-eighth or more African ancestry made one a Negro, Rachel would had to have been full-blooded African—something no witness could prove and several effectively disputed—in order for Davis to be an African American. The high court thus proclaimed Davis Knight legally white.[10]

The customary method of defining one's race differed, however, from the legal one. To most white Mississippians, many of whom believed a blood test could determine the proportions of one's "African" or "European" blood, a single drop of "tainted" African blood sufficed to make one black. Many whites considered even living among African Americans grounds for being socially defined as one.[11] Thus, although Davis Knight's legal ordeal was over, the local debate over the "purity" of the Knight family's blood raged on.

Two years after the state supreme court's decision, Newton Knight's grandniece, Ethel Knight, published *The Echo of the Black Horn,* a sensationalized "history" of Newton Knight that thinly disguised her effort to discredit Newton Knight's anti-Confederate uprising and rid the white branches of the Knight family of the taint of miscegenation. Touting her book as "an authentic tale" of "the free state of Jones," she dedicated it to "the memory of the Noble Confederates who lived and died for Jones County."[12] Her version of Jones County's Civil War uprising displaced Tom Knight's earlier *Life and Activities of Captain Newton Knight and His Company and the "Free State of Jones County"* (1946) as the "true" story of Newton Knight.

Ethel Knight cleverly gained Tom Knight's endorsement of her version of his father's life by showcasing Tom's bitter denunciation of his father's interracial relations on the dust jacket of *The Echo of the Black Horn.* The former storekeeper was over ninety years old and still peddling pencils, chewing

gum, candy bars, and copies of his book on the streets of Laurel.[13] Tom
Knight reportedly told Ethel that through God's help he had lived down
"the disgrace and the shame that my father heaped upon me when he went
to the Niggers!" Since he was "soon to die," Tom allegedly authorized her
"to tell it all, the whole truth about my father." Presumably, Tom had omitted
Rachel Knight from his own book out of shame, but the public trial of Davis
Knight had exposed this shame. The truth must now be told. Even old Tom
agreed.[14]

Ethel conceded that interracial marriages occurred between the children
of Newton Knight and Rachel Knight, but she seized the opportunity to
shape the events that preceded and followed these marriages. In her hands,
Rachel became a cunning, seductive, mulatto "Jezebel" who could not identify the fathers of her several white-skinned children.[15] Unlike Tom Knight,
whose book portrayed his father as a principled Robin Hood, Ethel portrayed Newton as a murderous Civil War outlaw whose wrongheaded rebellion against the Confederacy alienated all but a few of his neighbors and
relatives. According to Ethel, it was his increasing isolation from respectable society that pushed him ever closer to Rachel, who had provided him
crucial aid in resisting the Confederacy. After the Civil War, she revealed,
the two outcast Knight families, white and black, lived together on Newton's
land. The children of Rachel and Newton later intermarried, thus laying the
mixed-race foundations for Davis Knight's later miscegenation trial.[16]

Ethel Knight's fantastic "history" is a tangle of family memories, oral and
documentary history, and the racist catechism taught to New South school-
children during her girlhood.[17] She set out to dissociate those branches of the
Knight family descended from Newton's brothers and cousins from those descended from the children of Newton and Rachel Knight. Indeed, to further
quash rumors of the Knight family's "impure blood," Ethel claimed that except for Davis Knight the descendants of the mixed-race couples had "all left
the country and moved where they were not known, and married white." She
assured her readers that "there are no mixed people living today [in Jones,
Covington, and Jasper Counties] who have in them Knight blood." In other
words, with the exception of Davis Knight, the family's blood was "pure."[18]

Unwittingly, Ethel Knight breathed life into the long-buried story of
Rachel Knight. The Newton Knight rebellion has been told in histories,
folklore, fiction, and film, but all have erased Rachel from the drama. Early
chroniclers of the legend practiced a genteel silence in regard to this tale of

interracial intimacy in the slaveholding and segregated South. More recent historians who have mainly viewed the uprising through the narrow lens of battles and conflicts between white men probably concluded that Rachel was irrelevant to the "real" story of the Piney Woods uprising.

Rachel, like so many southern women who participated directly in the Civil War, must be included in the war's narratives. As historians increasingly focus their research on the homefront rather than the battlefield, on intraregional conflicts rather than just the conflict between the Union and the Confederacy, women like Rachel emerge center stage, vitally engaged in the struggles of war.[19]

In her effort to defuse an old scandal brought to life by Davis Knight's trial, Ethel Knight not only restored Rachel's historical role but she unveiled a powerful, larger-than-life woman who had endured slavery, sexual exploitation, the Civil War, Reconstruction, and Mississippi's mounting campaign for white supremacy and racial segregation. Most strikingly, Rachel Knight seemed to have had as much impact on the world around her as it had had on her.

Unfortunately, Rachel's historical reemergence was guided by the pen of a white segregationist whose own Knight ancestors fought and died for the Confederacy. Ethel Knight constructed a woman whose behavior and very existence embodied the lessons that she insisted the white South must learn once and for all: that the invading North's abolition of slavery destroyed the happiness of both blacks and whites in the South, and that Reconstruction under northern Republicans had brought ten years of ignorant "Negro rule" to Mississippi. In Ethel's view, racial integration defied the biblical word of God.[20]

Until we reimagine Ethel's narrative from the perspective of her subject, Rachel's life will remain defined by the inheritors of the very world she defied. Ethel's versions of events during the Civil War and Reconstruction are rooted in the Myth of the Lost Cause that she so revered[21] and in her commitment to maintaining white supremacy in the 1950s South. As Natalie Zemon Davis argues, the historian must address the "competing moral positions" of participants in past events, particularly when one of them—or, in this case, one of their descendants—is telling the story of the other.[22]

At present, intriguing mysteries surround Rachel's very identity. One white descendant of the Knight family claimed that Rachel could hardly speak English when brought from Georgia to Mississippi, suggesting she came from the coastal Sea Islands. Ethel Knight's descriptions of Rachel suggest the same. She portrayed Rachel as a conjure woman who prepared "magic potions" for Newton and told fortunes for the community by reading coffee grounds. To protect herself and her family from evil spirits, Rachel placed a whittled cedar pinwheel at the gate to her home.[23]

Witnesses at Davis Knight's trial variously described Rachel as Creole, Cherokee, Choctaw, or South African. Newton Knight's son Tom swore that she was "just an old Negro woman," with the "kinky hair," "flat nose," and "big thick lips" of a full-blooded African. In contrast, Dr. J. W. Stringer and Wiley W. Jackson, both white men, and Henry Knight, Rachel's grandson, remembered a "gingercake colored" woman who had long, curly, black hair that "swung across her shoulders" and who looked more Indian than African. Their memories suggest a striking woman likely of European, Native American, and African heritage.[24]

Although Rachel died eighteen years before Ethel Knight was born, Ethel confidently described her as "an unusual mulatto, almost beautiful," with "blue-green eyes" and hair that "hung down to her waist in waves of shining chestnut, . . . only a shade darker than her smooth face." Thus, Ethel confirmed, even exaggerated, the descriptions provided by Stringer, Jackson, and Henry Knight. She, like the judges of the high court, concluded that Tom Knight was too embittered by his siblings' interracial marriages to provide an honest description of the woman he held responsible for his family's shame.[25] Besides that, for Ethel's purpose, an "almost beautiful" green-eyed mulatto fit perfectly the tales of feminine wiles, seduction, and forbidden sex that enlivened the pages of *The Echo of the Black Horn.*

Records confirm that Rachel was the slave of Newton's grandfather. According to Ethel Knight, John "Jacky" Knight, a former Georgian who moved to Mississippi around 1817, purchased her in Augusta, Georgia, in April 1856. Jacky Knight was one of Covington and Jones Counties' wealthiest men. Although most of his neighbors were self-sufficient farmers or herders who owned few if any slaves, by 1850 he owned twenty-two slaves and several tracts of land in both counties. Despite some descendants' and a former slave's claim that he trafficked in slaves, Ethel emphatically denied it. She insisted that he was simply a soft-hearted horsetrader who had a penchant for buying slaves in order to ameliorate their condition.[26]

Ethel portrayed Jacky Knight as the quintessential paternalistic gentleman who "had as carefully reared his slaves as he had his own children." [27]

Such a man could not be a slave trader, for Ethel blamed all the evils that plagued the institution of slavery on this class. Slave traders, she explained, were social outcasts who obtained "filthy money by traffic[king] in human life." Men like Jacky Knight did not deserve this stigma because they spent money to buy slaves in order to "save" them from traders. They then treated the slaves like family members (pp. 29–30).

Ethel blamed slave traders for the beating of slaves (which she erroneously claimed was against the law) and for miscegenation. "From this type of men sprang the first Mulattoes," she declared. "In many instances, the females were bred, unwillingly, like beasts" (pp. 29–31). In her Old South, however, white gentlemen like Jacky Knight did not debauch defenseless slave women. Like the antebellum defenders of plantation slavery, she described a benevolent institution in which masters cared for and civilized a race "whose ancestors boiled and ate their sons" (p. 250).

Despite Ethel's defense of slavery, she did not deny that Rachel had been debauched by a white man and that this probably accounted for her being sold on the auction block. According to Ethel, Rachel identified her first two children's father as the "handsome, blond" son of her rich master (p. 284). Although Rachel was only sixteen years old in 1856, the year Jacky Knight allegedly bought her, she was already the mother of two-year-old Georgianne (whom Jacky also purchased) and she was pregnant with her first son, Jeffrey. The white appearances of both children indicated the mixed blood of their mother and their almost certainly white father or fathers (pp. 34–37).[28]

For all her identification with the South's white master class, as a woman Ethel deplored the rape of black women by white men. In writing the story of Rachel, she struggled to reconcile her defense of slavery with her awareness of black women's sexual vulnerability. In self-conscious prose, Ethel wrote that "sometimes even the best master would be forced to sell off a slave for an objectionable reason. . . . Many of the objectionable instances were never mentioned, such as rape." She denounced this "practice" as "horrible, since these unfortunate people were victims of circumstance, treated without any consideration whatsoever." Perhaps because she was close to admitting that slaveholders, too, molested slave women, Ethel turned abruptly to describing the horrors that awaited slaves at the hands of the evil slave trader. As always, they, not the institution itself, debased otherwise contented slaves (p. 31).[29]

Ethel did not consider that Jacky Knight might have purchased Rachel for economic and perhaps sexual purposes. She claimed that Jacky bought Rachel solely to prevent her separation from her children. At this point, Ethel added a strange twist to the story. She described how yet another of Rachel's daughters, Rosette, scrambled up on the auction block just as Jacky Knight made his purchase, thus forcing the soft-hearted planter to buy her, too. Ethel claimed that Rosette lived well into adulthood, but there is no evidence such a person ever existed (pp. 34–37).[30]

Ethel's contention that Rosette was Rachel's oldest child casts further doubt on Rosette's authenticity. Records show that Rachel gave birth to Georgianne at the age of 14 or 15, meaning she would had to have given birth to Rosette at the age of 13 or 14 and then immediately to have become pregnant and delivered another child. This is not impossible, but it is highly unlikely.[31]

Rosette's appearance in *The Echo of the Black Horn* is even more curious since she is the only child of Rachel described by Ethel as having black skin. Ethel may have sought to establish Rachel's Africanness as negatively as possible through this daughter. She described Rosette's father, for example, as "a full-blooded, blue-gummed African" from whom Rosette "inherited her negroid characteristics . . . even to that little odor peculiar to the full-blooded black race." Ethel's description of Rosette conjured up the demeaning images of black children popularized by various white media during the first half of the twentieth century. In Ethel's literary imagination, Rosette was a "banjo-bellied, spindle-legged waif" who "rolled her big eyes, and scratched her kinky head" (pp. 37, 262–63).[32]

These cruel caricatures revealed Ethel's revulsion for African Americans, notwithstanding her honeyed praise for those who "loved their white folks and were in turn loved by them, as members of families" (p. 30). When viewed in conjunction with Rosette's questionable authenticity, these caricatures suggest that Ethel manufactured or embellished the images of Rosette and her father in order to discourage her white readers from sympathizing with the green-eyed Rachel and her white-skinned progeny. Ethel's version of Rachel's history, a version that included a sexual relationship with a "blue-gummed African" and a black-skinned, kinky-haired child who was a product of that liaison, sealed Rachel's debasement. White Mississippians bred on vitriolic racist dogma no doubt recoiled in disgust at Rachel's doubly "polluted" sexual history. Through Rosette, Ethel reminded readers that the beautiful Rachel and her white-skinned children were, after all, "just another Negro family" (pp. 262–63).

Ethel Knight abhorred interracial sexual intimacy yet displayed a lurid fascination with it. She described Rachel's nights with Newton Knight's band of deserters in erotic, if horrified, detail. "Orgies [occurred], ghastly in obscenity, where Rachel and another black slave woman writhed and twisted their naked bodies in eerie dances, to the applause of the Deserters. Where fiddling and dancing went on for hours, undisturbed, . . . where there was feasting, drinking and pleasure. Where booze-crazed, prurient, sex-mad men indulged in fornication, and evil pleasures of a hideous nature" (pp. 283–84). Rachel became the female counterpart of the beastly black male rapist of white southern lore, the "Jezebel" who reduced white men to their basest instincts. Thus, Ethel and her white readers could simultaneously deplore and wallow in the forbidden sexual behavior of society's black and white "outlaws."

Rachel was indeed a sexually active woman who, between 1854 and 1875, gave birth to perhaps nine children without ever marrying.[33] Ethel's explanation for this was simple. She linked such promiscuity to Rachel's roots in Africa where "parentage was as varied and uncertain as that of the beasts of the forests." "It was the custom," she claimed, "for slave women to bear children of different fathers." Rachel simply continued that "custom" after gaining her freedom (pp. 250, 261). According to Ethel, Rachel became such a "strumpet" during the war that she could not even identify which of the 125 followers of Newton Knight fathered her white-skinned daughter Fannie. Although others gossiped that Fannie's father was Newton, Ethel preferred the image of Rachel's "satisfy[ing] the evil pleasures" of all 125 of Newton's men to that of Rachel's having a single sexual partner (pp. 253, 260).[34]

It is highly misleading to discuss Rachel's sexual activity without viewing it in the historical context of slavery. As a young slave girl, possibly not yet even a teenager, Rachel was impregnated by a white man. While still a teenager, and pregnant again, she and her child were sold and transported from Georgia to Mississippi, presumably severing whatever other kinships or friendships she had. She arrived in the Piney Woods of Covington County, Mississippi, powerless and alone except for her child. Light-skinned and physically very attractive, she was the sort of slave after whom many white men lusted. The fact that she had a white-skinned daughter conveyed to interested men that she had already been "initiated" into the world of interracial sexual relations.

Rachel gave birth to another child, Edmund, in 1857 or 1858, about two years after giving birth to Jeffrey. Until the Civil War erupted, she had no reason to anticipate that she would ever be free of slavery or the bearing of slave children. She apparently did not give birth to another child until March 1864. This suggests that the war brought her a respite from the unremitting sexual attentions of white men.[35]

Rachel's participation in the uprising led by Newton Knight catapulted her into the most powerful role she had ever known. Whether fact or fantasy, the campfire orgies described by Ethel Knight pale in comparison to the fantasies of freedom that the Civil War and Newton Knight's rebellion must have triggered for Rachel.

Ethel's account of Rachel's wartime behavior, though laden with racial invective and criticism of those who opposed the Confederacy, is filled with intriguing snapshots of a dynamic Rachel. In fact, these snapshots reveal a much more complex portrait than the "Jezebel" image so assiduously culti-vated by Ethel herself. For example, to explain how Rachel came to assist Newton Knight, Ethel said that Newton first learned from other slaves that Rachel possessed "great powers" as a conjure woman. Concluding that such a woman might be useful, he initiated their first meeting. They allegedly struck a bargain whereby Rachel promised to supply the deserters with food in return for Newton's promise to work for the liberation of all African Americans (pp. 73–75, 122).

Unlike other accounts of Newton Knight's rebellion that do not even mention Rachel, *The Echo of the Black Horn* has contributed significantly to our understanding of the wider role of women in the rebellion. Newton, shortly before his death in 1922, described the vital participation of women in his movement. In an interview with Meigs Frost of the *New Orleans Item,* he described how women poisoned the bloodhounds of the Confederate cavalry sent into Jones County to arrest deserters. "Yes," Newton grinned and recalled, "Those ladies sure helped us a lot. . . . They had 44 blood-hounds after us, those boys and General Robert Lowry's men. But 42 of them hounds just naturally died. They'd get hongry and some of the ladies, friends of ours would feed 'em. And they'd die. Strange, wasn't it?" Newton further described how the women sprinkled polecat musk and red pepper on the trails leading to the deserters' hideout.[36]

Ethel Knight claimed that Rachel had taught this trick to white women in the movement, that she had learned it while participating in the under-ground railroad of fugitive slaves. Rachel allegedly told Newton and his men to rub the musk, red pepper, and garlic on the bottoms of their shoes; the garlic would confuse the hounds, while the pepper would make them cough and sneeze. Soon after, wrote Ethel, the women friendly to the deserters were supplying them with dried, powdered red pepper (pp. 173–74).

Ethel gave no source to document this story, but it is likely that a slave woman would know better than a white farmwife how to throw off the scent of bloodhounds. This story may well have originated in oral accounts of the uprising passed down through the generations. Perhaps Rachel was omitted in later written accounts because the authors, particularly Newton's son Tom, wanted her role expunged from the record in order to bury the scandal of miscegenation. The gospel of racial segregation in the New South condemned Rachel to historical oblivion.

Ethel described several more instances during the Civil War in which Rachel aided Newton Knight, none of which can be substantiated, but all of which seem plausible. When Colonel Lowry's men murdered Newton's cousin Ben in the mistaken notion they had at last captured the elusive Newton Knight, Rachel reportedly brought the news to Newton, who in turn summoned his men by blowing his infamous black horn. Rachel further warned him that the cavalry would be returning to the deserters' swamp the next day and thus enabled him to ambush the cavalry at another location. Finally, in Newton's closest brush with death following a shoot-out, Ethel described how a doctor, brought to the deserters' hideout at gunpoint to tend Newton's wounds, was surprised to find "a pale ginger Mulatto" woman — Rachel — already nursing him (p. 193).

Ethel may have exaggerated Rachel's contributions to the Jones County uprising to "blacken" Newton's reputation. The lifelong connections of the couple and the intermarriages of their children, however, suggest that she did not exaggerate Rachel's role. Ethel apparently reported every tale she had ever heard about Rachel and Newton's Civil War exploits to denigrate both in the harshest terms possible. To this end, she told her stories carefully, though without regard for documentable fact, embellishing them whenever it served her needs.[37] Ethel was determined that Newton would never again be perceived as the courageous leader of a principled rebellion against the Confederacy. Adding Rachel to the story contributed to this goal but required that she break the Knight family's code of silence about the "white Negroes" who shared their blood. What had long been gossip was not part of the written record.[38]

Despite Ethel's pretensions, *The Echo of the Black Horn* is not historical scholarship. As folklore and folktales committed to print, however, it is invaluable. The best-known and most frequently read work on "the free state of Jones" in the entire state, it provides a window on the popular beliefs that it has helped to shape. "Miss Ethel" is an icon among many local people, and the book recently received its sixth printing. "I believe Miss Ethel is closer than anyone to the truth," one descendant of Newton Knight's Civil War associates concluded. "That Rachel, she was a beautiful animal—but she hoodooed Newton." [39]

From her modest white frame home, located on the edge of the Leaf River woods where Jones, Jasper, and Covington Counties intersect, and where Newton, Rachel, and the band of deserters evaded Confederate capture, Ethel Knight stands guard over her version of the story of their lives. Indeed, she has become as much a part of the area's living and volatile past as the people and events she chronicled.

More than simply a "version" of the past, however, her book embodies continued domination of whites over blacks and conventional authority over dissent in its imprisonment of Rachel and Newton within a "New South" glorification of the Old South's prerogatives of race and class. Rachel, resuscitated by Ethel on the one hand, is reenslaved by her caricatures on the other. Once the racial, class, and gendered discourses of *The Echo of the Black Horn* are deconstructed, however, Rachel's remarkable life and the sheer force of her personality captivate us. In fact, in many ways she has become the captor, not the prisoner, of her biographer. Rachel appears to have "hoodooed" Ethel Knight and her readers into a never-ending fascination with her memory.

## NOTES

I am grateful for Gregg Andrews's editorial assistance and for the comments and suggestions of Shearer Davis Bowman at the 1994 convention of the Texas State Historical Association.

1. *State of Mississippi v Davis Knight,* 13 December 1948, Case No. 646, court transcripts of the Circuit Court, Jones County, Miss., Clerk's Office, Mississippi Supreme Court.

2. Ibid. Mollie Knight's proper name was Martha Ann Eliza Knight; Jeffrey's was Jeffrey Early; Mat's was George Mathew. Fannie was listed as Frances in the 1900 Federal Manuscript Census. Family records and censuses indicate that the marriages took place

in 1878, although Ethel Knight claimed both couples were married on Christmas Eve, 1884. U.S. Federal Manuscript Censuses, 1880, 1900, Jasper County, Miss.; Jan Sumrall and Kenneth Welch, *The Knights and Related Families* (Denham Springs, La.: n.p., 1985), 12; Ethel Knight, *The Echo of the Black Horn* (n.p., 1951), 298.

3. *State v Knight*, court transcript; Thomas J. Knight, *The Life and Activities of Captain Newton Knight and His Company and the Free State of Jones County* (n.p., 1946). A copy of an almost identical manuscript, dated 1934 and entitled "Intimate Sketch of Activities of Newton Knight and 'Free State of Jones County,'" is contained in the Special Collections of the Mississippi Department of Archives and History, Jackson, Miss.

4. Knight, *Echo of the Black Horn,* 264. There is stronger evidence that Newton Knight became sexually involved with Rachel's daughter, Georgianne, after Rachel's death in 1889. In 1926, B. D. Graves, a lifelong associate of Newton, told a community gathering that Newton "took a negro woman [Georgianne] as his wife." From "Addresses Delivered at Hebron Community Meeting" (prepared and presented to the Eastman Memorial Foundation Library by the First National Bank of Laurel, 17 June 1926), Lauren Rogers Museum of Art, Laurel, Miss. In 1934, Martha Wheeler, a former slave of the Knight family, told a WPA interviewer that "Rachel was considered his [Newton's] woman." After Rachel's death, she claimed, Georgianne "took her place." Sometime between 1880 and 1900, Serena Knight moved out of the Newton household. George P. Rawick, ed., *The American Slave: A Composite Autobiography,* supplement, series 1, vol. 10, pt. 5, *Arkansas Narratives* (Westport, Conn.: Greenwood Press, 1972), 2268; Federal Manuscript Censuses, 1880, 1890, Jasper County, Miss.; Sumrall and Welch, *Knights and Related Families,* 161.

5. Jacquelyn Dowd Hall, "'The Mind That Burns in Each Body': Women, Rape, and Racial Violence," in *Powers of Desire: The Politics of Sexuality,* ed. Ann Snitow, Christine Stansell, and Sharon Thompson (New York: Monthly Review Press, 1983), 328–49. For an analysis of how dominant beliefs about appropriate race, class, and gender behavior converged to ignite mass hysteria and violence, see Nancy McLean, "The Leo Frank Case Reconsidered: Gender and Sexual Politics in the Making of Reactionary Populism," *Journal of American History* 78 (December 1991): 917–48. Elizabeth Young interprets the 1935 film *Bride of Frankenstein* as a "racist American discourse of the 1930s on masculinity, femininity, rape, and lynching" in "Here Comes the Bride: Wedding, Gender, and Race in *Bride of Frankenstein,*" *Feminist Studies* 17 (fall 1991): 403–37. For more comprehensive analyses of race relations during this era, see Joel Williamson, *Crucible of Race: Black/White Relations in the American South since Emancipation* (New York: Oxford University Press, 1984), and Neil R. McMillen, *Dark Journey: Black Mississippians in the Age of Jim Crow* (Urbana: University of Illinois Press, 1989).

6. William Gillette, *Retreat from Reconstruction, 1869–1879* (Baton Rouge: Louisiana State University Press, 1979), 166–235. Still useful on Mississippi is Vernon Lane Wharton, *The Negro in Mississippi, 1865–1890* (Chapel Hill: University of North Carolina,

1947). On southern law, race, and sexual relations, see Peter W. Bardaglio, "Lawyers, Lynching, and Governance in the New South, 1880–1900" (Paper delivered at the annual meeting of the Southern Historical Association, Louisville, Ky., November 1994), and Mary Frances Berry, "Judging Morality: Sexual Behavior and Legal Consequences in the Late Nineteenth-Century South," *Journal of American History* 78 (December 1991): 835–56. For a comprehensive overview of the era, see Eric Foner, *Reconstruction: America's Unfinished Revolution, 1863–1877* (New York: Harper and Row, 1988).

7. Paula Giddings, *When and Where I Enter: The Impact of Black Women on Race and Sex in America* (New York: Bantam Books, 1985), 17–31; Jacquelyn Dowd Hall, *Revolt against Chivalry: Jessie Daniel Ames and the Women's Campaign against Lynching* (New York: Columbia University Press, 1979).

8. *New Orleans Item,* 20 March 1921. Knight's death was reported in the *Ellisville Progressive,* 16 March 1922. The "Negro wife" referred to by the editor was probably Georgianne Knight. In 1920 Newton Knight lived with his white daughter Cora and his three white grandchildren. In the next household was Otho Knight, the mulatto son of Newton's daughter Mollie and Rachel's son Jeffrey. In yet another household was Georgianne, Rachel's oldest daughter, and Georgianne's daughter Grace. Former slave Martha Wheeler claimed that Grace, a schoolteacher "high in school circles," was Newton's daughter. U.S. Federal Manuscript Censuses, 1880, 1900, 1910, 1920, Jasper County, Miss.; Rawick, *American Slave,* suppl., ser. 1, vol. 10, pt. 5, *Arkansas Narratives,* 2268.

9. *State v Knight,* court transcript.

10. *Knight v State,* 207 Miss. 564 (1949).

11. In 1900, a census enumerator for Jasper County classified Newton Knight, Serena Knight, Mollie Knight, and various children of Newton and Serena as black, presumably because they were living among their mixed-race kin. Similarly, Ethel Knight alleged that Tom Knight told his mother, Serena, that "people who live with Negroes are no more than Negroes." *State v Knight,* court transcript; U.S. Federal Manuscript Census, 1900, Jasper County, Miss.; Knight, *Echo of the Black Horn,* 310. On the classification of misbehaving whites as blacks, see Williamson, *Crucible of Race,* 467.

12. Knight, *Echo of the Black Horn,* frontispiece and dedication page. Ethel, whose maiden name was Boykin, claims descent through her mother from James Knight, a brother of Newton. Her husband, Sidney Knight, was descended from Daniel Knight, an uncle of Newton. Both ancestors served and died for the Confederacy. Interview with Ethel Knight by Victoria Bynum, 10 August 1993, Covington County, Miss. See also Winnie Knight Thomas, Earle W. Knight, Lavada Knight Dykes, Martha Kaye Dykes Lowery, *The Family of John "Jacky" Knight and Keziah Davis Knight, 1773–1985* (Magee, Miss.: Robert and DeLores Knight Vinson, 1985), 25, 30.

13. Tom Knight was listed as the owner of a Laurel grocery store in the 1920 Fed-

eral Manuscript Census for Jones County, Miss. He was described as a peddler in the *Laurel Leader Call*'s 19 December 1951 review of *Echo of the Black Horn*. Earle Knight, the grandson of Newton Knight's cousin and fellow unionist William Martin "Dickie" Knight, remembered that Tom had once owned a store but in later years had operated a street stand. Interview with Earle Knight by Victoria Bynum, 28 July 1994, Laurel, Miss.

14. Quoted from the dust jacket of Knight, *Echo of the Black Horn*. According to Ethel, Tom Knight sold her his manuscript materials and copyright shortly after the Davis Knight trial. Though Tom presumably agreed that Ethel Knight should tell the story of Rachel, his cousin Earle Knight does not believe Tom expected his father's political principles and goals to be recast as well. Interview with Ethel Knight, 10 August 1993; interview with Earle Knight, 28 July 1994.

15. The image of the lascivious, cunning mulatto "Jezebel" was well entrenched by the time Ethel Knight employed it. For a historical overview of literary images of African American women, see Patricia Morton, *Disfigured Images: The Historical Assault on Afro-American Women* (Westport, Conn.: Greenwood Press, 1991). On black women as "Jezebels" see especially Deborah Gray White, *Ar'n't I a Woman? Female Slaves in the Plantation South* (New York: W. W. Norton, 1985), 27-61; see also Victoria E. Bynum, *Unruly Women: The Politics of Social and Sexual Control in the Old South* (Chapel Hill: University of North Carolina Press, 1992), 36-40, and Elizabeth Fox-Genovese, *Within the Plantation Household: Black and White Women of the Old South* (Chapel Hill: University of North Carolina Press, 1988), 292.

16. Knight, *Echo of the Black Horn*, 253-58, 289-90, 300.

17. On the literature of this era, see Williamson, *Crucible of Race*, 140-76. For an overview of the content of New South textbooks, see Carl Degler, "The South in Southern Textbooks," *Journal of Southern History* 30 (February 1964): 52-63.

18. Knight, *Echo of the Black Horn*, 279-314.

19. James Street, whose novel *Taproots* (Garden City, N.Y.: Sun Dial Press, 1943) formed the basis of the 1948 movie of the same name, created the mixed-blood character of Kyd, a member of the story's main family. In addition to the works of Thomas J. Knight and Ethel Knight, the most important histories include Rudy H. Leverett, *Legend of the Free State of Jones* (Jackson: University Press of Mississippi, 1984); Goode Montgomery, "Alleged Secession of Jones County," *Publications of the Mississippi Historical Society* 8 (1904): 13-22; G. Norton Galloway, "A Confederacy within a Confederacy," *Magazine of American History* 8 (1886): 387-90. Recent works that highlight southern women's participation in the Civil War include LeeAnn Whites, "The Civil War as a Crisis in Gender," in *Divided Houses: Gender and the Civil War,* ed. Catherine Clinton and Nina Silber (New York: Oxford University Press, 1992), 3-21; Bynum, *Unruly Women,* 111-50; Drew Gilpin Faust, "Altars of Sacrifice: Confederate Women and the Narratives of War," *Journal of American History* 76 (March 1990): 1200-1228; George C.

Rable, *Civil Wars: Women and the Crisis of Southern Nationalism* (Urbana: University of Illinois Press, 1989); Phillip Shaw Paludan, *Victims: A True Story of the Civil War* (Knoxville: University of Tennessee Press, 1981).

20. These themes run throughout *Echo of the Black Horn,* but see especially p. 19.

21. The most comprehensive revisions of New South history are Edward L. Ayers, *The Promise of the New South: Life after Reconstruction* (New York: Oxford University Press, 1992), and C. Vann Woodward, *Origins of the New South, 1877–1913* (1951; reprint, Baton Rouge: Louisiana State University Press, 1971). For an early review of "Lost Cause" historiography, see Bernard A. Weisberger, "The Dark and Bloody Ground of Reconstruction Historiography," *Journal of Southern History* 25 (November 1959): 427–47. The continued popularity of Ethel Knight's work in Mississippi is testimony that the "Lost Cause" version of southern history is still embraced by much of the nonacademic community.

22. Natalie Zemon Davis, "On the Lame," *American Historical Review* 93 (June 1988): 599.

23. Interview with Earle Knight, 28 July 1994; Federal Manuscript Censuses, 1870, 1880, Jasper County, Miss.; Knight, *Echo of the Black Horn,* 258, 263–64. On the language of Sea Island blacks, see Lawrence W. Levine, *Black Culture and Black Consciousness: Afro-American Folk Thought from Slavery to Freedom* (New York: Oxford University Press, 1978) 144–49; on the importance of conjuring, witchcraft, and carved wooden charms, see the Georgia Writers' Project, Works Progress Administration, *Drums and Shadows: Survival Studies among the Georgia Coastal Negroes* (1940; reprint, Athens: University of Georgia Press, 1986).

24. The only witness who corroborated Tom Knight's testimony was D. H. Valentine. The state supreme court discounted Valentine's testimony because, although he was born one year after Rachel Knight's death, he claimed to have seen her several times as a child. *State v Knight,* court transcript.

25. Knight, *Echo of the Black Horn,* 34, 312.

26. Jacky Knight married Keziah Davis in Columbia County, Georgia, 5 November 1798. By 1818, the couple lived in Covington County, Miss. In 1860, Jacky Knight owned real estate valued at $3,000 and personal property valued at $23,000. His estate papers indicate that he raised hogs and grew mostly corn, oats, and cotton. Descendant Earle Knight claims he grew rice and cotton for market, and contends that he did buy and sell slaves. No proof of this was found. U.S. Federal Manuscript Censuses and Slave Schedules, 1850, 1860, Covington County, Miss.; Thomas et al., *Family of John "Jacky" Knight,* 320, 340–43; "Legends of Ghosts, Treasures," *Laurel Leader Call,* 18 January 1993; interview with Earle Knight, 28 July 1994; Rawick, *American Slave,* suppl., ser. 1, vol. 10, pt. 5, *Arkansas Narratives,* 2267; Knight, *Echo of the Black Horn,* 32–37; Natchez Trace Slaves and Slavery Collection, 1793–1864, Center for American History, University of Texas, Austin.

27. Knight, *Echo of the Black Horn,* 24. (Hereafter, page numbers from Knight's book will be cited in the text.) Ethel's description of Jacky Knight's paternalism is corroborated by former slave Martha Wheeler's description of him as "good and kind" and his slaves as "wellfed and clothed." Rawick, *American Slave,* suppl., ser. 1, vol. 10, pt. 5, *Arkansas Narratives,* 2264-67.

28. The inscription on Georgianne's tombstone lists her birthdate as 14 October 1855; this would make her less than a year old when Jacky Knight purchased her and her mother.

29. Two particularly fascinating studies of the tangled web of kinships created by interracial relationships in the South are Adele Logan Alexander, *Ambiguous Lives: Free Women of Color in Rural Georgia, 1789-1879* (Fayetteville: University of Arkansas Press, 1991), and Pauli Murray, *Proud Shoes: The Story of an American Family* (1956; reprint, New York: Harper and Row, 1987).

30. No Rosette Knight appears in the Federal Manuscript Censuses for Jasper, Jones, or Covington Counties, Mississippi, between 1860 and 1920, nor is one mentioned in John Knight's will. Although several witnesses at Davis Knight's trial recalled the names of various children of Rachel, not one remembered a Rosette. Earle Knight, born in 1905 and a coauthor of *Family of John "Jacky" Knight,* does not recall seeing or hearing of Rosette before the publication of Ethel's book. Interview with Earle Knight, 28 July 1994.

31. James Trussell and Richard Steckel estimate that slave women's average age at menarche was fifteen years. See "The Age of Slaves at Menarche and Their First Birth," *Journal of Interdisciplinary History* 8 (winter 1978): 477-505. See also White, *Ar'n't I a Woman?* 104. The differences between Rachel's and Georgianne's ages were calculated from the U.S. Federal Manuscript Censuses, 1870, 1880, Jasper County, Miss., and from their tombstones' inscriptions.

32. The documentary film *Ethnic Notions* (San Francisco: Resolution Inc./California Newsreel, 1987) provides an excellent overview of negative media stereotypes of African American adults and children.

33. The 1870 federal manuscript census listed six children in Rachel's household: Georgianne, Jeffrey, Edmund, Fannie, Marsha (or Martha), and Stewart. In 1880, Edmund was gone, but three more children were listed: Floyd, A. A. (a daughter), and Henchy. U.S. Federal Manuscript Censuses, 1870, 1880, 1900, Jasper County, Miss.

34. According to the 1900 Federal Manuscript Census for Jasper County, Fannie Knight was born in March 1864.

35. U.S. Federal Manuscript Censuses, 1870, 1880, 1900, Jasper County, Miss.

36. *New Orleans Item,* 20 March 1921. Newton Knight referred to Robert Lowry as "General," but Lowry was still a colonel at the time their battles occurred. Tom Knight expanded on his father's accounts of women's participation. See *Intimate Sketch of Newton Knight,* 29-39. Col. Robert Lowry and his men were ordered into Jones County by T. M. Jack, Assistant Adjutant-General. See Special Order No. 80, Headquarters,

Demopolis, Ala., 20 March 1864, *Official Records of the War of the Rebellion* (Washington: Government Printing Office, 1891), ser. 1, vol. 32, pt. 3, p. 662.

37.  Shortly before his death at age 100 in 1952, Newton's first cousin George Knight (nicknamed "Clean Neck") insisted that Ethel's book was filled with distortions and lies. Interview with Earle Knight, 28 July 1994.

38.  Ethel Knight was particularly galled by James Street's portrayal of *Taproots*'s protagonist, Hoab Dabney, as a highly principled unionist because she believed that Street based this character on Newton Knight. Nevertheless, many members of the Knight family were upset when Ethel Knight not only vilified Newton Knight but told the story of Rachel. Not surprisingly, mixed-race Knights and other African Americans objected to the manner in which she told the story. Interview with Ethel Knight, 10 August 1993.

39.  Interview with Julius Huff, 8 August 1993, Covington County, Miss.

CAROLYN J. POWELL

# In Remembrance of Mira

## REFLECTIONS ON THE DEATH
## OF A SLAVE WOMAN

And, ye masters, do the same things unto them,
fore bearing, threatening: knowing that your master
also is in heaven. — Ephesians 6:9

LAVERY, the catalyst that forged the merging of black and
white in the pre–Civil War American South, also perpetuated
and sustained a way of life and a social value system that, according to some historians, was filled with "paradox, irony,
and guilt."[1] Slave masters felt that their actions with regards to their slaves
could be rationalized, since they viewed themselves as adhering to a moral
code and ethical standards that were traditionally sanctioned by the South.

In their quest to maintain a position of respect in society and to justify
their social value system, slave masters took on the role of the "paternalistic father," while trying to balance their most prized possession — honor. As
historian Eugene Genovese has pointed out, "Paternalism defined the involuntary labor of the slaves as a legitimate return to their masters for protection
and direction." Genovese has also argued, "Southern paternalism developed as a way of mediating irreconcilable class and racial conflict; it was an
anomaly even at the moment of its greatest apparent strength."[2] Coupled
with the "great father" image that the South sought to sustain, honor was
the mechanism that enabled this society to maintain slavery's appearance as
a legitimate institution supported by major social values. Wyatt-Brown has
pointed out that the meaning of "honor" was well defined by the contemporary American novelist Nathaniel Hawthorne in his book *My Kinsman,
Major Molineux* as comprising several overlapping values: "Honor is the

inner conviction of self-worth. . . . Second, . . . honor is the claim of that self-assessment before the public. . . . The third element is the assessment of the claim by the public, a judgment based upon the behavior of the claimant. In other words, honor is reputation." [3]

The South was historically more violent than other regions in America. As the South sought to maintain its "paternalistic image," it could in no way mask or blot out the extreme sadistic violence that permeated its very existence. This period in our history sadly gave us people like Madame LaLaurie of New Orleans, who maintained a torture chamber in her house: "Slaves were found mutilated, starved, [and] bound down with chains." [4] In fact, violence was at the very heart of slavery; it was the mechanism of lynching, castrating, maiming, raping, and yes, even torturing that supported a system so violent that it is hard to conceive that one human being could do these things to another. History has informed us about the violence that slave masters perpetuated on slaves. However, even the recent telling of slavery history is all too often reticent about the "unspeakable" violence that occurred during this period. Slavery historian Kenneth M. Stampp has suggested, "It would be pointless to catalogue the atrocities committed by psychopaths." [5] However, silence on any aspect of history can be detrimental, and it helps to solidify our ignorance on important issues like race, class, and gender; these same issues are at the very heart of the black and white struggle in America today.

A major underpinning of Southern society's violence was what Catherine Clinton has termed "the sexual dynamics of slavery." [6] And this essay argues that to investigate how the antebellum southern legal system dealt with the powerful, interlinked issues of sex and slavery provides a way of closely examining willful and malicious violence and its impact upon the important southern tradition of honor as integral to community values. In particular, an examination of the impact of such violence upon a typical small southern community in North Carolina as well as upon the state, and also upon a slave woman who tragically experienced and died at the hands of such violence, will reveal these dynamics.

In the case of *State v Hoover* (1839), an unspeakable, violent murder was committed by a slave master in the county of Iredell, in Statesville, North Carolina. The case of John Hoover and the murder of his slave, Mira, needs to be told, not because of the gore and the violent actions of this man who was truly psychopathic, but because violence is an act that does not occur in a vacuum. When violence occurs against one person within a community, it can either unite or divide its people, and it can change the course of its very existence. In the course of her research this author found obtaining primary sources no easy task, since the Hoover family did not leave diaries, letters, or anything that could offer more details about Hoover or his family. Living relatives, who are now quite elderly, could only remember bits and pieces of what they were told or heard as children. Nonetheless, sources of a different kind can be discovered.

Perhaps the two most important primary sources can be found in the superior court testimony given at Hoover's first trial and in his will. The court transcript paints a vivid picture not only of Hoover the man, but of how he affected his community. In fact, this important legal record shows that Statesville, North Carolina, in the name of "honor," responded in a way that no other southern community had ever done before: it condemned a slave master who was not simply violent but sexually deviant as well. During the course of my research into this case as it became necessary to seek out answers to many of my questions on sexual deviance, I found that the secondary resources were extremely helpful.

This story is not simply about the violent ways of one slave master and his disregard for his prescribed role as the paternal father. It also involves an institution that forced a town to cleanse its soul and to come to grips with the reality that surrounded the issues of race, class, and gender.

There are many cases that speak of the treatment of slaves by their masters, but *State v Hoover* (1839) is exceptional as perhaps the most heinous crime ever to be recorded in North Carolina history. It is also exceptional in its court verdict of guilty against a white man who chose to torture his female slave to death. In the fall term of 1839, the Superior Court of Iredell County charged John Hoover with the brutal murder of his slave Mira. The court record stated: "The witnesses called on the part of the state, testified to a series of the most brutal and barbarous whippings, scourgings and privations, inflicted by the prisoner upon the deceased from about the first of December to time of her death in the ensuing March, while she was in the latter stages of pregnancy, and afterwards, during her period of confinement, and recovery from a recent delivery."[7]

On May 5, 1840, after an unsuccessful appeal to the state supreme court, Hoover was hanged. In the previous forty years Iredell County had reported only five hangings, of three whites and two "negroes."[8] And it would appear that John Hoover was the only slave master ever to be hanged for killing a slave in the South. During this time period there were no newspapers in Statesville itself to report on Hoover's crime or his punishment. But it is significant that the surrounding area's press was silent regarding this trial. For example, the *Charlotte Journal* on March 5, 1840, simply stated, "Chief Justice Ruffin in *State v Hoover* from Iredell, judgment affirmed." [9]

The Hoover case is unique in the South because it says a great deal about race and gender relations and about how North Carolina chose to deal with these two volatile issues on the eve of the Civil War. Therefore, within the context of race and gender relations and slavery, I will examine why the community surrounding Statesville was so silent concerning Mira's death. Second, I will examine why North Carolina chose to hang this white man for killing his slave. And finally, I will ask what could have made John Hoover commit this vicious crime. Answering these questions will allow us to understand why North Carolina chose to step out from among all other southern states, at least in this instance, to recognize and defend this slave woman, albeit only after her death. We will also understand what such legal cases can tell us about the experience of enslaved women.

*At the time* of Hoover's trial, Statesville was a small town with a population of no more than two hundred people.[10] On the surface Statesville was probably typical of other developing southern communities, except that there were fewer slaves than elsewhere in this part of the state. Hoover, in comparison to his neighbors, was land rich; at the time of his death he had amassed a total of 1,914 acres of land, a considerable amount of property.[11] The records indicated that at various times he owned more land than he actually paid taxes on, and he also owned an undetermined number of slaves who never appeared in the census records or county tax lists.[12] Therefore, it would appear that Hoover was not only a master of the art of brutality but also a cheat. Research indicates that Hoover owned more land than those who were witnesses against him at his trial. Tax records for some of the members of the jury and for witnesses in the case show that the amount of land they owned varies. Henry Philer, a witness, owned 200 acres of land and no slaves, while Alfred Guy, a member of the jury, owned 736 acres and seven slaves.

The white residents of Statesville were generally no different from those in any other southern community during this period. Most were probably Protestant in their religious beliefs. They probably believed that fornication by white males in southern society was tolerable but not as acceptable with women of a darker skin color. However, those southern gentlemen who maintained quiet, unobtrusive liaisons with slave women were only whispered about behind closed doors. Yet those, like Hoover, who practiced promiscuous sexual liaisons coupled with extreme violent behavior with slave women could and did evoke the wrath of the community in which they lived. Many communities like Statesville clearly believed that the issue was not "thou shalt not fornicate with black women," but rather "thou shalt take care to do so at no other man's expense." [13]

As testimony presented to the Iredell County Superior Court shows,[14] John Hoover, a member of this community, systematically, willfully, and maliciously tortured his slave Mira to the point where her body was almost devoid of skin. In fact, the court record states that Mira's corpse, "from the back of her head to her heels was literally a continuous wound. . . . She was a perfect skeleton—the whole of the back was covered with scales some of which dropped off from six inches to a foot long" (pp. 18-20). Hoover was clearly relentless in his torture of Mira: "with his hands and his feet and with clubs, whips, chains, braces and sticks . . . the said John Hoover at various times aforesaid had held fire to against and upon the head, neck, breast, back, body and sides of her the said female slave Mira" (p. 2). Henry Philer, a witness for the State who at one time worked for Hoover, stated that Hoover "ordered the deceased to swing a maul (a heavy mallet for driving wedges and piles) over her head and the deceased [failed] to do so" (p. 12). Prior to this Philer had told Hoover he refused to work with the maul because it was too heavy. Jacob Hill, a witness for the State, testified that the defendant "ordered the deceased to rise a pile of snow and raise up her clothes and sit down in the snow and there remain for some time" (p. 14).

It would appear that Hoover was desperately and violently trying to make Mira abort her child, perhaps because he had fathered the baby or resented the man who had, or perhaps because he was driven by other deep-seated emotions that defied understanding, even for Hoover. In any case, the 1839 court transcript speaks volumes about the continued violence that led finally to this woman's death. On Tuesday morning, March 26, 1839, John Bales, a witness for the State who worked for Hoover, saw Hoover beat Mira with a stick. That evening when he came back to Hoover's place for dinner, he saw that Mira was chained by her neck to a log in the yard. As Mira tried to get up and make her way to the house, she fell and never regained consciousness. Mira died in Hoover's kitchen approximately 2 A.M. Wednesday,

March 27 (p. 16). The court record does not indicate whether or not Hoover ever exhibited abusive behavior toward other slaves.

It is evident by the testimony of witnesses and other members of the community that they knew Hoover was committing these cruel and inhuman acts against Mira. Why then did they not respond and come to the aid of this slave woman? Research does not provide a clear-cut answer. However, southern history shows us that white southern men have traditionally refused to interfere in the chastisement of slave property.

It seems that Statesville residents chose not to recognize the abuse of Mira. Instead, they responded to Hoover, who was intensely disliked within the community. According to the transcript, James Wordy, who worked for Hoover, "left on unfriendly terms with the defendant. . . . The overbearing conduct of the defendant towards the witness and [the] defendant's cruelty to the deceased was the causes assigned by [the] witness for leaving" (p. 10). Jacob Wooliver, who was at Hoover's house just before Christmas in 1838, said that he "was not on friendly terms with the defendant and had not been for the last three years" (p. 16). In fact, not one member of this community came to Hoover's defense at his trial.

The one factor that seems to be at the heart of why this community allowed the abuse of this slave woman but reacted against Hoover's antisocial violent personality centers around the system of "southern honor." According to Bertram Wyatt-Brown, "Honor . . . demanded family reticence, not to conceal anyone's wrong doing but to shield honor itself."[15] Through its silence, Statesville was trying to deal with the embarrassment and dishonor that Hoover brought. This seems the most plausible explanation of why none of the newspapers in the surrounding areas carried information on this incident nor its trial. A unified acceptance of silence meant no exposure of the inner fabric of a community which had been tainted by one of its own. Yet Hoover had violated North Carolina's law as it applied to the abuse of slave property, as well as offended the system of southern honor that rationalized the institution of slavery, because he visibly contradicted the paternal slave master's prescribed role. The only way in which Statesville itself then could regain its honor was to bring in a verdict of guilty. And we can learn through a similar case that the underlying issues of race and gender played a vital role in the decisions made by those in this southern community as well as those made in court.

Melton A. McLaurin's book *Celia, a Slave* sets the stage for us in Callaway County, Missouri, concerning a master-slave relationship in the 1850s, some ten years after Hoover's death. Celia was owned by John Newsome, who repeatedly raped her from the day he bought her at the age of fourteen. Within five years, Newsome's sexual violation of Celia had caused her to bear him two children. When Celia became involved with a slave named George, George insisted Celia end Newsome's nightly visits to her cabin. Celia herself had threatened to hurt Newsome if he continued his sexual practices. On the night of June 23, 1855, Newsome made his last demand. As he approached Celia in her cabin, she hit him with a stick, causing him to fall to his death. Celia then burned Newsome's body in her fireplace.[16]

Unlike Hoover's trial, Celia's trial was highly publicized, with the added focus on the debates over slavery that flared throughout Missouri during the 1850s. The key difference, however, between the two trials was that the Missouri courts upheld the ideology of the white social order, which was to maintain control over the lives of slaves, despite the sexual violation of slave women, which was all too common. Thus, on December 21, 1855, at 2:30 P.M., nineteen-year-old Celia was hanged.[17]

In this context I have two questions: Why was Celia executed in her case and Hoover in his case, and what do these cases say about Old South race and gender conventions? It seems that the white social order of Missouri, whose job it was to control slavery within its borders, saw Celia as the aggressor, not as the victim of five years of sexual exploitation. In the eyes of his community John Newsome did not violate the system, because Celia was insignificant. Therefore, as demonstrated by McLaurin, in Missouri such brutality to a slave woman was acceptable. What mattered most to Callaway County, Missouri, was that it had suffered the loss of one of its own at the hands of a slave woman. The death of Celia was immaterial to this community, while what was important was the position and power of the slave master.

On the other hand, in Statesville, North Carolina, John Hoover was clearly seen as the aggressor who not only broke the rules but also tainted a community in the process. He had exhibited violent behavior that destroyed human property. For the courts to sanction this type of behavior would have meant that North Carolina had lost all sense of honor. The comparison of these two cases shows us that the issues of race, gender, and slavery are internally intertwined. Slave women like Celia could be sexually exploited and legally condemned by the court to die for defending themselves, while in an important sense the fate of slave women such as Mira was the same. That is, Mira tried to survive sexual exploitation in a community that thought more of honor than of human life, whose silence sanctioned Hoover's sexual abuse and brutality, and in the end she died as well.

Yet in a legal context, the various and not necessarily complementary definitions of southern "honor" became evident. The drama that unfolded in Celia's trial was significantly unlike what was seen at Hoover's. Upon reading the lower court's testimony of Hoover's trial one quickly detects a staid community sense of collective coldness and acceptance of Hoover's impending guilt and death. In fact, the twelve witnesses one by one, without any visible emotion, methodically sealed Hoover's fate with a verdict of "guilty of murder." The North Carolina community had thus resolved their problem of honor in an arena that was legal and acceptable to all. This verdict meant, however, that Hoover could appeal to and hopefully face a more lenient audience.

If North Carolina had not humanized its slave codes between 1741 and 1817, Hoover might indeed have received a more sympathetic sentence. But by 1817 the state legislature had enacted a law that extended real protection to the life of a slave, by stating, "That the offense of killing a slave hereafter be denominated and considered homicide, and shall partake of the same degree of guilt when accompanied with the like circumstances that homicide now does at common law."[18] It is on this basis that the North Carolina Supreme Court under Chief Justice Thomas Ruffin, who was conservative in his interpretation and application of the law but also known for his ability to analyze facts that would render appropriate decisions, took a second look at Hoover's case on appeal. In this instance Ruffin faced his most challenging and possibly most heartwrenching case ever. According to Ruffin, "Next to the sin of disobeying a commandment of the bible [*sic*], it is a sin to violate the law of the state."[19]

In a previous case, *State v Mann* (1829), Ruffin had said, "A master may lawfully punish his slave, and the degree must, in general, be left to his own judgment and humanity, and cannot be judicially questioned. . . . But the master's authority is not altogether unlimited. He must not kill. There is at least, this restriction upon his power: he must stop short of taking life."[20]

When Ruffin wrote his opinion in the Hoover case for the North Carolina Supreme Court, he clearly did so with a sense of deep sorrow. According to Ruffin, "The court is at a loss to comprehend how it could have been submitted to the jury that they might find an extenuation from provocation. There is no opening for such hypothesis. There is no evidence of the supposed act, which it was thought, might be provocations. But if they had been proved, this court would not have concurred in the instructions given, doubtless, from abundant caution and laudable tenderness of life." [21] Ruffin's reaffirmation of the lower court's decision in the Hoover case sent a clear signal to the community as well as the state that it could not entertain the thought of changing Hoover's crime from murder to a lesser charge.

In trying to comprehend the sexual dynamics of slavery in relation to John Hoover's behavior, it should be noted that recently several historians have made important observations about how slave masters viewed slave women. Deborah Gray White suggests, "Once slaveholders realized that the reproductive function of the female slave could yield a profit, the manipulation of procreative sexual relations became an integral part of the sexual exploitation of female slaves." [22] Catherine Clinton notes, "Southern planters divided women into two classes: ladies, always white and chaste; and whores, comprising all black women (except for the saintly Mammy)." [23] These views, in turn, only enhanced the ability of the slave master to maintain total control. Therefore, it becomes clear that the supposedly paternalistic and in reality dominant position of the slave master over the slave woman has always been in large part a sexual one. Moreover, paternalism, according to Genovese, "grew out of the necessity to discipline and morally justify a system of exploitation." [24]

Certainly an exploration into the sadistic mind of Hoover can give us the opportunity to explore other ways of viewing master-slave relationships that depart from the customary form of "paternalism." Hoover's case gives us an opportunity to look at some of the psychological aspects of the master-slave relationship that have not yet been really explored. However, there will always be unanswered questions, which will only allow us to speculate about what caused Hoover to become a torturer and killer. Historian Earl E. Thorpe has carefully drawn upon Shulamith Firestone's *Dialectic of Sex* to point out that "the oedipus complex so fragments the mind and emotions of men that, in a 'sexual schizophrenia,' they must have one woman to put on a nearly sexless pedestal and another degraded person at whom they can direct their 'lower' passions." [25] In the antebellum American South clearly enslaved women provided manifold opportunity for the unleashing of such tortured and tortuous emotions. The court records indicate that Mira carried her pregnancy to term despite the repeated beatings and cruel treatment she received. There is no indication from these records that this child whom Hoover had wanted aborted was his, if this child was a boy or girl, if the child had been fathered by another slave, or if Mira had any other children prior to this particular birth. But, according to Mr. Allison, a witness for the State, "his father raised the deceased—that [the] witness and his brother sold her to the defendant, [and] that she was an obedient and humble negro when his father owned her." [26] What is known about the sexual habits of slaveholders and about Hoover's psychopathic and sexually perverse behavior certainly indicates that he could well have been the father of her child—an occurrence which, as we know, was by no means unusual in the master–slave woman relationship in the American South.

Yet it still seems important to ask what made Hoover torture and murder this woman. It was not until the mid-nineteenth century that "the subject of sexual perversion became a matter of crucial concern to scientists and the public alike." [27] The doctors during this period did not know anything about abnormal psychology. Yet, if Hoover had been diagnosed by a psychoanalyst in the 1990s, he would likely have been considered to have what is known as a perversion—a term which "implies an irresistible attraction toward some abnormal or bizarre sexual behavior." As Louise Kaplan states in her book *Female Perversions,* "What distinguishes perversion is its quality of desperation and fixity." [28] In this context it seems probable that Hoover was fixated on inflicting a constant methodical form of pain on Mira, from December 15, 1838, until March 27, 1839, when she died. [29]

According to criminologist Hans Toch, Hoover likely falls into a category described as "comprising persons who see themselves (and their own needs) as being the only fact of social relevance. Other people are viewed as objects rather than as persons whose needs must be taken into account (or must be countered or anticipated)." [30] Such persons are naturally prone to violence. And when we think of abnormal sexual behavior, one of the things that instantly comes to mind is sadomasochism, a behavior which involves the use of whips and chains, such as the ones Hoover used to inflict pain on Mira. Yet Toch's observations could also suggest the same reasons why the North Carolina white community could not tolerate Hoover's flagrantly abnormal behavior. The community of Statesville saw Hoover's violent actions as being self-serving, contributing in no positive way to the social order of the community, as well as destroying their sense of "honor" amongst its people.

The existing records tell us nothing about Hoover's childhood or his relations with his wife, Regina, children, or the community.[31] Therefore, we are left to explore those avenues that tend to reflect as closely as possible similar human behavior. Hoover's behavior does suggest that he was living a life of deception, which is an important factor in trying to understand the strategy of sexual perversity. Accordingly, this type of strategy will typically "deceive the onlooker about the unconscious meanings of the behaviors he or she is observing."[32] It probably would be safe to say that Hoover constantly tried to restrain those inner inexplicable erotic passions, but could not. Therefore, he was most likely driven to rape, torture, and finally murder as ways to suppress the inexplicable. Sexually deviant behavior probably dictated that Hoover abused his wife and children and that Mira was only an extension of his sexual abuse, because she was a slave woman who was an outcast in southern society and who was absolutely powerless within the Hoover household.

However, John Hoover's behavior leads to many questions that cannot be definitively answered, while unfortunately we are not in a position to definitely evaluate why he committed such an atrocious crime. Nonetheless, to investigate his psychological makeup does provide opportunity to explore untapped avenues that have been traditionally untouched, and thus to examine the extremes of sexual perversion and violence that could at any time be unleashed by the institution of slavery.

The Hoover legal case with its verdict of guilty also raises numerous questions. For example, would John Hoover have been similarly punished and hanged if he had murdered a male slave? Did Mira's gender play a role in Statesville's tortured combination of silence and support for the guilty verdict?

What is clear is that to examine the case of *State v Hoover* enables us to focus on the kinds of submerged but extremely compelling issues that forced the American South to reassess its approach to slavery and that underpinned its constant struggle to legitimize this institution within both the context of race and gender conventions and important communal social values led by "honor." Certainly, the Statesville community's response to the Hoover case demonstrates that honor was a major value and that the community could not risk any dismissal of this value, which suggested that this essential tradition had lost its meaning and worth. The Hoover case severely tarnished Statesville's desired reputation for righteousness and social morality, and meant that this southern community could respond only by casting this publicly deviant slave master from its midst and from life, while simultaneously maintaining an embarrassed silence. Thus, the torture and murder of Mira by this sadistic and sexually perverted killer ultimately forced the state of North Carolina to respond to the silent cry of a community that wanted to rid itself of its pain and to restore its honor.

Yet we should never forget that even though North Carolina chose to hang this slave master, it in no way rectified the torture and murder of this woman. Moreover, the Hoover case compels us to remember that slave women like Mira were seen as immaterial with regard to their sexual exploitation and abuse. Mira's murder was preceded by a history of monstrous suffering at Hoover's hands, while Celia's resistance against her master's abuse was punished by hanging. In short, such cases illuminate the tragic impact of the sexual dynamics of slavery upon slave women and confirm that slave masters could abuse and violate these women with virtual impunity in private. However, it was seemingly not equally acceptable publicly to violate the Old South's professed and major social conventions and communal values.

As the Hoover case shows, to violate the tradition of honor that masked the violent underpinnings and moral bankruptcy of the institution of slavery and that held together white southern society and its emphasis on community could not be tolerated. In this context, the Statesville community's response to the Hoover case can best be understood as revealing the painful paradoxes and essential fragility of a society built upon slavery that desperately needed to maintain its self-image of moral worth and honor.

What is clear is that John Hoover himself represented a dying institution that had fallen out of step with a social order that could not and would not support or defend a man who, in effect, chose to destroy not only slave property but a community as well. And while the Statesville community's and the state's response to the Hoover case should not be misinterpreted as vindicating Mira's rights to life and dignity, it is hoped that this essay's attention to her real and tragic experience does provide this vindication.

## NOTES

1. Bertram Wyatt-Brown, *Southern Honor: Ethics and Behavior in the Old South* (New York: Oxford University Press, 1982), 3.

2. Eugene D. Genovese, *Roll, Jordan, Roll: The World the Slaves Made* (New York:

Pantheon Books, 1972), 5, 6. See also Peter Kolchin's discussion on paternalism in *American Slavery, 1619–1877* (New York: Hill and Wang, 1993).

3. Bertram Wyatt-Brown, *Honor and Violence in the Old South* (New York: Oxford University Press, 1986), 14.

4. Lyle Saxon, *Fabulous New Orleans* (1928; reprint, Gretna, La.: Pelican, 1988), 210.

5. Kenneth M. Stampp, *The Peculiar Institution* (New York: Vintage Books, 1956), 182.

6. Catherine Clinton, *The Plantation Mistress* (New York: Pantheon Books, 1982), 199.

7. *State v Hoover,* 20 N.C. 393 (1839).

8. *Landmark Newspaper,* Statesville, N.C., Friday, 13 February 1880.

9. The silence that surrounded Statesville was an insulating force that prevented those on the outside of this community from learning about the embarrassment that was probably felt by the people of Statesville, as well as the damage that this trial had done to the concept of "southern honor." Recognition of the trial in the *Charlotte Journal* on 5 March 1840 in many ways reflected simply an afterthought.

10. Homer M. Keever, *Iredell-Piedmont County* (Iredell County Bicentennial Commission, 1976), 2.

11. Iredell County Deed Book 10, 26 August 1847, 546.

12. The federal census records from 1830 through 1860 do not list the Hoover family as owning any slaves. However, it appears that John's wife, Regina, was still living in Statesville during the 1840 census. Despite the fact that the federal census records are devoid of information, there is further evidence of Hoover owning other slaves. In his will, John Hoover stated, "[I]f a slave should become troublesome or behave in a troublesome manner some fit person is to be employed to sell him or her."

13. Wyatt-Brown, *Southern Honor,* 298, cited in Wyatt-Brown as R. J. Walker to Hiram G. Runnels, 6 July 1835, RG 21, Miss DAH; also see Thomas H. Garret Case, 25 January, 18 October 1860, RG 27, ibid.; Daniel Greenleaf to Runnels, 1 May 1834, RG 21, ibid., J. J. Lyons, dry goods, 7 August 1835, Abbyville, S.C., vol. 6, D. B. Baker.

14. North Carolina (Iredell County) Superior Court Testimony, fall term 1839 [hereafter cited as Court Testimony].

15. Wyatt-Brown, *Southern Honor,* 310.

16. Melton A. McLaurin, *Celia, a Slave* (Athens: University of Georgia Press, 1991), 28–30.

17. Ibid., 114.

18. 1817 N.C. Sess. Laws, 949.

19. Ernest James Clark, "Slave Cases before the North Carolina Supreme Court" (master's thesis, University of North Carolina, Chapel Hill, 1959), 12, citing Thomas Ruffin in Samuel A. Ashe, *Cyclopedia of Eminent and Representative Men of the Carolinas of the Nineteenth Century,* 3 vols. (1892; reprint, Spartanburg, S.C.: Reprint, 1972), 2:44.

20. *State v Mann,* 20 N.C. 395 (1839).

21. Paul Finkelman, *The Law of Freedom and Bondage: A Casebook* (New York: Oceana, 1986), 228–29, citing *State v Hoover,* 4 Dev. and Bat. 365 (1839). It should be noted that early American court reports were named after the editors who were reporting these cases as they were decided in court, hence the citation of Dev. and Bat. (Devereux and Battle).

22. Deborah Gray White, *Ar'n't I A Woman? Female Slaves in the Plantation South* (New York: W. W. Norton, 1985), 68.

23. Clinton, *The Plantation Mistress,* 204.

24. Genovese, *Roll, Jordan, Roll,* 4.

25. Earl E. Thorpe, *The Old South: A Psychohistory* (Westport, Conn.: Greenwood Press, 1979), 143.

26. Court Testimony, 17.

27. Louise J. Kaplan, *Female Perversions: The Temptations of Emma Bovary* (New York: Doubleday, 1991), 7.

28. Ibid., 6, 9–10.

29. Court Testimony, 2.

30. Hans Toch, *Violent Men: An Inquiry into the Psychology of Violence* (1969; reprint, Washington: American Psychological Association, 1992), 136.

31. The records are silent on John Hoover's personal life, as well as the life of his slave Mira. However, we do know that the Hoovers had nine children, which included a set of twin boys. Herbert C. Hoover, the thirty-first president of the United States, was a descendant of this family.

32. Kaplan, *Female Perversions,* 9.

JOHN C. INSCOE

# The Civil War's Empowerment of an Appalachian Woman

## THE 1864 SLAVE PURCHASES

## OF MARY BELL

N MARCH 11, 1864, with the Civil War approaching its fourth and final year, Mary Bell, the wife of a dentist in the remote southern highland community of Franklin, North Carolina, entered the ranks of slaveholders by purchasing a family of three slaves. This was a move she made independently and announced only after the fact to her husband, then serving with his Confederate regiment in Alabama, in a letter that proclaimed: "Well, I believe I told you that you need not be surprised if [I] made a nigger trade. Well I have done it."[1]

Mary Bell's ill-fated "nigger trade" was at one level a function of what were, for at least one section of Confederate Appalachia, unusual socio-economic opportunities created by the Civil War. But this transaction also reflects the degree to which the war provided unique opportunities for southern white women left at home to act in what were otherwise almost exclusively male spheres of influence and authority. That this woman chose to use her new empowerment to purchase slaves carries other implications in terms of the opportunities and aspirations generated by the war and of the gender distinctions that characterized those aspirations, particularly as they related to slavery.

Much has been written about the devastation and deprivation that southern mountaineers suffered during the Civil War, with considerable emphasis on the extent to which women were the ultimate victims of both.[2] Mary Bell was among that group, and yet her experience offers a very different per-spective—that of a wife who, when left by her husband, took full advantage of her region's fluid labor force and resilient economic structure not only to fend for herself and her family but also to fulfill a goal far more meaningful to herself than to her husband—joining their community's very slim ranks of slaveholders.

Finally, Mary Bell's story offers a revealing variation on the experience of slaveholding women during the Civil War. To take upon themselves the discipline and management of an enslaved labor force just as the peculiar institution's disintegration began was among the most burdensome challenges faced by plantation mistresses. That dilemma has become a central theme of the growing literature on Confederate women. As George Rable has noted, "All their other problems—whether with crops, livestock, or overseers— paled in comparison with having to deal with the decay and eventual death of slavery."[3]

Drew Gilpin Faust has observed that "on a microcosmic level, the daily interactions of particular women slaveholders with specific slaves yield a striking vision of the master-slave relationship in a new wartime guise, of war-born redefinitions of social power and social roles."[4] In the Bells' case, that power shift from master to mistress was not quite so neatly made, since Mary's husband, Alfred, was never really involved in the daily interaction with a slave force as she was. Having only acquired slave property during Alf's wartime absence, Mary Bell's situation offers instead a means of examining her own redefined status and role, first as a supervisor of others' slaves and then, only briefly, as the sole authority over her own. In both capacities, she wrestled with problems of management and discipline common to most southern plantation mistresses. What made Mary's experience so distinctive was that she propelled herself into the ranks of slave ownership and began relishing her new status and its benefits at the very point in the war when slavery was collapsing in much of the rest of the Confederacy, just as many slaveholders were coping for the first time without the black workforces on which they had been so dependent. Because slave ownership was the goal that Mary Bell worked hardest to achieve and, having done so, that in which she took the greatest satisfaction, the very temporary nature of that achievement suggests certain ambiguities, and even ironies, in her own wartime empowerment and that of other southern mistresses as well.

*It was just* a few months before the Civil War broke out that Alfred Bell moved with his wife, Mary, and their two small daughters from northern Georgia back to his birthplace, Franklin, just over the state line in North

Carolina's remote and mountainous southwestern corner. Alf quickly established a dental practice, shared in his father's jewelry business, and bought a small farm about a mile from their residence in town. Because of Alf's professional and business concerns, hired labor was vital to the Bells' farming operation even before he left for war in November 1861.[5]

Agricultural labor took a variety of forms in antebellum Appalachia. Options ranging from tenant farming both on rental and sharecropping terms and short-term "day labor" to wage paid overseers offered highland landowners several readily available means of utilizing a significant nonlandholding white populace.[6] Slavery provided additional options for even nonslaveholding landowners. While slaveholders made up only about 10 percent of the North Carolina mountain population in 1860, the political, social, and economic clout they wielded was fully as hegemonic as that enjoyed by lowland planters. The limitations imposed on mountain agriculture by climate and terrain would neither have justified nor supported even the region's small slave labor force. Thus, perhaps the most distinctive variation in the institution in southern Appalachia was that its slaveholders were, as Frederick Law Olmsted once observed, "chiefly professional men, shopkeepers, and men in office who are also land owners, and give only divided attention to farming."[7]

But equally as vital to slavery's viability in this mountain environment was the demand for slave labor among nonslaveholders. The hiring out of slaves was a far more common practice in highland communities than elsewhere because it worked to the advantage of both negotiating parties. For owners, renting out the labor of their bondsmen and women for either short or long terms provided not only considerable income but also an easy outlet for what often proved to be surplus labor. For a large segment of the region's nonslaveholding or small slaveholding populace, hiring offered an affordable means of benefiting directly from the locally available black labor supply and of working farm acreage beyond the capacity of a family unit alone.[8]

In 1860, Macon County's populace included 62 slaveholders (6.5 percent of household heads) and 519 slaves (8.6 percent of the population). Only two residents owned more than 20 slaves. Dillard Love owned 95, which made him the fifth largest slaveholder in all of western North Carolina. In Franklin, slavery's presence was more apparent than elsewhere in the county, with 66 slaves (divided among 11 owners) making up almost a third of the village's 215 residents.[9]

The Bells were not among those eleven slaveholders when they moved to

Franklin, but like many of their nonslaveholding neighbors, they took advantage of both the white and black manpower sources available in the community. From their arrival in 1860 until at least the end of 1862, they entrusted their farm to a white tenant, Bill Batey, the twenty-one-year-old son of a local blacksmith, who lived and worked on the Bells' land in exchange for his own use of an adjacent plot. They also employed two slaves, Tom and Liza, both hired on an annual basis from the county's largest supplier, Dillard Love. Tom farmed with Batey, while Liza helped Mary with household duties and child care and was often sent to aid the men with their fieldwork.[10]

After Alfred Bell's enlistment for Confederate service in November 1861, Mary in fact never suffered seriously from labor shortages during the ensuing years in which she assumed full responsibility for managing their farm and household. She drew on a variety of local sources in addition to her tenant and her hired slaves. Alfred's father and brother, both Franklin residents, were regular sources of support and advice, as well as occasional manpower. Mary sometimes hired other men, black and white, for particular jobs or by the day or week, but for the most part, Batey, Tom, and Liza formed the Bell farm workforce for the first half of the war. Mary's relationship with Batey remained somewhat tentative. She never felt fully secure in her role as his employer or supervisor, and her role remained essentially that of an intermediator between her husband and their tenant; she dutifully passed on Batey's questions to Alf and Alf's instructions to Batey.[11]

Far more of a responsibility and source of worry for Mary were the two hired slaves. Despite the fact that they referred to Batey as an "overseer," there is little indication that he bore any of the burden of supervising or disciplining either Tom or Liza. Though their behavior proved a constant source of irritation, Mary felt far freer to exert her own authority and judgment over them than she ever did over their white counterparts. Much of the problem with both Tom and Liza lay in their proximity to their own home. Mary complained of her lack of success in keeping either in place with the slave community of Dillard Love, their owner, so nearby. "Tom has been at Dillard's all week," she informed Alf in May 1862. "I do not know what he is doing or whether he intends coming back or not. He does as he pleases." By this point, the problem had become such that she wrote Love and asked him to either send Tom back or send another hand. She also asserted that Alf's father was part of the problem, in that "he does not control Tom as he ought to. He lets him have his own way too much." Such statements suggest that she was at least partially dependent on a male authority figure to control her male workers.[12]

The implications of Tom's association with other local slaves was more serious than merely depriving the Bells of a few days' work. Late in January 1862, a plot involving the theft of meat by several local slaves was uncovered. Several slaves of William McCoy were caught stealing meat—over six hundred pounds—from their master's smokehouse and selling or bartering it to the slaves of Dillard Love. McCoy forced confessions from at least six of his slaves by whipping them, and in the process he found that Tom was among several others, black and white, involved in these transactions. Exposure of this activity apparently put a stop to it. That, along with the fact that the ultimate responsibility for punishing their miscreant property lay with McCoy and Love, evoked a rather casual reaction from the Bells. In response to Mary's matter-of-fact account of what she called "a big scrape up in town," Alf stated, "I hope the negroes have not commenced stealing your bacon yet," and he instructed her to apply the best padlocks she had to their smokehouse.[13]

In spite of this disturbing evidence of Tom's role in such subversive activity, Mary Bell seemed more perturbed by her inability to control Liza. At first her offenses were much the same as Tom's lesser ones: "It is a hard matter to get Liza to do her work, she always has to gad about with Dillard's niggers when they are in town, which you know is often." But Liza proved far more strong-minded than Tom, and by the end of the summer her moodiness, volatile temper, extracurricular activities, and even menstrual cycle had driven her mistress to total exasperation. Mary reported to her husband in September, "I have concluded to send Liza home before long. She has got to be so careless and impudent and always on the pad. She has got so that I hardly dare to speak to her any ways cross. . . . She goes when she pleases and comes when she pleases." In a typical incident, Mary complained that she had granted Liza a pass to go across the river to the Love plantation on a Saturday night, only to have her show up two days after her designated Sunday night return. After such "tramps," as Mary called them, when Liza "runs herself to death and looses sleep," she "always grunts about for two or three days," making any effort to get work from her futile.[14]

It is difficult to tell from Mary's reports whether or not the ineffectual work habits, sullen attitudes, and subversive activity of both Tom and Liza reflected a new spirit of independence among the local slave community brought on by the disruptions of the war and the absence of much of the county's white male population. Other factors seem just as likely; inherent in the hiring of local slaves by nonslaveholding neighbors had always been the potential for restless and unruly behavior. Complaints by hirers to owners about the conduct of their contract labor were common throughout the antebellum period, particularly in this region where such arrangements accounted for much of the application of the slave workforce.[15]

Another explanation for the problem Mary Bell faced with these particular slaves lay in the fact that she was a woman. Despite having a white male tenant in her employ and various other men at her disposal, including her husband's father and brothers, Mary seems to have borne the bulk of responsibility for supervising her black employees. There is little doubt that both Tom and Liza sensed this as well as her lack of experience in exerting authority over hired hands. Perhaps already resentful at having been removed from their families and slave community, neither seemed to have any qualms about the challenges they posed to their temporary mistress, and they took full advantage of the disciplinary leeway the situation offered them.

The situation continued to plague Mary to the extent that, by early fall of 1862, she was ready to dispense with hired slave labor altogether and to pursue other options to fulfill the labor demands of her farm. The correspondence in which she weighed with Alf these alternatives from late 1862 until well into 1864 suggests the presence of an unusually flexible workforce in this section of Appalachia, thus contradicting our notions of a ravaged and disintegrating wartime economy plagued by depleted manpower that was so apparent elsewhere in the Confederacy.

It was at that point that a new and more attractive option (at least to Mary) presented itself—that of purchasing slaves. As a result of certain profitable investments, some sizable back payments collected by Mary for dental services performed by Alf before his enlistment, and his share of the family jewelry business, the Bells were in the unusual position of having accumulated considerable capital. He was rightfully nervous about the future value of the cash accrued and urged Mary "not to keep much money on hand," but rather to "invest it in land or property." As he went on to explain, "There is too much money for it to be good long after the war closes." Even with his faith that the Confederacy would emerge victorious and that "the yanks will reckognis us," Alf feared that "our congress wil kill our money and it will be like the old continental money."[16]

Mary agreed that their growing cash stockpile should be invested wisely, but she had very different ideas as to how to do so. She saw slave property as far more desirable than real estate and pushed hard to convince Alf to see likewise. He had told her of his particular interest in buying "the old Joe Welch farm down the river," and she was quick to discourage that venture, informing him of complications in a family estate settlement involving that property. She was equally quick to raise the prospect of a slave purchase instead. In the same letter in which she nixed the Welch property, she continued to complain about her hired slaves, and she used that pretext to conclude that she had once considered buying Liza, but would not now "own her as a precious gift." If she ever bought a slave, she continued, she would buy Martha, another of Dillard Love's slaves who is "a long ways ahead" of Liza. It was two months later before Mary broached the subject again, but this time she did so much more directly. "I would like to buy Martha and her child," she informed Alf on November 20, "if Mr. Love would take a reasonable price for them and it would be advisable to buy negroes at this time." She was quick to assure him that she was "not a judge of such things" and would make no move until Alf came home or wrote to Love with an offer.[17]

Martha was not the only slave woman available on the local market at that time. She was in fact part of a surprisingly dynamic slave trade in the mountains and among Macon County residents during the war years. While such activity was in part a continuation of local slave exchanges throughout the late antebellum period, it also reflected a more substantial demographic shift brought on by the uncertainties of war. Like a number of highland and upcountry communities, Franklin was among the beneficiaries of increasingly desperate efforts by slaveholders in South Carolina and Georgia to move their slaves beyond the reach of Union occupation forces along the coast or out of the path of Sherman's troops. Through connections already established between mountain merchants and lowcountry agents, and through local contacts with South Carolina planters who summered in highland resorts, slaves were moved into the region for either hire or sale for what western Carolinians considered bargain prices and what by 1864 desperate owners saw as welcome alternatives to total property losses.[18]

With increasing frequency, Mrs. Bell reported on purchases and sales of slaves among Franklin residents. They usually involved only an individual— and far more often than not, a woman—in itself a reflection of one of Mary's primary motives in entering this market. Among several available late in 1862, she singled out Dr. Lyle Siler's Sarah as a potential purchase, but noted that the physician would only take gold or silver for her, which was apparently beyond the Bells' capacity. Mary shrugged off this prohibitive factor, stating, "I would rather have Martha any how if we were to buy any."[19]

Acquiring Martha was further complicated by the fact that she had attracted interest from other prospective buyers. The Bells' most likely rival was John Ingram, who already owned at least four slaves and had an advantage over Alfred Bell in that he was at home and seemed likely to interfere with Bell's attempts to negotiate a long-distance deal from his company's camp in East Tennessee. Martha herself seemed to have been fully aware of the negotiations under which she was likely to change hands, and she indicated to Mary that she would much rather become the first Bell slave than the property of John Ingram, who she feared was not willing to acquire her child as well. She assured Mary that she herself would "beg Mr. Love to sell her" to them, and Mary urged Alf to write Love "and tell him that I am anxious to buy her and child and that you are willing." Mary, by this point, was already considering alternative purchases should they not obtain Martha, and by December had even convinced herself that even the once detested Liza would be acceptable. Rationalizing such a change of mind to Alf, she explained, "I am making a pretty good spinner out of her and I think perhaps if you were at home and we were out in the country she would do better." She concluded on a note of practicality by pointing out that "it would be better at least to own her than to spend money on hands that would be worth nothing."[20]

Due perhaps to the competitive nature of this opportunity combined with Alf's sense of urgency in transforming his cash into property of one sort or another, he was very willing to follow his wife's lead and even entrusted her with carrying out the transaction. "As to buying Marthey or Liza or any thing else you and my sweet babes want," he wrote, "I want you not to ask me anything about it. Its enough for you to know that I want you to buy it. I am more than willing. I have a wife, and I thank god for it, who is not extravegant and [is] always trying to lay something up for the futur." But as much as he trusted his wife's judgment, he also made his impatience and his own priorities quite apparent, for he followed these assurances by instructing: "I want the money payed out. If you fail to by her you had better pay Allman some on our land debt and try to buy the adjoining land to ours from Jules Siler even if you have to pay a big price."[21]

Despite the eagerness of Mary and the willingness of Alf to become slave-holders, none of the variety of options they discussed in the fall of 1862 ever materialized. But at some point over the next year the Bells did come into possession of a female slave named Eve. Because Alf managed to spend much of 1863 at or very near home, there is almost no correspondence between the Bells for that year. It only becomes apparent as their regular exchange of letters resumed early in 1864, after Alf had moved with his company into Georgia, that Eve, as payment for accumulated debts owed to Alf, had joined Mary's household on what they assumed then to be a permanent basis.[22]

By that point, Mary had had to face the hard reality that ownership — as opposed to the rental — of a slave did not necessarily ensure either a better working relationship between mistress and bondswoman or more respect or cooperation on the part of the latter. She complained in March 1864: "I never could put up with Eve, she was so hateful and she had made her braggs that if we kept her a hundred years she would never do us any good and she was making her words true. . . . There was always something the matter with her or she was pretending." Alf, by then certainly familiar with these complaints from his wife, was as patient and as compliant as ever in responding to them. He wrote that if she wished to sell Eve, she should do so, and he suggested the names of two likely buyers, both already Franklin slave owners. Yet he was just as quick to suggest that instead of selling this seemingly hopeless bondswoman, Mary might trade her to the Silers for "that land." "Try them first," he wrote, "give any price for it that you think we can pay and live after-ward." His final word on the subject: "I want the land bad."[23]

Alf was then stationed with his company in Pollard, Alabama, his greatest distance yet from home, and his advice to his wife arrived too late. A week earlier, she had made the "nigger trade" that so excited her: with the help of Alf's brothers, she "swaped Eve for a man, woman, and child . . . and gave $1,800 to boot." The transaction was a complicated one that Mary explained to her husband in detail. She paid $250 in cash, her brother-in-law Ben con-tributed $50 that he owed Alf, and the $1,500 balance was held as a note by Mr. Kilpatrick, with whom Mary made the exchange. According to her account and Ben's, Kilpatrick had purchased the family only a few months earlier through an agent in Charleston. Worried about his mounting debts and concluding that he had overextended himself with his new slave prop-erty, he agreed to these terms with the Bells. Mary's role in negotiating the terms of this transaction was minimal, although Ben made clear that it had been done with her full approval and her own letters indicate that she fully understood all aspects of the exchange. She was so excited at her sudden situation of multiple slave ownership that she assumed Alf would be equally pleased. Only the cost she felt might concern him, as she suggested with a combination of humor and guilt, "I recon you will have to petition for your wages to be raised until you can pay up the debts that your extravagant wife contracts." [24]

But Mary quickly followed that comment with assurance: "I know you will be pleased with them when you come home," and she filled what was among her lengthiest letters with detailed descriptions of their new family. Trim was a thirty-five-year-old cooper, a "smart quick fellow" who had made paint buckets in Charleston. Mary was sure he would be a good farmer, and if she could acquire the tools he needed (his had been left behind when he left Charleston), he could spend wet days putting those skills to good use. Trim's wife, Patsy, was about forty years old, "a fat old jolly thing" who was acquired with the added bonus of being pregnant. "I like her a great deal better than Eve," Mary wrote, but followed with a revealing statement as to the adjustment it would take to make this lowcountry native an effective mountain worker: "She is like all the other south niggers — don't know much about such work as we do, says she never cooked any only for herself and her family but she is willing to try to learn to do anything." Patsy could card pretty well, her mistress reported, and was already learning to spin. Mary showed herself to be a tough taskmaster or at least gave Alf that impression: "I have told them both," she confided to him, "that if they do not make my crib full of corn that I will sell them both in the fall for enough to fill it." Their daughter, Rosa, was a three-year-old, "a smart pert child" a little larger than their own little girl Maggie. After further details on the rearrangement of rooms to make living space for the three newcomers, Mary closed her letter by telling Alf, "I have showed the darkies your likeness. They think you quite handsome and are anxious to see you." [25]

Alf was taken aback by news of Mary's purchase. But comforted by his brother's insistence that the deal had indeed been a bargain, he stifled criticism of his wife, limiting his initial comments to: "I supose you will have negroes enough to make corn and rye this year. . . . Well, if they will suit you I am glad for the trade. I will try and pay the money." A week after that he seemed even more resigned to his new status. "I hope we now can get along without having any thing to do with Loves negroes," he wrote. "I do crave to be independent and unbeholding to any body." [26]

Mary continued to stress that she was "so well pleased with my darkies" during their first few months as Bell slaves. Her letters were filled with praise for Trim's initiative, work habits, and variety of skills: "He is none of your poke easy sort, but one of them smart quick sort. . . . I would not take $3,000 for him in confederate money," Mary declared. He "has not a lazy bone in him, every chance he has, in morning before breakfast and on wet days he is working away at his trade. He can do most anything . . . he knows as much about farming as Andy," a white tenant still in the Bells' employ who seemed gratified by the labor reinforcements of the new slaves. And despite her age, Aunt Patsy too was a big improvement over her female predecessors. "I would not begin to swap her for Eve," Mary stated, noting that she was not only a "good cook, a splendid washer and ironer," but also "so nice and so agreeable and likeable," and finally, "she is not wasteful, but very saveing far ahead of Liza or Eve either in that." [27]

Mary seemed to revel in her new situation. At the end of the first of her glowing descriptions of her new workforce, she declared to Alf, "If this war would just end and you could be at home, I would be satisfied." As late as July she wrote: "I like my darkies better I believe than I did at first," explaining that she had discovered that Trim could cut and make his own clothes, which "suits me very well." She even teased Alf by telling him that their own two-year-old daughter thought that Trim was her father. "She calls Trim Pa, she says my Pa has gone to war but her Pa is at home." She summed up her situation in that letter by stating, "I feel so good that evrything went right with me. I do not think any person could have made me mad for two or three days if they had spit in my face." [28]

Such euphoria of course could not be sustained. By fall, Mary found herself pregnant—for at least the fourth time—just as Aunt Patsy, who it turned out was not pregnant, suffered a series of fainting spells, which along with a more general deterioration in health made her more of a burden than a help to her expectant mistress. Even Mary's high regard for Trim was tempered by the fact that, with Andy's departure at the end of October, management of the farm proved too much for Trim alone. In direct contradiction to her summertime assessment of him, she concluded in November that "these low country negroes are not like ours in their work nor anything else. . . . I have almost lost confidence in anybody." [29]

Yet Mary's disillusionment was not with the burdens of slave ownership. It was merely the continual "sickliness" of Patsy that dampened her earlier enthusiasm. Beginning in the fall, she proposed to her husband further slave purchases to either supplement or replace the family she owned. "I believe that Trim would be of great service to us," Mary wrote, "but Aunt Patsy never will be any more I am afraid and it will be a long time before Rosa will be any." She admitted, "It does seem like that people never can be fixed as they want to be. We craved a man and when we got one, we lack a woman."[30]

In particular, Mary had her eye on a slave couple, Betts and Alfred, that she felt would meet her needs. She wrote Alf on several occasions that "if they were still for sale and if you have money enough I think they would suit us as well as any we could get. They both know how to manage pretty well, as well as any negroes I recon." Finally admitting what had seemed to be her highest priority in acquiring slaves all along, she stated, "I want a woman that can get up and get breakfast," the chore she most detested having to do herself.[31]

Mary learned that Mr. Kilpatrick, from whom she had purchased Trim, Patsy, and Rosa, was willing to buy back at least the father and daughter, though even he admitted he would have to accept the sickly Patsy as well. Such a sale would have included reclaiming Eve, who apparently had not satisfied Kilpatrick any more than she had Mary. Mary was even willing to agree to supervise that recalcitrant charge again if she could have Bett and Alfred as well, her rationalization being, "I know Bett could make her [Eve] smart if any body can and then I can have one in the house and one to work out of doors." In spite of her eager desire for these new slaves, she admitted having qualms about giving up the family she had so enthusiastically embraced several months earlier. "I should not be so anxious to trade these off if I thought Aunt Patsy would not be a burden on our hands in her old days. She always tries to do all she can when she is well and always tried to please me but she is very slow about her work. I like her disposition better than Trim's although I can get along with him very well."[32]

Despite the urgency of her tone, there is no indication that any such trade or purchase ever took place, but we cannot know for sure. Unfortunately, Alf's return home in February 1865 ended Mary's vivid record of their slave-owning experience, leaving us with far too many unanswered questions. The story of emancipation in this or virtually any other part of Southern Appalachia is a story yet to be told, and with the sudden halt to the richly detailed correspondence spawned by the Bells' wartime separation, it is unlikely that we can ever know how they coped with the sudden and involuntary loss of their prized property; whether or not Trim, Patsy, or any other freedman or woman stayed with the Bells to provide the same sort of labor under new contractual arrangements; or whether they, like hundreds of their counterparts, took to the road, perhaps returning to their roots in coastal South Carolina.[33]

What then does Mary Bell's experiences with slaves — hired, sought, and purchased — bring to our understanding of the empowerment that the Civil War provided southern white women as owners and supervisors of black labor? In some respects, of course, the Bells' situation was atypical because of their continued affluence during the war and because of their Appalachian setting. As businessman and professional, even in enterprises as marginal as jeweler and dentist, Alfred Bell quickly established a lucrative position upon his return to his highland hometown on the eve of the war. He did so effectively enough within his year and a half of residency before his enlistment that, under his wife's conscientious guardianship, he continued to reap the rewards of his efforts even during his prolonged absence. Their letters regarding the intricacies of his business affairs reveal a dynamic local economic structure, based on a viable — though often informal and personal — system of credit and debt that continued unabated in Macon County, where the war had little or no physically disrupting effect, most likely a function of its relative remoteness. Despite guerrilla activity that wreaked havoc on many areas of the Carolina highlands, Franklin found itself insulated from even those instrusions.

Such insulation also meant more stability for the peculiar institution in the region, which allowed the Bells, as late as 1864, to acquire slaves of their own while continuing to hire the slaves of others. None of the tensions or hardships imposed on their community by the war proved so serious or destructive as to threaten either their slave property or their slaves' behavior. The system remained viable and, with a depletion of manpower, slaves became a commodity more in demand than ever at least until the conflict's closing months.

But if the opportunities available to the Bells during the war years were exceptional, their reaction to their success took a more traditional form. Like most southerners, Alfred and Mary Bell equated financial prosperity with slaveholding and moved, as soon as they could, into those ranks. This step merely raised the number of Franklin's slaveholding households from eleven to twelve; yet it linked the Bells with the most influential and respected members of their community in a way they had not quite enjoyed before, as full-fledged members of that modest but undeniable local elite.

There was no gender gap in the value placed upon such heightened stature; Mary was as intent upon achieving it as Alfred, and her awareness that slave ownership would provide such entrée very likely factored into her desire to enter those ranks. Among the headaches she faced with her hired black workers was having to complain to and request intervention from the owners of her charges. This surely served as a constant reminder that while it was very much a business relationship, it was also a less egalitarian client/patron situation in which she was cast into the role of dependent supplicant to her wealthier neighbors for use of the very product that most visibly demonstrated that wealth. For Alf, too, the advantages of being "independent and unbeholding to any body" was the first rationalization he expressed in resigning himself to his wife's new investment. Thus, the war had done little by its final year to alter the terms that defined class and status, however subtle, even in this remote mountain community. Like thousands of their upwardly mobile counterparts throughout the South, the goals of this couple in 1860, shared equally by husband and wife, had been to acquire slaves and land and the respect and position that accompanied both. The upheaval of the war did nothing to dampen their optimism or thwart their opportunity to achieve those ambitions.

The Bells' correspondence also provides a revealing portrait of a marital partnership and of a woman who grew considerably in the new roles demanded of her on the homefront. Just as it would have been unimaginable for an American president prior to 1862 to have single-handedly proclaimed the emancipation of slaves, so it would have been almost inconceivable for Mary Bell or any other wife to have made a slave purchase without seeking approval from her husband. The fact that she did so serves as a particularly dramatic and perhaps extreme example of how the war empowered some southern white women as both wives and as household fiscal agents. The war's upheaval, along with an unusually tolerant and even encouraging husband, allowed Mary Bell a sense of independence and initiative within that partnership that she would probably never otherwise have known. The wartime prosperity she enjoyed and her entry into the ranks of slaveholders just as many were being deprived of that status distinguishes her experience from the plight of many Confederate, and certainly most Appalachian, women, who as Gordon McKinney has documented suffered more physical abuse and economic deprivation than those in other parts of the South.[34]

In contrast to that majority whose suffering was intensified as the war was prolonged, Mary Bell's situation improved over the course of the conflict.

Increasingly self-assured, she thrived on her achievements and was far less despondent in 1864 than she had been in her first few months on her own in late 1861 and much of 1862. Her acquisition of slaves was both a result and a source of her vastly expanded self-confidence. While she remained vocally apathetic and even contemptuous of the Confederate cause throughout the war, she adapted to its demands and changing dynamics with exceptional flair. If, as Drew Gilpin Faust has suggested, "white women's actions as slave mistresses were critical to Confederate destinies," then Mary Bell ultimately served the southern nation as well as or better than most.[35]

The gender gap in the Bells' investment priorities is also suggestive. The fact that through gifts, dowries, and inheritances, slaveholders were more likely to bestow slaves to daughters and land to sons suggests that Mary Bell, like other southern women, may have acquired a greater affinity for human over real property. Or perhaps, as the mother of three daughters and no sons, she may have been thinking of future bequests to them.[36] Yet the far more likely incentive behind Mary's determination to purchase slaves was her desire for immediate relief from the domestic burdens she bore. Alf, on the other hand, while not unsympathetic with his wife's situation, was far more interested in land ownership and both the long-term prospects it offered as a real estate investment and the more immediate returns its agricultural output promised. Yet, due to wartime circumstances, it was she, not he, who determined the form their investment would take and her priorities and proclivities that ultimately prevailed.

Alfred's absence in itself created a need for manpower to maintain the Bells' newly acquired farm acreage merely to keep their growing family fed and clothed. While Mary fully recognized the necessity of male slaves to fill that void, female slaves were always more central to her ambitions, and they dominated her reports and plans to Alf regarding first the hiring, and then the purchase, of slave labor. She seemed far more preoccupied with Liza, Eve, Martha, Betts, and Patsy than she ever did with Tom, Trim, or the various men she viewed as prospective property. There was never any suggestion that she felt more empathy or intimacy with these women than she did with their spouses; there was certainly no interracial "sisterhood" in evidence in the Bell household. If anything, relationships with her female charges Eve and Liza were more fraught with tensions and frustrations than were those with Tom or Trim, which may have resulted from the more constant contact and closer supervision she maintained over them. Nor did common maternal instincts make Mary empathetic toward the slave mothers with whom she dealt. She was indifferent to the parental bonds at stake when confronted with Martha's personal appeal to purchase her and her child, treating it only as an advantageous ploy in her efforts to outbid the other potential buyer who was interested only in the mother.[37] It is obvious that, ultimately, Mary's greater attention to these women resulted from their capacity for relieving her own workload in the house, garden, or field. Considering the fact that in addition to those new responsibilities, she spent most of the war either pregnant or with newborns to care for (she bore two children during the war and lost a third), her craving for such relief was natural. In 1860, James D. B. DeBow delineated the reasons nonslaveholders sought to acquire slaves and mentioned first not what they could contribute to agricultural productivity but rather the domestic services they could provide. "The non-slaveholder," he wrote, "knows that as soon as his savings will admit, he can become a slaveholder, and thus relieve his wife from the necessities of the kitchen and the laundry, and his children from the labors of the field."[38] As Mary Bell's actions indicate, such priorities were even more pronounced when it was the wife of the nonslaveholder who initiated entry into the slaveholding ranks.

It is revealing that for all her praise of Trim's skills, hard work, and contributions to the farm's maintenance, Mrs. Bell was ready to sell him and his family once Patsy's deteriorating health made her less and less useful to her mistress. By the same token, Mary was willing to retake charge of the "hateful" Eve when the opportunity presented itself simply because two women in her employ seemed too tempting a prospect to resist. The choices she made suggest that her intense desire to own slaves stemmed more from their use in alleviating the physical burdens of family and farm than from considerations of financial security or social status. Her exhaustion seemed almost palpable as she proclaimed her desire for "a woman who can get up and get breakfast."[39]

Finally, it is tempting to judge the Bells' purchase of slaves in 1864 as foolish and short-sighted or at least to suggest that Alf exhibited greater foresight than his wife in sensing the precarious future the war imposed on this particular form of property. But there is no evidence that he had any doubts as to either the Confederacy's ultimate victory or slavery's continued, and even safer, existence under that new government. Had he had any qualms about the risk involved, he certainly would not have been so quick to encourage Mary in her pursuit of slave property. The vitality of the highland slave trade hinged on ever increasing threats to black property elsewhere; Mary Bell sensed this and joined numerous other western Carolinians in acquiring or exchanging slaves at what they thought to be bargain rates.

Just as the war imposed new challenges and responsibilities on Mary Bell and other southern women, it also provided them with new opportunities of which Mary took more advantage than most. In describing the plight of southern womanhood at war, Anne Firor Scott laid out the essence of Mary Bell's experience with almost uncanny precision. "Husbands hurrying off to the army," Scott stated, "sent back all kinds of instructions about the planting, harvesting, and marketing of crops, the management of slaves, the education of children, the budgeting of money, the collecting of old debts, and every other aspect of their business, apparently in perfect confidence that their wives would somehow cope. The women, in their turn, were polite about asking advice and begged for guidance, while carrying on as if they had always been planters, business managers, overseers of slaves, and decision makers."[40]

Indeed, Mary rose to the challenge of assuming all of those roles and took considerable satisfaction in so doing.[41] Yet it was her acquisition and management of a slave force that provides the most dramatic reflection of how the war and the peculiar circumstances of her highland locale allowed her to fulfill what were intensely personal ambitions. She considered this her greatest success, and yet, because it was tied so to an institution already disintegrating and soon to be extinguished completely, her empowerment probably proved more ephemeral than that of other "strong-minded" women for whom, Scott suggested, "the experience of self-sufficiency during the war had opened the door [of further empowerment] a crack."[42]

It is ironic that the Bells' material success and Mary's own determination and newfound independence enabled her to take the single step that rendered her family's financial future most precarious and gave it far more of a stake in the outcome of a war for which she had long professed nothing but apathy. One can only speculate on how much of the blame for that loss she had to shoulder; on what recriminations she faced—from Alfred or self-imposed—and what they ultimately cost her in terms of her newly acquired liberation and self-confidence; and on whether or not she herself ever recognized the sad irony of the fateful step that her new status had allowed her to take on March 11, 1864.

## NOTES

1. Mary Bell to Alfred W. Bell, 11 March 1864, Alfred W. Bell Papers, Manuscript Department, Perkins Library, Duke University. All subsequent citations to the Bells' correspondence are to letters in this collection.

2. On the plight of Appalachian women during the Civil War, see Gordon B. McKinney, "Women's Role in Civil War Western North Carolina," *North Carolina Historical Review* 69 (January 1992): 37–56; Phillip Shaw Paludan, *Victims: A True Story of the Civil War* (Knoxville: University of Tennessee Press, 1981); Durwood Dunn, *Cades Cove: The Life and Death of a Southern Appalachian Community, 1818–1937* (Knoxville: University of Tennessee Press, 1988), chap. 5; Barbara Howe, "The Impact of the Civil War on Women in Wheeling, West Virginia," paper presented at the Second Southern Conference on Women's History, Chapel Hill, N.C., June 1991; Ralph Mann, "Guerrilla Warfare and Gender Roles: Sandy Basin, Virginia as Case Study," in Tyler Blethen, ed., *Diversity in Appalachia: Images and Realities,* vol. 5 of *Journal of Appalachian Studies Association* (1993), 59–66; and Mann, "Family Group, Family Migration, and the Civil War in Sandy Basin, Virginia," *Appalachian Journal* 19 (summer 1992): 374–93.

More general studies of nineteenth-century Appalachian women include Sally Ward Maggard, "Class and Gender: New Theoretical Priorities in Appalachian Studies," in *Impact of Institutions in Appalachia: Proceedings of the Appalachian Studies, Eighth Annual Conference,* ed. Jim Lloyd and Anne G. Campbell (Boone, N.C.: Appalachian Consortium Press, 1986), 100–113; Milton Ready, "Forgotten Sisters: Mountain Women in the South," in John C. Inscoe, ed., *Southern Appalachia and the South: A Region within a Region,* vol. 3 of *Journal of Appalachian Studies Association* (1991), 61–67; and Mary K. Anglin, "Errors at the Margins: Rediscovering the Women of Antebellum Western North Carolina," paper presented at Southern Historical Association meeting, Fort Worth, Texas, November 1991.

3. George C. Rable, *Civil Wars: Women and the Crisis of Southern Nationalism* (Urbana: University of Illinois Press, 1989), 115.

4. Drew Gilpin Faust, " 'Trying to Do a Man's Business': Slavery, Violence and Gender in the American Civil War," *Gender and History* 4 (summer 1992): 198. Faust's essay focuses on a Texas woman and the problems she faced with her slaves and overseer during the wartime absence of her husband. The rapidly expanding literature on the challenges faced by slaveholding women in the Confederacy also includes Rable, *Civil Wars;* Anne Firor Scott, *The Southern Lady: From Pedestal to Politics, 1830 to 1930* (Chicago: University of Chicago Press, 1970), chap. 4; Clarence L. Mohr, *On the Threshold of Freedom: Masters and Slaves in Civil War Georgia* (Athens: University of Georgia Press, 1986), 214–32; Marilyn Mayer Culpepper, *Trials and Triumphs: The Women of the American Civil War* (East Lansing: Michigan State University Press, 1991), chap. 2; and Joan E. Cashin, " 'Since the War Broke Out': The Marriage of Kate and William

McLure," in *Divided Houses: Gender and the Civil War,* ed. Catherine Clinton and Nina Silber (New York: Oxford University Press, 1992), 200–212.

5. Information on the Bells' prewar situation comes from the inventory description to the Bell Papers, Duke.

6. On antebellum agriculture in the North Carolina mountains, see H. Tyler Blethen and Curtis W. Wood Jr., "The Pioneer Experience to 1851," in *The History of Jackson County,* ed. Max R. Williams (Sylva: Jackson County Historical Society, 1987), 67–100 [Jackson County adjoins Macon County to the east]; and John C. Inscoe, *Mountain Masters, Slavery, and the Sectional Crisis in Western North Carolina* (Knoxville: University of Tennessee Press, 1989), chap. 1. On tenant labor in antebellum Appalachia, see Joseph E. Reid Jr., "Antebellum Southern Rental Contracts" [on Haywood County, N.C.], in *Explorations in Economic History* 13 (1976): 69–83; and Blethen and Wood, "Pioneer Experience to 1851," 83–95.

7. Frederick Law Olmsted, *A Journey in the Back Country in the Winter of 1853–54* (1860; reprint, New York: Schocken Books, 1970), 253. See Inscoe, *Mountain Masters,* chap. 3, for a discussion of slave utilization in antebellum western North Carolina.

8. On the hiring of slaves, see Clement Eaton, "Slave Hiring in the Upper South: A Step toward Freedom," *Mississippi Valley Historical Review* 46 (March 1960): 663–78; Inscoe, *Mountain Masters,* 76–92; Randolph B. Campbell, "Slave Hiring in Texas," *American Historical Review* 93 (February 1988): 107–14; and William A. Byrne, "The Hiring of Woodson, Slave Carpenter of Savannah," *Georgia Historical Quarterly* 77 (summer 1993): 245–63.

9. *Eighth U.S. Census,* 1860: Schedule 2, Macon County, N.C.

10. The Bells' correspondence began in November 1861 and continued through February 1865. On labor arrangements, see her letters of 13 November 1861, 5 March, 4 April, 28 April, 15 May, 29 May, 13 June, and 20 June 1862. For other aspects of Mary Bell's situation during the Civil War, see Inscoe, "Coping in Confederate Appalachia: A Portrait of a Mountain Woman and Her Community at War," *North Carolina Historical Review* 64 (October 1992): 388–413.

11. Although Mary's relationship with Batey was not that of a slaveholding mistress and an overseer, her discomfort was not unlike that experienced by other women in those relationships. See, for example, Elizabeth Fox-Genovese, *Within the Plantation Household: Black and White Women of the Old South* (Chapel Hill: University of North Carolina Press, 1988), 187–90, 205–7; Rable, *Civil Wars,* 114–15; Catherine Clinton, *The Plantation Mistress: Woman's World in the Old South* (New York: Pantheon Books, 1982), 191; and particularly Faust, " 'Trying to Do a Man's Business,' " 202–10 passim.

12. Mary to Alfred Bell, 22 May 1862. On gender differences in controlling slaves, see Clinton, *Plantation Mistress,* 192–93; Fox-Genovese, *Within the Plantation Household,* 135, 140–45; and Faust, " 'Trying to Do a Man's Business.' "

13. Mary to Alfred Bell, 30 January 1862; Alfred to Mary Bell, 8 February 1862.

14. Mary to Alfred Bell, 22 May, 21 September 1862.

15. For other examples of such complaints, see Inscoe, *Mountain Masters,* 76–80, 89–90; and Byrne, "The Hiring of Woodson," 249–59.

16. Alfred to Mary Bell, 17 August 1862.

17. Ibid.; Mary to Alfred Bell, 21 September, 20 November 1862.

18. For references to the movement of slaves from coastal plantations to inland and upcountry areas, see B. H. Nelson, "Some Aspects of Negro Life in North Carolina during the Civil War," *North Carolina Historical Review* 25 (April 1948): 157–59; Mohr, *On the Threshold of Freedom,* chap. 4; Wayne K. Durrill, *War of Another Kind: A Southern Community in the Great Rebellion* (New York: Oxford University Press, 1990), chap. 3; Lynda Morgan, *Emancipation in Virginia's Tobacco Belt, 1850–1870* (Athens: University of Georgia Press, 1992), 112–13. On the increased slave trade in the Carolina Highlands during the war, see Inscoe, "Mountain Masters as Confederate Profiteers: The Profitability of Slavery in Western North Carolina, 1861–1865," *Slavery and Abolition* 16 (April 1995): 85–110.

19. Mary to Alfred Bell, 20 November 1862.

20. Mary to Alfred Bell, 6 December 1862.

21. Alfred to Mary Bell, 28 November, 19 December 1862. See also his letter of 29 December 1862.

22. Mary to Alfred Bell, 19 February 1864.

23. Mary to Alfred Bell, 11 March 1864; Alfred to Mary Bell, 17 March 1864.

24. Mary to Alfred Bell, 11 March 1864; Benjamin W. Bell to Alfred Bell, 11 March 1864.

25. Mary to Alfred Bell, 11 March 1864.

26. Alfred to Mary Bell, 31 March, 8 April 1864.

27. Mary to Alfred Bell, 19 March, 8 April, 15 April, 5 June 1864.

28. Mary to Alfred Bell, 8 July 1864. See also her letter of 8 December 1864.

29. Mary to Alfred Bell, 17 November 1864.

30. Ibid.

31. Mary to Alfred Bell, 24 November 1864.

32. Ibid. It is worth noting that in their negotiations over Trim, Patsy, and Rosa, neither the Bells nor Kilpatrick ever considered splitting the family, despite the fact that only Trim was of much immediate value in terms of his capacity for labor. This may reflect a greater respect for slave family ties among highland slaveholders than is evident elsewhere. On the debate over the more benevolent treatment of slaves in mountain areas, see Inscoe, "Race and Racism in Nineteenth-Century Southern Appalachia: Myths, Realities, and Ambiguities," in *Appalachia in the Making,* ed. Dwight Billings, Mary Beth Pudup, and Altina Wallers (Chapel Hill: University of North Carolina Press, 1995).

33. Freedmen's Bureau agent John W. De Forest noted, "The Negroes who had been brought to the up-country during the war by white families were crazy to get back to

their native flats of ague and country fever. Highland darkies who had drifted down to the seashore were sending urgent requests to be 'fotched home again.' " De Forest, *A Union Officer in the Reconstruction* (New Haven: Yale University Press, 1948), 36–37.

34. McKinney, "Women's Role in Civil War Western North Carolina."

35. Faust, " 'Trying to Do a Man's Business,' " 198. See also Faust's "Altars of Sacrifice: Confederate Women and the Narratives of War," *Journal of American History* 76 (March 1990): 1200–1228. On Mary Bell's attitude toward the war and toward the Confederacy, see Inscoe, "Coping in Confederate Appalachia," 393–99, 410–11.

36. Jane Turner Censer provides the most definitive evidence of gender-distinctive inheritance patterns in her study of North Carolina planters. Censer, *North Carolina Planters and Their Children, 1800–1860* (Baton Rouge: Louisiana State University Press, 1984), 105–7, 110–11. See also Jean E. Friedman, *The Enclosed Garden: Women and Community in the Evangelical South, 1830–1900* (Chapel Hill: University of North Carolina Press, 1985), 90.

37. For other examples of slave women making special appeals to the sympathy of white women, see Clinton, *Plantation Mistress,* 187–92; and Fox-Genovese, *Within the Plantation Household,* 131–32.

38. [James D. B. DeBow], *The Interest in Slavery of the Southern Non-Slaveholder* (Charleston: Evans and Cogswell, 1860), 9, quoted in Matthew G. Schoenbachler, " 'Good Cooks and Washers': Slave-hiring, Domestic Labor, and the Market in Bourbon County, Kentucky," an unpublished paper that suggests that slave women were more in demand for hire than men by nonslaveholding yeomen because they most valued the relief from "household drudgery" such hirings provided their wives.

39. These were by no means the last slave purchases made. As late as 4 May 1865, a woman in Lawrenceville, Georgia, bought a slave girl for $50 in gold. "I think the institution about gone, but she had not a relative in the world. Seems affectionate and well disposed, and if she remains with me I will do my duty towards her, and it will be no great loss if I lose the $50." Quoted in Culpepper, *Trials and Triumphs,* 385n.

40. Scott, *Southern Lady,* 82.

41. See Inscoe, "Coping in Confederate Appalachia," for a fuller account of various other aspects of Mary Bell's responsibilities and achievements during the war—including, just as Scott suggests, the management of Alf's business, the collection of debts owed him, the planting, harvesting, and marketing of crops, and the care and education of their children.

42. Scott, *Southern Lady,* 101.

W I L M A   K I N G

# The Mistress and Her Maids

## WHITE AND BLACK WOMEN
## IN A LOUISIANA HOUSEHOLD,
## 1858-1868

"M Y HEALTH is quite good now—but *my temper is quite bad*," wrote Tryphena Blanche Holder Fox (1834-1912) on July 9, 1858, to her mother, Anna Rose Holder (1808-1895), in Pittsfield, Massachusetts. "These darkies," the source of disquiet, she explained, " 'do plague me to death' sometimes." Fox referred to enslaved women, especially Susan, who worked by "fits & starts—good three or four weeks & then so ugly & contrary that an angel could hardly keep mild & pleasant." Differences in perceptions about gender-related experiences including childbearing and domestic work figured prominently in her disappointments.[1]

In 1852 Tryphena Holder accepted a position as tutor for the George Messenger family near Vicksburg, Mississippi. Much of her salary went back to Massachusetts to help support her widowed mother and dependent siblings. When George Holder, a textile mill supervisor, died in 1849, his resources were not adequate to support his family of six children. The size of the Messengers' holdings made the eighteen-year-old teacher ever conscious of their class differences. The young woman saw herself as a "stranger in a strange land," socially and economically. Seeking to improve her status, she married David Raymond Fox (1822-1893), a physician and son of a local planter, after a brief 1856 courtship. They made their home in Plaquemines Parish, Louisiana, where the new bride struggled to transcend the ranks of a northern working-class woman to that of a "southern lady."[2]

This essay focuses on the intersection of class, race, and gender as

Tryphena Holder Fox and African American women, largely slaves, negotiated the boundaries of their mistress-maid relationships between 1858 and 1868. The control/resistance dynamics were never far from the surface. A succession of maids lived and worked at "Hygiene," the Fox home along the Mississippi River. However, she wrote especially about Ann, a slave woman hired between 1857 and 1860; Susan and Maria, slaves owned by Fox from 1858 to 1863 and 1860 to 1863, respectively; and Milly, a free woman, employed there between 1865 and 1868.[3]

The mistress's northern working-class background, her marriage to a professional rather than to a planter, and her relationship with slave and free servants before and after the Civil War make her worthy of study. The "time has never been better to explore the lost worlds and recapture voices of southern women's history," writes Catherine Clinton in the *Georgia Historical Quarterly*'s special 1992 issue, "The Diversity of Southern Gender and Race: Women in Georgia and the South." In more than one hundred letters from Tryphena Fox to Anna Holder there are detailed discussions of gender-related experiences. The correspondence sheds light on the life of a southern, albeit transplanted, white woman during the slave era.[4]

Tryphena Fox, like many of the women portrayed in Clinton's *Plantation Mistress,* complained of loneliness. To be sure, Hygiene was a distance from the nearest neighbors, but the mistress's perceptions of her improved social status isolated her even more. Because of condescending views about local whites, she had few friends. Of the Stackhouse family, she wrote: "I do not like them at all, for though the Messrs Stackhouse are the wealthiest planters here, the whole family is exceedingly illiterate." She visited them only to "keep on the right side, on account of the Doctors practice there." Fox dubbed other whites as "good-hearted people, but not very intelligent or refined"; therefore, one did not "gain much by visiting them." She wished to have "a few nice families" nearby. Educated and refined neighbors with parallel social interest would have pleased her.[5]

Fox's marriage and relocation elevated her above the ranks of a hired servant—"only the teacher"—and placed her in the world of wealthy sugar planters. "When I think of my former position," she wrote in late 1856, "I am so glad that I am no longer dependent upon this one or that for food & shelter." Earning a living by teaching except under the most dire circumstances "was not a fit occupation for a lady." The upwardly mobile woman easily imagined herself as a plantation mistress, but she never had the assets to

move firmly into that position. Dr. Fox was a salaried physician, hired annually to treat slaves owned by planters in the surrounding area, rather than a
"rich man." In 1860 he owned Hygiene and the lot it stood upon, which was
worth $5,000, along with personal property worth $2,500. Dr. Fox never
owned more than four adults and several children at any one time between
1856 and 1864.[6]

By contrast, the physician's clients and neighbors had greater holdings.
The value of Oscar Vellere's real estate was $50,000, and his personal prop-
erty was worth $60,000. Another planter, Auguste Reggio, valued his hold-
ings at $70,000 real and $90,000 personal. William Stackhouse's holdings
were less than Vellere's and Reggio's, yet he was not a poor man. His real
property was worth $45,000, and the personal property was estimated at
$35,000.[7]

Notwithstanding the size of the doctor's real and personal property, the
northern-born woman was "mistress" at Hygiene. She held firm notions
about the role of "southern ladies" gained at Baconham Plantation where
Messenger owned hundreds of acres of cotton fields and ninety-seven slaves
in 1850. During Sophia Messenger's absence in December 1855, the tutor
acted as "housekeeper and the 'general inspector.'" Once in a home of her
own, she drew upon ideas gained at Baconham and from her own childhood
experiences. The Holders ran a boarding house in Pittsfield where medical
students and mill hands sought such housing arrangements.[8]

Tryphena Fox's success or failure as a housekeeper depended on labor
management skills. Shortly after her June 1856 marriage, the twenty-two-
year-old bride explained her role in the mistress-maid relationship: "Having
two servants to do the work, I do but little myself and that particular things
which I do not like to trust to them, but I have to watch them and tell them
every little item to be done, for a negro never sees any dirt or grease, so if a
*Southern lady* does not do much manual labor, she has head-work enough
to keep her busy." There was a direct link between the quality of her life and
the quality and quantity of their work. Dr. Fox, who owned the manservant
Reuben at the time of the marriage, initially hired maids for his wife. If they
worked efficiently and remained physically fit, the mistress had leisure time
for reading or letterwriting. Otherwise, chores remained "behind hand" as
she struggled to combine the roles of maid and mistress. In this respect she
was no different from many of her contemporaries.[9]

The mistress had little control over hired servants. Besides, the tenuous nature of "teaching & looking after other peoples' [servants]" was bother-some. However, Fox assumed owning slaves ended such aggravations. In December 1857, she announced: "We are obliged to save every dollar he [Dr. Fox] can 'rake & scrape' to pay for a negro woman." Owning humans did not appear to disturb her. Although the mistress had come of age after the abolition of slavery in Massachusetts, she must have been aware of racial prejudices against northern blacks. Nevertheless, ownership of slaves was consistent with "a fundamental premise of the southern ideal of woman-hood: Women, to be ladies, had to have servants." Furthermore, it reflected material well-being.[10]

Servants satisfied both personal and status needs, but to hire or own them did not guarantee satisfaction. The highly personalized nature of mistress-maid relationships often resulted in discord. At Hygiene, a maid's failure to internalize the mistress's ambitions was not unusual. Bondservants pre-cipitated conflicts in subtle but deliberate ways. Their inabilities or illnesses often forced the mistress to assist or complete their work. Inexperience as a housekeeper along with the struggle to maintain New England standards in the plantation South put her at odds with Susan, a servant Dr. Fox bought in late 1857.[11]

Susan belonged to a Frenchman in the parish who was eager to sell her. His family spoke no English, and Susan did not understand French. Moreover, "like most foreigners," Fox wrote, the owner was "very hard on negroes." Susan did all the work for the family of ten, collected her own wood, and hauled water from the river. She also "gave them a great deal of trouble."[12]

The mistress assumed that the amount of work was the source of the prob-lem and inferred it would be different at Hygiene with its three occupants: Tryphena Fox, her husband, and their daughter, Fanny Otis (1857-1918). The mistress believed she could "get along with [Susan] passable well." She underestimated Susan's penchant for day-to-day resistance. Historians Ray-mond and Alice Bauer concluded that slaves used this method of protesting their condition routinely. Moreover, the mistress appeared oblivious to this practice and the ongoing amount of give and take involved in creating work-ing relationships with slaves.[13]

Blinded by what she considered an excellent price for Susan, the mis-tress dismissed the warning signals about the woman's will to resist control. Dr. Fox paid $1,400 for Susan and her daughters, five-year-old Adelaide and three-year-old Margaret. Dr. Fox believed he could sell the family for $2,000, which was reasonable considering market prices in the 1850s. Tryphena Fox soon understood that Susan's price reflected the Frenchman's interest in ridding himself quickly of "troublesome property." Within months the mistress had a litany of complaints about Susan. Certainly, the turbulent interactions between the two women destroyed any basis for friendship or sisterhood.[14]

Age and class as much as race were responsible for their disaffection. Besides, there were no special acts to meld their differences. When the twenty-eight-year-old Susan began work New Year's Day, 1858, the mistress, who was several years younger, described her as "slow and 'nigger.'" Fox explained, "If she were not such a monstrosity as she is just now she would have to step a *little* faster." Susan, pregnant with her third child, was due to deliver in February. Slaveowners often required lighter work if they were aware of the relationship between heavy work and infant mortality. However, Dr. Fox, who knew the pecuniary value of reproduction, did not reduce her workload.[15]

Susan bore several children while at Hygiene. Her son Buddy was born February 2, 1858; another child, "a fine mulatto boy," arrived February 28, 1860; and "a very fine large boy" was born in March 1861. The birthdate of another child, Maria, is unknown. In that same period, the mistress gave birth to Edward Randolph on January 16, 1860, and to Anna Rose on July 12, 1861. Pregnancy created no special bonds between the women. Tryphena Fox wrote about her own pregnancies, but she said almost nothing of Susan's. Note the terseness of her March 17, 1860, comments: "Susan managed to be quite smart . . . concluded she would *have a baby*—" The letter conveys neither an awareness of the pregnancy nor concern about Susan's well-being.[16]

Childbearing in nineteenth-century America was perilous regardless of the pregnant woman's race or class. Aside from physical concerns, a study of childbirth and the psychological experience of labor by Natalie Shainess argues that an expectant mother's attitude about her femininity, values, and the relationship with the unborn child's father determines how she views pregnancy.[17]

The mistress described her husband as "devoted to his family" and "a husband, in every sense of the word," yet she was apprehensive about each of her ten pregnancies. The source of anxiety was the absence of her mother and sister at the time of delivery, but Fox was not alone. Aside from her husband, his sisters, Emily or Lucy, were usually present. Their visits broke the monotony and reunited her with women of her own race, class, and age. Besides, the young mother was secure knowing that if she did not survive the lying-in, they would care for her infant as if it were their own.[18]

Conditions surrounding the birth of slave children were different. Enslaved women had little to say outside their own worlds about femininity or values. Unlike white husbands who could be present at the time of delivery, many slave fathers were absent because of forced separations. The women generally gave birth with the assistance of other slave women unless emergencies arose. Susan had a community of slave women, albeit a small one, who shared her interest, but she had no husband present. By contrast, the mistress's husband was there, but she had no community of women of her own race and class. At bottom, both women experienced a kind of separation and isolation during childbirth.

The historical documents are silent about the father or fathers of Susan's children. Questions about his/their race(s), residence(s), and relationship(s) with the children remain unanswered. Records are equally mute about Susan's parents or siblings. She had no family to visit and provide a supportive atmosphere, yet she was not alone. Ann, the hired woman, assumed her chores in 1858 along with bathing and nursing the infant. In short, she "waited upon" Susan. Fox complained that it was too much for her " 'to play nigger' to everybody," implying that Ann's first responsibility was to her family rather than to Susan's. When Susan's fourth child was born in 1860, Emily Fox assumed all of the "housework & nursing" for two weeks. The mistress had gone to Mississippi and the newly acquired Maria, an eighteen-year-old slave, went along to attend to Fanny. By the time Susan's fifth child was born in 1861, she and Maria had lived at Hygiene together for more than a year. Perhaps she assisted Susan as had the other women.[19]

Fox, whose daughter was under two years of age when Buddy was born in 1858, officiously watched over Susan, the mother of three children. Occasionally she complained of having to instruct Susan about nursing practices or to "make" her care for her own child. The mistress firmly believed that slaves "were like so many children to be clothed & nursed & fed & were constantly to be looked after." She accused Susan of "looking for an excuse to 'lay up' two or three weeks more." Reasons abound for Susan's postpartum lethargy. The reality of passing a lifetime of servitude on to her child may have depressed her. Possibly she resented the younger, less-experienced mother monitoring her behavior. It is also possible that Susan was avoiding work.[20]

Neither Susan nor the mistress experienced difficulty breastfeeding; therefore, neither neglected her own child for the other's. To be sure, there are more examples of black women suckling white children than of white women breastfeeding black babies, yet it occurred. Given the disdain the mistress had for her maid, it is unlikely that Fox would ever use Susan as a wet nurse. Besides, Fox had other alternatives. In 1861 her mother-in-law and a sister-in-law were also pregnant, and they could have served as wet nurses if she needed one.[21]

Care of the Fox children remained in the hands of their mother with assistance from Maria, who took Fanny on daily walks and acted as caregiver when they traveled. Ann remained the mistress's "*main-stay* in the servant's line." She performed any necessary chores for the smooth operation of Hygiene even if it meant ignoring the division of labor. She also helped with child care. These childless servants gave the Fox offspring their undivided attention. Susan had children of her own. When she returned to work, her infants either went along to the kitchen or remained in the nearby cabin with Adelaide or Margaret. Susan probably crossed the yard periodically to attend to them. Perhaps Ann and Maria managed to help her.[22]

The mistress busied herself with her own children and paid little attention to the slaves unless sicknesses occurred. When they fell ill, the mistress intimated that she alone could care for them. She charged that Susan was "worthless" as a nurse. Despite the quality of care or who gave it, one black and two white children died between 1860 and 1863.[23]

The deaths of the Fox children tested her mettle greatly. The weight of her grief when two-year-old Rose died April 3, 1863, was no different from the pall covering her on January 30, 1860, when the two-week-old Edward Randolph Fox died. Although the premature baby suffered immensely, the devastated mother lamented, "He was a beautiful child & I never, *never loved* anything as I did him." Sorrowfully, she complained that Susan and Ann "handled the baby so roughly for such a little delicate thing" that she could not "bear to have them touch him." The mistress associated their care with his death and blamed them for her "sickness & feebleness" afterwards. Lying-in did not foster closeness between the mistress and maids, especially as Susan was also pregnant.[24]

The situation hardly changed when Susan's infant, a "fine mulatto boy," died several weeks later. Poor prenatal care and low infant birth weight, common factors in infant mortality rates, were not considerations in this case. The mistress claimed that Susan "neglected the child & it took cold and died from the effect of it." The bereaved woman felt "badly about its death for it was a pretty baby." Moreover, she "took a fancy to it." Unlike slaveholding women who mourned the death of a favorite slave, the mistress grieved because he was near the age of her recently deceased son. Her sentiments did not transfer to Susan, who inhabited a different sphere, defined by race and class. This experience did not alter the mistress-maid relationship.[25]

The deaths of slave children precipitated a myriad of responses from their mothers. Those who harbored death wishes for their children saw it as a dream fulfilled. Some women consoled themselves quietly with religion and believed death was the will of a supreme being, a liberator freeing the deceased from a life of drudgery and abuse. It was a grantor of eternal rest and peace. In its finality death erased uncertainties and provided hope for a heavenly reunion. Susan left no record of her response to the child's death or that of her owner's son.[26]

Whether Susan's children lived or died, she returned to work one month later. It was not unusual for slave women to receive such time off after parturition. By comparison, the mistress had little special time for convalescence after childbirth and seemed to resent it. Although Susan had the time off, the mistress was eager to know if she were a "good servant or not" since childbirth shortly after the 1858 purchase had interfered with her work. Again in 1860, Fox allowed Susan one month to recuperate, but she was eager for her "to work in downright good earnest." Owners defined the quantity of time slave parents spent with their families; therefore, parents had to determine the quality of that time.[27]

By 1861 Fox's eagerness for Susan to return waned. "For my sake," she wrote, "I am glad the law allows her a month & hope I shall hardly see her during the time." This change of attitudes resulted from their emotionally draining relationship. The mistress hoped to "be pretty well rested" at the end of the month. During the reprieve, she hired "an excellent negress" two days each week at fifty cents per day. The woman arrived early, finished the laundry one day and the ironing the next. Of importance, she caused no trouble.[28]

Fox probably recalled the trying exercise when Susan laundered clothes after the birth of her son Buddy. She wrote: "To day it has been push, hurry, push, to get the washing any where near done & though it is four o'clock

[Susan] is just hanging out the colored clothes. The white things have only been washed in *one* water & boiled — she has done nothing but wash since six o clock this morning, so you may know how slow she is — only three, Dr R — , baby & myself to wash for." Susan's productivity paled when compared with the laundress's, who worked without interruptions from any offspring. She could not afford anything less than diligence if she wanted other work at Hygiene. Susan had no such options. Besides, she had an infant and other children to care for. It is also possible that her sluggishness was a deliberate act of resistance.[29]

Susan's recalcitrant behavior was more obvious in the kitchen where she was responsible for preparing the family's meals. She was a good "pastry cook & able to cook plain, every day meals"; however, the inexperienced mistress insisted that she prepare dishes "her way" based on recipes obtained from Anna Holder rather than dishes she perfected. Susan probably viewed this as interference with her culinary talents and registered discontent through slow or haphazard work. The clash of the wills in the kitchen subjected her to a loss of self-esteem while her daughter Adelaide, who also worked in the house, looked on.[30]

Additionally, Fox's view about managing the kitchen held potentials for friction. "In this country," she explained, "all provisions are kept under lock and key, and one of the principal duties of a southern lady's housekeeping is to carry the key and give out the proper quantities of groceries for each meal, otherwise the cook would waste twice as much as was needed and pilfer as much more." A gulf existed between reality and myth. Carrying keys symbolized her power, and that was more important than theft, real or imaginary. Susan, a mature woman, was hardly unaware of this stereotypical notion about slaves.[31]

With the expectations of a lady, the mistress rarely approved the maids' skills and work ethic, whether they washed, cooked, or sewed. She turned herself into a "human sewing machine" to keep everyone clothed. Neither she nor the slave women spun thread or wove cloth. Fox either bought it in New Orleans or asked Anna to send it from Pittsfield where textile mills produced voluminous amounts of cloth annually. The mistress reserved "fine sewing" for herself and the "coarse sewing" for Maria, since she believed the maid was incapable of anything else. Fox also ripped out Maria's stitches when they did not meet her approval. If Susan sewed or quilted, it was within the confines of her own cabin. It was not unusual for white and black women to sew separately.[32]

Attention to housekeeping outdistanced many activities at Hygiene. Inclement weather and guests created additional chores. The mistress turned the whole house "topsy-turvy" with "cleaning & scrubbing" in preparation for winter guests in 1860–61. To impress the visitors described as "very wealthy people," she bought wallpaper, paint, and carpet that the doctor could ill afford. Working in tandem with the servants, she cut all paper and made the paste. When their energy flagged, she used her *"Yankee* elbow & fingers & determination" to finish the job. Based upon their work habits, it appears that the slowdowns were related more to resistance than to fatigue.[33]

The constant attention to housekeeping chores required close contact with and supervision of servants. The quality of such interactions often depended on a maid's age and status. If hired women proved unsatisfactory, the mistress replaced them. When her own slaves failed to meet expectations, Dr. Fox whipped them. On occasions she also wielded the strap. No one created as much trouble as Susan, an active agent rather than a passive victim in the power relationship for control of her labor.[34]

A close reading of Fox's correspondence suggests not only that her relationship with Susan was stormy but that she was ambivalent about her roles. For example, in September 1858 Fox wrote: "Susan would see the horses starve & everything go to ruin before she would do [anything about] it, unless ordered." Yet, according to the division of labor at Hygiene, Rueben was responsible for the outside work. Nevertheless, the following sentence explained, "She makes a very good servant though & tries to please more than she did at first." This raises questions about the clarity of gender-related work, Susan's defiance, and Fox's propensity for hyperbole.[35]

The mistress aspired to be a writer and believed she could describe familial incidents with aplomb equal to the Swedish writer Fredrika Bremer. The desire to hone her skills invited embellishment. Ordinarily mistresses' comments about servants' deficiencies were more frequent than accolades touting their strengths. In this respect she did not differ from other women with servants in antebellum America.[36]

The mistress's most vociferous complaints about the maids' recalcitrance came when guests were present. The slaves insulated themselves from extra work and foiled Fox's efforts at gracious hospitality. Southern ladies prided themselves on that attribute, but they could not boast about unkempt houses or disobedient servants. Additionally, when taken away from regular routines, Susan and Maria could not think for themselves, according to the mistress. When Susan fell ill more than once when guests arrived, Fox accused her of malingering. Whether the ailments were real or imagined, they ordinarily forced the mistress to cater to guests and attend to Susan as well.[37]

The scenario changed abruptly in June 1859 when four guests were staying at Hygiene. Susan, who had "a little sore on her finger," refused to work. "The more there was to be done the more she shirked," the mistress complained. Dr. Fox whipped Susan, but the "unheard of impudence" continued. Rather than resolving the matter herself, Fox, who was pregnant, threatened to tell the doctor. Susan, who was also pregnant, knew that he would not tolerate such insolence; therefore, she ran away.[38]

Susan probably intended to return when calmer tempers prevailed. Leaving her children speaks volumes about her actions and the conditions at Hygiene. On the one hand, Susan left the children to protest her treatment. On the other, she was confident that they would be taken care of because of the owners' financial interest in them and because, like other slave women, she knew Ann would help her. Generally, slave mothers were less prone to run away than childless women because of an unwillingness to leave their offspring behind. The psychological impact of deserting them was too great. Besides, "Nobody respects a mother who forsakes her children," said Molly Horniblow to her granddaughter Harriet Jacobs when she considered running away alone.[39]

Two years after Susan's flight, Maria ran away under similar circumstances. When ordered to make a fire in the room for a guest, Maria absented herself for a lengthy period before the mistress found her "sprawled out on the hearth-rug *fast asleep*." Maria's behavior embarrassed the slaveholding woman, who whipped her without showing any repulsion. It was more important to establish some semblance of power in the eyes of the guest, especially Aunt Ellen, a "very lady-like amiable woman." This "very gentle & quiet, but firm & dignified" lady, a relative of Dr. Fox's, was visiting Hygiene for the first time. Like Susan in 1859, Maria was obstinate after the whipping. Her behavior threw the mistress into a quandary. "I disliked to say anything to her master," Fox wrote, because "he whips her so severely." Concerned more with the degree than with the kind of chastisement, she beat Maria again, but "not very severely." The extenuating circumstances mattered little. Maria ran away.[40]

Without family ties at Hygiene to compel her return, Maria remained in hiding for six months. Once Dr. Fox located her and reestablished usual routines, the mistress wrote: "She has been severely whipped, and has come back evidently resolved to do her best that she can; as to her being a runaway, we have forgiven and shall forget. As Dr. R says she is a negro and now that she has been punished, it is enough." It was different when Susan ran away in 1859. Dr. Fox located her the following week and sent her directly to Woodburne, a plantation owned by his father, the Reverend James A. Fox, in Warren County, Mississippi. Tryphena Fox claimed immediate relief and declared that Susan would never return.[41]

Financial concerns governed Fox's reaction to Maria's absence. Had it not been for the $1,500 paid for Maria, the mistress maintained she would "not care a picayune" if she ever saw her again. The cost assumed greater importance since Dr. Fox bought a thirty-year-old woman, Elizabeth, in March 1861 to replace Maria. Susan's cost was insignificant because the mistress's emotional well-being was priceless. Susan had become the pregnant woman's "greatest annoyance." Furthermore, the slave children, tangible assets from the 1857 investment, remained at Hygiene. During Susan's five-month absence, Ann cared for them at no extra cost.[42]

The flogging and flight probably frightened and confused the children, but the mistress ignored any emotional stress they endured while basking in her own comfort. She believed the seven-year-old Adelaide could "take care of herself," complete "many useful errands around the house," and assist with Fanny's care. Ann was totally responsible for Buddy and Margaret's care. With certainty the mistress wrote, "I know that when I tell Ann to do this or that for them my orders are promptly obeyed."[43]

To her dismay Tryphena Fox soon reported that Ann was shirking her responsibilities by not keeping the children covered at night, and she did not "dress them soon enough in the morning to prevent them from taking cold & having chills." Ann had become "slack about taking care of them," she wrote. Given Fox's propensity for hyperbolic writing and her perception of the maids, it is likely that she overstated the case. The deliberate neglect of the children was not consistent with Deborah Gray White's study regarding the "female slave network," which suggests that they helped each other when needed. If Ann neglected them, perhaps it was to make the slaveholding woman rethink the circumstances. Both women knew the value of the children as human beings and property too well to allow them to suffer.[44]

Because of their health, the mistress involved herself more with their care by having Buddy brought to her room every night. She was sometimes "up with him & Fanny five or six times." The exhausted woman soon announced: "My health is so delicate [Dr. Fox] will be obliged to bring Susan back; *the worst of all evils.*" Beneath the callousness that allowed the separation, she relented. "If it were not for her children she would never come back." They need "a Mother's care these cold nights," Fox wrote. Moreover, she was not willing to jeopardize her own health by caring for them.[45]

The mistress noted a marked transformation in Susan once she returned. "I could not wish for a better servant," she wrote. One year later Fox observed, "Susan has turned over quite a new leaf." Fear of further separations from her children along with gratitude for her return prompted this change. Furthermore, the mistress had instituted new management tactics: "I have learned the secret that a great deal depends on Mistress' temper & let others give way & shirk & try her as much as they will, she must always command herself, be firm & yet gentle; treat her servants like wayward children, when they do badly, & reward them when they do well—always gently & calm & self-possessed herself when they are around her, let her feel as badly & low-spirited as she may when out of sight." This approach raises questions about why the mistress adopted the new tactic. As an avid reader of popular novels and magazines that extolled the concept of the "Cult of True Womanhood," which emphasized purity, piety, domesticity, and submissiveness in white females, Tryphena Fox probably decided that the new policy was more in keeping with the behavior of a lady.[46]

The new tactic also reads like a capitulation to Susan's recalcitrance rather than her belief in the possibility of a viable paternalistic master-slave relationship. Eugene D. Genovese argues that paternalism defined the relations between superordination and subordination or master and slave wherein each party had rights, duties, and responsibilities. The "special sense of family shaped southern culture," writes the historian, wherein blacks and whites welded "into one people with genuine elements of affection and intimacy." The mistress and her maids did not share such an affiliation. Additionally, there is no evidence to suggest that Dr. Fox forged such a paternalistic relationship with the slaves, male or female.[47]

Regardless of the motives that prompted this new policy, it was more complicated than it appeared. Besides, it would ease their financial strain since Reverend Fox paid his son six dollars per month for Susan's labor while it cost Dr. Fox twelve dollars to hire a replacement. Because of Susan's reputation as "troublesome property," he could not sell her. Hygiene had no fieldwork; therefore, Susan either worked inside the house or she did not work. Fox had no choice other than "to put up with many things which would otherwise be intolerable." The nonbinding truce trapped the mistress. On one hand was Susan's ostensible accommodation, and on the other was the lack of money to hire or buy a new servant. Perhaps both women understood the choices and consequences and silently "negotiated" a peace.[48]

Despite the new tactic, tensions remained. "It is not pleasant to live on the same place & in as close proximity," the mistress concluded, "as one is obliged to do with the cook & be all the time at enmity with her & feel angry, whether I say anything or not." She claimed Susan was "impudent & lazy & *filthy.*" She could not overlook such behavior. "Perhaps," Fox reflected, "it is not all Susan's fault." Although admitting that she did "not treat her right" in one breath, the mistress justified her actions in the next. "I do not like her & never did, & *never shall.*" Comments made by Mary Boykin Chesnut seem appropriate here: "People can't love things dirty, ugly, and repulsive, simply because they out to do so, but they can be good to them at a distance; that is easy." [49]

Their relationship was a pathetic imitation of the one Fox's sister-in-law Lucy Fox Newman shared with Betty, a maidservant. Enviously, Fox described her as "the most trusty of servants—a perfect treasure—devoted to her mistress & takes as much interest in everything as if she owned it all." Of greater importance, she "never caused a moment's trouble." The length of time with the Newmans made a difference. The septuagenarian had matured along with her owners.[50]

Such a mistress-maid relationship at Hygiene was improbable. "After five years' experience in housekeeping with black people," Fox wrote, "I have found that I must give up my notions of a very nice & orderly house or scold & watch & oversee all the time." Her expectations and images of a southern lady versus the realities ruined her temper and made the servants "really dissatisfied and the more careless from being looked after." The ongoing and multifaceted struggle of housekeeping and controlling servants overwhelmed her. Because it was not "ladylike" and seemed "so trivial too for a woman to be always on the lookout for a dirty dish on a dusty mantle piece," she decided to abandon her ideas about housekeeping and resolved to "let it go" if the house were "passably decent." [51]

The mistress felt submerged "beneath a chaos of brooms, dusters & dishcloths, chickens, eggs & darkies, with or without clean hands, faces & aprons." It was exasperating. Furthermore, the isolation of the plantation South left little leisure to reinforce old or gain new knowledge. By 1861, as she noted, she had forgotten much of the "history, the natural sciences, biography, & even what poetry" she had learned at Maplewood Young Ladies' Institute in Pittsfield. She had lost command of what had been an important part of her life. And while she attributed the frustration to willful servants, the isolated rural river community without "society" and financial security befitting her ideals were equally exasperating. [52]

Moreover, the Civil War jolted the mistress from the constant disquiet over servants and made permanent changes in their lives. Immediately before the April 25, 1862, fall of New Orleans, Dr. Fox moved his family and slaves to his father's plantation. Their sojourn in Mississippi put them in the midst of the war since Woodburne was near Vicksburg. As Union soldiers approached, slaves knew it was simply a matter of time before they were freed. Elizabeth, Maria, and Reuben fled after the July 4, 1863, Confederate defeat at Vicksburg. Ironically, Susan remained. Her hesitancy reflected the difficulty of fleeing with four youngsters rather than any loyalty to her owner. [53]

As a result of the war, the flow of mail between Fox and her mother nearly stopped; therefore, details about their daily lives become sketchy. It is known that Dr. Fox joined the Confederate States of America Army in 1863 and became president of the medical board in De Kalb, Kemper County, Mississippi. Susan inevitably overcame the barriers and left Woodburne. The circumstances surrounding her relocation are not known, but she obviously took advantage of her owner's absence and the fluid conditions. Fox simply wrote: "I have heard that Susan went to Memphis." She showed no interest in finding the maidservant. [54]

"I am happier & should be ten years younger," Fox wrote scornfully in July 1864, "in looks & feelings had there never been such a thing as *slave.*" She claimed that owning them was hardly worthwhile. "No one can tell the trouble that four or five around the house can give one, until they have tried it." The devastation of war and the loss of personal and real property added to her bitterness. Under different circumstances it is unlikely that Fox would have made such a statement. Although many northern women supported the abolition of slavery, she was no abolitionist—secret or otherwise. She had complained once that she would rather do her own work than depend upon the enslaved women, but she never spoke in favor of ending slavery. Her economic and social welfare was intricately connected to it. Once slavery ended, Fox forged a new life without this segment of her past.[55]

An assessment of the relationship between the mistress and the slave women shows that it was not vastly different from the experiences of her white contemporaries. To be sure, hired servants caused less trouble and the quality of their treatment was better than that meted out to slaves. Anything to the contrary would bring reproof from owners. Curiously, Fox intervened with respect to Maria by punishing the maid herself. The single concession on Susan's behalf, allowing her back at Hygiene in 1859, benefited both women. Susan's return relieved the mistress of nursing the children while guaranteeing that they would receive good care.

In fact, any modicum of amicability between the women resulted from a mutual interest in the slave children. They were the magnet that pulled the women together and also the force that pushed them apart. The children were an investment in their owner's future while they were emotional assets to Susan. Fox hated the woman, but she demonstrated sustaining interests in the slave children, which Susan appeared to resent. When the mistress made the six-year-old Adelaide her "little pet house maid" in 1859, it deprived Susan of her help. Enslaved children ordinarily worked alongside parents before assuming jobs elsewhere when nine or ten years of age. Moreover, Adelaide was now more readily subjected to the owner's authority, and Susan's ability to protect her from the realities of slavery eroded.[56]

Fox delighted in having Adelaide as a servant while her dislike for Susan continued. The mistress's 1864 remark after hearing that one of Susan's children had died illustrates the point: "They needed 'Mistress [*sic*] nursing & care.'" This comment suggests Fox's continuing perception of Susan as a "worthless" nurse and unfit mother. Although the mistress's concern about the children had initially emanated from their monetary value, it evolved into a broader interest in their welfare. Moreover, the children were tractable and did not challenge her authority. Susan was not a child nor was she childlike. Just as she recognized the mistress's lack of experience in the kitchen, she knew that the mistress was not of "quality folk" nor the lady she pretended to be. Perhaps Susan would have been more accommodating to a "real" southern lady.[57]

With the demise of slavery in 1865 and the change in labor relationships between former slaveowners and slaves, Fox resolved to "take life a great deal more easy & really enjoy it." In part, the hardships endured in the war years and the maturation process caused her to view life differently. Additionally, changes in her financial status along with new priorities of recently freed women were major factors in her decision to have fewer servants. The widespread withdrawal of ex-slave women from the labor force made hiring difficult since many women remained at home to care for their own children, to work as sharecroppers with their families, or to attend school.[58]

In the years immediately following the war, Fox concentrated on restoring Hygiene to its former condition. During the family's stay in Mississippi, vandals had entered the house and removed most of its furnishings. The task of relocating or replacing household goods left little time for writing about servants or playing the lady. Since slavery had shaped her perceptions, its demise and the loss of personal and real property eradicated much of what she believed was important in the making of a southern lady. Additionally, soon after Fox restored Hygiene, fire razed it and she began rebuilding anew.[59]

Beyond focusing on restoring or rebuilding Hygiene, Fox hired an exceptional servant who did not require an extraordinary amount of her attention. The rare find, Milly, a young childless freed woman, began work at Hygiene shortly after the Fox family returned to Louisiana in June 1865. "You know she knew nothing about ironing when she came here," Fox wrote, "but has learned quite well—that—as well as everything else." Touting her attributes frequently, Fox said Milly was an excellent servant, who worked cheerfully without pouting or shirking. Furthermore, she was "perfectly honest."[60]

Of more importance than honing domestic skills, Fox bragged that Milly remained "the same as the first day she came, true and faithful." Differences between Susan and Milly's treatment contrasted sharply. Milly's illnesses received serious consideration, but she lost no time from work because of pregnancy, parturition, or childcare. Before the Civil War the mistress had concluded that "negroes were *so* peculiar—so utterly void of white folk's habits of cleanliness & energy!" Yet after the war, in her view, Milly was different. She was "very neat as a *black* person" and "so much more like white folks" than "any other negress" in the vicinity. Fox claimed that she provided a "good home" for the "very faithful & industrious" woman whom she hoped Milly would "have sense enough to stay."[61]

In fact, these women shared a relationship unlike any other mistress-maid relationship at Hygiene. Milly, a self-supported woman, was interested in pleasing her employer. She accepted three years of tutelage without complaint or resistance. The maidservant was a "splendid cook & I am quite proud of her as one of *my pupils,*" Fox boasted. The two women sometimes worked side by side. The mistress helped "Milly iron & keep the house in order, so she would have an extra day" to help with the roses and strawberries.[62]

The best explanation for this postwar relationship between a mistress and her maid was the relative absence of the control/resistance dynamic of slavery. Fox commented:

> Milly has stood by me like a Trojan & though half sick sometimes has worked through it all & waited upon everybody & everything. Of course I have hired the washing & ironing done & Rachel helped keep the house in order while she stayed & dressed & waited upon George, still Milly has had a great deal to do & has done all faithfully without being told or without grumbling — has worked Sundays & evenings & all times. I am going to make her a present of a pretty barege dress which I have & I send you a .50 cts, & wish you would make or buy her some simple but pretty collar & send to her — she will be so proud of it as coming from my sister.

Fox was now more concerned about the amount of work at Hygiene; therefore, she was willing to hire additional help. This is ironic since the size of her family remained the same. Perhaps her sensitivity emanated from the loss of leisure time along with servants during the war when she was reduced to working with her own hands.[63]

Certainly Fox's postemancipation affinity for Milly was striking. She was above reproach in the mistress's eyes. Moreover, Fox was now an older, experienced housekeeper while Milly, who was in her late teens or early twenties, was eager to please and had no quarrel about the amount of cooking, laundry, or cleaning. She seemed to inculcate Fox's ideas about housekeeping and was sorely distressed when she could not save more of the furnishings when the fire engulfed Hygiene in February 1866. After building a new kitchen, Fox wanted it kept clean. "If Milly spills a drop of grease," she wrote, "I tell her she must get a corn-cob & ashes & scrub it up & give *herself* a good scolding." Such banter seemed to amuse Milly, who never spoke "a cross word."[64]

The accolades continued until October 1868 when Milly wanted to visit her ailing godmother. Certain that she could never replace Milly, the mistress then "played housemaid & cook." Fatigued at the end of the day as she waited for Milly's return, Fox wrote: "It discourages me to think how dependent I am & sometimes I wish I had been kept at hard work all my life, then I should be used to it & shouldn't mind what a smart New England woman would call *light work.*" The letter implies that routine housekeeping exhausted her, but it was not as distressing as recognizing the extent of her dependency upon Milly.[65]

Milly returned after a week of "vexation & fussing" for the mistress, who retired to her "little sitting room (where I belong I'm thinking)," she wrote. Immediately afterwards, Fox was "looking & feeling quite decent." The reprieve ended when Milly's godmother died and the maid needed further time off to attend the funeral. Milly assured Fox that she would return but continued postponing it well beyond what the employer considered a normal bereavement. She then learned that Milly inherited "two lots in Algiers & a small house, with all new furniture & clothing." Fox concluded that the woman was now too independent to work. Frustrated because the housekeeping was "behind hand" and angered over Milly's new independence, Fox condemned the entire race as "*treacherous, difficult & unreliable.*" Clearly Milly's change in status greatly unsettled the mistress. Hastily Fox fired Milly and demanded the immediate removal of her personal effects from the servant's cabin. The mistress now decided to hire white servants, preferably Irish or Dutch. This choice was related as much to Fox's negative perception of persons without English ancestry as it was to her imperious attitude.[66]

Feeling betrayed because she "worked like a darkey rather than hire a fresh hand," Fox then vowed never again to put such confidence in servants. This raises questions about the nature of her sentiments for Milly and the hostility with which she severed their connection. The language describing Milly's behavior was as acerbic as her castigations of Susan. What caused such an emotional outburst? Was it losing a servant, or was it the servant gaining independence? Certainly, Fox dreaded beginning anew and teaching a new servant "her way." Losing Milly, the "scholar," meant combining the roles of mistress and maid until she found a suitable replacement.[67]

Milly's legacy was disturbing on another level. Marriage liberated the mistress from the dependency of her own salaried employment while the inheritance freed the maid from a similar dependency. The servant's response to the situation is not known. Milly's independence was more far-reaching. She was secure financially and was now beyond her employer's control. By contrast, economic security evaded Fox. The privileged status of southern white mistresses had depended on the subjugation of black women. And in this context Milly's inheritance made the continuation of a pleasant working relationship untenable, for it made the mistress face a common fear that "the elevation of the blacks will be the degradation of the whites." In short, while the differences with Susan were essentially based on race, Fox's new attitude toward Milly was essentially governed by class as well as race. Regardless of the causes for the differences, Tryphena Fox saw herself as superior to women from a race of *"treacherous, difficult & unreliable"* people.[68]

Nevertheless, it is clear that her maidservants, slave and free, acted in their own interest when opportunities arose. The mistress experienced greater feelings of betrayal when Milly left, since they had shared a maid-mistress relationship without obvious resistance dynamics. Milly pleased the mistress as much as Susan had displeased her. In any case, following Milly's departure, there were many black and white servants at Hygiene. Of more importance, Fox's attitude about Milly softened with time, and she judged other servants with her standards in mind. The mistress claimed that the maid Celestine, who began work at Hygiene in early 1869, never took "that Motherly care of the children that Milly used to." By late 1869, Tryphena Fox compared "Milly [who] used to do the cooking half the housework, all the ironing & then nurse Georgy" with Celestine's replacement.[69]

Looking back over the decade of interaction with maids, it is clear that slavery shaped Fox's behavior and her notions about southern ladies. Beyond that, the control/resistance dynamic that was so evident in the relationship between the mistress and enslaved adults became less obvious. The redefinition of ownership of labor was responsible for changes in the dynamics between the mistress and newly freed maids.

Fox continued to believe that a workable relationship could exist with domestic servants if she could either "control or command labor." Emancipation had removed that option. Besides, the mistress knew that to control another's labor was impossible. In a moment of solemn reflection Tryphena Fox struggled with the tension created by her ideas about southern ladies with efficient servants and leisure time on one hand and the exasperating reality of being overburdened with household chores and drained mentally by conflicts with servants on the other hand. The northern-born woman resentfully concluded that a viable solution to her dilemma was to live in a place and time where it was "the fashion for *ladies* to do their own work." [70]

Fox never considered returning to the North because of her "ingrafted hatred of Yankees." She continued to cling to an old way of life while many of her contemporaries "were changing to meet the changed times." Eventually, the mistress contented herself with malleable black adolescent servants, children, with whom she was likely to forge a more reciprocal relationship. Moreover, they, more readily than adult servants, would complement her role of a southern lady. [71]

*NOTES*

1. Tryphena Blanche Holder Fox (hereafter cited as TBHF) to Anna Rose Holder (hereafter cited as ARH), 9 July 1858, Mississippi Department of Archives and History (hereafter cited as MDAH). See Anne Firor Scott, *The Southern Lady: From Pedestal to Politics, 1830–1930* (Chicago: University of Chicago Press, 1970).

2. TBHF to ARH, 7 December 1855, MDAH. For discussion of Tryphena Fox's formative years see Wilma King, ed., *A Northern Woman in the Plantation South: Letters of Tryphena Blanche Holder Fox, 1856–1876* (Columbia: University of South Carolina Press, 1993), which contains 81 of the 187 letters from Fox to her mother.

3. Scott, *Southern Lady,* 46–47.

4. See Catherine Clinton, "In Search of Southern Women's History: The Current State of Academic Publishing," *Georgia Historical Quarterly* 76 (summer 1992): 420–27. See also Ruth Currie-McDaniel, "Northern Women in the South, 1860–1880," *Georgia Historical Quarterly* 74 (summer 1992): 281–312; Lawrence N. Powell, *New Masters: Northern Planters during the Civil War and Reconstruction* (New Haven: Yale University Press, 1980).

5. TBHF to ARH, 7 January 1857, 24 June 1860, MDAH. See Catherine Clinton, *The Plantation Mistress: Woman's World in the Old South* (New York: Pantheon Books, 1982), especially chap. 9, "Every Woman Was an Island."

6. TBHF to ARH, 18 November 1856, MDAH; U.S. 8th Census, 1860 Slave Schedule, Plaquemines Parish, Louisiana, National Archives, Washington, D.C. (hereafter cited as NA).

7. U.S. 8th Census, 1860 Population, Plaquemines Parish, Louisiana, NA.

8. TBHF to ARH, 7 December 1855, MDAH; obituary, *Berkshire Eagle,* 18 December 1922.

9. TBHF to ARH, 14 July 1856, MDAH (emphasis added); Scott, *Southern Lady,* 8.

See Jean E. Friedman, *The Enclosed Garden: Women and Community in the Evangelical South, 1830–1890* (Chapel Hill: University of North Carolina Press, 1979), 81–82.

10. TBHF to ARH, 3 December 1857, 27 December 1857, MDAH; Elizabeth Fox-Genovese, *Within the Plantation Household: Black and White Women of the Old South* (Chapel Hill: University of North Carolina Press, 1988), 197; Bettina Aptheker, "Domestic Labor: Patterns in Black and White," in *Woman's Legacy: Essays on Race, Sex, and Class in American History* (Amherst: University of Massachusetts Press, 1982), 114. For a discussion of discrimination against free persons of color in the North see Leon Litwack, *North of Slavery: The Negro in the Free States, 1790–1860* (Chicago: University of Chicago Press, 1965), 66–112.

11. TBHF to ARH, 1 November 1857, 3 December 1857, 27 December 1857, MDAH; David M. Katzman, *Seven Days a Week: Women and Domestic Service in Industrializing America* (New York: Oxford University Press, 1978), 146. See Susan Strasser, *Never Done: A History of American Housework* (New York: Pantheon Books, 1982). See also Virginia Ingraham Burr, ed., *The Secret Eye: The Journal of Ella Gertrude Clanton Thomas, 1848–1889* (Chapel Hill: University of North Carolina, 1990), for comments about enslaved women by a contemporary of Tryphena Fox.

12. TBHF to ARH, 27 December 1857, MDAH.

13. Ibid. See Raymond A. and Alice H. Bauer, "Day to Day Resistance" *Journal of Negro History* 27 (October 1942): 388–419.

14. TBHF to ARH, 27 December 1857, MDAH. See Edmund L. Drago, ed., *Broke by the War: Letters of a Slave Trader* (Columbia: University of South Carolina Press, 1991).

15. TBHF to ARH, 17 January 1858, MDAH; "Rules for Government of Plantation, *Negroes,*" Cornhill Plantation Book, 106, Duke University, Durham, N.C.; Greenwood Plantation Record, 25 June 1861, Library of Congress, Washington, D.C. (hereafter cited as LC). See John Campbell, "Work, Pregnancy, and Infant Mortality among Southern Slaves," *Journal of Interdisciplinary History* 14 (spring 1984): 793–815.

16. TBHF to ARH, 17 March 1860, MDAH.

17. See Natalie Shainess, "The Psychologic Experience of Labor," *New York State Journal of Medicine* 63 (15 October 1963): 2923–32; Sally G. McMillen, *Motherhood in the Old South: Pregnancy, Childbirth, and Infant Rearing* (Baton Rouge: Louisiana State University Press, 1990).

18. TBHF to ARH, 6 June 1856, 1 November 1857, 29 March 1861, 16 June 1861, 22 August 1865, MDAH; Judith Walzer Leavitt, *Brought to Bed: Childbearing in America, 1750 to 1950* (New York: Oxford University Press, 1986), 87–115; Joan E. Cashin, "The Structure of Antebellum Planter Families: 'The Ties That Bound Us Was Strong,'" *Journal of Southern History* 56 (February 1990): 58–60; Fox-Genovese, *Within the Plantation Household,* 27; Clinton, *Plantation Mistress,* 154–55.

19. TBHF to ARH, 19 February 1858, 15 November 1858, 17 March 1860, 29 March 1861, MDAH.

20. TBHF to ARH, 19 February 1858, 15 November 1858, 15 July 1865, MDAH.

21. TBHF to ARH, 17 November 1859, MDAH. See Sally McMillen, "Mother's Sacred Duty: Breast-feeding Patterns among Middle- and Upper-Class Women in the Antebellum South," *Journal of Southern History* 52 (August 1985): 333–56.

22. TBHF to ARH, 5 September 1858, 20 February 1860, MDAH. See Deborah Gray White, *Ar'n't I a Woman? Female Slaves in the Plantation South* (New York: W. W. Norton, 1985), 126–28.

23. TBHF to ARH, 8 August 1861, 26 July 1864, MDAH.

24. TBHF to ARH, 1 February 1860, MDAH. See McMillen, "Their Sorrowing Hearts: Infant Mortality and Maternal Bereavement," in *Motherhood in the Old South*, 165–79.

25. TBHF to ARH, 1 February 1860, 17 March 1860, MDAH; Fox-Genovese, *Within the Plantation Household*, 131.

26. Harriet Jacobs, *Incidents in the Life of a Slave Girl, Written by Herself*, ed. Jean Fagan Yellin (Cambridge: Harvard University Press, 1987), 76.

27. TBHF to ARH, 19 February 1858, 3 March 1858, 17 March 1860, MDAH. See Greenwood Plantation Record, 25 June 1861, LC; Jacqueline Jones, *Labor of Love, Labor of Sorrow: Black Women, Work and the Family, from Slavery to the Present* (New York: Vintage Books, 1986), 19; Leslie Howard Owens, *This Species of Property: Slave Life and Culture in the Old South* (New York: Oxford University Press, 1977), 38–40.

28. TBHF to ARH, 29 March 1861, MDAH. Rather than a "law," Tryphena refers to the accepted practice of allowing slave women to have one month for recovery after childbirth.

29. TBHF to ARH, 31 July 1857, 9 July 1858, MDAH. See Strasser, *Never Done*, for a discussion of laundering clothes.

30. TBHF to ARH, 27 December 1857, 15 November 1858, MDAH.

31. TBHF to ARH, 29 June 1856, MDAH. See Clinton, *Plantation Mistress*, 19–20; Alex Lichtenstein, " 'That Disposition to Theft, with Which They Have Been Branded': Moral Economy, Slave Management, and the Law," *Journal of Southern History* 21 (spring 1988): 413–40.

32. TBHF to ARH, 27 December 1857, 16 November 1860, MDAH; Josiah Gilbert Holland, *History of Western Massachusetts* (Springfield, Mass.: Samuel Bowles, 1855), 2:560; Fox-Genovese, *Within the Plantation Household*, 120, 184.

33. TBHF to ARH, 3 March 1858, 12 December 1859, 28 October 1860, 16 November 1860, MDAH; Aptheker, "Domestic Labor," 115.

34. See TBHF to ARH, 20 February 1860, MDAH.

35. TBHF to ARH, 5 September 1858, MDAH.

36. TBHF to ARH, 12 June 1866; Fox-Genovese, *Within the Plantation Household*, 136. See Daniel E. Sutherland, "The Servant Problem: An Index of Antebellum Americanism," *Southern Studies* 18 (winter 1980): 488–503; Daniel E. Sutherland, *Americans*

*and Their Servants: Domestic Service in the United States from 1800 to 1920* (Baton Rouge: Louisiana State University Press, 1981).

37. TBHF to ARH, 3 March 1858, 5 September 1858, 15 November 1858, 8 August 1861, MDAH.

38. TBHF to ARH, 13 June 1859, MDAH.

39. Jacobs, *Slave Girl,* 91; White, *Ar'n't I a Woman?* 22. See Judith Kelleher Schafer, "New Orleans Slavery in 1850 as Seen in Advertisements," *Journal of Southern History* 47 (February 1981): 33–56; Michael P. Johnson, "Runaway Slaves and the Slave Communities in South Carolina, 1799 to 1830," *William and Mary Quarterly* 38 (July 1981): 418–41.

40. TBHF to ARH, 29 March 1861, MDAH. See Marli F. Weiner, "Plantation Mistresses and Female Slaves: Gender, Race, and South Carolina Women, 1830–1880" (Ph.D. diss., University of Rochester, 1985), 120–21; Fox-Genovese, *Within the Plantation Household,* 97.

41. TBHF to ARH, 13 June 1859, MDAH; Fox, 12 August 1861, Tryphena Blanche Holder Fox, diary transcript, MDAH.

42. TBHF to ARH, 13 June 1859, 29 March 1861, MDAH.

43. TBHF to ARH, 13 June 1859, MDAH.

44. TBHF to ARH, 17 November 1859, MDAH: White, *Ar'n't I a Woman?* 128.

45. TBHF to ARH, 17 November 1859, 12 December 1859, MDAH.

46. TBHF to ARH, 20 February 1860, 22 May 1860, 24 June 1860, 12 July 1860, 14 October 1860, MDAH.

47. Eugene D. Genovese, *Roll, Jordan, Roll: The World the Slaves Made* (New York: Vintage Books, 1976), 3–7, 74. See Peter Kolchin, *American Slavery, 1619–1877* (New York: Hill and Wang, 1993), 111–32.

48. TBHF to ARH, 17 November 1859, 12 December 1859, 16 December 1860, MDAH.

49. TBHF to ARH, 16 December 1860, MDAH; Aptheker, "Domestic Labor," 116.

50. TBHF to ARH, 5 March 1860, MDAH.

51. TBHF to ARH, 8 August 1861, MDAH. See Scott, *Southern Lady,* 28–34.

52. TBHF to ARH, 8 August 1861, MDAH.

53. TBHF to ARH, 3 July 1863, MDAH; Daniel E. Sutherland, "A Special Kind of Problem: The Response of Household Slaves and Their Masters to Freedom," *Southern Studies* 20 (summer 1981): 152–54. For discussions of the Civil War and Reconstruction see James M. McPherson, *Battle Cry of Freedom: The Civil War Era* (New York: Oxford University Press, 1988); Eric Foner, *Reconstruction: America's Unfinished Revolution, 1863–1877* (New York: Harper and Row, 1988); Catherine Clinton and Nina Silber, eds., *Divided Houses: Gender and the Civil War* (New York: Oxford University Press, 1992).

54. TBHF to ARH, 18 January 1864, 26 July 1864, MDAH.

55. TBHF to ARH, 26 July 1864, MDAH. See Leon Litwack, *Been in the Storm So*

*Long: The Aftermath of Slavery* (New York: Vintage Books, 1980), 196–97; Burr, *The Secret Eye,* 168–69.

56. TBHF to ARH, 15 November 1858, 14 October 1860, MDAH. See Weiner, "Plantation Mistresses and Female Slaves," 102–3.

57. TBHF to ARH, 26 July 1864, MDAH.

58. TBHF to ARH, 15 July 1865, MDAH; Litwack, *Been in the Storm So Long,* 244–45; Sutherland, *Americans and Their Servants,* 57.

59. See TBHF to ARH, 17 February 1866, MDAH.

60. TBHF to ARH, 17 February 1866, 22 July 1866, MDAH.

61. TBHF to ARH, 15 November 1858, 3 October 1866, MDAH; TBHF, diary transcript, 31 July 1866, MDAH.

62. TBHF to ARH, 22 July 1866, MDAH.

63. TBHF to ARH, 7 February 1867, MDAH.

64. TBHF to ARH, 17 February 1866, 5 November 1866, MDAH.

65. TBHF to ARH, 28 March 1866, 3 October 1866, MDAH.

66. TBHF to ARH, 2 October 1868, MDAH; Jones, *Labor of Love,* 53, 68–72; Sutherland, "A Special Kind of Problem," 154, 158–59. See TBHF to ARH, 21 August 1865, MDAH, regarding comments about an Irish soldier.

67. Sutherland, "A Special Kind of Problem," 160, 162.

68. Aptheker, "Domestic Labor," 116.

69. TBHF to ARH, 13 February 1869, 30 December 1869, MDAH.

70. TBHF to ARH, 2 October 1868, MDAH (emphasis added); Sutherland, "A Special Kind of Problem," 162.

71. Scott, *Southern Lady,* 102.

MARGARET M. R. KELLOW

# The Divided Mind of Antislavery Feminism

## LYDIA MARIA CHILD AND THE CONSTRUCTION OF AFRICAN AMERICAN WOMANHOOD

S THE FIRST day of August 1833 approached, the date of Emancipation in the British West Indies, the most celebrated American woman author of the day, Lydia Maria Child, published a carefully wrought condemnation of American slavery and race relations, *An Appeal in Favor of That Class of Americans Called Africans.*[1] Perhaps hoping to spur her compatriots to follow the British example, perhaps wanting to foster the tiny abolitionist movement then emerging in the northeastern United States, and almost certainly as a consequence of her own growing convictions regarding the injustice of slavery, Child constructed a detailed critique of the South's peculiar institution, one studded with vivid images carefully calculated to persuade her readers to reconsider their attitudes toward slavery. Among the most potent of these was the figure of the female slave, abused, exploited, and violated. Here Child made no concessions to northern sensibilities. "The negro woman is unprotected either by law or public opinion. She is the property of her master, and her daughters are his property. They are allowed to have no conscientious scruples, no sense of shame, no regard for the feelings of husband, or parent; they must be entirely subservient to the will of their owner, on pain of being whipped as near unto death as will comport with his interest, or quite to death, if it suit his pleasure."[2] Probably no other American woman did more sooner to bring the image of the African American women in southern slavery to the attention of the northern public. Despite the harsh criticism her *Appeal* engendered, Child's juvenile fiction, her antislavery catechisms, and her short stories repeatedly portrayed the particular injuries slavery and discrimination inflicted on black women.

Child lobbied vigorously in person, in print, and in petitions to various legislatures on behalf of African American girls and women facing a variety of challenges arising out of slavery and discrimination.[3] Her research, from private correspondents throughout the country, in court records, and in newspaper accounts and in interviews conducted with enslaved women sojourning in the North with southern masters, provided fuel for her own work and for Theodore Dwight Weld's 1838 attack on slavery, *Slavery as It Is*.[4] In the 1840s, her fiction and her newspaper editorials kept the image of the female slave before the American public. Although Child was at pains to describe the whole enormity of slavery, its devastating impact on men, women, and children, nevertheless, the image of the enslaved African American woman that took shape in the minds of northern abolitionists in the 1830s and 1840s was to a significant extent crafted by Lydia Maria Child.

Child shared this undertaking with several other white female abolitionists. Through their publications and speeches, Child, the Grimké sisters, Abby Kelley, and Lucretia Mott brought enslaved black women to the attention of northern society, a society whose prejudices regularly allowed it to ignore or disparage the African American women in its midst.[5] Initially, these abolitionists justified their public activism by claiming to speak for their sisters in bondage. As Jean Fagan Yellin has demonstrated, in the discourse of antislavery, much of it constructed by women, the figure of the female slave, kneeling and enchained, became a powerful emblem for fostering support for abolitionism.[6] It was a figure that spoke directly to deeply held assumptions about gender and femininity in antebellum society.

This discovery of African American women took place in the context of the self-discovery of white middle-class northern women. Mott, Kelley, the Grimkés, and Child all found in American slavery an arresting metaphor for the condition of American women, and they did not hesitate to exploit its strategic potential. As Abby Kelley observed, "We have good cause to be grateful to the slave. In striving to strike his irons off, we found most surely, that we were manacled ourselves."[7] "The investigation of the rights of the slave," wrote Angelina Grimké, "has led me to a better understanding of my own."[8] By this representation of black women in the cause of antislavery, white abolitionist women transcended prevailing conventions regarding femininity and facilitated their own self-creation as autonomous individuals. In the cause of the slave, some women found themselves motivated to act, to write, and ultimately to speak out publicly.

In claiming the right to speak for their sisters in bondage, women abolitionists constructed themselves as autonomous, responsible subjects. Some of these women, among them Harriet Beecher Stowe, author of *Uncle Tom's Cabin*, developed their concern for the slave in an overtly nonpolitical framework. Imbued with prevailing cultural prescriptions about the sympathizing nature of woman, these women saw in the oppressed and downtrodden slave a worthy object for their tenderness. As a number of authors have pointed out, Stowe's work contains a substantial critique of antebellum gender relations as underlying the moral challenges facing the young nation. However, Stowe's critique was grounded in maternal rather than egalitarian feminism. In her view, the challenges facing the young nation, slavery among them, could best be met by extending the domestic virtues of piety and self-sacrificing concern for others to the nation as a whole. Woman's moral influence could redeem America's promise.[9]

Such antislavery feminists as Kelley, the Grimkés, and Child grounded their commitment in a belief in individual liberty and equality. These convictions, like those of many American men, derived from the republicanism of the Revolution, but also resonated with the economic liberalism of the emerging urban bourgeoisie. Regarded from this position, slavery could not be reconciled with American liberty. As they observed the incorporation of all (white) adult males into the body politic which mass political movements and Jacksonian democracy had effected, these abolitionist women refused to remain aloof from what they perceived as questions touching on the moral and political health of the nation. Although antislavery women made no formal claim for the vote until 1848, they did see themselves as full and equal citizens with a right and a duty to participate in debates on issues of national importance.

In the process of challenging American slavery, Lucretia Mott, Abby Kelley, Sarah and Angelina Grimké, and Lydia Maria Child mounted a significant challenge to prevailing antebellum gender prescriptions that excluded women from public life. Through their antislavery activities they created new careers and identities for themselves. However, comparisons between the self-creation of antislavery feminists and their representations of African American women often reveal striking contrasts. As an icon of antislavery, the figure of the enslaved woman was unquestionably an effective symbol, but an exploration of the dissonance between the self-creation of white antislavery feminists and their representations of black women discloses significant tensions and ambiguities. The work of abolitionist author Lydia Maria Child (1802–1880) offers an excellent opportunity to explore these tensions. By contrasting Child's own self-creation with her depictions of African American women, the problematic nature of these images of black womanhood becomes apparent.

Throughout a long and prolific career, Child brilliantly manipulated the tropes and symbols of antebellum culture to attack slavery and racism and to claim full personhood for herself. An unwillingness to accept any contradiction between the ethos of equality she espoused and the gender constraints and subordination she experienced in her own life underwrote her public career.[10] Although the growing strength of antebellum gender prescriptions frequently buffeted Child's resolve, she held firm to her principles. In 1833, her awareness of her responsibilities as a citizen induced her to speak out on the subject of slavery. Her *Appeal* not only criticized American slavery and race relations but articulated Child's growing concern about the threat slavery posed to the well-being of the Republic. Recognizing that slavery and race prejudice were grounded in a presumption of the inherent inferiority of African Americans, Child argued that the perceived inferiority of black Americans was a consequence of enslavement. Only Emancipation would permit a fair assessment of the capacities of African Americans, a test in which Child was convinced African Americans would acquit themselves well. To subjugate an entire race on categorical grounds flew in the face of Child's beliefs about individualism and opportunity. Thus, Child's views on racism and sexism flowed from the same source, her commitment to individual liberty.[11]

Child's convictions and the actions that stemmed from them brought down a storm of controversy on her. Ministers rebuked her from the pulpit and exhorted her to confine herself to domestic concerns.[12] However, these attacks failed to shake Child's principles. Instead they sharpened her awareness of the oppressive nature of antebellum gender prescriptions. In response Child linked the flawed state of American politics to the silencing of women by social convention. By excluding women from discussions of serious matters, women's capacities were stunted and their abilities wasted, and thus they came to conform to the stereotypes that oppressed them. It was this aspect of sexism (and racism) on which Child focused her attention. Oratory about woman's rights she left to others. Child's strategy was to demonstrate what a competent and intelligent woman could *do*.[13] Whether addressing a legislature or editing a national newspaper, Child spoke with the voice of "a free-born woman, sharing moral and intellectual advantages with all the sons and daughters of this intelligent Commonwealth."[14]

Unlike Harriet Beecher Stowe and many of the rank and file among abolitionist women, Child did not couch her arguments in prevailing views of women as inherently more sensitive to moral issues than men. Although Child certainly encouraged women to exert their moral influence on behalf of the slave, she enjoined this responsibility on men as well. Nor could moral influence be the limit of women's participation in antislavery. Women must claim and exercise their place as fully developed coworkers in the antislavery struggle. They must be free to do whatever they felt they could. Neither was sympathy for the enslaved the only motivation for women's commitment to abolitionism. For Child, justice constituted a far more compelling incentive for women's activism. Like Sarah Grimké and Lucretia Mott, Child grounded her commitment to woman's rights solidly in the same commitment to egalitarianism that underwrote her commitment to antislavery.[15] Child did not believe men and women were identical, but such differences as existed between them did not justify the subordination of women in antislavery or anywhere else.[16]

Child's commitment to the equality and autonomy of individuals, male or female, echoed through her writing for much of her life. In editorials for the *National Anti-Slavery Standard,* in the social commentary of her enormously successful *Letters from New York,* and in her fiction, Child reiterated her ideal of American womanhood, of a woman not identical to man but equally intelligent, equally competent, and equally responsible. Although Child's true woman loved and cared for her home, Child constantly warned of the cramping, wasteful, and destructive consequences of confining women who aspired to more solely to the domestic realm.

For Child the parallels between slavery, racial prejudice, and the situation of women included this environmental aspect. In each instance she attacked the constricting and debilitating aspects that hampered the full development of the individual. In 1842, in an editorial entitled "Coincidences," Child detailed these parallels in a superb and revealing example of the resonances between antislavery and woman's rights.[17] Child summoned up each argument for the subordination of African Americans and white women and showed the similarities between them and the faulty logic that underlay them all.[18] The apparent dissipation of the lively intelligence shown by black children and often by little white girls was not a sign of shallowness, as was often argued, but a consequence of lack of opportunity or, in the case of white girls, disincentives. Black children were barred from developing their abilities, and white girls were told "that gentlemen in general do not like intellectual ladies." Physical force and scriptural quotations kept both black slaves and white women in subordination, Child maintained. Although women's supposed physical weakness purportedly justified their inferior position, Child noted that in many countries women frequently performed heavy physical labor.[19] The inherently affectionate and docile nature of black people particularly suited them to submission, it was argued, and as Child pointed out, "The parallel between them and women is sufficiently obvious." Similar, too, was the supposedly inherent affinity of black people and white women for religious sentiment. Both classes, she noted, were systematically excluded from politics and government.

After examining the ways in which the positive qualities of both groups served to disadvantage them, Child pointedly examined the other side of the coin. She noted that slaves were said to boast when high prices were paid for them; likewise, she noted their supposed fondness for gaudy finery. With mocking restraint, she forbore to extend these observations to white women, but the implications were unavoidable. Child noted that slaves and white women were awarded *privileges* whereas citizens had *rights*. Slaves and white women had to obey laws they had no say in making or suffer the consequences. "Both women and colored people are taught that it is not becoming to form opinions for themselves; that it is going out of their place; that they should receive their opinions from others; and if they shine at all, shine with a reflected light."[20] If these conditions had been brought about by physical force, Child believed that moral sentiment, which had hitherto rendered white women and black people vulnerable to force, would ultimately transcend it. When that process was complete, individuals of whatever color or sex would be free to develop their full humanity.

Child's analysis embodies the individualist critique of slavery that characterized immediatist abolitionists in the 1830s. Slavery gave unfair advantage to some individuals (i.e., slaveholders), while obliterating any possibility of individual achievements for others (i.e., slaves). Although, as Richard O. Curry has pointed out, abolitionists were philosophically inclined to this argument, it served a concrete strategic purpose as well. Southerners insisted that African Americans could not look after themselves without slavery, that if slaves were emancipated, they would starve. These southern apologists for slavery received support for their position in northern cities as increasing discrimination began to swell the number of indigent free blacks. Child rebutted these assertions by arguing that slaves were not shiftless — they had no reason to work hard. Child insisted that blacks were every bit as capable as whites when given the same opportunities. Her publications frequently presented examples of accomplished black artists, scientists, entrepreneurs, and leaders to dispel these misconceptions. Child argued that freedom, not slavery, would nurture independence and self-reliance in African Americans.[21]

However, the discourse of independence and self-reliance as constructed by Child, crucial though it was to undermining the defense of slavery, had very little to do with black women. Child's calls for the individual rights of African Americans are overwhelmingly male oriented.[22] When she compared black people to white women she implicitly asserted that, just as it was inappropriate to enslave blacks because they were men, it was also inappropriate to treat white women like slaves. Making white women's claim for self-constituted individualism by juxtaposing their situation to that of black men in slavery proved a compelling strategy (albeit one with potentially racist undertones as the debate over the Fifteenth Amendment would show).[23] However, the resonances between antislavery and woman's rights tended to write African American women out of the discourse of individual autonomy. In this discourse, although extremely effective in terms of its intended goals, black women figured hardly at all. Antislavery women, Child among them, sympathized genuinely with the plight of the slave woman, but there was little rhetorical advantage to be gained by identifying with a truly powerless group. Moreover, in the decade after Fanny Wright's highly publicized career, which yoked so-called free love to abolitionism in the public mind, attacks on the sexual exploitation of black women couched in the language of individual autonomy and self-ownership were certain to backfire on any white woman impolitic enough to make them.[24] Thus, the discourse of autonomy and individualism, which informed important aspects of antislavery and woman's rights, for the most part ignored black women.

The portrayal of the black man as at least a potentially autonomous individual contrasts sharply with that of his victimized and violated sisters, daughters, mother, and wife, for that is the way in which African American women appeared in the discourse of white antislavery feminists. Child's work contains dozens of portrayals of black women, from her earliest antislavery work to her last novel.[25] Few nineteenth century authors understood better the subtleties and significance of image and representation. Moreover, Child understood the polemical value of various images of African American women, and she consciously manipulated these to reshape public opinion.

In Child's work, faithful nurses, grieving mothers, cast-off wives, and rejected daughters articulated a vision of black womanhood that epitomized prevailing ideals of femininity in antebellum America. Her black heroines embodied the virtues of true womanhood and as such were intended to move the hearts and consciences of Americans. True stories such as those of Charity Bowery and Annette Gray contrasted the innate goodness of black women with the arrogance and venality of their white southern masters, whose behavior violated the canons of domesticity and nineteenth-century public moral standards at every turn.[26] These depictions challenged and appealed to Christian and republican virtue. However, they also invoked an image of black women that laid the groundwork for the stereotype that would later be canonized in post–Civil War reminiscences and fiction as "Mammy."[27] This nonthreatening construction of women who were selfless, loving, and devoid of sexual feeling was an effective counter to repugnance toward the supposed sexual voracity of black women. Similarly, this image offset deep-seated fears concerning black retribution. The image of African American women as inherently true women also served to rebut predictions of the potential for anarchy in post-Emancipation society by demonstrating the strong commitment of black women to ties of family and affection. If black women aspired to nothing so much as the chance to shape their personal relations into conventional nuclear families, then freedom would bring, not chaos, but the reconstruction of southern society after the model of the northern bourgeoisie.

In asking to what extent the discourse of white antislavery feminists empowered African American women, it must be acknowledged that much of the abolitionist critique of slavery was intensely patriarchal. Slavery violated the family; black men were unable to protect, defend, or support their families. Slavery obstructed "proper" family formation. Although Child struggled long and hard in her own life to limit the claims of husband, father, and home, her vision of Emancipation saw as the ideal for black families the model of the American bourgeois family. Although Child did not

(as later generations have sometimes done) blame black women for the obstacles slavery posed to conventional family formation, she did assume that
this was the norm to which black women should aspire.[28] Child challenged
"patriarchalism" explicitly for the ways in which it limited the freedom and
individualism of women, including herself, but much of her idealization of
black women deals with the extent to which they conformed to patriarchal
ideals of womanhood. As LeeAnn Whites has demonstrated, by the 1850s,
affirmations of the manhood of African American men were juxtaposed to
attestations to the motherhood of African American women.[29]

It is difficult to find direct evidence that Child had come in contact with
southern stereotypes of black women as sexually voracious, except that her
depictions were almost never without didactic if not polemic purpose.[30]
What is certain is that her portrayals of African American women almost invariably conformed at least in principle to prevailing antebellum standards
of female sexual morality. Child's 1841 editorial in the *National Anti-Slavery
Standard,* entitled "Annette Gray," demonstrates a thorough understanding of the sexual exploitation of slave women and the power relationship in
which it was situated. Child has Gray articulate feelings of victimization and
shame in which there is not hint of lasciviousness. "I cannot be thankful
enough that my master was not young and handsome; for it would have been
a sin to love him.—As it was, though I could not help myself, and would
gladly have done so if I could, yet I could not look my mistress in the eye. . . .
I never could help hanging my head for shame."[31]

Although like Gray they are frequently exploited sexually, Child's black
female subjects are virtuous, pure-minded, and affectionate rather than pas-
sionate. Their affections may be engaged, but this only serves to make them
more vulnerable. "Slave mistresses do sometimes love their masters," Child
quotes Gray as saying, "and it almost kills them when they are turned away
for somebody else." Child simply does not allow for the possibility that such
relationships could be anything other than degrading for the slave woman
and opportunistic on the part of the master. Seeing slave women in sexual
relations with their masters only as exploited victims, Child denies them any
agency. She is blind to the reality that within the broad spectrum of such
relationships, granted most of which contained some element of exploitation, there existed a space in which some African American women might
choose to use their sexuality to mitigate the conditions of their enslavement.

When Child portrays liaisons involving female slaves positively in her fiction, as in "The Quadroons" (1842) and *A Romance of the Republic* (1867), the heroines believe themselves to be truly married, but are deceived by their white southern suitors, who turn out to be their masters as well. When in each case these men abandon them for wealthy white spouses, it is a clear breach of faith against a trusting and innocent heart. In "The Quadroons," the discovery of this desertion leads to silent grief and death and, for the daughter of the relationship, disaster. In *A Romance of the Republic,* written after Emancipation, the betrayed woman almost dies of grief, but then recovers, and the novel moves toward a more optimistic resolution.[32]

In both stories, Child casts her heroines entirely in the role of true women and thereby forecloses meaningful exploration of any ambivalence they might have experienced. Although Child is well aware that desire and attraction could transgress conjugal bonds, and she is willing at times to portray white women in unconventional relationships, Child's African American heroines are never motivated by attraction and desire.[33] Likewise, Child's depictions give no sense of the ways in which sexual desire could give a black woman some leverage in her enslavement. Given the public moral standards of the day, these would have been difficult points to make, but Child's conceptualization of black women as invariably victims assumes that the question of their motivation is moot.

Child's dealings with Harriet Jacobs reveal the primacy she placed on fostering socially acceptable images of black women. Jacobs (1813–1897) had been born into slavery in North Carolina and willed into the possession of a sexually predatory master. Spurning his advances, she formed a relationship with a young white lawyer with whom she had two children. When her master attempted to use her children to extort sexual favors from Jacobs, she hid herself in the home of her freed grandmother, remaining there for seven years, before managing to escape to the North where she was eventually reunited with her children.[34]

When Jacobs sought Child's endorsement to expedite the publication of her autobiography, *Incidents in the Life of a Slave Girl*, in 1860, Child readily agreed. Recognizing the polemical advantages of a truly autobiographical account of female slavery, she seized on the opportunity to put the story of this "much-injured woman" before the public. In her brief introduction to Jacobs's work, Child envisioned and presented Jacobs as (one more) long-suffering, much abused woman struggling to protect her family and her personal safety. In discussing her own motivation for involving herself in

Jacobs's undertaking, Child invoked her "sisters in bondage, who are suffering wrongs so foul, that our ears are too delicate to listen to them." [35] At no time in her introduction did Child even allude to a subject that was clearly of great importance to Jacobs, namely, the affectionate relationship she had with the man who fathered her two children.

Child's determination to control and shape the public presentation of black women becomes even more apparent when her editorial advice to Jacobs is contrasted with her own activities. [36] Jacobs's original manuscript contained a chapter that referred to John Brown's raid on Harper's Ferry. Child advised Jacobs to delete this, saying: "It does not naturally come into your story, and the M.S. is already too long. Nothing can be so appropriate to end with, as the death of your grandmother." [37] Child's advice counseled Jacobs to confine her narrative to issues that affirmed domestic and sentimental ideals of womanhood and not to link herself as a black woman with an individual who had attempted to foment servile war.

It was advice Child chose not to apply to herself. Following Brown's arrest after Harper's Ferry, she had written to Gov. Henry A. Wise of Virginia offering to come and nurse Brown. Although she professed to regret Brown's methods, she eagerly and publicly committed herself to his cause. The ensuing correspondence, including letters to and from Margaretta Mason, wife of Senator James Mason of Virginia, was published first in the *New York Tribune* and later as a pamphlet by the American Anti-Slavery Society, eventually selling 300,000 copies. [38] Child's aggressive defense of Brown's principles signaled a determination to participate in national political discourse regardless of her sex. Thus, the public role Child appropriated for herself, that of activist and partisan, differed substantially from that which she enjoined on black women.

In her conceptualization of black women, as trusting and virtuous souls, deceived and exploited by weak men corrupted by wealth and pride, Child mobilized traditional social values surrounding women, marriage, and family to claim for female slaves the same moral entitlements as those embraced by white middle-class women. At the same time, by contrasting the fidelity of black women with the perfidy of white southern men, Child constructed a powerful metaphor for American treatment of Africans. Her purposes were laudable, but the consequence was not so much the empowerment of individual black women as simply the construction of an alternative and presumably more favorable stereotype.

Child has also been closely identified with another central figure of anti-slavery discourse, the so-called tragic octoroon.[39] From the publication of her *Appeal* to *A Romance of the Republic*, Child wielded this powerful symbol of sexual exploitation and betrayal to foster public indignation about slavery.[40] The figure of the tragic octoroon tapped deeply felt assumptions about domestic virtue and female sexuality; however, Child, almost alone among white women writing, acknowledged the racist underpinnings of this symbol. Depictions of light-skinned female slaves aroused sympathy precisely because they were almost white.[41] Child looked for a day when stories of women of recognizably African descent would be welcomed into the American canon, as black Americans became fully integrated into American society.[42]

Despite this awareness, Child was too shrewd a propagandist not to exploit the evocative power of the image of the tragic octoroon. She manipulated racial and sexual stereotypes brilliantly to demolish prejudice and challenge hidebound thinking. Beginning in the *Appeal*, Child discussed the question of miscegenation with considerable frankness and refused to be dissuaded by concerns about female delicacy. She had few qualms about interracial relationships in principle and portrayed several of these positively in her fiction. She spoke out publicly against antimiscegenation laws.[43] In Child's work, the mulatto woman could be not just a symbol of what was wrong with slavery, although she was surely that, but also a metaphor for the regenerating possibilities of racial integration.

Child's positive attitude toward interracial relationships found little support even within antislavery. The American Anti-Slavery Association had bound itself at its founding meeting in 1833 to combat racial prejudice as well as slavery. In response antiabolitionist Northerners charged that Garrisonian abolitionists promoted "amalgamation," or race-mixing. Antislavery activists took great pains with northern sensibilities (prejudices) on this subject, and beyond criticizing the licentiousness of southern planters, which fostered the growth of the mulatto population, they generally avoided the subject of interracial relationships. However, Child recognized the significance of the connection between concerns about miscegenation and prejudice.[44] Her analysis of public hostility to such relationships flowed inexorably from her determination to negate the constraining impact of gender as a category. The same reasoning that rejected sexual discrimination had also to negate race as a limiting category and miscegenation as an abomination. As Child attempted to attack and undermine sexual prejudice, the logic of her position negated any defense of racial barriers. Acceptance of interracial relationships flowed from her insistence on gender equality.[45] However, it must also be noted that at no time was Child's willingness to countenance interracial relationships grounded in support for female sexual autonomy.

Child's fullest exploration of interracial relationships came in her last novel, *A Romance of the Republic.* Her intention in writing was to stem the rising tide of racism emerging in the wake of Emancipation.[46] The novel begins with a conventional evocation of the "tragic octoroon." The genteel and protected daughters of a Louisiana businessman learn on their father's death that their mother was a slave and was never manumitted. As a consequence of their father's business debts, Rosa and Flora are to be sold at auction. In their distress, the young women accept the protection of Gerald Fitzgerald once he agrees to honor Rosa's promise to her father that she will not entrust herself to any man except her husband. After arranging for marriage to Rosa, Fitzgerald hides the two girls on his Georgia plantation. In time Rosa bears him a son, but not before she learns that her marriage was a sham and Fitzgerald has married a white woman, and not before Fitzgerald begins to make sexual overtures to Flora. Flora escapes to the North, and eventually Rosa flees to Europe. Before she leaves, however, Rosa sacrifices her maternal feelings to guarantee a better life for her own child by switching him with Fitzgerald's legitimate son.

To this point, the plot follows the standard abolitionist themes of violated black womanhood and southern white male debauchery.[47] Rosa and Flora are by turns innocent victims entrapped in the coils of slavery and, following their escape, exemplars of respectable domesticity. The two children who are switched shortly after birth articulate Child's attack on racial prejudice. Her basic premise is that the apparently immutable characteristics that white Americans associated with African blood were in fact illusory, depending in her characters not on the reality but on the awareness of one's racial heritage. Race then should form no barrier to integration.

The experiences of the two children who have been switched and of the children of Rosa and Flora's marriages make explicit Child's assumptions about racial characteristics and her hopes for the future. As the plot unfolds, Child's prescriptions go beyond attempts to eradicate race prejudice. Rosa and Flora marry white men fully aware of their ancestry, and it is here that Child's vision of the future of American society and the role black women

will play in its formation becomes clear. When Child advocated the eradica-
tion of discrimination and the full integration of blacks and mulattoes into
American society, she, unlike most of her contemporaries, was willing to extend that integration to include assimilation.[48] Yet despite Child's sincere
commitment to equality, her thinking on race manifests all the ambiguities
and complexities of what George Fredrickson has called romantic racial-
ism.[49] Having striven at length to challenge and undermine pejorative stereotypes of black Americans, Child unwittingly perpetuates categorical thinking on race by substituting positive but nevertheless stereotypical assertions
about the inherent nature of African Americans, particularly about women.

Fitzgerald's legitimate son, although he has not a drop of African blood,
has been raised in slavery unaware that he is actually white. Child implies
that being spared such morally dubious parenting has in fact been an advantage for George Falkner, as he is known. Slavery has not extinguished
his desire for liberty. Implicitly, George's Anglo-Saxon heritage drives him
toward freedom. He attempts to escape once, only to be sent back into
slavery by his own grandfather. Eventually, having finally freed himself,
George marries a black woman and enlists to fight for the Union in the Civil
War. While George fights, Henrietta, his wife, is taken under the tutelage
of Rosa and Flora, where she quickly learns the domestic arts. In Child's
narrative, Henrietta does not emerge as a distinct character. She serves only
to demonstrate that even a slave woman accustomed to fieldwork can and
presumably will embrace the domestic ideal. By the same token, Child's pes-
simism about American racial prejudice is apparent in that she has George
and Henrietta travel to France after the war to establish a business and a
home, because she assumes the social barriers such a couple would face in
America would be insurmountable.

Gerald, in truth Rosa's son, has been raised with all of his (supposed)
mother's and his father's prejudices, and so he is profoundly shocked when
he learns of his African heritage. Yet, despite his upbringing, his innate de-
cency and kindness allow him to come to terms with this and to forgive Rosa
for her deception. He too enlists in the Union Army where, after encounter-
ing George, he is wounded and dies. In having the only true mulatto male in
the story die without issue, Child articulated prevailing racial attitudes more
closely than she realized.[50]

Child's depiction of the children of Rosa and Flora's marriages underscores her acceptance of assimilation, an acceptance that was grounded in romantic racialist assumptions about the inherent nature of African Americans. These children are healthy and attractive individuals who experience no sense of inferiority or caste. They have become to all intents and purposes white, residing in middle-class comfort and rectitude in Massachusetts. Implicit in Child's prescription is a hope that through the union of the best qualities of black and white Americans the millennial potential of American society might be realized.[51] It seems likely that by portraying black women as home-loving paragons of true womanhood, Child hoped she could at least remove one obstacle to this process.

That this agenda might ignore the goals and aspirations of individual African Americans, particularly women, does not seem to have occurred to Child. Yet, in the work of contemporary black writers such as William Wells Brown, Frances Ellen Watkins Harper, and Harriet E. Wilson, there is ample evidence that among African Americans, racial solidarity rather than assimilation seemed a wiser course. Despite a genuine interest in the well-being of black Americans, it is difficult to describe as anything other than paternalistic Child's failure to comprehend that autonomy and self-definition might reflect the aspirations of African Americans more accurately than assimilation.

In addition, her narrative makes clear that the literal absorption of the African race into the mainstream of the American populace would be through the medium of black women and not black men. Violent southern responses to sexual relations between white women and black men, responses which frequently found sympathetic echoes in northern society, made Child's stance prudent as a polemical strategy. However, apart from the inherent superiority of white Americans that her position implied, it denied to black women the agency and self-determination Child had insisted upon for herself. In arguing that there was no reason why white men should not choose black or mulatto women given their innate domestic and affectionate natures, the choices and desires of African American women seem to warrant little attention. Moreover, by simply substituting a more acceptable stereotype for the reality of African American women's lives, Child failed to address the double discrimination that left so many black women both sexually and economically vulnerable and put the comforts of domesticity far beyond their reach. Lastly, Child's construction of African American women as either victims or domestic paragons, although undoubtedly well intentioned, held at least the potential to render the experience of nonconforming black women as doubly deviant.

*Lydia Maria Child* envisaged an America where the ideal of individual opportunity could be realized. For her the democratic promise of the Revolution, now hallowed by the Civil War, could only be fulfilled when the artificial barriers created by prejudice, arrogance, and elitism were dismantled. To this end she devoted all her energies and talents. That the images of black women she created in order to serve her polemical purposes might have had negative consequences for the African American women she portrayed would surely have surprised her. Although utterly committed to ending both slavery and racial discrimination, Child's rhetorical strategies and political objectives shaped her depiction of black American women in ways that tended to flatten, to stereotype, and at times almost to negate the experience of the very women she strove to liberate. In her fiction and her prescriptive work, in order to make her case for integration, Child required her black heroines to be either hapless victims or paragons of respectability. Where the choices made by actual African American women fell outside these narrow confines, Child excused or ignored them. Thus, she failed to appreciate that even within the oppressive structures of slavery, African American women like Harriet Jacobs could at times experience choice and sexual autonomy and might at times find the conventions of bourgeois respectability irrelevant to their lives.

Bourgeois constructions of womanhood could be both oppressive and empowering for African American women. Where their experience did not embody the domestic ideal, this discrepancy could serve as a rationalization for their enslavement, for sexual exploitation, and for denial of the protection that law and custom accorded "true" women. This part of the dynamic Child understood. What she failed to grasp, or felt it politic to deny, was that within the framework of this reality, African American women made choices, espoused values, and lived their lives in accordance with their own priorities. When it suited their purposes, African American women did consciously embrace bourgeois standards of respectability.[52] At other times they rejected them with the same frequency and for the same variety of reasons as did their white counterparts.

## NOTES

1. Lydia Maria Child (hereafter LMC), *An Appeal in Favor of That Class of Americans Called Africans* (1833; reprint, New York: Arno Press, 1968). For LMC's public reputation in 1833, see *North American Review* 37 (1833): 138.

2. LMC, *Appeal*, 23.

3. See for example LMC to Esther Carpenter, 4 September 1836, and LMC to Jonathan Phillips, 23 January 1838.

4. See for example LMC to Theodore Dwight Weld, 18 December 1838. . . . Weld, *Slavery as It Is: Testimony of a Thousand Witnesses* (1839; reprint, Salem, N.H.: Ayer, 1991).

5. See for example Gerda Lerner, *The Grimké Sisters from South Carolina: Rebels against Slavery* (Boston: Houghton Mifflin, 1967), 7 and 186–87; Dorothy Sterling, *Ahead of Her Time: Abby Kelley and the Politics of Antislavery* (New York: W. W. Norton, 1992), and Otelia Cromwell, *Lucretia Mott* (Cambridge: Harvard University Press, 1958), 123–35.

6. Jean Fagan Yellin, *Women and Sisters: The Antislavery Feminists in American Culture* (New Haven: Yale University Press, 1989), 3–26.

7. Quoted in Blanche Glassman Hersh, *The Slavery of Sex* (Urbana: University of Illinois Press, 1978), 34.

8. Angelina E. Grimké, *Letters to Catherine E. Beecher, in Reply to an Essay on Slavery and Abolitionism, Addressed to A. E. Grimké* (Boston: Isaac Knapp, 1838), 114.

9. For an analysis of Stowe's political agenda see Jane P. Tompkins, *Sensational Designs: The Cultural Work of American Fiction, 1790–1860* (New York: Oxford University Press, 1985), 141–46.

10. For an exploration of the dissonance between the Revolutionary rhetoric of individualism and egalitarianism and the experience of American women see Linda K. Kerber, "Can a Woman Be an Individual? The Discourse of Self-Reliance," in *American Chameleon: Individualism in Transnational Context,* ed. Richard O. Curry and Lawrence B. Goodheart (Kent: Kent State University Press, 1991), 154–58.

11. See for example Margaret M. R. Kellow, " 'Duties Are Ours': A Life of Lydia Maria Child, 1802–1880" (Ph.D. diss., Yale University, 1992), 264–65.

12. See Samuel J. May, *Some Recollections of Our Antislavery Conflict* (1869; reprint, New York: Arno Press, 1969), 98, 100.

13. See for example LMC to Lydia Bigelow Child (sister-in-law, 1807–1878), 12 December 1839. All letters to and from LMC are from *The Collected Correspondence of Lydia Maria Child, 1817–1880,* ed. Patricia Holland and Milton Meltzer (Millwood, N.Y.: Kraus Thomson, 1980). Microfiche. Reproduced with permission.

14. LMC to the Legislature of Massachusetts, 20 March 1839.

15. See for example Sarah Grimké, *Letters on the Equality of the Sexes* (Boston:

I. Knapp, 1838), quoted in *The Feminist Papers*, ed. Alice S. Rossi (Boston: Northeastern University Press, 1988), 306–16, and Lucretia Mott's "Address at Marlboro Chapel," 23 September 1841, reprinted in *National Anti-Slavery Standard* (hereafter *NAS*), 28 October 1841.

16. See for example LMC to Angelina Grimké Weld, 2 October 1838.

17. LMC, "Coincidences," *NAS*, 6 October 1842.

18. That Child's own logic was also flawed in her determined comparisons between women (meaning white and usually middle-class women) and slaves (meaning African American men) is apparent from a reading of Elizabeth V. Spelman, *Inessential Woman: Problems of Exclusion in Feminist Thought* (Boston: Beacon Press, 1988), 1–17, 114–32.

19. It is significant that in making this point, LMC opted not to draw attention to the fact that African American women performed heavy physical work, work that was deemed inappropriate for white women, on cotton and sugar plantations in the American South.

20. LMC, "Coincidences," *NAS*, 6 October 1842.

21. For the individualist critique of antislavery see Richard O. Curry, "The Right to Self-Government: Anti-Institutionalism and Individualism in Abolitionist Thought," in Curry and Goodheart, *American Chameleon*, 108–9; for Child's articulation of these views see LMC, *Appeal*, 76–77. See also Louis S. Gerteis, *Morality and Utility in American Antislavery Reform* (Chapel Hill: University of North Carolina Press, 1987). Regarding concerns about indigence of free blacks in northern cities see George M. Fredrickson, *The Black Image in the White Mind: The Debate on Afro-American Character and Destiny* (New York: Harper and Row, 1971), 49.

22. LMC was not unique in this regard. See for example Angelina Grimké's discussion of African American intelligence in Grimké, *Appeal to the Women of the Nominally Free States* (1838; reprint, Freeport, N.Y.: Books for Libraries Press, 1971), 33.

23. See for example Ellen Carol DuBois, *Feminism and Suffrage: The Emergence of an Independent Woman's Movement in America, 1848–1869* (Ithaca, N.Y.: Cornell University Press, 1978), 177–78.

24. For a summary of the impact of Fanny Wright's career see Glenna Matthews, *The Rise of Public Woman: Woman's Power and Woman's Place in the United States, 1630–1970* (New York: Oxford University Press, 1992), 108–11.

25. See for example LMC, "The Little White Lamb and the Little Black Lamb," *Juvenile Miscellany*, 3d Series, 4 (March/April 1833): 53–56 and *A Romance of the Republic* (Boston: Ticknor and Fields, 1867).

26. LMC, "Charity Bowery," *Liberty Bell*, 1839 and *Letters from New York, Second Series* (New York: C. S. Francis, 1845), 48–56. For a less romanticized but still affectionate depiction of Bowery see LMC's letter to Thomas Wentworth Higginson, 17 March 1860. See also LMC, "Annette Gray," *NAS*, 22 July 1841.

27. See Deborah Gray White, *Ar'n't I a Woman? Female Slaves in the Plantation*

*South* (New York: W. W. Norton, 1985), 46–50. Child's work illustrates Patricia Morton's observation that antiracist writing can at times mythologize supposed racial characteristics. See Morton, *Disfigured Images: The Historical Assault on Afro-American Women* (Westport, Conn.: Greenwood Press, 1991), 1–15.

28. Child's own bourgeois values made it difficult for her to appreciate that, for some black women, the lack of legal "protections" available to white women may have militated against conventional family formation. By the same token this situation may have permitted black women to retain traditional African patterns of kinship and family structure. See Suzanne Lebsock, *The Free Women of Petersburg: Status and Culture in a Southern Town, 1784–1860* (New York: W. W. Norton, 1984), 90, and Christie Farnham, "Sapphire? The Issue of Dominance in the Slave Family, 1830–1865," in *"To Toil the Livelong Day": America's Women at Work, 1780–1980*, ed. Carol Groneman and Mary Beth Norton (Ithaca, N.Y.: Cornell University Press, 1987), 76–83. For a discussion of the Moynihan Report (1965), which identified assertive black women as an underlying cause of the "tangle of pathology," which had supposedly beset the African American family see Morton, *Disfigured Images*, 3–5, and Paula Giddings, *When and Where I Enter: The Impact of Black Women on Race and Sex in America* (New York: William Morrow, 1984), 325–35. For a discussion of the enormous obstacles confronting freedwomen who attempted to command respect from their former masters see Catherine Clinton, "Reconstructing Freedwomen," in *Divided Houses: Gender and the Civil War*, ed. Catherine Clinton and Nina Silber (New York: Oxford University Press, 1992), 306–19.

29. See LeeAnn Whites, "The Civil War as a Crisis in Gender," in Clinton and Silber, *Divided Houses*, 3–21.

30. For an exploration of the myth and reality surrounding this image see White, *Ar'n't I a Woman?* 27–46.

31. LMC, "Annette Gray," *NAS*, 22 July 1841.

32. LMC, "The Quadroons," *Liberty Bell*, 1842 and *A Romance of the Republic*.

33. See for example LMC's short stories "Hilda Silfverling" and "Rosenglory" in LMC, *Fact and Fiction* (New York: C. S. Francis, 1846). For evidence that LMC may have experienced these tensions in her own life, see Kellow, "Duties Are Ours," 375–79, 428–32.

34. Harriet A. Jacobs, *Incidents in the Life of a Slave Girl, Written by Herself*, ed. Jean Fagan Yellin (Cambridge: Harvard University Press, 1987). See in particular Yellin's introduction (xv–xx), in which she corroborates and documents Jacobs's account.

35. LMC, introduction, in Jacobs/Yellin, *Slave Girl*, 4–5.

36. Although her political agenda varied markedly from LMC's, Harriet Beecher Stowe's portrayal of Sojourner Truth as the "Lybian Sybil" provides another example of the determination of some abolitionist women writers to shape the image of African American women. See Patricia R. Hill, "Writing Out the War: Harriet Beecher Stowe's Averted Gaze," in Clinton and Silber, *Divided Houses*, 271–78.

37. See LMC to Harriet Jacobs, 13 August 1860.

38. See *Correspondence between Lydia Maria Child and Gov. Wise and Mrs. Mason, of Virginia* (New York: American Anti-Slavery Society, 1860).

39. See for example Yellin, *Women and Sisters*, 71–76.

40. See for example LMC, *Appeal*, 23.

41. See for example "Highly Interesting Facts," *NAS*, 3 February 1842. See also Judith R. Berzon, *Neither White nor Black: The Mulatto Character in American Fiction* (New York: New York University Press, 1978), 52–53.

42. See for example LMC to [Oliver Johnson] Editor of *NAS*, pre-14 January 1865, reprinted as "A Chat with the Editor of the *Standard,*" in the *Liberator*, 20 January 1865.

43. See for example LMC to the Legislature of Massachusetts, 20 March 1839.

44. On more than one occasion Child quipped that eventually a sufficient amount of money in the pockets of a black bride or groom would overcome the strongest northern biases in this regard. See for example LMC, *Appeal*, 132–33.

45. James Kinney has pointed out that the approach to miscegenation in the work of antebellum polemical writers varied according to whether one was using it to attack slavery (Miscegenation is a consequence of slavery and therefore bad) or racism (Revulsion toward miscegenation is a consequence of prejudice and therefore miscegenation in and of itself is not wrong, although resulting mulatto children will encounter problems). See Kinney, *Amalgamation! Race, Sex, and Rhetoric in the Nineteenth-Century American Novel* (Westport, Conn.: Greenwood Press, 1985), 100–101.

46. See for example LMC to Theodore Tilton, 27 October 1867.

47. In Fitzgerald's self-congratulatory description of himself as the "Grand Bashaw," echoes of Wendell Phillips's condemnation of the South as one great brothel can be clearly heard. Cf. Jules Zanger, "The 'Tragic Octoroon' in Pre-Civil War Fiction," *American Quarterly* 18 (spring 1966): 67.

48. Cf. Kinney, *Amalgamation!* 113.

49. See Fredrickson, *Black Image in the White Mind*, 97–129.

50. For a discussion of nineteenth-century "scientific" thinking on mulatto fertility see Robert Brent Toplin, "Between Black and White: Attitudes toward Southern Mulattoes, 1830-1861," *Journal of Southern History* 45 (May 1979): 197–99.

51. It is quite telling that this was an option that was already being rejected and would continue to be rejected by less optimistic, but certainly more realistic, African American writers such as William Wells Brown, Frances Ellen Watkins Harper, and Harriet E. Wilson dealing with these same themes. See Brown, *Clotel* (1853), Wilson, *Our Nig,* (1859), both reprinted (New York: Mentor, 1990) and Harper, *Iola Leroy* (1892; reprint, New York: Oxford University Press, 1990).

52. For a perceptive example of this strategy see Evelyn Brooks Higginbotham, *Righteous Discontent: The Women's Movement in the Black Baptist Church, 1880–1920* (Cambridge: Harvard University Press, 1993), 185–229.

# 2 Worlds of Women and Slavery

D A V I D  S H E I N I N

# Prudence Crandall, Amistad, and Other Episodes in the Dismissal of Connecticut Slave Women from American History

I N APRIL 1984, the Connecticut Historical Society (CHS) opened a major exhibition on African American women in the history of the state. Conceived as fifteen large display panels, "Black Women of Connecticut: Achievements against the Odds"[1] was the first (and last) CHS exhibit to highlight the history of African American women. The exhibit enjoyed the success its organizers anticipated. It toured the state after a showing at CHS buildings in Hartford, introducing hundreds of visitors to African American achievers. Yet, despite this uncommon focus by the Connecticut historical community on African American women, the show offered few insights into their history. In its companion book, organizers described the exhibit as "biographical sketches of eighty-one women who symbolize three centuries of black triumph over adversity." The word *symbolize* was used ambiguously. But the CHS wished to suggest that the eighty-one exceptional women portrayed— many still living—represented the history of African American women in the state over three centuries. Since 1975, the historical literature on African American women has exposed the limitations of a historical methodology that documents those who have "made it" by the Horatio Alger-like measures of white male society. All the same, the CHS offered precisely such a representation of African American women's history.[2]

"Black Women" reinforced existing scholarly stereotypes in the Connecticut literature—and that of other New England states—that discount the roles of slave women. And it is important to recognize that both before and after 1984, the historiography has ignored and remained lastingly dismissive of Connecticut women slaves. Most commonly, historians have explained Connecticut's past through the accomplishments of white men and the institutions they founded. Most authors touching on slavery have done so sparingly. They have stressed the actions of white male abolitionists and other opponents of forced labor, exploring only briefly the cultural, social, and economic qualities of slave life in Connecticut and the elements that distinguished slavery in Connecticut and the rest of New England from slavery in the American South. Still serving as a CHS traveling exhibition in 1994, "Black Women" reflected and reaffirmed weaknesses and longstanding rigidities in the historical literature of Connecticut. That the exhibit could not offer an understanding of slavery stemmed ultimately from the exclusivity of a state historiography that has long denied the historical role of women slaves. This chapter will examine the Connecticut literature in an effort to explain the absence of slave women from the histories of the state.

A reference to slavery in the introductory passage to the 1984 exhibit's companion book conceded an important insight into one limiting historiographical theme: "Slavery, even in Connecticut, attempted to enchain both the bodies and the minds of black people." In a state historical tradition that predates the Civil War, scholars have downplayed the ferocity of slavery for both men and women, ignoring social and cultural processes of resistance and violence that have been documented in the literature of other states and regions. Despite this preliminary reference to slavery, the exhibit all but ignored women slaves. A section on "Art" depicted slave life in a quilt pattern and made reference to "black people torn from their homes in Africa." Yet there was no mention of the art and culture of slave women. Folk medicine appeared as "primitive treatments." In another important reflection of the Connecticut historical literature, exhibit subsections on "Civil Leadership," "Business," "Journalism," and "Law and Law Enforcement" defined accomplishment in historical terms more relevant to white men than to black women. A section on "Politics and Government" ignored the ways by which slave women led in families, in communities, in the workplace, and in other contexts. "Civil Rights" panels highlighted slavery in both a preamble paragraph and an illustrative design. But visitors learned nothing of the lives of women slaves or civil rights issues in the context of unfree labor.

To be sure, slave labor was never as important to New England society as it was to southern economies. Historians believe that there were far fewer slaves in New England than in the South, that the proportion of the total population they represented was much smaller, and that they rarely worked in the large groups that characterized relations of production and living conditions on many southern plantations. By most accounts, African slaves first reached New England in the mid-sixteenth century—1639 in Connecticut. Although fewer than 1,000 slaves had reached New England before 1700, by 1775 there were some 16,034 slaves within a total regional population of 659,446. Censuses taken between 1771 and 1776 showed that African Americans represented only 2.4 percent of the population. In Connecticut, that figure was 3.2 percent—higher than each of the other New England colonies, with the exception of Rhode Island at 6.1 percent. Pressures for abolition in white New England society came much earlier and were much more effective than in the southern states. In the 1770s, leading Congregationalist ministers published sermons denouncing slavery. This and the participation of African Americans in the Revolutionary War helped convince many white New Englanders of slavery's injustice. In 1780, Massachusetts abolished slavery by judicial decision. Connecticut adopted a series of measures that gradually ended slavery by 1830. These included an act of gradual emancipation (1784) and a prohibition against the slave trade (1788).[3]

Before 1760, the slave population of Connecticut was more evenly distributed across the colony than in other parts of New England. But over the next two decades, the slave population was increasingly concentrated in and around larger towns, particularly Connecticut's ports. Through the mid-eighteenth century, several hundred slaves lived in New Haven, Hartford, and Norwich. The 1774 census showed that New London ranked first among Connecticut counties for its slave population; there were almost twice as many African Americans (2,036) in New London as in the most populous county in Massachusetts. As in other parts of New England, in Connecticut there was a disproportionately large number of male slaves. In 1774, there were 1,572 men in the colony, compared to 1,042 women, with an excess of males in Hartford, New Haven, New London, Fairfield, Windham, and Litchfield Counties. Women were, however, present in significant numbers working as spinners, weavers, seamstresses, and in other functions. On farms, women worked in various capacities, though there is very little information available in the historiography concerning rural life for slave women. As in the southern colonies, slave women were commonly the victims of sexual and physical abuse; in addition, court records of fornication and bastardy charges suggest that families not sanctified by church marriages were not uncommon among Connecticut slaves.[4]

Despite the unique elements of Connecticut and New England slavery, in the place of a substantive analysis of slaves' lives, authors have repeatedly focused on two frequently discussed episodes to explain Connecticut slavery—the Prudence Crandall case and the *Amistad* incident. In the historical literature, these episodes serve as object morality lessons on how African Americans should be and should have been "treated." Both cases neglect slave women. Moreover, the predominance of these incidents in state scholarship has contributed to a complacency both in the historical community and in Connecticut culture more generally. Over several generations of scholarship, "Prudence Crandall" and "*Amistad*" have been described repeatedly in a manner suggesting that these incidents tell us all that is important to know about Connecticut slavery.

The *Amistad* mutiny is about men. More important, its predominance in the historical literature has contributed to a sense that uprisings and resistance concern men only. As told for decades, the story begins with a nineteenth-century slave mutiny aboard a Spanish ship, *La Amistad*. Cinque, the leader of the uprising, and his fellow captives brought the ship to Connecticut, where they were charged with murder and piracy. Abolitionists rallied to their defense. For almost nineteen months, the trial of the mutinous slaves was a national and international cause célèbre. The slaves' counselor, John Quincy Adams, won a Supreme Court decision in 1841 clearing the defendants of all charges. In over a century since these events, there has been little variation in how authors have analyzed this topic. In the historical literature, the case centers on the valiant leadership qualities of Cinque, the legal arguments in the case against the slaves, and the triumph of abolitionist sentiment in Connecticut.[5]

Like the *Amistad* case, Prudence Crandall is discussed frequently in historical works on Connecticut, as well as in works not specifically concerning the state. Both cases have been described by historians in a manner that perpetuates an ambiguous understanding of African American women. Scholars have written about these episodes in a context that conceives of events in Connecticut as informing a larger "American" history of abolitionist sentiment, rather than in the regional or local context of Connecticut's past. In 1833, Prudence Crandall opened a school for African American girls in Canterbury. "If she had announced that she contemplated opening a college for the spread of contagious diseases . . . ," the journalist Archibald H. Grimké wrote, "Canterbury could not possibly have been more agitated and horrified."[6] In spite of the animosity of most town residents, angry opposition from state legislators, and legal action taken against her, Crandall kept the school open until September 1834, when vandals damaged the property so badly that it had to be abandoned.

The historical actors in these episodes were, for the most part, white men who debated the rights of African Americans, with defenders of oppression cast as villains in the historical accounts. In the two decades since Eugene Genovese and John Blassingame wrote their seminal works on slave lives and families,[7] the historical literature of Connecticut has set aside debates on community, culture, family, and gender in slavery. Scholars have cast Connecticut as a supposed bastion of white antislavery, while dismissing the lives and actions of slave women. In fact, very little is known of slavery in Connecticut. Scholars have written almost nothing on slave women, the slave family, or the social and cultural components of slave life that have constituted the chief emphasis in the historical literature of slavery in the South since 1972.

In part, and in this context, scholars have ignored women slaves in Connecticut because they represented a small percentage of the population, never more than 4 percent. Even so, during the late eighteenth century African Americans likely represented one of every eight lower-class Connecticut residents. Moreover, the historian Frederick Turner Main noted that toward the end of the colonial period, in the southeastern towns along the Long Island Sound, more than 20 percent of male heads of family owned one or more slaves at some point in their lives. Slaves lived in Middletown, New London, and Norwich, the principal trading centers of colonial Connecticut. They also inhabited the richest agricultural towns including Groton, Fairfield, Colchester, and Stratford. This and other evidence manifests that even though the population of Connecticut African Americans did not approximate that of Old South states such as Virginia or North Carolina, women slaves made vital contributions to their society.[8] Beyond this data, supplied for the most part by census records, our understanding of men and women slaves remains tentative. Some authors briefly discuss the work of men slaves as personal servants, farm laborers, and skilled workers (in tanneries, mills, and elsewhere). But such references are frequently ambiguous and only made in passing. In 1942, historian Lorenzo J. Greene wrote that "negro women served as cooks, laundresses, maids, nurses, and household workers." This is in keeping with the gendered division of labor in other slave societies. But remarkably, in the half-century since Greene's work on New England slavery, no study has returned to reassess how Connecticut slave women lived and worked.[9]

## The Literature of Connecticut History

Christopher Collier's 1983 annotated bibliography of Connecticut history demonstrates the absence of slave women from the historiography of the state. A chapter on "Slavery and the Black Experience" is limited to 10 of 376 pages in the volume, accenting the scant attention to slavery, African Americans, and women in the historical literature. Collier warns his readers about the scholarship between the end of Reconstruction and the Second World War, the period of "national consensus." During this time, "white Northerners and Southerners agreed to leave black Americans to the mercies of 'local custom.' . . . Local histories . . . are full of patronizing and pejorative comments about Negroes."[10] Despite this admonishment, most works written on African Americans in the state were published during this time. More important, the impact of that historical literature continues to be felt. Forrest Morgan's *Connecticut as a Colony and as a State* is representative of national consensus period literature that claimed a comprehensive historical approach but conceived of African American women as a footnote in state history. References to slavery in this largely institutional history are few; they assess the actions of white men in regard to abolition, important national debates on slavery, and the Civil War.[11] Similarly, while in Connecticut and elsewhere religion played a central role in the lives of African Americans, M. Louise Greene's important study, *The Development of Religious Liberty in Connecticut,* omitted any consideration of women and African Americans.[12]

In another key study of this period, *Connecticut in Transition, 1775–1818,* Richard J. Purcell discussed the early stages of industrialization in the state with no reference to African Americans, although race-based tension and violence pervaded many parts of New England during this time as an influx of African Americans sought work. Purcell restricts his analysis of agriculture in the state to a review of the Connecticut Agricultural Society and a range of other institutions organized and dominated by whites. As in many other pre-1950 studies, references to African Americans are in passing only. In a discussion of animal husbandry Purcell notes that "larger rewards were offered for the return of lost sheep than for runaway negroes." Nothing is said of African American farmers, male or female.[13]

Written in 1977, Jackson Turner Main's *Connecticut Society in the Era of the American Revolution* illustrates the persistence of the methodological rigidity in the historical literature of the state. Like most of those written since the Civil War, this book conceives of the American Revolution as a period in which African American women were of little consequence to historical change. Main's introduction signals the author's intention to go beyond the long-standing methodological emphasis on "high society." But *Connecticut Society* launches quickly into the myth of a Connecticut history without African Americans, and slave women more specifically. For "practical reasons" the author does not make clear, "women and children appear in this account only peripherally." Main's assertions that Connecticut had no social inequalities and that "any respectable small property owner could vote and hold office" are inaccurate, ignoring African Americans who owned property but could not vote. In a reflection of the larger historiography, Main writes as though African Americans were not part of the social fabric. Still more troubling are the author's questionable depictions of African American sexual relations: "Except perhaps in the southeast, the black population was simply too sparse to permit normal sexual activity and formation of stable families." Not only does Main present no information on the relatively common practice of intermarriage among African American and native peoples, but his notion of "normalcy" is based on no documentary or other evidence of how African Americans lived.[14]

Many local histories, while hinting at the presence of women slaves in the colony and state, follow the lead of the conservative state historiography. There are few references to women. An emphasis on town and colonial institutional structures precludes a consideration of African American women by virtue of both their race and gender. E. B. Huntington's *History of Stamford, Connecticut* makes one brief reference to slaves in a section of "miscellaneous" material. He describes two documents pertaining to slavery as "specimens of those which remind us of an institution never again to be revived in Stamford. They are here preserved as a part of the history of earlier times in this old puritan town." Writing in 1868 with a lingering abolitionist fervor, Huntington consigned slavery to a past better left shrouded.[15] More recent local histories have continued to deny that slave women played a notable part in Connecticut history. Although there were 120 African Americans in Stamford in 1756, Estelle S. Feinstein's *Stamford from Puritan to Patriot* contains only brief passages on slavery, always in the context of white society and its institutions. A chapter on "The Family" concerns the white family only. Feinstein writes that the population of African Americans dropped by 50 percent between 1756 and 1774, but she cannot explain why. Though she touches on the subject of women in Puritan society, she proffers no insights into the lives of African American women or men in her discussions of industry, agriculture, taxation, and incomes.[16]

Like Feinstein's history of Stamford, Gail E. Smith's "A Little Band of Chosen Spirits: Windham County Abolitionists, 1835–1850," is more valuable for what it intimates about the potential for research on women slaves than for the data it provides. Smith notes that by 1837 there were nine antislavery societies operating in Windham, more than any other county in the state. Readers learn of white abolitionism, but this article offers no comment on the presence of African American women or whether the activities of slaves had impacted upon the local abolitionist movement. Through the observations of white abolitionists, the author notes that "all across the state incidents of racial and anti-abolitionist violence flared up throughout the 1830s" and that, in 1834, white workers petitioned the Connecticut Assembly protesting the influx of free blacks into the state. But there is no indication of what this migration and social tension meant to African Americans in Windham or in the state more generally.[17]

Some local histories have included important references to African Americans and slaves. But these works lack a methodological rigor that might inform our understanding of the lives of slave women. In *East Granby: The Evolution of a Connecticut Town*, Mary Jane Springman and Betty Finnell Guinan define a local history much in keeping with other histories of the state, stressing the institutional structures of white society. They make clear, however, that slaves were not uncommon in East Granby. Wills, censuses, and other documents record events relating to women slaves, such as the 1790 baptism of "Catherine a Negro child daughter to London Freebody deceased." Yet, in this and other local histories that do not conceal slave women entirely, scholars do not reach beyond anecdotal references. Springman and Finnell report that an increase in the African American population from 55 to 107 between 1800 and 1850 was the result of fugitives from the South. While some of the new arrivals lived with local families, working as domestics and farm laborers, others had small homesteads. There is no additional information on what impact the newcomers had on the existing African American community, the larger impact of the migration on the town, or the roles of slave women in the area. For East Granby, as for other parts of the state, historians have not yet begun to uncover or analyze how slave women lived.[18]

## The Literature of African Americans in Connecticut

Like the literature of Connecticut more generally, the historiography concerning African Americans in the state tells little about the daily lives, beliefs, or cultures of women slaves. There is no shortage of terse and intriguing references to slave women in many works.[19] In the late eighteenth century, for example, an African American from New London appeared before the governor to argue that she and her children had been lawfully freed by her former master, so her refusal to yield herself as a slave to his grandson was justified. In the mid-nineteenth century, in a more important case, the slave Nancy Jackson initiated a suit against her master, J. S. Bulloch, a citizen of Georgia, for unjust confinement. Bulloch had brought Jackson to Connecticut from the South. Jackson argued that the state's 1774 prohibition against the importation of slaves into the colony and a 1784 act that provided that any person born in the state after March 1 of that year would be freed at age 25 guarded against her enslavement. In this important precedent, the court found in favor of Jackson, who was freed.[20] Nonetheless, scholars have made little use of these and other case studies to understand women or the gendered significance of their actions. In addition, historians have rarely attempted to consider how such data might inform a gendered understanding of resistance and culture in Connecticut society.[21]

Many scholars have sidestepped a gendered analysis of slavery, or a methodology of any sort that might probe slave culture, by falling back on the two most frequently discussed themes in the history of African Americans in Connecticut: *Amistad* and Prudence Crandall. These cases are cast in the literature in a manner that focuses on the institutions, ideologies, and "heroes" of white society. The persistence of Prudence Crandall and *Amistad* as central themes in writings on slavery reflects the more generalized tendency in the Connecticut scholarship to ignore African Americans, while building the mythology of "Yankee abolitionism" as the defining feature of African American history in colony and state. Works on the *Amistad* affair share a polemical and moralizing quality with studies of Prudence Crandall. Both bodies of literature seek to define the state in a larger national context: "Connecticut" assumes the character of a progressive people who struggled with and confronted ugly incidents of racism, then overcame them.

Written in 1955, Elizabeth Yates's *Prudence Crandall: Woman of Courage* affirms this high moral tone and conceives of African American history through the actions of white men and one white woman. In so doing, Yates contributes to a historical literature that dismisses African American women as notable historical actors. Although the Prudence Crandall story is ostensibly about the education of African American girls, like other historians interested in this theme, Yates concentrates on the actions of a "heroic" white woman. Almost nothing is known about the girls who faced the fury and violence of the Canterbury community or where they went after vandalism shut down Crandall's school in 1834. But Yates provides copious information on all stages of Crandall's life, the central legislative and court arguments for and against the school, and the means by which this became an event of national importance through publicity in William Lloyd Garrison's weekly paper, *The Liberator,* and other national abolitionist publications. Like others who have written on Crandall, Yates did not see her work as an opportunity to explore the lives of African American women in the state but, rather, as a chance to present a historical morality lesson about white society.[22]

There is an implicit denigration of African American women—slave and free—in this literature. In an introduction to *Prudence Crandall,* Dorothy Canfield Fisher writes that Crandall was "no imaginary heroine. She was a slender young woman, with bright blue eyes, soft blond hair, and a special way of speaking, quiet, controlled—, 'lady-like,' as people said in the early part of the 1800's,—but firm as granite." Yates ascribes a fanciful and undocumented dialogue to Crandall's students. On the first day of class, Crandall ostensibly taught ladylike behavior to her students, while one African American girl, Sarah Harris, identified 'submissiveness' as a virtue in class. Historians have cast Crandall as the antithesis to the late nineteenth- and twentieth-century racist stereotypes of African American women, including the "Mammy"—a supposed antithesis to ladylike conduct. Historians have suggested that Crandall's "white" features explain her courage and persistence in defense of African Americans. A still more disturbing feature of the historical literature is the long-standing and implicit assumption that follows: Crandall achieved for African American women what African American women could not achieve for themselves.[23]

Several more recent works on Prudence Crandall are better researched and less blatant in their juxtaposition of the "white" teacher and her African American followers. However, even where the current historiography has challenged older works, newer studies continue to neglect a consideration of the African American girls who formed the core of this story. In *Three Who Dared: Prudence Crandall, Margaret Douglass, Myrtilla Miner — Champions of Antebellum Black Education,* Philip S. Foner and Josephine F. Pacheco write in militant admiration of the education of African American girls. However, each of these three case studies concerns the "unique" courage of white women educators. For Foner and Pacheco, these cases represent important historical aberrations for two of the same reasons Yates writes with fascination about Crandall. First, the authors are inclined to view African American men and women as historically passive. Second, they do not conceive of a distinct African American educational tradition in Connecticut and elsewhere during the eighteenth and nineteenth centuries. Foner and Pacheco assume that apart from these rare cases, there was virtually no education of African American women. While the authors mean to remove this history from a morality play framework — stressing instead a celebration of interracial cooperation — they maintain the paradigm of African American women's history explained through the actions of white men.

In "Racism and Sexism in Ante-bellum America: The Prudence Crandall Episode Reconsidered," Lawrence J. Friedman goes farther than most in identifying methodological limitations that have hindered a more ample consideration of African American women. While he underscores the early nineteenth-century conflict between the racial doctrines of the Colonization Society and the Garrisonian abolitionists as central to this problem, he reasons that a gendered analysis of the Crandall case is crucial. Friedman points out that most historians of this time have ignored the sexual dimension of the problem. Many studies are little more than polemical defenses of Crandall and the Garrisonian position. Yet, although Friedman goes on to offer an effective criticism of white male fears of race mixing and African American sexuality in Connecticut — as well as how this affected the positions of Crandall's opponents — his focus remains on white men. Friedman delivers no new data on the young women who attended Prudence Crandall's school.[24]

More general studies on Connecticut slavery have been influenced by the prominence of the *Amistad* and Prudence Crandall stories. Indeed, many works of the national consensus period conceived of a progressive Yankee abolitionism in Connecticut as defining the history of slavery. All the same, these scholars frequently present racist stereotypes of African Americans, while ignoring the presence of women slaves. Writing in 1875, William C. Fowler explained a reliance on Scripture as how otherwise thoughtful colony residents could support slavery. Like other studies of slavery that focus on the actions of white men, this work reviews the slave trade and character- izes as spiritually uplifting the influence of white masters, in contrast to the "moral degradation" of Africa. Where he discusses African Americans, Fowler is dismissive in his references to an "imitative race" and his belief that "many were musicians."[25] Historian Ralph Foster Weld also conceived of slavery through the actions of white men. Because he held that slavery- related legislation and religious beliefs defined the institution, Foster found no compelling reason to understand the lives of African Americans. Weld helped perpetuate the myth that, in the absence of a plantation system, a "mild" form of slavery predominated in Connecticut. Not only did Weld and others not investigate or consider the lives of women, but their references to "slaves" almost always referred to men.[26]

Several important studies allow a moderately deeper understanding of women slaves, not by what they investigate in regard to women's lives but, rather, by what they reveal almost incidentally. Writing in 1940, Robert Austin Warner stressed white abolitionism, but also provided information on disease in the African American community, the antagonism of African Americans to colonization schemes, and other details of African American life that remain unexplored by historians. Many puzzling references hint at the richness of the histories of slave women. Warner referred to the more than one thousand women who asked that the nineteenth-century Connecti- cut statute forbidding mixed marriages be repealed. Yet readers do not learn how many of the women were African Americans. Detailed descriptions of schooling and churches in the African American community ignore the pres- ence of women.[27]

In Lorenzo J. Greene's classic study, *The Negro in Colonial New England,* extensive data on population changes over time reveal almost nothing about women slaves. Chapters on "Machinery of Control" and "Crimes and Pun- ishment" are founded on a review of judicial and other legalistic controls that leaves out women. Details of the Revolutionary War and its impact on slaves in the state hint at violence against women slaves but disclose nothing concrete. Greene underlines the range of slave skills in the diverse colonial economy, many being "equally at home in the cabbage patch and the corn-field." But like other sections of the book, this understanding of diversity in job skills disregards women while at the same time making clear that women slaves were present and active in New England society. During the Salem witch purge, for example, women slaves were arrested and charged with witchcraft. In the late seventeenth century an African American girl tried to blow up the house of her Boston master by dropping a live coal into a cask of gunpowder. And in one of several eighteenth-century slave conspiracies, a woman named Kate set fire to a house.[28]

Horatio T. Strother exposes some of the depth and richness of slave life — without doing more than touching on slave women. *The Underground Railroad in Connecticut* concentrates on the routes, obstacles, and participants in slave escapes, but makes only vague references to the women who ran and assisted others. That slave flight in Connecticut was relatively common in the eighteenth and early nineteenth centuries brings into question much of the state historiography by implying that harsh conditions prompted flight. But even as Strother disarms one historical myth, he confirms another by relegating slave women to an incidental role. One runaway, William Grimes, reached New Haven in the early nineteenth century. In his writings, Grimes made brief references to his wife, Clarissa Caesar, describing her as "lovely and all accomplished." He credited her with teaching him to read and write, and the couple farmed for a while in rural Litchfield. But as in other cases where women are mentioned, nothing more is known of Clarissa Caesar.[29]

In a similar vein, Alfred M. Bingham's "Squatter Settlements of Freed Slaves in New England" provides telling but restricted information on the social history of slavery. Bingham exposes a particularly grim component of slavery in colonial Connecticut; he assesses stone structures in the southeastern part of the state that were built by slaves as a temporary refuge, once they had been turned loose by masters who no longer found their labor useful. Bingham speculates that many must have died during the winter months, in light of the limited protection afforded by these shelters. But beyond challenging the conventional wisdom on a benign form of slavery in Connecticut, this study offers only a small clue into the lives of slaves. Like other authors, rather than undertaking an investigation of this slave community, Bingham retreats to a discussion of white society and the conditions under which slaves were brought to southeastern Connecticut.[30]

Writing in 1973, historian David O. White chastised scholars of the revolutionary period in Connecticut for having failed to acknowledge the contributions of African American soldiers. In *Connecticut's Black Soldiers, 1755–1783,* White renders a stinging criticism of the dismissive racism in the works of William C. Fowler, Bernard Steiner, and others. But, like many scholars who have written in the past two decades on Connecticut slavery, he makes historical assumptions that have dismissed African American women. White's references to the status of eighteenth-century free African Americans and his consideration of the range of employments for slaves relate strictly to men. White does describe in detail the actions of African American soldiers in the Revolutionary War effort. But his methodology is as rigid as those he criticizes; this is a listing of African American soldiers in Connecticut regiments and their movements as part of those units. White's understanding of how and why African Americans participated is conditioned by his views on white soldiering. He argues that African American leadership was "not highly developed" in Connecticut in comparison to Boston's African American community, which boasted a number of Revolutionary War enthusiasts. This assumes that the Connecticut African American community had no conception of war or leadership outside the parameters by which white society envisioned the conflict. Locked into a methodology that examines the war effort only through soldiers' actions, White rejects a variety of likely contributions by African Americans to the war effort through agricultural labor and other forms of work. As a result, like much of the literature on the Revolutionary War in Connecticut, there is no attention to the roles of African American or white women.[31]

Very few works specifically address and document the history of African American women, slave or free, in pre–Civil War Connecticut. In "Addie Brown's Hartford," for example, David O. White makes clear that Addie Brown's account is not the typical description of Hartford by nineteenth-century European travelers or political leaders; he argues that this version, as told by a young African American woman in letters she wrote to a friend, offers a unique vantage point by virtue of the author's race and background. All the same—and like the Connecticut historiography more generally— White stresses the actions of an exceptional personality to illustrate the collectivity. He describes the emerging African American community of mid-nineteenth century Hartford, the creation of two African American churches, and formal schooling for African Americans. Yet despite the fact that the letters under review were written by an African American woman, the article brings to light almost no material on daily life for African American women in the city. White states that Hartford's African Americans were among the first city residents to participate in the abolitionist movement after 1820, and he notes that an African American, William Saunders, was the first Hartford agent for the abolitionist newspaper *The Liberator*. In her letters, written between 1865 and 1868, Addie Brown described her work as a housekeeper, dye house worker, and seamstress in a manner that charts the complex interplay between work inside and outside the home. Yet White offers no consideration of the Connecticut equivalent to the gendered analysis of southern African American labor in the current historiography. Determined to defy a rigid orthodoxy in state history that devotes insufficient attention to African Americans, White does not step beyond the organizing premise of the 1984 CHS exhibition: an important case of African American achievement is significant in and of itself.[32]

## Finding Connecticut Slave Women

In its methodologies, the work that goes farthest in addressing the conservatism of the Connecticut scholarship also reflects the limits of that literature, as well as the areas for potential research and analysis that might improve our understanding of women slaves. William D. Piersen's *Black Yankees: The Development of an Afro-American Subculture in Eighteenth-Century New England* posits that slave culture in New England was distinct and can be characterized as such. "Far more than we might have imagined," Piersen writes, "during the eighteenth century the region's black population maintained African values and approaches to life. . . . The Afro-American subculture . . . was not the product of isolation but, instead, a body of shared traditions and values that black New Englanders purposefully maintained to give themselves a double identity, a positive sense of themselves within the larger Yankee community."[33] Despite this promising start to an important study, Piersen falls back on research methods and analytical approaches that continue to reduce Connecticut slave women to bit players in the region's history. He chastises those who reach conclusions about "black attitudes" on the basis of "generalizations drawn from impressionistic glimpses assumed to be typical." Yet he then goes on to adopt a methodology that only provides a glimpse of slave women. Advancing a circular logic that brings his analysis into question and continues to exclude Connecticut African-Americans and women slaves from historical investigation, Piersen argues that generalizations can be "bolstered" by comparative evidence taken from "similar cultural developments among black populations elsewhere." Like generations of scholars, Piersen leaves readers with the question, How can we know that cultural developments outside Connecticut are "similar" to what took place in Connecticut when there is such sparse information on how Connecticut slaves lived?

Piersen's caveat on the paucity of available evidence ("at least as I collected it") is telling. Though the extent of his research in archival and manuscript collections is path-breaking by comparison to most works on New England slavery, he has studied no primary materials from the Connecticut Historical Society collections or any other Connecticut archival source. Like other works on New England slavery, *Black Yankees* assumes that what goes for Massachusetts — and to a lesser extent Rhode Island — goes for Connecticut. "Little distinction," Piersen asserts, "is made between the culture of coastal or urban blacks and that of those residing in the relative isolation of the rural, agricultural interior." But what also becomes clear is that a methodology that blurs these distinctions will blur other important historical variables, including that of gender.[34] Because of this tendency toward ambiguity, the conclusions Piersen draws about Massachusetts and Rhode Island are extended to Connecticut without sufficient concern for regional and local variations. Piersen provides some interesting examples and cases of Connecticut slavery, but conveys nothing new in regard to slave culture and life in the colony. Like many works on New England and Connecticut slavery, Piersen's study devotes much attention to how white society conditioned slavery through the work forms expected of slaves and the contacts allowed between a master's family and a slave family. But the evidence is selective. In arguing that a "slave with a strong personality and superior talents could dominate his master," Piersen cites the case of a slave woman, Violet, and her master, the Reverend Mose Parsons of Byfield, Connecticut. He reports that Violet was described "as the autocrat of her family, and the presiding genius of her household." Not only does this smack of the "Mammy" imagery of physically domineering African American women, but the citing of one or two cases to make a larger point about Connecticut slave women leaves questions unanswered. For scholars to reach answers or even develop questions about slave women in the state, they must begin with a thorough review of available primary sources—as yet undone.[35]

The CHS recently published a guide to its holdings relating to African American history. There are few references to women; this suggests that there is an urgent need for a critical review of CHS collections with an eye to gender.[36] Moreover, there is no general bibliography of manuscript and narrative sources for African American women in the state. No scholar has prepared a guide to historical sources available for the study of African Americans in Connecticut history. And no systematic review has been undertaken for many possible sources including church records, newspapers, court records, probate files, account books, town treasurers' records, pension papers, cemetery records, war records, local histories, family genealogies, published diaries, slave autobiographies, personal papers, travelers' reports, federal census records, tax lists, and city directories.[37]

Writing in 1987, Sterling Stuckey wondered how a single African American national culture had formed out of the interaction of African ethnic groups in North American slavery. While it has been increasingly possible to speak of a national African American culture in twentieth-century American society, Stuckey's evidence points to unique regional differences for some parts of the United States. Though the number of Africans and African Americans in Pennsylvania, for example, represented only 2 percent of the state's population of 333,000 in 1790, Stuckey counters the rationale long used to dismiss a consideration of slavery in Connecticut—that there were too few slaves to matter. The maintenance of African culture by so few slaves in Pennsylvania, in his words, raises "a question regarding the relationship of slave culture to demography that deserves an answer different from the one offered until now." Stuckey's work on African culture, spirituality, and syncretism from Pennsylvania to South Carolina signals the need for similar investigations into Connecticut slavery and the experience of the enslaved woman.[38]

Debra Newman's "Black Women in the Era of the American Revolution in Pennsylvania" presents another Pennsylvania case study that evinces the kinds of research questions that might well be posed for Connecticut history. Newman explains that the Gradual Abolition Law in Pennsylvania made a significant difference in the lives of African Americans, although the material aspects of freedom were worse for some. In a study without a parallel in the Connecticut historiography, Newman's "Black Women" establishes that African American women were a small but significant segment of eighteenth-century Pennsylvania society and that although few records were generated by African Americans themselves before the Gradual Abolition Law, many documents afford a window into the lives of these women. These include baptism and marriage records, wills, deeds, newspaper advertisements for the sale of slaves, censuses, and merchants' records. While none of these records alone gives a well-rounded view of African American women in Pennsylvania, taken together they provide much information, and equivalent records for Connecticut could be expected to do the same.[39]

A seeming contradiction in Robert J. Cottrol's *Afro-Yankees: Providence's Black Community in the Antebellum Era* reinforces the shortcomings of a historical literature that dismisses slave women in Connecticut. Cottrol excuses the southern states' focus in the historical literature "where the great majority of the black population lived and worked." In the North, the author maintains, slavery was an insignificant economic institution—as though this renders less important the history of slaves there. Yet in his study of Rhode Island, Cottrol argues that it is important to study the northern slave experience not only in pursuit of the history of a state or region but to inform our understanding of the slave experience in the United States more generally. Although Cottrol has little to say about Connecticut or women slaves in New England, many of his insights into the culture and society of Rhode Island slaves offer potential starting points for research on Connecticut slave women. In Rhode Island and other parts of New England, Cottrol found that slaveholding patterns and the cultures of Puritan slave owners allowed for the emergence of a semiautonomous slave culture. Slaves had a high degree of freedom compared to their southern counterparts. This led to frequent mingling with whites and natives. And Cottrol notes that street clashes and tension between blacks and whites were common. But unlike other works that document the roles of women in street violence, this work makes no reference to the participation of black women.[40]

A series of questions form the basis of Cottrol's consideration of work forms: "In what occupations were blacks engaged? From what occupations were blacks absent or excluded? Which occupations offered blacks the greatest chances for economic success and perhaps social and political leadership as well?" However, Cottrol addresses these questions for men only, and no historian has addressed them for slave women in any of the New England states. The author goes on to write that "just looking at the community's occupational structure gives some sense of what the population was like, but the sources can tell more. They can provide glimpses of day-to-day relations between people of different races. They also reveal literacy, institutionaliza- tion, family patterns, population fertility, pauperism, and patterns of prop- erty holding" — though not, in this case, for slave women.[41]

The paucity of information on women slaves in the literature of Con- necticut history and on African Americans in the state explains, in part, the limited references to Connecticut in the broader literature of African Ameri- can women in American history. While the literature of Connecticut history has excluded slave women, the literature of African American women and slavery has devoted marginal space to Connecticut. Even as scholars in the past twenty years have found compelling new means of exploring the histo- ries of women slaves in the South, much work remains to be done on most regions outside the South. Before 1970, few works on the history of African American women beyond Connecticut undertook a rigorous analysis of slave women in the North or South.[42] A handful of important recent works have made vital criticisms of traditional perceptions of African American women. Yet, in the absence of a strong body of literature on Connecticut slavery, authors have had to rely on social and cultural models from plantation soci- eties to explain the lives of Connecticut slave women.[43]

For example, Shirley J. Yee's *Black Women Abolitionists* focuses on the participation of free African American women in the struggle to end slavery and racial oppression. Yee's pioneering study reveals a dynamic history of these women's activities in abolitionist movements, complete with a com- mentary on the gendered segregation of abolitionist societies and the nature of African American female leadership. In addition, this work illuminates the potential for discovering these historically excluded women. But Yee men- tions only briefly the roles of African American women in this movement in Connecticut. In the absence of a Connecticut historiography that outlines the regional history of nineteenth-century African American life, Yee in- cludes Connecticut African American women in historical models founded in an understanding of the southern states and, to some extent, urban cen- ters in the northeast. Until scholars undertake analyses of Connecticut slave women, their history will be subsumed in a historiography heavily influ- enced by the southern plantation experience.[44]

## Conclusion

When the 1984 exhibition on "Black Women of Connecticut" opened, the CHS hoped that visitors would understand achievement in the context of severe obstacles against which African American women had had to struggle in Connecticut's past. According to the display book, these included the "social disapproval" that "prevented all but a handful of women from seeking roles other than those of wife, mother, or, in some cases, unskilled worker. Often, black women were denied even the fulfillment of home and family . . . since slavery could rip the black family physically apart." [45] While these assertions may be true, no study before or since 1984 has undertaken to document the work of women slaves in Connecticut or the nature of slave family life. What exhibition visitors read in regard to slavery had no foundation in scholarly research in the state, but seemed to be loosely drawn from the literature on slavery in the southern states. In this and in other respects, it becomes clear that the exhibit reflected equivalent crude assumptions in the historiography—rigidities that have left the history of slave women in Connecticut, and in New England more generally, undiscovered. Like the historical literature of Connecticut, the 1984 exhibition exposed three major problems in interpretation and method: the illustration of African American women's history through the roles of a handful of outstanding individuals, the weak commitment of the CHS to identifying a "representative" group of women, and the paucity of information on this subject in the historical literature.

In 1982, Elizabeth Fox-Genovese challenged historians to break down decades-old models of historical, institutional, and political change. She juxtaposed women's history and official history, reasoning that the latter was founded on a poor understanding of gender systems as essential to historical analysis and to the formation of political institutions. Social systems could be explained effectively only when historical methods analyzed gender roles and identities. Fox-Genovese encouraged historians to set aside the methodological functionalism that "passed verdict" on the nature of women's history before work on a project began, assigning women familiar roles that complemented the activities of their men. [46] Many historians have made the changes Fox-Genovese suggested in state and regional history contexts. The literature of Connecticut history, though, has made few advances in this regard. In the decade following the "Black Women" exhibition, the CHS initiated no reinterpretation of the display. In fact, in 1994, as a series of circulating exhibition panels, the exhibition remained one of the society's most popular traveling exhibits. Moreover, in 1990, the CHS sponsored "Free Men: The *Amistad* Revolt and the American Anti-Slavery Movement," a new display that reflected each of the traditional areas of historiographical neglect. Recent historical works persist in methods of research and analysis that exclude African American women. The Connecticut historiography continues to draw on the traditional and functionalist models of institutional and political change that refuse a gendered analysis and, more specifically, a deliberation that might contemplate the roles of African American women. At the same time, historical writing on slavery and African American women in the United States neglects slave women in Connecticut and, to a significant extent, New England, because of an ongoing focus on the plantation South—and the absence of a strong regional historiography in this field.

## NOTES

1. During the final months of the exhibit's preparation, I was hired by the CHS as a research assistant to ensure that there would be no glaring omissions of prominent Connecticut African American women from the displays. As a research assistant, I did not have the opportunity to contribute to the selection of exhibit subjects or to the design of the show.

2. *Black Women of Connecticut: Achievements against the Odds* (Hartford: Connecticut Historical Society, 1984). Ignoring the role of African American women is by no means unusual in recent exhibits or "display books" on state histories. See, for example, Joan N. Burstyn, ed., *Past and Promise: Lives of New Jersey Women* (Metuchen, N.J.: Scarecrow Press, 1990).

3. Lorenzo Johnston Greene, *The Negro in Colonial New England* (1942; reprint, New York: Atheneum, 1968), 74, 317–24; Robert Austin Warner, *New Haven Negroes: A Social History* (New Haven: Yale University Press, 1940), 38–62.

4. Greene, *Negro in Colonial New England,* 90–93; David O. White, *Connecticut's Black Soldiers, 1775–1783* (Chester: Pequot Press, 1973), 9–11; Barbara W. Brown and James M. Rose, *Black Roots in Southeastern Connecticut, 1650–1900* (Detroit: Gale Research, 1980), xiii.

5. See Eleanor Alexander, "A Portrait of Cinque," *Connecticut Historical Society Bulletin* 49 (winter 1984): 31–51; Howard Jones, *Mutiny on the Amistad: The Saga of a Slave Revolt and Its Impact on American Abolition, Law, and Diplomacy* (New York: Oxford University Press, 1987).

6. Philip S. Foner and Josephine F. Pacheco, *Three Who Dared: Prudence Crandall,*

*Margaret Douglass, Myrtilla Miner—Champions of Antebellum Black Education* (Westport, Conn.: Greenwood Press, 1984), 13.

7. Eugene Genovese, *Roll, Jordan, Roll: The World the Slaves Made* (New York: Random House, 1972); John W. Blassingame, *The Slave Community: Plantation Life in the Antebellum South* (New York: Oxford University Press, 1972).

8. Jackson Turner Main, *Connecticut Society in the Era of the American Revolution* (Hartford: American Revolution Bicentennial Commission of Connecticut, 1977), 17–18.

9. Main, *Connecticut Society in the Era of the American Revolution,* 18; Ralph Foster Weld, *Slavery in Connecticut* (New Haven: Yale University Press, 1935), 7; Greene, *Negro in Colonial New England,* 110; Oscar Zeichner, *Connecticut's Years of Controversy, 1750–1776* (Chapel Hill: University of North Carolina Press, 1949), 247.

10. Christopher Collier, *The Literature of Connecticut History,* Occasional Papers of the Connecticut Humanities Council, no. 6 (Middletown: Connecticut Humanities Council, 1983).

11. Forrest Morgan, ed., *Connecticut as a Colony and as a State, or One of the Original Thirteen,* vol. 3 (Hartford: Publishing Society of Connecticut, 1904).

12. M. Louise Greene, *The Development of Religious Liberty in Connecticut* (1905; reprint, Freeport, N.Y.: Books for Libraries Press, 1970).

13. Richard J. Purcell, *Connecticut in Transition, 1775–1818* (Washington, D.C.: American Historical Association, 1918), 166.

14. Main, *Connecticut Society,* 7–18.

15. E. B. Huntington, *History of Stamford, Connecticut* (Stamford: Author, 1868), 456.

16. Estelle S. Feinstein, *Stamford from Puritan to Patriot: The Shaping of a Connecticut Community, 1641–1774* (Stamford: Stamford Bicentennial Corporation, 1976), 92, 120.

17. Gail E. Smith, "'A Little Band of Chosen Spirits': Windham County Abolitionists, 1835–1850," *Connecticut Historical Society Bulletin* 48 (summer 1983): 100–109; Gary L. Whitby, "Horns of a Dilemma: The Sun, Abolition, and the 1833–34 New York Riots," *Journalism Quarterly* 67 (summer 1990): 410–19.

18. Mary Jane Springman and Betty Finnell Guinan, *East Granby: The Evolution of a Connecticut Town* (Canaan, Conn.: Phoenix, 1983), 66, 99, 238–42.

19. There are few published narrative sources written by Connecticut African Americans; most such works are written by men and offer a diffident understanding of the lives of African American women in the state. There are no Connecticut cases in Ruth Edmonds Hill and Patricia Miller King, eds., *Guide to the Transcripts of the Black Women Oral History Project* (Westport, Conn.: Meckler, 1991). Well-known Connecticut slave narratives include Venture, *A Narrative of the Life and Adventures of Venture, A Native of Africa* (New London, Conn.: C. Holt, 1798); Ann Plato, *Essays: Including Biographies and Miscellaneous Pieces, in Prose and Poetry* (Hartford, Conn.: n.p., 1841); and Hagar Merriman, *The Autobiography of Aunt Hagar Merriman* (New Haven: n.p., 1861).

20. Bernard C. Steiner, *History of Slavery in Connecticut* (Baltimore: Johns Hopkins University Press, 1893), 19, 52–53.

21. A recent issue of the *Connecticut Historical Society Bulletin* represents the only comprehensive effort to document the lives of African American women in Connecticut. The author of the issue, Ruth Barnes Moynihan, adopted an approach at odds with that of the 1984 CHS exhibit: she stressed the lives of "ordinary women of various backgrounds, circumstance, and status." Yet, in both her methodology and conclusions, Barnes does not free her work from the constraining features of the Connecticut historiography, and she does little to advance our understanding of women's lives in slavery. Moynihan, "Coming of Age: Four Centuries of Connecticut Women and Their Choices," *Connecticut Historical Society Bulletin* 53 (winter/spring 1988): 1–82.

22. Elizabeth Yates, *Prudence Crandall: Woman of Courage* (New York: Aladdin Books, 1955), 13.

23. Ibid., 97.

24. Lawrence J. Friedman, "Racism and Sexism in Antebellum America: The Prudence Crandall Episode Reconsidered," *Societas* 4 (summer 1974): 211–28.

25. William C. Fowler, *The Historical Status of the Negro in Connecticut* (1875; reprint, Charleston: Walker, Evans, & Cogswell, 1901), 20.

26. Weld, *Slavery in Connecticut*. See also Thomas J. Davis, "Emancipation Rhetoric, Natural Rights, and Revolutionary New England: A Note on Four Black Petitions in Massachusetts, 1773–1777," *New England Quarterly* 62 (June 1989): 248–63; Lewis P. Simpson, "Slavery and the Cultural Imperialism of New England," *Southern Review* 25 (winter 1989): 1–29.

27. Warner, *New Haven Negroes*, 51.

28. Greene, *The Negro in Colonial New England*, 71–76, 94, 101, 150–62.

29. Horatio T. Strother, *The Underground Railroad in Connecticut* (Middletown: Wesleyan University Press, 1962), 46.

30. Alfred M. Bingham, "Squatter Settlements of Freed Slaves in New England," *Connecticut Historical Society Bulletin* 41 (July 1976): 65–80.

31. White, *Connecticut's Black Soldiers*, 10–14, 21–29, 54.

32. David O. White, "Addie Brown's Hartford," *Connecticut Historical Society Bulletin* 41 (April 1976): 56–64A.

33. William D. Piersen, *Black Yankees: The Development of an Afro-American Subculture in Eighteenth-Century New England* (Amherst: University of Massachusetts Press, 1988), x.

34. Ibid., x–xi.

35. Ibid., 30.

36. "An Annotated Guide to Sources for the Study of African-American History in the Museum and Library Collections of the Connecticut Historical Society," *Connecticut Historical Society Bulletin,* special series, no. 1 (1994): 5–251.

37. White, *Connecticut's Black Soldiers*, 10–14, 20–29.

38. Sterling Stuckey, *Slave Culture: Nationalist Theory and the Foundations of Black America* (New York: Oxford University Press, 1987), 16–19, 23.

39. Debra Newman, "Black Women in the Era of the American Revolution in Pennsylvania," *Journal of Negro History* 41 (July 1976): 276–89.

40. Robert J. Cottrol, *The Afro-Yankees: Providence's Black Community in the Antebellum Era* (Westport, Conn.: Greenwood Press, 1982), xiii, 4–5, 53.

41. Ibid., 112, 113.

42. See, for example, C. F. Graves, *The Negro Woman's Fifty Years of Freedom* (Elizabeth: Linotype Printery, 1918).

43. Many important recent works include Connecticut in a general discussion of African American women's history, but without attention to the specifics of regional and local variations. See, for example, Elizabeth A. Peterson, *African American Women: A Study of Will and Success* (Jefferson: McFarland, 1992). See also K. Sue Jewell, *From Mammy to Miss America and Beyond: Cultural Images and the Shaping of U.S. Social Policy* (New York: Routledge, Chapman, and Hall, 1993).

44. Women outnumbered men forty-five to thirty-two at the founding of the Hartford Colored People's Society, but Yee provides no additional information on the roles of women in this movement. Shirley J. Yee, *Black Women Abolitionists: A Study in Activism, 1828–1860* (Knoxville: University of Tennessee Press, 1992), 83, 37. See also Rosalyn M. Terborg-Penn, "The Historical Treatment of Afro-Americans in the Woman's Movement, 1900–1920: A Bibliographical Essay," *A Current Bibliography of African Affairs* 7 (summer 1974): 245–59; Jacqueline Jones, *Labor of Love, Labor of Sorrow: Black Women, Work, and the Family from Slavery to the Present* (New York: Basic Books, 1985), 11–43; Ira Berlin, Steven F. Miller, and Leslie S. Rowland, "Afro-American Families in the Transition from Slavery to Freedom," *Radical History Review* 42 (1988): 89–121.

45. *Black Women of Connecticut*, 1.

46. Elizabeth Fox-Genovese, "Placing Women's History in History," *New Left Review*, no. 133 (May–June 1982), 5–29.

KIMBERLY S. HANGER

# "The Fortunes of Women in America"

## SPANISH NEW ORLEANS'S FREE WOMEN

## OF AFRICAN DESCENT AND THEIR

## RELATIONS WITH SLAVE WOMEN

DURING THE SPANISH PERIOD of New Orleans's history (1763–1803) free women of African descent actively participated in the city's economic, familial, and cultural life, even though they, like slave women, experienced oppression both as women and as blacks. Free *pardo* and *moreno*[1] women were retailers, domestics, business owners, producers, and consumers. They bought and sold, borrowed and loaned, rented and exchanged real estate, personal property, slaves, and services. Some of them inherited, accumulated, and transferred to their heirs sizable estates. Although their life cycles varied considerably from white and slave women and even among themselves, most free women of color strove to realize what their society prescribed: forming stable relationships with men and other women, white and black; bearing, baptizing, raising, and educating their children; and procuring property and patronage so that present and future generations might advance their status, or at least survive.

Free women of African descent in colonial New Orleans and other American slave societies confronted discriminatory laws and practices, abusive individuals, and unjust, unwarranted perceptions. Whites, free black males, and even the occasional slave subordinated, exploited, or mistreated free and slave women of color. Even though some free black women benefited from friendship and kinship networks and close associations with whites, particularly through manumission and inheritance, they had to muster much energy, cunning, and determination in order to maintain their material wealth and other advantages for themselves and succeeding generations.

This essay, examining the lives of free and slave women of African descent in New Orleans during the Spanish regime, looks at the ways in which slave women became free, the efforts of free black and slave women to liberate friends and family, the accumulation of real, personal, and slave property, and the relationships that free black women had with slave women, free black men, and white men and women in their community. Several scholarly works examine African slavery in Louisiana, the most recent and thorough being that of Gwendolyn Midlo Hall, *Africans in Colonial Louisiana,* Ann Patton Malone, *Sweet Chariot,* and Roderick A. McDonald, *The Economy and Material Culture of Slaves.*[2] Others look at free blacks but place little emphasis on women, mainly because there are more records available for free black men, who served in militias and had what society considered "valuable" occupations.[3] Even fewer works concentrate on colonial women.[4] Although in her dissertation and forthcoming book Virginia Gould focuses on free women of color, she concentrates on the antebellum period.[5] Other topical approaches to Louisiana history often fail to incorporate women into their story line. For example, one recently published book on criminal activity in Spanish Louisiana devoted one chapter to "Free Men of Color and Slave Defiance" with hardly a mention of women, who made up half of the slave and two-thirds of the free black populations of New Orleans at the time and who are found throughout the records resisting authority.[6]

Indeed, sources for the study of free black and slave women in colonial New Orleans are incredibly vast and in many respects still untapped. Careful recordkeepers, Spanish administrators documented everything they could, usually in triplicate. Nevertheless, most materials are in eighteenth-century French and Spanish, many are in poor condition, others are located only in Spanish archives, and some—most notably the sacramental records of the Archdiocese of New Orleans[7]—were inaccessible until very recently. Great opportunities await the diligent scholar. Primary sources utilized in this essay include censuses, tax lists, property damage claims, militia rosters, criminal and civil cases, sacramental (baptismal, marriage, and funeral) records, and notarial registers. The latter are most useful for delving into the everyday lives of "common folk" and include property transactions, slave manumissions, wills and estate inventories, marriage contracts, and suits for debt, recovery of property, separation, and divorce. Even to begin to comprehend what colonial New Orleans society was like, one needs to employ a combination of many types of sources, because any one gives an incomplete, sometimes inaccurate, picture.[8] In addition, because of the massive quantity of documents, reconstitution of any segment of the society can only be accomplished by utilizing computerized data analysis. Such projects are under way but take much time and many resources.

Although it is more difficult to reconstruct the lives of colonial New Orleans women than men, especially black women, the richness of Spanish sources makes such a project possible. This author's past work has examined the free black population as a whole and is now concentrating on free women of color and their relations with slave and white women. It is part of the process of "discovering" women of African descent who lived in freedom and slavery in the fascinating world of colonial New Orleans.

*Founded in 1718* on the site of a long-established American Indian portage point where the Mississippi River comes closest to the shores of Lake Pontchartrain, New Orleans was Louisiana's principal urban center and port. France held Louisiana and its capital city of New Orleans from 1699 until 1763, when it ceded the colony to Spain under provisions of the Treaty of Paris. Spain, in turn, governed Louisiana until 1803.

Under French and Spanish rule Louisiana's value was mainly strategic. Both Bourbon monarchies viewed Louisiana as useful primarily within the context of larger geopolitical considerations: neither wanted Britain to seize it. Although Spain, like France, considered Louisiana an economic burden, the crown hoped to utilize it as a protective barrier between mineral-rich New Spain and Britain's increasingly aggressive North American colonies. Spain thus actively endeavored to attract settlers and slaves to the region, not only to defend it but also to balance the somewhat hostile French population remaining in Louisiana and to promote agricultural and commercial growth.[9]

In Louisiana, as in many areas of Spanish America, the crown fostered the growth of a free black population in order to fill middle sector roles in society, defend the colony from external and internal foes, and give African slaves an officially approved safety valve. Africans took advantage of the legal, demographic, economic, and political conditions prevailing in Louisiana to gain freedom, secure decent living conditions, and advance their social status. The labor shortage dilemmas that plagued New Orleans throughout the colonial period were for the most part solved by Africans, both slave and free. Free blacks were especially suited for the skilled, petty commerce, and transportation jobs that whites accepted reluctantly and mistrusted their black slaves to carry out. In addition to playing an essential role in the New Orleans economy, free black men also performed vital defense and public service acts. Their militia formed part of Spain's circum-Caribbean defense system. On a daily basis they repaired breaks in the levee, fought fires, and chased runaway slaves. Free people of African descent also contributed to New Orleans's rich cultural diversity and participated in the region's complex cross-cultural exchange networks.[10]

Although census figures conflict and provide only approximate accuracy, they point to a growing population over the Spanish period of New Orleans's history (Table 1). White males consistently outnumbered white females; the opposite held true for slaves and free blacks. During the period the white population of New Orleans almost doubled, while the slave population grew 250 percent. As a result of restrictions on slave importations, the number of slaves in New Orleans decreased in the 1790s, but then multiplied in the early 1800s in response to the growing demand for slave labor on sugar and cotton plantations and the lifting of import bans.[11] The number of free blacks increased sixteenfold, and this group reportedly was undercounted throughout the era![12] Also significant, the percentage of free persons of color in the total, free, and nonwhite populations increased under Spanish rule (Table 2). Manumission, reproduction, and immigration (particularly from Saint-Domingue in the 1790s and early 1800s) contributed to this rise in number and proportion of New Orleans free people of African descent.

Among free blacks, females outnumbered males two to one, a proportion that paralleled the sex ratio within the manumitted population (about 58 males for every 100 females). It was lower, however, than the sex ratio for the city's slaves, which hovered around 82 and rose to 95 in 1805 (refer to Table 1). Thus, compared to their proportion of the total New Orleans slave population, bondwomen secured freedom more frequently than did bondmen. Both unconditional and conditional (upon service or money) manumission favored female slaves in late eighteenth-century New Orleans. Although for the Spanish period as a whole, the majority of slaves received their liberty by way of acts instituted by the master, as they had under French rule, a rising proportion initiated manumission proceedings themselves or with the help of a relative or friend.[13]

Slave women, like men, attained free status in a number of ways. Some ran away and joined the maroon communities that proliferated in the swamps surrounding New Orleans; others escaped from plantations to the city, where

*Table 1: New Orleans Population, Year by Status by Gender*

| Year | Whites | | | Free Blacks | | | Slaves | | |
|------|---|---|-------|---|---|-------|---|---|-------|
| | M | F | Total | M | F | Total | M | F | Total |
| 1771[a] | — | — | 1803 | — | — | 97 | — | — | 1227 |
| 1777[b] | 1104 | 632 | 1736 | 101 | 214 | 315 | 518 | 633 | 1151 |
| 1788[c] | 1310 | 1060 | 2370 | 233 | 587 | 820 | 956 | 1175 | 2131 |
| 1791[d] | 1474 | 912 | 2386 | 324 | 538 | 862 | 871 | 918 | 1789 |
| 1805[e] | — | — | 3551 | — | — | 1566 | — | — | 3105 |

[a] Lawrence Kinnaird, *Spain in the Mississippi Valley, 1765–1794*, 3 vols. (Washington, D.C.: GPO, 1946–1949), 2:196.

[b] Archivo General de Indias, Papeles Procedentes de Cuba (hereafter cited as AGI PC), legajo 2351, 12 May 1777.

[c] AGI PC 1425, 1788.

[d] Census of New Orleans, 6 November 1791, Louisiana Collection, New Orleans Public Library.

[e] Matthew Flannery, comp., *New Orleans in 1805: A Directory and a Census Together with Resolutions Authorizing Same Now Printed for the First Time* (New Orleans: Pelican, 1936).

they tried to pass as free or to sneak passage to another territory.[14] Avenues to freedom deemed more legitimate by the dominant society included manumission initiated by masters (during their lifetimes or on their deathbeds) and manumission initiated by slaves or third parties (self-purchase either with the master's approval or forced before a tribunal). In keeping with its aim of encouraging growth of a free black population in Louisiana, the Spanish crown implemented a practice common in its American colonies known as *coartación:* the right of slaves to purchase their freedom for a stipulated sum of money agreed upon by their masters or arbitrated in the courts. Confronted with a reluctant owner, the slave, a relative, or a friend could request a *carta de libertad* (certificate of manumission) in front of a government tribunal. Two and sometimes three assessors declared the slave's monetary value, and upon receipt of that sum, the tribunal issued the slave his or her carta. Thus, under Spanish law slaves did not have to depend upon the generosity of masters to attain freedom; rather, they relied on their own efforts and the aid of a favorable legal system.[15]

Even within an environment conducive to manumission, slave women often struggled long and hard to become free. Purchase of a carta represented a major investment for the slave or a third-party white, free black, or other slave. In Louisiana the price of freedom increased during the Spanish period and rose even higher in the antebellum era as officials closed the foreign slave

*Table 2: Proportion of Free People of Color in the Total Free, and Nonwhite Populations, New Orleans*

| Year | % of Total Population | N | % of Free Population | N | % of Nonwhite Population | N |
|---|---|---|---|---|---|---|
| 1771[a] | 3.1 | 3127 | 5.1 | 1900 | 7.3 | 1324 |
| 1777[b] | 9.8 | 3202 | 15.4 | 2051 | 21.5 | 1466 |
| 1788[c] | 15.4 | 5321 | 25.7 | 3190 | 27.8 | 2951 |
| 1791[d] | 17.1 | 5037 | 26.5 | 3248 | 32.5 | 2651 |
| 1805[e] | 19.0 | 8222 | 30.6 | 5117 | 33.5 | 4671 |

[a] Lawrence Kinnaird, *Spain in the Mississippi Valley, 1765–1794,* 3 vols. (Washington, D.C.: GPO, 1946–1949), 2:196.

[b] Archivo General de Indias, Papeles Procedentes de Cuba (hereafter cited AGI PC), legajo 2351, 12 May 1777.

[c] AGI PC 1425, 1788.

[d] Census of New Orleans, 6 November 1791, Louisiana Collection, New Orleans Public Library.

[e] Matthew Flannery, comp., *New Orleans in 1805: A Directory and a Census Together with Resolutions Authorizing Same Now Printed for the First Time* (New Orleans: Pelican, 1936).

trade and restricted opportunities for manumission. Many people of color labored long years and used most of their scarce resources to free themselves or friends and kin, indicating the premium they placed on freedom.

Upon request, masters usually allowed slave women to purchase themselves and their family members. María Luisa, a thirty-two-year-old parda slave, paid her master 500 pesos (the peso was equivalent to the dollar at the time and was the monetary unit upon which the dollar was based) in 1772 for her carta and that of her four children, ages seven, five, two, and three months. A more complex kin group purchase involved the morena Magdalena, fifty-three years old, who bought her own liberty for 350 pesos and within the next few days purchased cartas for her twenty-year-old son Francisco (300 pesos), twenty-three-year-old daughter Lileta (350 pesos), and Lileta's two young sons for 150 pesos each.[16]

In 1775 the thirty-nine-year-old morena Francisca Montreuil reimbursed her master, don Roberto Montreuil, 800 pesos for her freedom and that of her parda daughter Naneta, more commonly known in later documents as Ana Cadis. Francisca also registered her obligation to pay Montreuil an additional 300 pesos within one year; he canceled the note one year and two days later. By 1777 the morena libre Francisca Montreuil had accumulated the 300 pesos needed to purchase from her former master the carta of her son Carlos, a twenty-year-old pardo blacksmith.

When Francisca died in 1803, she possessed an estate valued at 10,459 pesos, which when debts of 3,157 pesos 3 reales (8 reales to the peso) were subtracted, left 7,301 pesos 5 reales to be divided among her three living children (Carlos, María Genoveva, and Agata) and her three living grandchildren by her deceased daughter, Naneta. A native of Louisiana and the natural[17] daughter of Francisco Rancontre and Susana, Francisca was about seventy years old when she died. Among her substantial estate were five slaves worth 2,650 pesos, one slave who was promised his freedom, a house and lot in New Orleans worth 2,825 pesos, two plantations along Bayou Road worth 1,735 pesos, livestock, furniture, and household goods.

Francisca's daughter Naneta died in 1800 and also left a large estate acquired during her quarter century of freedom. Naneta married Pedro Bahy (Bailly), also a recently freed pardo, in 1778 and brought a dowry of 350 pesos in silver and four cows worth forty pesos given by her mother, Francisca. Naneta's father was a white man, don Pedro Cadis. She gave birth to five legitimate children, two of whom died before they reached the age of ten, and all of whom had leading white citizens and officials as their godparents. Naneta was left to care for her family, properties, and slaves — and was given power of attorney to do so — while her husband spent over two years in prison in Cuba, convicted of espousing radical French ideals and of conspiring to overthrow the Spanish government in 1794. Pleading for the welfare of her children, Naneta successfully petitioned the Spanish crown to release her husband in 1796. These children, second-generation free blacks, benefited greatly from the business acumen of their parents and grandmother when they inherited their estates in the early 1800s.[18]

As seen from the cases above, relatives and friends often paid the price of a slave woman's freedom. After soliciting don Joseph Villar on many occasions, the parda libre Marion finally convinced him to liberate her son Janvier, a nineteen-year-old creole pardo, for 400 pesos and her daughter Luisa, a creole grifa about twenty years of age, for 200 pesos.[19] When she wrote her will in 1798, the free negra Janeton, a native and citizen of New Orleans, instructed her executor, don Francisco de la Rua, to collect the money owed her by another white man and use it to purchase the freedom of her youngest child, María. In addition, la Rua was to give María what remained from the estate so that she could use it to earn money with which to purchase the freedom of her three other slave siblings.[20] Why Janeton did not try to collect the debt and manumit her children while she was still alive is unclear.

Free women of color occasionally had to bring reluctant masters before tribunals in order to purchase freedom for loved ones and protect them from abuse. In 1792 María Laveau, a free morena, petitioned the court to manumit her daughter Roseta, parda slave and concubine of Francisco Aimé. Documents supported Laveau's contention that Roseta had lived "en calidad de muger con su amo" (with her master as his wife) and had borne him three children, all of whom had died as a result of mistreatment. Laveau thus requested that the court manumit Roseta without compensation to Aimé. Aimé fought the petition, however, and in the end Laveau had to pay 425 pesos for Roseta's freedom.[21]

In one unusual case a free black woman, Clemensia Demasilière, fought through the court system to free her half-sisters, who were slaves owned by her brothers or half-brothers, Pedro Baltazar and Pedro Agusto. The two Pedros were the free pardo natural children of don Francisco Emanuel Demasilière and the free morena María Bienvenu. Don Francisco had manumitted without conditions his slave María and her four-year-old son Pedro Agusto in 1782, and Pedro Baltazar was born free. It is not clear whether Clemensia was don Francisco's daughter, even though she took his name. A year after don Francisco died in 1787, María Bienvenu purchased the freedom of Clemensia, then fifteen years old, a move one would imagine don Francisco would have made if he were her father. Clemensia was not mentioned in his will. When don Francisco wrote his will, he stipulated that in remuneration for her services, María Bienvenu was to receive nine moreno slaves, three of whom — Basilio, Rosalia, and Iris — were her children by another man. Bienvenu could enjoy the use of these slaves during her lifetime, but she could not sell them, and when she died they were to go to the two Pedros. Bienvenu died in 1791. Her three slave children passed to their free half-brothers, Pedro Baltazar and Pedro Agusto, along with the six other slaves, a house in New Orleans, a plantation and sawmill downriver from the city, household goods, twenty pigs, and eight cows. Bienvenu's own possessions included another negra slave, twelve chairs, one cypress armoire, three cypress tables, six pots, two dozen plates, 150 empty bottles, and her personal clothing, all of which she left to her mother, the free negra Luisa.

Thus, the free parda Clemensia was excluded from both her mother's and probable father's wills. In 1794 she appeared before a tribunal in New Orleans to obtain the freedom of her half-sister Iris and paid 450 pesos to her brothers for it. Seven years later Clemensia brought her brothers, or rather their guardians, before a tribunal again, this time to request the freedom of their other half-sister, Rosalia. Clemensia had saved 400 pesos to manumit Rosalia; she apparently preferred to free her half-sisters than her half-brother or could more easily afford their cartas. However, two years later in 1803, Pedro Baltazar Demasilière freed his half-brother Basilio gratis and without conditions.[22]

Like whites and free blacks, slave women paid masters to issue cartas for loved ones, but most likely such purchases involved much greater personal and material sacrifice. When slaves used scarce resources to manumit others, they placed a desire to liberate fellow bondpersons above their own freedom in true acts of compassion, consideration, and selflessness. Examples include the parda slave Margarita, who gave her master 200 pesos to manumit her cuarterón son Pedro, two years of age.[23] One slave mother convinced her free brother to purchase the freedom of her child, and another requested the carta of her daughter with funds provided by the child's godmother, a free black woman.[24] When the mulata libre María Angela Tribiño was baptized in March 1795, the priest noted that the child's mother, a negra slave, had purchased her freedom two months prior.[25]

Sometimes free black women purchased slave relatives but did not free them. At age twenty-six the parda Naneta Chabert was freed by her master without conditions in 1772. One year later she purchased two slaves: her mother—a parda named Henrieta, forty-five years old—and her grandmother—a morena named Gäy, seventy-three years old. Three months later Naneta manumitted her mother, but she never freed her grandmother. Perhaps enslavement by caring kin held advantages for the elderly, or possibly Gäy died soon after the purchase. In her will dated one day before she died in April 1786, Chabert did not mention her grandmother but noted that her mother lived in Mobile. Chabert's goods consisted of one plantation near New Orleans and another between Baton Rouge and Pointe Coupee on the Mississippi River; she also owned four slaves, one of whom cared for her mother in Mobile. Chabert owed various sums to three white men, one white woman, one free black woman, and one male slave. It is interesting to note that Chabert did not leave her estate to her mother but rather to her goddaughter and her goddaughter's husband.[26]

As the Chabert case demonstrates, free black women purchased and freed or kept slave kin, but they also owned slaves for purposes of service and speculation, just as their white neighbors did. The holding of African slave property by free people of color was customary throughout the Americas,

*Table 3: Free Black Purchases of Nonkin and Kin Slaves,
New Orleans, 1771–1803*

| | Purchase of Nonkin | | Purchase of Kin | |
| --- | --- | --- | --- | --- |
| Years | FW | FFB | FW | FFB |
| 1771–1773 | 7 | — | 3 | — |
| 1781–1783 | 58 | 3 | 12 | — |
| 1791–1793 | 106 | 11 | 15 | — |
| 1801–1803 | 92 | 7 | — | — |

FW=From White          FFB=From Free Black
*Sources:* Acts of: Juan Bautista Garic, vols. 2–4, 1771–1773; Andrés
Almonester y Roxas, 1771–1773, 1781–1782; Rafael Perdomo, 1782–1783;
Leonardo Mazange, vols. 3–7(1), 1781–1783; Fernando Rodríguez,
vols. 7(2), 1, 1783; Francisco Broutin, vols. 7, 15, 25, 1791–1793; Pedro
Pedesclaux, vols. 12–19, 1791–1793 and vols. 38–45, 1801–1803; Carlos
Ximénez, vols. 1–5, 1791–1793 and 17–19, 1801–1803; Narciso Broutin,
vols. 3–6, 1801–1803. Orleans Parish Notarial Archives, New Orleans.

and most colonial governments guaranteed the property rights of their free
black citizens. Ownership of black slaves fostered free black identification
with white society and thus dissipated white fears of racial collusion. The
pattern of free black ownership of slaves in Spanish Louisiana closely resembled that of other Spanish American colonial regions and Brazil, where
free black populations were large and valuable and there were no legal restrictions on manumission. In these areas free blacks primarily owned slaves
to help them in their trades in both cities and fields. As long as slave prices
remained low, free people of color who could afford bondpersons used them.
In addition, as noted above, free blacks could afford to purchase their slave
relatives and could free them with few constraints, and thus did not need to
hold them as slaves.[27]

New Orleans free blacks purchased rising numbers of slave laborers into
the 1790s, with a slight dip in the 1800s as prices rose (Table 3). Comparison of free black purchases of slave nonkin with those of kin reveals the
prevalence of the former, a trend that increased over time. Analysis of the
notarial records also indicate that almost two-thirds of the slaves whom free
blacks acquired were females. In addition, the gap between gender ratios
in the free black population and that of free black purchasers closed until
the ratios were almost on parity. Initially, a disproportionately large percentage of slave buyers were free morenas and pardas, but with each decade

the percentage of female purchasers declined while that of males increased. Census and purchasing data show that in 1777 females comprised 67.9 percent of the free black population in New Orleans but purchased 77.8 percent of the slaves between 1771 and 1773. Respective proportions for the 1780s were 71.6 percent and 75.8 percent; for the 1790s 62.4 percent and 64.8 percent; and for the 1800s 60.2 percent and 60.4 percent. The percentage of males in the free black population in 1777 (32.1 percent) and in the universe of free black buyers 1771–1773 (22.2 percent) rose to 39.8 and 39.6 percent, respectively, in the first years of the nineteenth century. Given the total available slaves purchased and free black buyers by gender and phenotype, it appears that free morenas and pardas purchased greater numbers of female and fewer male slaves than would be expected, whereas free morenos and pardos preferred moreno slaves. Most likely, intended use of the slave based on occupational gender divisions, along with higher prices for male slaves, influenced this pattern. Free black women used slaves to perform domestic chores and peddle their trade goods; they augmented their income by hiring out skilled slaves; and they bought and sold slaves for speculative purposes. Take María Teresa Cheval, a free parda tavernkeeper, for example: she purchased a morena bosal (newly imported African) from one man for 90 pesos and sold her the next day to another man for 300 pesos![28]

In addition to procuring bondpersons through purchase, free persons of color acquired slave property by way of testamentary and *inter vivos* acts. Heirs rarely contested these generous bequests to free blacks, and Spanish colonial courts usually upheld the deceased's wishes as long as there existed a written, witnessed last will and testament. According to the December 1779 will of Henrique Mentzinger, who was a sergeant in the white militia, the pardito libre Juan Baptista, two years old, was to receive Mentzinger's twenty-six-year-old morena slave named Fatima. In addition, Mentzinger left to the parda libre Luison, eight years of age, his eight-year-old moreno slave named Manuel. Both Juan Baptista and Luison were the children of the morena libre Gabriela, Mentzinger's former slave and probable common-law mate. Mentzinger willed 200 pesos to Gabriela.[29]

Doña Magdalena Brazilier's will stipulated that María Luisa, a parda libre about seven or eight years old, was to receive two slaves—Batista (twenty years old) and Luisa (eighteen years old)—along with Brazilier's residence in New Orleans and all her clothes, jewelry, household goods, kitchen utensils, and furniture. María Luisa was the daughter of Brazilier's "mulata mestiza" slave Maneta. In the will Brazilier freed seven of her slaves, many of them other children of Maneta, but she did not manumit Maneta. Maneta's children joined María Luisa and their brother Poiquon, a pardo libre whom Brazilier had manumitted prior to making her will.[30]

A native of Coruña, Spain, don Marcos de Olivares bestowed upon his natural daughter, the free parda María Josepha de los Dolores, ownership of a morena slave and her two children, along with another morena slave. Olivares also willed her 2,000 pesos, two houses, furniture, clothing, silver, and various household effects. He donated to María Josepha's mother, the free morena Mariana Voisín, a small house and land, a morena slave, and 1,000 pesos and instructed her to administer their daughter's inheritance until she reached majority. Other free persons of color, including María Josepha's grandmother, also benefited from Olivares's generosity.[31]

Free persons of color also donated slave property to friends and kin in their wills. Near death in 1793, the fifty-six-year-old free morena criolla Mariana Meuillon designated her natural son as her only heir. Bautista Meuillon, a twenty-five-year-old free pardo, thus acquired his mother's silverware, two lots and houses in New Orleans, a seven-by-forty-arpent tract of land eight leagues upriver from the city, and a morena bosal named Mariana. The last two items Mariana had received from don Luis Meuillon, her likely consort. Several people owed Mariana money, including one white woman, four free black women, and one free black man.[32] Unmarried and without heirs, the morena libre Margarita Momplessir stated in her testament that she owned thirteen *"piezas de esclavos"*: the morena Juli, her ten children (ages twenty-two years to eight months), and the three children of Juli's oldest daughter, Clarisa (six to one years of age). Momplessir distributed this slave family to free and slave female friends and relatives: Clarisa to Catalina, a morena slave belonging to the estate of don Francisco Momplessir; one of Clarisa's daughters to a pardita libre named Eufrosina Dimitry, daughter of don Andrias Dimitry; and the remaining slaves to the free cuarterona Francisca Momplessir. She also donated 100 pesos to each of the three children (two girls and a boy) of another free black woman.[33]

Though not as common as testamentary bequests, inter vivos donations of slaves to free people of color occasionally appeared in the notarial registers. Among these benefactors was don Francisco Raquet, who in 1782 donated two young morena slaves and two pieces of land to Adelaida, free cuarterona, daughter of the free parda Francisca Lecler, alias Raquet. Four years later don Francisco donated a plantation next to his own holdings downriver from New Orleans to Adelaida and her cuarterón brother Honorato. In his will written in 1802 don Francisco recognized the now twenty-four-year-old Adelaida as his natural daughter; donated 3,000 pesos to her, 400 pesos to her mother Francisca, and 1,000 pesos to each of Adelaida's two sons; and named as heir to his plantation and twelve slaves Adelaida's daughter, Adelaida Dupry.[34] Apparently don Francisco preferred his granddaughter to his grandsons; his generosity improved the material well-being of three generations of free black women.

New Orleans free women of color acquired slave, real, and personal property by working for wages, operating successful business enterprises, and receiving inheritances or donations from whites, slaves, and other free blacks. Within their own lifetimes or over generations some free black women amassed sizable estates, although it is difficult to assess these estates because no comparable study has been conducted for free black men or whites of either sex. No matter how much or what they owned, however, most free black women actively endeavored to protect and expand their resources in order to improve their own material conditions and social standing and that of their kin and friends. Numerous court cases attest to their struggle to protect their rights within a society that exploited them both as nonwhites and as women. As will be seen in the case of María Gentilly, slaves too challenged the prerogatives of New Orleans free women of color.

Much of the wealth that free blacks in Spanish Louisiana possessed was passed on to them by whites and other free blacks through intricate kinship and friendship networks.[35] Associations with whites—be they sexual, paternal, friendly, or business in nature—benefited free people of color, women in particular. In New Orleans's corporate society, advantages accrued to those free women of color who were linked by kin and patronage to leading white families. Some white males publicly acknowledged their free black consorts and offspring and donated personal and real property to them. For example, in his testament dated 1794, don Pedro Aubry declared that he was single but that he had two natural children by the morena libre María Emilia Aubry; all three were his former slaves. As his only heirs, the children received a farm seven leagues from New Orleans, two slaves, livestock, furniture, and household goods.[36]

Although free women of color most commonly acquired property from white benefactors, other free blacks also willed them material goods. Free persons of color passed their goods to lineal and lateral kin and to friends, thereby contributing to others' well-being. Second- or third-generation free blacks usually inherited the accumulated riches, no matter how meager, of past generations, and slaves who had well-established free black friends or relatives stood a better chance of being "rescued" from slavery than those with no ties to the free black population. For example, Juan Bautista Hugón, born free and captain of the free pardo militia when he died in 1792, purchased the freedom of four out of five of his children (one son and four daughters) and at least one of their mothers during his lifetime. On the day of his death Hugón's goods consisted of a house and land in New Orleans, one slave, furniture, and clothes. He donated to a morena slave named Magdalena (most likely one of his consorts) a bed, a stoneware fireplace ornament, one pig, and the chickens on the patio of his house. Hugón also requested that his testamentary executor purchase his fifth child's carta de libertad. Hugón's goods sold at public auction for 1,095 pesos. After paying for the carta, outstanding debts, and burial and court costs, the executor turned over 227 pesos, 5 reales to Hugón's children.[37]

Testaments and estate inventories illuminate the extent of property free black women could accumulate during their lifetimes and bestow upon relatives and friends when they died. They also reveal intricate kinship and patronage ties among free blacks, whites, and slaves. Perrina Daupenne, parda libre, drew up her will in August 1790. She was the natural daughter of a white man she confessed not to know and the parda libre María Daupenne; she was single and without any children. Daupenne owned a house in the city and ten slaves, five of whom she freed without conditions, including a morena woman from Guinea and her two parda daughters. She also instructed her executor to purchase the freedom of a pardo slave belonging to a white man. In addition to leaving Charity Hospital ten pesos and giving a priest thirty pesos to say thirty masses for her soul, Daupenne donated slaves, livestock, clothes, furniture, linen, household goods, and a cypress grove to her friends, aunts, and cousins, all of them women. To her brother she gave her share of their dead brother's estate. Daupenne's white godmother, doña Sinfora Prado y Navarete, received all her gold jewelry and a mahogany armoire. Daupenne appointed another white person and government official, don Andrés Manuel López de Armesto, to act as her executor. Finally, Daupenne named as her heir the moreno libre Candio Tomás, legitimate son of her cousin María Juana Pierre Tomás and of Pedro Tomás, morenos libres.[38] Few free black women went to their graves this wealthy, but those who did usually raised the material level of at least some free blacks and slaves who remained behind.

The parda libre María Francisca Riche also died without any children, and she too distributed her estate among her closest kin and longtime friends, as well as the poor. A natural daughter of the free morena Carlota Riche, native of Pointe Coupée, and resident of New Orleans, Riche donated 10 pesos to indigent patients at Charity Hospital and 100 pesos and a harness decorated with silver to doña Julia Bauvais of Pointe Coupée (Riche had served as Bauvais's nurse when she was a child). She ordered her executor to sell her household goods and a morena slave and spend the proceeds to liberate her brother and sister, Pedro and María Luisa. In turn, the siblings were to use what funds remained to purchase the cartas of María Luisa's two daughters, and these nieces were to inherit Riche's estate.[39]

Unlike Daupenne and Riche, the free morenas Janeton Laliberté and María Belair had living children, and their estates can be traced down through at least two generations during the Spanish period. A native of Senegal, Laliberté wrote her will in 1771 and noted that thirty years earlier she had married a moreno named Gran Jacot (also known as Luis) and that they had a daughter named María Juana. She later married another free moreno, but this union produced no children. Laliberté willed to her daughter her half lot in New Orleans, a plantation downriver from the city at English Turn and located adjacent to lands of Pedro Tomás, her son-in-law, and four cows with their calves. Thirty years later María Juana Tomás wrote her will. Her marriage to Pedro Tomás had produced seven children, six of whom were still living, the oldest forty-four years and the youngest twenty-five. Tomás's only property consisted of the half lot and house inherited from her mother, and she left this to her children and the one son of her dead child.[40] Prior to her marriage to the pardo libre Luis Daunoy, María Belair had two natural daughters, Carlota and Martona, to each of whom she willed one-fifth of her estate when she died in 1794. The rest of her estate she left to her and Daunoy's legitimate son, also named Luis. María's property consisted of her dowry (500 pesos) and half the goods communally owned with her husband, which included a half lot and cabin in New Orleans. Martona Belair followed her mother to the grave one year later and left her one-fifth share of María's estate to her six natural children, ranging in age from thirteen years to twenty months. Martona made her living as a dry goods retailer and had acquired much more property than her mother. Appraisors valued her estate—furniture, household goods, personal clothing, a half lot and house in New Orleans, a promissory note, and dry goods for her business—at 1,572.5 pesos. Martona owed one white woman and eight white men (most of them wholesale merchants) 553 pesos, thus leaving 1,019.5 pesos for her six children. In addition, Martona held as guardian one female slave (valued at 400 pesos) for two of her minor children and another female slave (valued at 350 pesos) for one of her other minor children. Two white men, probably the respective fathers, had donated the slaves to the children.[41]

Marriage contracts that specify dowries hint at the material well-being of free black women earlier in their life cycles than do wills and estate inventories. On January 10, 1779, Pedro Langlois wed Carlota Adelaida, both pardos libres, and on January 23 they entered into a marriage contract. Langlois declared his possessions as three slaves and cash totaling 1,800 pesos. A widow with a young child, Carlota Adelaida declared both the property she brought from her former marriage and her daughter's inheritance. This included land, slaves, and debts worth a net total of 1,350 pesos. While Langlois administered his new wife's and stepdaughter's possessions, he could not alienate them without their consent.[42] In a second example the husband, cuarterón libre Francisco Alexandro Colombe, was marrying for the second time and made clear in the prenuptial agreement that half of his goods—valued at 3,000 pesos—belonged to the three children from his previous marriage. His new wife, parda libre Henriqueta Toutant, also carefully delineated the possessions her family—in particular her wealthy white father don Bartolomé Toutant Beauregard—had bestowed on her. Hard currency, jewelry, clothes, furniture, and household utensils valued at 1,200 pesos comprised Toutant's dowry.[43] The cuarterona libre María Constancia's dowry was also appraised at 1,200 pesos and included 540 pesos worth of stamped silver (which she had acquired "through personal work in an honest manner"), 360 pesos worth of clothes and furniture, and the remainder the value of a young female slave. She entered into a marriage contract with Carlos Lavibarière, a free pardo, but their marriage is not recorded in the sacramental records for St. Louis parish.[44]

Although many free black women increased their material worth between the time of their marriage and that of their death, some experienced a decline in wealth and status. Among them was Luison Brouner (Mandeville), a parda libre who in many documents is recorded as a mestiza. Into her marriage to pardo libre Francisco Durand in 1785 Brouner brought a plot of land and a house with a separate kitchen in New Orleans, much furniture, personal clothing, and five slaves. Brouner was the natural daughter of Mr. Mandeville and María Juana, an *"india mestiza libre,"* and she had had a common-law relationship with don López de la Peña, which had produced four natural daughters, prior to her marriage to Durand. Brouner and Durand had no children. When she died in 1794, Brouner's holdings had been reduced to one slave, plus a half interest in a slave and plantation near Baton Rouge that her godmother, the parda libre Naneta Chabert, had donated to Brouner and Durand. Brouner owed don José de la Peña 400 pesos, an amount somewhat offset by the 200 pesos that one of her daughters owed her.[45] Most likely, Brouner had dispersed the majority of her properties over her lifetime or had faced some misfortune, thus indicating that wills made at the end of a lifetime were sometimes not representative of one's maximum material value.

A list of losses incurred in the first great fire to sweep colonial New Orleans (March 1788) is another useful source for estimating at least the real and personal property holdings of the city's free black women and for comparing them with those of free black men and white men and women. In September 1788 a list of 496 claims was submitted to the Spanish crown for damage to buildings and interior furnishings (plus 10 claims on government property) totaling more than 2.5 million pesos. Fifty-one of these claimants were free black women, and their average estimated loss in real and personal property was 1,770 pesos. Free black men made up only 21 of the claimants, with an average loss of 1,723 pesos. Another 67 of the claimants were white women (average loss of 2,880 pesos), and the remaining 357 claims were made by white men. The white male average claim of 6,090 pesos was more than double that of white females and about three and a half times greater than that of free black women or men.[46] Clearly, white men possessed the vast majority of material wealth in late eighteenth-century New Orleans, and while there were more free black women holding property than free black men (which one would expect given the demographic makeup of the city), the men possessed more valuable or larger amounts of property.

Maintaining and expanding property holdings, which free blacks in turn passed on to kin and friends, required much business acumen and an understanding of legal procedures. María Gentilly was one such free black woman who tried—but failed—to preserve her property from what she perceived as malicious deception on the part of an inept husband, unjust favoritism toward slaves, and discrimination against women, married women in particular. In January 1793 Luis Dor, the moreno slave of don Joseph Dusuau, sued the cuarterón libre Estevan Lalande, a carpenter and member of the free pardo militia, for collection of 230 pesos loaned in June 1791.[47] Lalande admitted before the tribunal that he owed Dor 230 pesos but could not pay it until he sold a house that belonged to his wife, the parda libre María Gentilly. Authorities placed Lalande in jail and seized the house in which both Lalande and Gentilly resided.

At this point Gentilly appeared before the tribunal to present evidence that the house belonged to her and indeed constituted part of her dowry. Prior to Gentilly's marriage to Lalande, don Luis Gentilly Dreux had manumitted his twenty-four-year-old slave María and donated to her a plantation with thirty oxen, twenty sheep, some thirty pigs, twelve horses, and a slave. He also gave her all the wood needed to build a house in New Orleans and 300 pesos to pay for its construction. Gentilly used 100 of the 300 pesos to purchase another plantation, and after her marriage to Lalande, he sold it for 450 pesos. They subsequently used the 450 pesos, plus the 200 remaining pesos and the wood, to build the house that the court later seized. Claiming that the house was part of her dowry and belonged solely to her, Gentilly ordered the court to release her property, *"en virtud del de prelación que las Leyes conceden a las Mugeres, para el cobro de los bienes que trahen al matrimonio, y demas no pertenecientes a la comunidad que tienen con sus maridos"* ("in virtue of the priority that the law concedes to women so that they may recover the goods that they bring into the marriage and that do not belong to the community of goods they share with their husbands").

Dor, however, argued that the documents Gentilly presented as proof of her ownership to the above-mentioned holdings were not notarized and thus were invalid in a court of law. Moreover, both Lalande and Gentilly had marked the promissory note for the 230-peso loan with their *X*s (because neither could sign his or her name). Thus, Gentilly was as responsible for the debt as was Lalande, and even property she solely owned could be seized.

Gentilly responded with a poignant plea for justice. First, she presented witnesses to validate the unnotarized documents that gave her her freedom and property from Gentilly Dreux. Second, she argued that the cross made at the bottom of the promissory note executed in Dor's favor by Lalande was not hers and that nowhere in the note was her name mentioned. In addition, such a note required two witnesses but was signed by only one. Finally, Gen-

tilly challenged Dor's assertion to first claim on her property simply because
he intended to use the money to purchase his freedom:

> My adversary also says that I well know the money he claims is to pur-
> chase his liberty, and that as respects my dowry, even if my demands
> were legitimated, his rights to payment prevail, principally because it
> would be invested to ransom him from the slavery and captivity in which
> he finds himself. I ask: From what code did he take this law? Who told
> him, that a debt contracted by a husband to a slave who wants to free
> himself with it, that for this reason a wife is obligated to pay the debt
> from her goods, if the husband himself is insolvent. Perhaps my oppo-
> nent's lawyer does not know that the dowry a woman and the rest of
> her goods have the right of precedence in all possible cases, that even
> the Royal Treasury itself sacrifices that to which it is owed by the hus-
> band, to leave intact that belonging to the wife, which it views as a sacred
> thing. . . . [If husbands could use their wives' belongings to free slaves,]
> the woman would be stripped of her properties with such fraudulent
> proceedings that the law would be barbaric if this were allowed. What
> then would happen to the fortunes of women in America where there
> are so many slaves? What woman would be dumb enough not only to
> weigh herself down by the heavy yoke of matrimony, subject to the capri-
> ciousness and fantasies of a disordered and unjust husband as she runs
> the risk of doing, as well as exposing [herself] to losing the goods with-
> out any power and subject herself to tyranny because the law does not
> authorize her to resist?

The law, however, did authorize Gentilly to resist, and resist she did. In
August 1793, one month after Gentilly presented the above petition, Lalande
admitted that he had fraudulently made a cross at the bottom of the promissory note in his wife's name but without her consent. He and he alone owed
Dor the 230 pesos. It appears that Lalande also lied about not being able to
sign his name, because documents from the 1770s and 1780s clearly show his
signature.[48] People rarely forget how to sign their own names.

The case took a turn when Lalande died a few days later and Dor had
to begin proceedings against Lalande's estate in order to collect the debt.
Once again Gentilly contested what she perceived as Dor's unjust pretensions on her dowry, reiterating that "the woman's dowry is always sacred,
and protected by royal laws and natural laws" no matter what it was used

for, even the manumission of a slave. Nevertheless, Dor convinced the tribunal that Lalande and Gentilly had both contributed to the purchase of the previously seized house in New Orleans and that it should be considered community property. Judge Manuel Serrano ordered Gentilly's house sold at public auction, with half the proceeds going to Gentilly and half to satisfy Lalande's debts.[49] Thus, in addition to losing her husband (perhaps not such a loss after all), Gentilly reluctantly relinquished much of the holdings she had brought into her marriage twenty years before.

In their efforts to free themselves, friends, and kin and to acquire and protect real, personal, and slave property, New Orleans free and slave women of African descent both succeeded and failed and in the process were exploited. They, in turn, exploited other women and men, free and slave. While some free women of color amassed large property holdings, which they astutely used to improve their own living conditions and that of their heirs, others experienced persistent dependency and even downward mobility, especially those who were newly freed. Within a colonial slave society that was stratified by race, socioeconomic and legal status, and gender, the interests of New Orleans free black and slave women were subordinated to whites of both sexes and to free black and slave men.

When given the opportunity, though, these women struggled on their own volition to attain freedom for themselves, their families, and their friends; to accumulate material possessions through employment, donation, and inheritance; and to maintain and expand their estates in order to benefit future generations. In many significant ways slavery connected the experience of both enslaved and free black women. Many free black women were once slaves, had friends and family still in slavery, labored to manumit such friends and family, worked and socialized with slave women, left goods to slave women in their wills, and/or owned women as slaves. Like other white and free black New Orleanians, free women of color acquired slaves for purposes of service and speculation and acted to further their own self-interest. Slave ownership more closely identified them with propertied and influential white citizens and often enhanced their chances for prosperity within the constrained setting of a three-caste slave society.

In addition, many slave and free black women did not hesitate to use the legal system, along with kinship and patronage networks, to improve their status and material circumstances. Despite widespread illiteracy and vulnerability as women, nonwhites, and in some cases slaves, women of color had the courage, will, and talent to take on the legal system. During long and hard struggles, they skillfully utilized patron and kin connections, including those forged through interracial sexual liaisons, to advance their own conditions and thus those of their offspring and relatives. Facing great odds, some failed, but enough succeeded so as to provide inspiration for their own and future generations of free and enslaved women of African descent.

## NOTES

Much of this research was carried out as a result of the generosity of several programs and institutions: the University of Florida Department of History, the Spain-Florida Alliance, the Program for Cultural Cooperation between Spain's Ministry of Culture and United States Universities, the American Historical Association, the University of Tulsa Faculty Research Grant and Faculty Development Summer Fellowship Programs, the Oklahoma Foundation for the Humanities, and the American Philosophical Society.

1. Throughout this work I use the inclusive somatic terms "free black" and "free person of color" to encompass anyone of African descent, be he or she pure African, part white, or part American Indian (*indio*). The exclusive terms *pardo* (light-skinned) and *moreno* (dark-skinned)—preferred by contemporary free blacks over *mulato* and *negro*—are utilized to distinguish elements within the nonwhite population. Occasional references delineate further between *grifo* (offspring of a pardo[a] or an indio[a] and a morena[o]), *cuarterón* (offspring of a white and a pardo[a]), and *mestizo* (usually the offspring of a white and an American Indian but in New Orleans sometimes meaning the offspring of a pardo[a] or moreno[a] and an india[o]). Racial terminology, however, was often variable and confusing. About two-thirds of New Orleans's free women of color were pardas, the offspring or descendants of mixed white and black unions. Only about one-fifth of slave women were pardas: see for example the Census of the City of New Orleans, 6 November 1791, New Orleans Public Library (hereafter cited NOPL).

2. Gwendolyn Midlo Hall, *Africans in Colonial Louisiana: The Development of Afro-Creole Culture in the Eighteenth Century* (Baton Rouge: Louisiana State University Press, 1992); Ann Patton Malone, *Sweet Chariot: Slave Family and Household Structure in Nineteenth-Century Louisiana* (Chapel Hill: University of North Carolina Press, 1992); Roderick A. McDonald, *The Economy and Material Culture of Slaves: Goods and Chattels on the Sugar Plantations of Jamaica and Louisiana* (Baton Rouge: Louisiana State University Press, 1993). See also Hans W. Baade, "The Law of Slavery in Spanish Louisiana, 1769–1803," in *Louisiana's Legal Heritage,* ed. Edward F. Haas (Pensacola: Perdido Bay Press, for the Louisiana State Museum, 1983), 43–86; Thomas Neil Ingersoll, "Old New Orleans: Race, Class, Sex, and Order in the Early Deep South, 1718–1819," 2 vols. (Ph.D. diss., UCLA, 1990); James Thomas McGowan, "Creation of a

Slave Society: Louisiana Plantations in the Eighteenth Century" (Ph.D. diss., University of Rochester, 1976); Judith Kelleher Schafer, *Slavery, the Civil Law, and the Supreme Court of Louisiana* (Baton Rouge: Louisiana State University Press, 1994).

3. Donald E. Everett, "Free Persons of Color in Colonial Louisiana," *Louisiana History* 7 (winter 1966): 21–50; Laura Foner, "The Free People of Color in Louisiana and St. Domingue: A Comparative Portrait of Two Three-Caste Slave Societies," *Journal of Social History* 3 (October 1970): 406–30; Kimberly S. Hanger, "Personas de varias clases y colores: Free People of Color in Spanish New Orleans, 1769–1803," Ph.D. diss., University of Florida, 1991; H. E. Sterkx, *The Free Negro in Ante-Bellum Louisiana* (Rutherford, N.J.: Fairleigh Dickenson University Press, 1972).

4. One of the few is Vaughan B. Baker, "Cherchez les Femmes: Some Glimpses of Women in Early Eighteenth-Century Louisiana," *Louisiana History* 31 (winter 1990): 21–37.

5. Lois Virginia Meacham Gould, "In Full Enjoyment of Their Liberty: The Free Women of Color of the Gulf Ports of New Orleans, Mobile, and Pensacola, 1769–1860" (Ph.D. diss., Emory University, 1991).

6. Derek N. Kerr, *Petty Felony, Slave Defiance, and Frontier Villainy: Crime and Criminal Justice in Spanish Louisiana, 1770–1803* (New York: Garland, 1993). Another excellent recent work on colonial Louisiana, which unfortunately does not include women, is Daniel H. Usner Jr., *Indians, Settlers, and Slaves in a Frontier Exchange Economy: The Lower Mississippi Valley before 1783* (Chapel Hill: University of North Carolina Press, for the Institute of Early American History and Culture, 1992).

7. Starting in the early 1970s the Archdiocese of New Orleans closed its sacramental records to the public; reasons given included claims that the records were in litigation or that the Archdiocese archives were understaffed. A change in policy came in November 1992. "Serious" scholars (those pursuing a doctorate or holding one) can now examine colonial baptismal, marriage, and burial registers, kept in separate books for whites and nonwhites during the Spanish regime.

8. For example, a list of persons who claimed losses in a fire that swept through New Orleans in March 1788 gave the phenotype (negro or mulato) and free status (*libre*) of most, but apparently not all, free black claimants (see ff. 46).

9. For a survey of Louisiana's colonial history, refer to Bennett H. Wall, ed., *Louisiana: A History,* 2d ed. (Arlington Heights, Ill.: Forum Press, 1990).

10. A more in-depth look at free people of African descent is provided by Hanger, "Avenues to Freedom Open to the New Orleans Black Population, 1769–1779," *Louisiana History* 31 (summer 1990): 237–64; "Personas de varias clases y colores"; and "A Privilege and Honor to Serve: The Free Black Militia of Spanish New Orleans," *Military History of the Southwest* 21 (spring 1991): 59–86. See also Hall, *Africans in Colonial Louisiana;* Usner, "The Frontier Exchange Economy of the Lower Mississippi Valley in the Eighteenth Century," *William and Mary Quarterly* 44 (April 1987): 165–92; and Usner, *Indians, Settlers, and Slaves.*

11. Paul F. Lachance, "The Politics of Fear: French Louisianians and the Slave Trade, 1786–1809," *Plantation Society in the Americas* 1 (June 1979): 162–97, examines Louisiana's slave trade policy in the context of the French Revolution.

12. In New Orleans and other Spanish cities, census counts were very low for free blacks. The Spanish government conducted most censuses for military service or tax reasons and thus undercounted women as well. See Cecilia Wu, "The Population of the City of Querétaro in 1791," *Journal of Latin American Studies* 16 (1984): 277–307.

13. Hanger, "Personas de varias clases y colores," chap. 2.

14. Hall, *Africans in Colonial Louisiana*, 201–36, 317–42.

15. Baade, "Law of Slavery"; Herbert S. Klein, *African Slavery in Latin America and the Caribbean* (New York: Oxford University Press, 1986), 194–95.

16. Acts of Andrés Almonester y Roxas, f. 251, 10 September 1772; Acts of Carlos Ximénez, no. 2, f. 229, 231, 5 May 1792 and f. 234, 235, 237, 7 May 1792. The slaveholder, dona María Julia de la Brosse, legitimate wife of don Francisco Carrière and childless, let several other slaves purchase their cartas at the same time. Two months later she wrote her will and donated to Magdalena, now a free morena, a fully outfitted bed and to Magdalena, her three daughters, and another former slave all the clothes of her use, divided equally five ways (Acts of Ximénez, no. 2, f. 331, 6 July 1792).

17. Spaniards distinguished between types of illegitimacy, as deliniated in *Las Siete Partidas,* a thirteenth-century law code that formed the basis for legal decisions in the New World as well as the Old. A natural child (*hijo natural*) was the illegitimate offspring of single parents, who often recognized the child as theirs. An illegitimate child of a married parent was known as an *adulterino,* and the child of a priest was labeled an *espurio.* Natural children often had higher social status and more legal rights than did other types of illegitimate children (Ann Twinam, "Honor, Sexuality, and Illegitimacy in Colonial Spanish America," in *Sexuality and Marriage in Colonial Latin America,* ed. Asunción Lavrin (Lincoln: University of Nebraska Press, 1989), 118–55.

18. Acts of Almonester y Roxas, f. 4, 5, 8 January 1775 and f. 17, 19, 10 January 1777; Court Proceedings of Narcisco Broutin, no. 59, f. 1028–76, 28 June 1803; Court Proceedings of Ximénez, f. 246–63, 28 May 1804; Acts of N. Broutin, no. 2, f. 13, 29 January 1800; Acts of Almonester y Roxas, f. 25, 25 April 1778; Black Baptisms, book 2, f. 290, 17 July 1782, book 3, f. 51, 31 May 1784, and book 4, f. 220, 15 April 1791; Archivo General de Indias, Papeles Procedentes de Cuba (hereafter cited AGI PC), legajo 211-A, f. 160, 1796. For more on Bahy (also Bailly) see Hanger, "Conflicting Loyalties: The French Revolution and Free People of Color in Spanish New Orleans," *Louisiana History* 34 (winter 1993): 5–33.

19. Acts of Juan Bautista Garic, no. 9, f. 595, 597, 29 December 1778.

20. Acts of Francisco Broutin, no. 47, f. 460, 15 November 1798.

21. Court Proceedings of N. Broutin, no. 11, f. 74–100, 17 March 1792. Laveau had at least one other daughter by a white man named Patricio Conway. An unmarried wholesale merchant from Ireland, Conway stated in his will that his one natural daughter was

María Conway, the fourteen-year-old child of María Laveau (Acts of N. Broutin, no. 5, f. 172, 16 March 1803).

22. Acts of Leonard Mazange, no. 5, f. 12, 7 January 1782; Acts of Mazange, no. 7, f. 282, 29 March 1783 and f. 290, 1 April 1783; Acts of Fernando Rodríguez, no. 13, f. 1143, 6 December 1787; Acts of Rodríguez and Pedro Pedesclaux, no. 2, f. 335, 11 March 1788; Acts of Pedesclaux, no. 13, f. 436, 30 June 1791; Acts of Ximénez, no. 7, f. 325, 18 August 1794; Acts of N. Broutin, no. 3, f. 131, 22 April 1801; Acts of Ximénez, no. 19, f. 21, 18 February 1803.

23. Acts of Garic, no. 10, f. 78, 1 February 1779.

24. Acts of Ximénez, no. 17, f. 3, 7 January 1801 and f. 197, 5 November 1801.

25. Black Baptisms, book 5, no. 750, 8 March 1795.

26. Acts of Garic, no. 3, f. 28, 1 February 1772; Acts of Garic, no. 4, f. 264, 16 September 1773 and f. 358, 23 December 1773; Acts of Rafael Perdomo, no. 7, f. 189, 21 April 1786.

27. David W. Cohen and Jack P. Greene, eds., *Neither Slave nor Free: The Freedmen of African Descent in the Slave Societies of the New World* (Baltimore: Johns Hopkins University Press, 1972); Mary C. Karasch, *Slave Life in Rio de Janeiro, 1808–1850* (Princeton: Princeton University Press, 1987), 211, 335-70; Michael P. Johnson and James L. Roark, *Black Masters: A Free Family of Color in the Old South* (New York: W. W. Norton, 1984) are just a few of the works that discuss free blacks as slave owners. For more information on free black ownership of slaves in colonial New Orleans that will be included in the discussion below, refer to Hanger, "Personas de varias clases y colores," 200-242.

28. Acts of Pedesclaux, no. 17, f. 295, 18 April 1793 and f. 297, 19 April 1793; Hanger, "Personas de varias clases y colores," 203-7. In another case Fanchon Montreuil, negra libre, bought a female slave for 475 pesos and sold her three weeks later for 600 pesos (Acts of Rodríguez, no. 8, f. 437, 12 April 1786 and f. 553, 4 May 1786).

29. Acts of Almonester y Roxas, f. 683, 22 December 1779 and f. 684, 23 December 1779.

30. Acts of F. Broutin, no. 15, f. 344, 14 November 1792.

31. Acts of Pedesclaux, no. 13, f. 764, 18 December 1791.

32. Acts of N. Broutin, no. 25, f. 108, 4 May 1793.

33. Acts of Ximénez, no. 19, f. 76, 2 April 1803 and f. 152, 11 August 1803.

34. Acts of Mazange, no. 5, f. 283, 18 March 1782; Acts of Rodríguez, no. 9, f. 945, 18 July 1786.

35. Free and slave persons of African descent could inherit property from whites. According to the *code noir,* which governed slaves and free blacks in Louisiana under French rule, free blacks could not inherit property. Louisiana judges rarely enforced this provision of the code, and when Spain established its rule in Louisiana, Spanish codes replaced French ones (Baade, "The Law of Slavery in Spanish Louisiana," 43-86). In 1774 the free morena Angélica Perret tested the extent of Spanish law regarding free black

inheritance rights. She petitioned to obtain the goods and property that Juan Perret had left her in his will. One of Perret's white grandchildren requested that the court deny Angélica's petition based on Article 52 of a royal edict pertaining to persons of African descent, which stated that free or not, they could not receive property from whites. The judge ruled in favor of Angélica (*Angélica v Heirs of Juan Perret*, 25 May 1774, Spanish Judicial Records, Record Group 2, Louisiana State Museum Historical Center [hereafter cited as SJR]).

36. Acts of F. Broutin, no. 30, f. 328, 23 December 1794.

37. "Autos fechos por fin y Muerte de Juan Bta Hugón," 8 August 1792, SJR.

38. Acts of F. Broutin, no. 7, f. 1, 23 August 1790.

39. Acts of Pedesclaux, no. 12, f. 47, 21 January 1791. Riche's household goods included (besides the silver harness): a walnut armoire, a bedstead with two feather mattresses and two Spanish moss mattresses, two feather pillows, four pairs of sheets, one linen mosquito net, two woolen blankets, one cotton blanket, four chairs, eight pots, one frying pan, and her personal clothing.

40. Acts of Garic, no. 2, f. 181, 1 June 1771; Acts of N. Broutin, no. 3, f. 367, 24 November 1801.

41. Acts of Pedesclaux, no. 21, f. 728, 1 August 1794; Acts of Pedesclaux, no. 25, f. 614, 14 August 1795; "Autos fechos por fallecimiento de Martona Belair," SJR, 15 August 1795. In 1787 don Santiago Fortier Jr. donated to Eugenia, the three-year-old cuarterona daughter of Martona Belair, a negrita named Eulalia (Acts of Rodríguez, no. 13, f. 852, 5 September 1787).

42. Black Marriages, book 1, no. 11, 10 January 1779; Acts of Almonester y Roxas, f. 57, 23 January 1779. For a discussion of dowry rights under Spanish law see Edith Couturier, "Women and the Family in Eighteenth-Century Mexico: Law and Practice," *Journal of Family History* 10 (fall 1985): 294–304, and Twinam, "Honor, Sexuality, and Illegitimacy," 118–55.

43. Acts of F. Broutin, no. 25, f. 144, 22 May 1793. The couple wed four days prior (Black Marriages, book 1, no. 65, 18 May 1793).

44. Acts of Almonester y Roxas, no. 1, f. 224, 15 June 1781.

45. Black Marriages, book 1, no. 27, 27 September 1785; Acts of Ximénez, no. 6, f. 27, 27 January 1794. In 1799 Brouner's youngest daughter Clarisa (Clara) López de la Peña instituted proceedings before an ecclesiastical tribunal to prove that she was of Indian descent and to have her daughter Luisa's baptismal record transferred from *El Libro de los Negros y Mulatos* to *El Libro de los Blancos*. Luisa's natural father was don Luis Declouet, a lieutenant in the fixed infantry regiment of Louisiana. The court granted Clarisa's request (Proceedings by Clara López de la Peña, Records of the Diocese of Louisiana and the Floridas, on microfilm at Louisiana Historical Center, Roll 8, 14 September 1799).

46. "Relación de la perdida que cada Individuo ha padecido en el Incendio de esta Ciudad . . . ," Archivo General de Indias, Audiencia de Santo Domingo, legajo 2576,

f. 532, 30 September 1788. The document gives phenotype and status for free blacks but not for whites, yet other documents indicate that some individuals who were not identified as free blacks were such. For example, in a separate petition for damage re-muneration, María Methode is identified as a parda libre, whereas in the "Relación" she is not. Thus, the "Relación" may include more free blacks and fewer whites than those who appear.

47. Materials for the Dor/Lalande/Gentilly trial are drawn from "Luis Dor, negro esclavo contra Estevan Lalande, pardo libre," 31 January 1793, Court Proceedings of F. Broutin, f. 1–99, and "Luis Dor, negro esclavo de Dn. Joseph Dusuau contra la Sucesión de Estevan Lalande, mulato libre," 10 January 1794, Court Proceedings of F. Broutin, no. 31-A, f. 1–43. Special thanks to Jane Landers for her invaluable help in translating these documents.

48. See, for example, Acts of Rodríguez, no. 8, f. 671, 24 May 1786.

49. In all fairness to Dor, it appears that Lalande and Gentilly had entered into joint agreements on numerous occasions (for example, see Acts of Pedesclaux, no. 15, f. 721, 10 December 1792). Records indicate that Gentilly and Lalande had no children together. Once Lalande died and Dor won the case, Gentilly would have to use what assets re-mained to support herself, although given her assertive nature, previous high standing in the community (as indicated by the witnesses who supported her claims), and property base, she probably did well.

VIRGINIA MEACHAM GOULD

# "If I Can't Have My Rights, I Can Have My Pleasures, And If They Won't Give Me Wages, I Can Take Them"

## GENDER AND SLAVE LABOR IN ANTEBELLUM NEW ORLEANS

**T**HE EXPERIENCES of urban slave women have unfortunately been overlooked by historians who are interested in understanding the lives of slave women in the antebellum South. Indeed, the experiences of the slave women who lived in the towns and cities of the South have been virtually ignored. Failing to view slavery as an institution and a personal condition that by necessity changed over time and place, women's historians have not considered the various expressions that slavery took. And in so doing, they have ignored the influence that differing conditions of slavery had on the day-to-day lives of women. Instead, they have assumed that the identities of plantation slave women were applicable to other slave women in the South. Yet the conditions of slavery on the plantation must be understood as unique to the plantation and should not be transposed onto other forms of slavery. Nowhere is it more obvious that slavery could mean different things to different women than when comparing the day-to-day experiences of slave women living in antebellum New Orleans to those living on the plantations outside the city.

In fundamental ways, the lives of urban slave women throughout the Americas were circumscribed by a complex set of social relations. No matter whether they were enslaved in the city or on the plantation, slave women in the New World were encumbered with a double burden. As slaves, they were defined as property that could be bought and sold, as well as stripped of the products of their labor. As women, they were viewed as subordinate to men, both slave and free, and thus dominated by them. In short, slave women in the South's entrepôts, like those on the plantations, were exploited not only by race but also by gender. Yet, even though urban slave women were bound within the same exploitive system, the nature of that system, as redefined by the exigencies of the city, reshaped their lives.

In general, the day-to-day experiences of plantation women depended on the plantation's location, its size, and its crop. In the district around New Orleans, the crop was usually sugar cane and the work was done in gangs, with women working beside men, clearing the fields, planting them with cuts of cane, and finally cutting and grinding the cane. The production of sugar was the most labor intensive of the systems of plantation agriculture. More than any other large-scale crop production, it brutalized and dehumanized slaves. It especially devalued the identities of women, requiring them to work in gangs, performing the same labor and working the same hours as men. Typically, women on sugar plantations were only able to reestablish their identities as women in the quarters and even then conditions placed extreme limits on the time and energy they could devote to their households and families.[1]

Frederick Law Olmsted described the fieldhands he saw returning from work on a sugar plantation near St. Francisville in 1854. "First came, led by an old driver carrying a whip, forty of the largest strongest women I ever saw together; they were all in a simple uniform dress of a bluish check stuff, the skirts reaching little below the knee; their legs and feet were bare; they carried themselves loftily, each having a hoe over the shoulder, and walking with a free, powerful swing. Behind them came the cavalry, thirty strong, mostly men, but a few of them women, two of whom rode astride on the plough mules."[2]

The organization of labor that Olmsted described on the sugar plantation in St. Francisville contrasts dramatically with that found in New Orleans. Slaveholders in the city certainly benefited from slave labor, as did those on the plantations and farms outside the city. But the benefits that planters and farmers expected from their slaves were different from those expected by urban slaveholders. Planters and farmers depended on the income their slaves could produce. Their financial status, or class, was determined by the capabilities, or production, of their slaves. Only a few urban slaveholders, however, depended on the income of their slaves. Instead, they generally relied on their slaves for the production of goods and services for consumption within the household; many if not most of the city's slaves were domestics.

Slave women in the city, therefore, unlike those on the plantations, existed in a world in which their gender-specific skills were highly desirable and, in many cases, preferable to those of men. It was only within that context, where the gender division of labor was informed by early modern European and African gender conventions, that women were prized for their capabilities. It was also only in the cities where women routinely capitalized on the gender division of labor to improve their economic conditions, without men. Yet, even though some of the conditions of urban labor could present slave women with social and economic advantages not commonly found in the plantation district, other conditions, in significant ways, rendered urban slavery an especially oppressive institution for slave women.

The absence of studies on urban slave women cannot be explained by a scarcity of resources. Slave women in the South's cities left clear traces of their lives. The records that include information about slaves in New Orleans, for instance, are extraordinary. The early Episcopal, Baptist, Methodist, Unitarian, and AME churches kept records of slave baptisms, marriages, and burials. The most inclusive sacramental records of urban slave women, however, are those of the Catholic Church. Since Louisiana was administered during its colonial period by the French and then the Spanish, the official Church and most of its population were Catholic; furthermore, this Catholic tradition continued into the antebellum period. Consequently, the identities of most of the population, including slaves, were recorded in the region's sacramental records. The births, marriages, and deaths of many of the city's slave women are recorded and housed at the Archives of the Archdiocese of New Orleans. It is with just such records that scholars will be able to reconstitute much about the lives of the women in the city.[3]

The Notarial Archives contain millions of property records of Orleans Parish. The records begin in the colonial period and continue nearly uninterrupted until today. The majority of the records are the wills, dowries, marriage contracts, and property sales—including those of slaves—on the local population. Many of the documents also include information of the manumission of slaves. Records of slave sales often include each slave's name, age, gender, color classification, occupation, and ownership. Physical descriptions, place of birth, and other interesting and useful bits of information are often included. By using the notarial records, scholars should be able to trace individual slaves and perhaps even slave families.[4]

Another important collection of records is housed in the Louisiana Division of the New Orleans Public Library. Most of the library's records date from the Louisiana Purchase and include invaluable information about the activities of the city's slaves. The collection includes city and state censuses, tax assessors' records, civil and criminal court records, police jail records, mayors' reports, death certificates, emancipation records, arrest records, passports, and licenses issued to peddlers. Taken together, these records paint a remarkable portrait of urban slavery and its consequences for women.

Besides their growing collection of documentation and illustrations, the archivists at the University of New Orleans have preserved and cataloged the records of the Supreme Court of the State of Louisiana. Many court records include remarkable descriptions of the slave women in New Orleans who waged desperate battles for their freedom. Others include detailed descriptions of women who had been freed and were subsequently fighting for property rights. Taken together, the court records make visible much about the lives of urban slave women.

In addition, scholars associated with the Ethel and Herman Midlo International Center for New Orleans Studies and the Gulf South Database Group are in the process of databasing records that identify much of the population living in the colonial, territorial, and antebellum Gulf South, including New Orleans. By capturing the names and other identifying characteristics, such as place and date of birth, godparentage, family relationships, and owners' identities, the database will provide as complete a description as possible of the slaves who inhabited early Louisiana. Other archives that house documents relative to slave women are the Historic New Orleans Collection, Tulane University, the Amisted Collection, and Hill Memorial Library at Louisiana State University.[5]

Despite such a wealth of available sources, as yet, few studies on slavery in Louisiana include specific information on the experiences and identities of slave women. Delores Labbé's dissertation, "Women in Early Nineteenth-Century Louisiana," includes a chapter on slave women and free women of color. Gwendolyn Midlo Hall's *Africans in Colonial Louisiana* also includes invaluable information for anyone attempting to understand the specific experiences of slave women in New Orleans. Ann Patton Malone does an excellent job of examining the forms and function of slaves on several of ante-bellum Louisiana's plantations in *Sweet Chariot*. In a more general work on New Orleans, John Blassingame touches on the experiences of slave women.[6]

Most of the studies on urban slave women in the Americas concentrate on women in Latin America and the Caribbean. For example, Mary Karash's examination of slaves in Rio de Janiero and their life-and-death struggle with disease and exploitation is an excellent study of slavery in the urban setting. Barbara Bush's *Slave Women in Caribbean Society, 1650–1838,* and Marietta Morrissey's *Slave Women in the New World* study women in the urban cen-ters of the Islands. Hilary Beckles offers *Natural Rebels: A Social History of Enslaved Black Women in Barbados.* Barry Higman's *Slave Populations of the British Caribbean, 1807–1834* primarily considers slave populations on the plantation, but it also includes a section on the activities of urban slaves.[7]

Perhaps one reason so little attention has been paid to slave women in the urban South is that so little is known about most of the Old South's urban centers. The limited number of studies that focus on urban slavery is more than likely a reflection of the scarcity of urban centers in the ante-bellum South. The South was overwhelmingly rural during its antebellum years. According to the 1860 census, only 7.1 percent of the South's popu-lation was urban while urban residents in the rest of the country comprised 19.8 percent of the population. Yet, even though the urban centers in the South were generally smaller and certainly fewer, they played a central role in the region's economy. Southern towns and cities like Richmond, Charles-ton, Savannah, Natchez, and New Orleans served as the region's entrepôts. They provided the facilities and labor for the exportation of the region's crops and the importation of the many necessary goods not produced in the South. The region's entrepôts also served as the centers for the importation and sale of slaves.[8]

Strategically located near the mouth of the Mississippi River, New Orleans was the fastest growing urban center in the South. A census taken in 1805, one year after the city was officially ceded to the United States, recorded its population at 8,222. Within five years, the number of inhabitants had grown to 17,242. Between 1820 and 1830, the city's population only increased from 27,176 to 29,737. But between 1830 and 1840, it boomed. The census of New Orleans in 1840 listed 102,193 inhabitants. The population had reached 116,375 by 1850 and 168,675 by 1860.

The growth of the city's population mirrored its commercial growth. By

1830, the port of New Orleans had begun to compete commercially with the older, more established ports of the United States. In fact, by 1830, New Orleans was second only to New York in commercial imports. By 1840, its exports had exceeded those of New York. Its inhabitants readily accepted its importance as a commercial center. To them, New Orleans had become "without exertion the metropolis of America, if not eventually of the world."[9]

The economy of the booming port provided the demand for the labor of tens of thousands of slaves. The 1805 census listed 3,105 slaves living in the city. Since the total population in that year, including slaves, free people of color, and whites, was approximately 8,222, the slave population represented 37.8 percent of the total population. By 1810, the number of slaves in the city had nearly doubled to 5,961, or 35 percent of the city's total population. In 1820, there were 7,355 slaves in the city. That number comprised nearly 27 percent of the population. By 1840, the city's slave population had grown to 23,448, a number that was approximately 23 percent of the total population. Thus, even though their raw numbers had grown, the percentage of slaves in the population had begun to shrink. When the 1850 census was taken, the percentage of slaves had not only declined but their raw numbers had decreased also. In that year, there were 17,011 slaves recorded in the city, a number that amounted to 14.6 percent of the entire population. The declining trend continued throughout the following decade. Therefore, by 1860 the city's slave population had decreased to 13,385, a number that amounted to only 7.9 percent of the population.[10]

The pattern of slaveholding in the city was a reflection of the nature of urban labor. Urban slaveholders generally held far fewer slaves than did plantation owners. The 1837 Tax Assessor's records for the First Municipality of New Orleans lists 279 slaveholders (excluding businesses), who owned 785 slaves. Those numbers, consistent with data obtained from the slave schedules included in the U.S. Census Records, suggest that even though slaveholding was widespread, urban slaveholders owned fewer slaves. The majority of slaveholders (175) owned only one or two slaves. The rest (85) owned between three and five slaves. The pattern of slaveholding for the First Municipality in New Orleans was generally consistent for the other municipalities of New Orleans as well as other southern urban centers.[11]

Southern industry proved the only exception to this pattern. The 1837 Tax Assessor's Records for the First Municipality of New Orleans reported that nineteen companies owned thirty-nine slaves in that year. Most industrial slaves were men, but women and children also labored in the South's industries. For instance, of the thirty-nine slaves owned by companies reported in the 1837 tax records, ten were women and children. The S. W. Oakley and Co. owned four men (Octave, Roy, Pethien, and Lucien) and one woman (Ester).[12]

Gender also distinguished the general pattern of slaveholding in New Orleans from those of the plantations and farms that surrounded the city. The first census record that reports data for gender in New Orleans was the Spanish census of 1771. Of the 1,288 slaves in the city in that year, 568 were males and 720 were females. Those numbers constitute a sex ratio of 126.8, which means that there were 126.8 female slaves for every 100 male slaves. The census taken in New Orleans in 1805 reported that of the 3,105 slaves in the city that year, 1,343 were males and 1,762 were females. That year the sex ratio was 131.2. By 1850, the U.S. census lists more than 10,193 slave women living in the city, but only 6,818 slave men living there. Thus, in 1850, the sex ratio had reached 149.5.[13]

Another difference in the pattern of urban slaveholding was especially significant for women. In particular, slaves were more likely to be owned by women in New Orleans than by those in its hinterlands. Of the 513 inhabitants in the First Municipality of New Orleans in 1837 who owned property (excluding companies), 107, or 21 percent, were women. Of those, 82 owned real estate, 25 owned real estate and slaves, and 43 owned slaves. Furthermore, according to the 1837 Tax Assessor's records, the 68 women who owned slaves in the First Municipality in that year owned a total of 154 slaves. In other words, the 21 percent of the slaveholding population who were women owned 20 percent of the slaves.

Female slaveholders in New Orleans demonstrated a strong preference for female slaves. Again, the 1837 Tax Assessor's records demonstrate the trend. Of the 154 slaves owned by women, 116 were females and only 38 were males. In short, 75 percent of the slaves owned by women were women and many owners were free women of color. In the First Municipality of the city in 1837, 62 free people of color were listed as property holders. Therein, 12 percent of the property holders listed were free people of color. Of those, 30 owned real estate only, 12 owned real estate and slaves, and 20 owned slaves only. A further analysis of the property records of free people of color demonstrates that the majority of the property holders, or 42 of 62, were women. The free women of color who were slaveholders owned a total of 40 slaves, 5 of whom were men and 35 of whom were women. For example,

*Table 1: Ratio of Female Slaves to Male Slaves
in the Urban Centers of the South*

|  | 1830 | 1850 |
|---|---|---|
| Baltimore | 1.4849 | 2.1109 |
| Charleston | 1.2216 | 1.2630 |
| New Orleans | 1.5167 | 1.4950 |
| Washington | 1.2821 | 1.8827 |

*Source: The Fifth Census or Enumeration of the Inhabitants of the
United States, 1830; Statistical View of the United States, . . . Being
a Compendium of the Seventh Census, 1850.*

Pouponne Wiltz owned one slave man, Jerry, and two women, both named
Sally. Rosseline Topin owned a woman named Marie, and Angelique Ony
owned Sophie, Marie, and Annette.[14]

The 1837 Tax Assessor's records for the First Municipality suggests the
predominant patterns of slaveholding by free people of color. In that year,
245 white slaveholders owned 715 slaves. That number amounts to 2.92
slaves per slaveholder. In the same year, 32 free people of color owned 59
slaves. That number amounted to 1.84 slaves per owner. Of the women who
owned slaves, 42 who were white owned 114 slaves, or each white slaveholding woman owned 2.71 slaves. Of the 32 free people of color who owned
slaves, 26 were women who owned 40 slaves, or the women owned 1.54
slaves each. Interestingly, the data demonstrates that of the whites who held
slaves 82.9 percent were men while the reverse was true for the free people
of color. In that segment of the population, 81.2 percent of the slaveholders
were women.

Occasionally free people of color owned family members. Sometimes
they purchased members of their families or friends in order to free them.
For instance, in February 1834 Marianne purchased her twenty-one-year-old
daughter, Julie, for the sum of 400 piastres (dollars). She paid 200 piastres
to Julie's owner and signed a mortgage for the rest. In February 1845 Louis
Houlin, a *negre libre,* purchased an infant, Orpheline, and the four-year-old
Marie Louise, from Euphrasie Barron, a *femme de couleur libre.* The condition of the sale was that Houlin would pay Barron 200 piastres for the children after which he would free them. Houlin had a personal stake: Orpheline
and Marie Louise were his natural children with a deceased slave, Adeline.
In that same month, Mr. Jeremiah, an *homme de couleur libre,* purchased

Eliza from Mr. Alexander Periera for 350 piastres on the express condition that he would free her. A few slave women were fortunate enough to be purchased out of slavery by their relatives, but not all could depend on their kin to free them.[15]

Most slave or free men who were related or married to slave women could not afford to purchase their freedom. Therefore, a considerable number of slave women who were never legitimately freed went free or lived in de facto freedom. A few women slipped into freedom in the busy urban environment, passing either as free women of color or as white women. Those women had to depend on their free friends or relatives to ensure their de facto freedom and thus their safety, but even though that usually worked, it could also prove to be extremely risky. Euphemié Lemelle Moran left the details of her struggle for freedom when she had to fight her own sister-in-law in court to prove her freedom. Euphemié Lemelle was born in St. Landry parish from the union of a free man of color and a slave woman. Even though she was legally defined as a slave, since her mother was a slave, Euphemié was raised as free by her free grandmother. Protected by her father's free family, she never knew the conditions of slavery and, indeed, she probably never would have if she had stayed with her birth family. Instead, she married Charles Moran, a free man of color. Unfortunately for Euphemié, even though she remained married to Charles Moran for many years and bore him seven children, he did not legitimately manumit her. Evidently, he, like her birth family, believed that he could protect her freedom. But Charles Moran did not, could not, protect her. He died, leaving her and their children as a part of his estate to be inherited by his sister, Juliette Moran, a free woman of color of New Orleans. Juliette's attitude toward Euphemié and her children did not reflect that of her brother. After convincing Euphemié to come to New Orleans with her children to "straighten out her free papers," Juliette had the sheriff arrest Euphemié and her children so that they could be sold into slavery. Euphemié sued, however, and after a lengthy court battle she satisfactorily proved to the court, with the help of her neighbors in New Orleans and St. Landry Parish, that she had lived as free for more than twenty years. Euphemié was legally declared free, and since the condition of her children followed her condition, they too were free.

Euphemié, however, was not the only woman who was threatened with reenslavement by her own family. Records in the city demonstrate that several women had to go to court to prove their freedom. Most won their cases and were declared legally free by the court. Those who could not prove their freedom were sold into slavery. After all, the labor of the women in question was becoming increasingly valuable.[16]

Although a few of the city's inhabitants owned their own relatives, most owned slaves for the benefit of their labor. The urban environment provided a variety of skilled and unskilled occupations traditionally defined as women's work, which is the primary reason that most urban slaves were women. The sexual division of labor that was less obvious on the sugar plantations was rarely ignored in the city. A few men worked as domestics. But most household chores were performed by women. Most of the city's slave women, the records suggest, worked at an endless round of domestic chores from before dawn until after sundown. A few very wealthy slaveholders who owned large numbers of domestic slaves assigned them individual tasks. In those households, slave women were assigned duties either as housekeepers, cooks or laundresses, or seamstresses or nurses. But many urban slave women lived in households where they were expected to perform a vast variety of domestic chores. Certainly, in the middle-class households of New Orleans, slave women performed all of the chores necessary for the operation of the household. They cleaned, cooked, nursed, washed, sewed, marketed, and gardened. It appears that slaveholders did as little of the work as possible.

But the city's slave women were not only to be found in private households. Many labored at domestic work in the city's hotels, inns, and boardinghouses. One slave woman who performed a variety of tasks belonged to Madame Tremoulet, an innkeeper in the city. When asked in 1818 about her favored slave by Benjamin Henry Latrobe, who later wrote extensively on the inhabitants of New Orleans, Tremoulet described her as "by far the best house servant of her sex that I know of, famous also as a seamstress and for her good temper." Besides waiting on boarders and making beds, Latrobe noted, the slave woman "made two shirts a day (and night) for the benefit of her mistresses purse." Indeed, she was of such value "that she could be sold for $2,000, and Tremoulet actually asks $3,000." Slave women who were especially skilled as seamstresses, laundresses, cooks, or merchants, Latrobe added, could produce enough income for a small white or free-colored family to live on.[17]

Female slaves did not just perform their chores and duties in the presence of their owners. Their work often carried them into the bustling streets, alleyways, and markets of the city. The city's domestic slaves, whom Lyle Saxon described as "old negro women with bright stripped *tignons* on their heads and with baskets on their arms, wandered about buying a little of this and a little of that." They evidently purchased most if not all of the goods for the household. In fact, in 1835, one New Orleans resident wrote that the "only purchasers in the markets were Negroes and generally slaves."[18]

But slaves were more than just the buyers in the markets. The New Orleans resident who described the market's purchasers as mostly slaves also noted that the sellers were also often slaves. "Almost the whole of the purchasing and selling of edible articles for domestic consumption [is] transacted by colored persons," he wrote. "Our Butchers are Negroes; our fishmongers Negroes, our vendors of vegetables, fruits and flowers are all Negroes." Benjamin Henry Latrobe also described their domination of the trade in the 1830s when he wrote that "in every street, during the whole day, women, chiefly black women, are met carrying baskets upon their heads and calling at the doors of houses." The baskets, according to Latrobe, "contained an assortment of dry goods." The women sold rugs, shawls, fabrics, kerchiefs, and other dry goods. They also peddled fresh produce, coffee, baked goods, and confections. The women transformed the early morning streets and alleyways, shouting and singing, "*Belle fromage! Belle cala! Tout chaud!*" as they sought to entice city dwellers into making purchases from the baskets of food they carried on their hips or balanced gracefully on their heads. Some of the peddlers, Latrobe wrote, belonged to inhabitants who kept dry-goods stores. But others belonged to residents who were too poor to furnish a store with goods. The baskets, Latrobe noticed, were their shops.[19]

Ellen Call Long, another visitor to antebellum New Orleans, described the economic importance of the marketers. It was the slave women, she noted, dressed "in bright bandanas," who dominated the city's marketing trade as they "presided over tables." The slave women, according to Long, were "laughing and chatting, and apparently as free as the customer who ordered his omelet or fruit." Most of the women sold "beer, cakes and fruit at street corners, or with baskets of fancy goods which they carried to the houses of patrons; and a more free, rollicking set of creatures I never saw — slavery at least with them had little significance." Then directly contradicting her own statement, she noted that the same *marchandes,* or marketers, whom she had described as so carefree, worked for the livelihood of their owners. Their sales, she observed, often supported entire families.[20]

Marketing offered *marchandes* much more than an occupation or liveli-hood. The streets and alleyways, market stalls and levees, or the high earth embankments that edged the waterways around the city, provided the women with a public place in which they could freely communicate with each other and with the world. As Barbara Bush points out, "The public Sunday market was an important institution . . . from the very beginning of slavery." As Bush has observed as well, marketing activities gave slaves ample opportunity to disseminate information among themselves, since vigilance by their masters and mistresses was practically impossible. They created a community where none was expected, finding a measure of anonymity in the bustling market-place.[21]

That the city's slave women dominated petty marketing was no accident. Slave women in the city, or their mothers or grandmothers, transported their knowledge of marketing with them from Africa to the New World. That transference is particularly obvious in Louisiana where the earliest African women from the region of Senegal also dominated the market trade. More-over, the tradition of slave women as marketers in the urban centers of the New World was also reinforced by the traditions in early modern Europe where women also served as society's petty marketers.[22]

Yet it is no less important to recognize that slave women themselves care-fully guarded the economic and political power they earned through their roles as petty marketers. Responding to a debate over closing the Sunday slave market, Benjamin Latrobe pointed out that the retail trade in dry goods had always been carried on by slave women "in this way before the United States got possession of the country." It had never been the "fashion for ladies to go shopping." Furthermore, according to Latrobe, there was a very practical reason that white New Orleanians encouraged the slave women to continue the practice. As he pointed out, there was so little land in or near the city for the cultivation of food that, were it not for the "vegetables and fowls and small marketing of all sorts, raised by the negro slaves, the city would starve." Slaves who raised produce on their allotted plots of ground or fished in their spare time, he noted, were allowed to keep some if not all of the money their labor produced. Moreover, Latrobe observed, despite the complaints of the slaveholders, they managed to live comfortably from the "labor of their slaves upon this traffic." And all the while, the peddlers were able to keep some control over their profitability.[23]

In fact, the dedication of slave women to peddling underscores their determination to retain as much power over their own lives as possible and the ways in which women in the city made opportunities for themselves. Slave women who peddled were left much to their own devices. Away from their master or mistress, the marketers were free to roam the port and even the countryside. After paying their masters or mistresses their fee, some could use the rest of their earnings to support themselves and their children. Moreover, some women were even able to save enough out of their earnings to purchase their de facto, if not legitimate, freedom. One such woman was Marie, the slave of Jean Baptiste Laporte. A contract drawn up between Laporte and Marie, who was described as about 40 years of age, documents that Laporte purchased Marie from Charles White on March 30, 1827, for the sum of 200 piastres. The contract stipulated, however, that Laporte owned Marie on the "express condition" that he free her when she had reimbursed the sum (200 piastres) plus interest at the rate of 10 percent.[24]

Fanny had also arranged to purchase her freedom from her owner. She agreed to pay Thomas McGovern $140, after which he would free her. But after receiving Fanny's money, McGovern broke the contract and refused to free her, claiming that she was a troublemaker, that she had run away and was living in another man's household. Denying McGovern's claims and refusing to remain in bondage, Fanny sued, claiming that she was free under the terms of the contract. Certainly, Fanny's court testimony demonstrates the day-to-day struggles of slave women in the city. It also shows that she did not reside with her owner. Louis Lamie testified that Fanny had rented a room from him in the yard and "paid me $5 for it." And, according to Lamie, Fanny "is very capable of gaining her living because she is a good washer & ironer." Fanny made her point and was allowed to go free.[25]

Since most of the city's slaves were household domestics or worked with their owners in commercial enterprises, their living arrangements usually resembled those of house servants on plantations. Most of Louisiana's planters normally housed their slaves in cabins arranged together some distance from the big house. The cabins served as basic shelter for the slaves, as their households, and, taken together, as quarters which usually represented a community. Slaveholders in New Orleans created living space for their slaves in the cramped conditions of the city where the residents were crowded together in every block. Slaves were sometimes housed in the main house, in a room at the back of the house, or in the attic. In 1842, Monsieur Isidore Löwenstern described the housing arrangements that he observed on his visit to New Orleans. Many of the houses in the American district of the city, he wrote, were very tall, with each floor having only two rooms. Slaveholders in that district economized on the upper floors where they housed the children and the servants. But, he added, slaveholders rarely resorted to that measure, since it was desirable for them to provide their slaves with a separate living space in order to enforce the distances between the races.[26]

Houses in New Orleans were usually constructed at the front of the lot with their front doors opening directly onto the street. Each house was adjoined to one of the houses next door and opened on the other side with an alleyway that led to the back yard, or courtyard. Most of the courtyards contained dependencies where slaves were housed. The dependencies inside the compounds were generally narrow two-story brick buildings, one room deep and two rooms wide. Verandas or balconies usually spanned the length of the building. Generally, the lower floor served as the kitchen for the entire household, with the upstairs serving as the slaves' living quarters.

The courtyards surrounded by the main house, walls of other houses, and other tall walls have been perceptively described by Richard Wade as compounds that served to constrain the movements of urban slaves in much the same way as the boundaries on plantations constrained slaves. There, urban slave women were not isolated by distance from others, but rather by the high walls that surrounded them. Urban slave women, therefore, spent as much time as possible outdoors, on the veranda, in the courtyard, or, if possible, abroad in the city.[27]

The dense living arrangements in New Orleans intensified relations between slave women and their owners. With living quarters in the house or within a few feet of it, slaves, and especially domestic servants, could spend much of their time under the watchful eyes of their masters and mistresses. Such intimacy could lead to love and caring as well as to hate and cruelty. Benjamin Latrobe described one woman who maintained a close relationship with her mistress. "I know . . . an old, decrepit woman who is maintained entirely by an old slave whom she formerly emancipated, but who, on her mistress getting old and helpless, returned to her and devoted her labor to her support." [28]

Such physical intimacy could also lead to sexual liaisons between slave women and their masters or landlords. Some slave women participated in sexual liaisons with their masters or with other white men or free men of color for the relative or legitimate freedom or social mobility that such relationships could offer. Such relationships are difficult to prove, yet the patterns that suggest them appear regularly throughout the records. The freed slave woman Sarah Valentine had more than likely formed a liaison with her white master before he freed her. In her will in which Sarah Valentine left her master her house on Terpsicord Street and her slave, Harriet, she wrote, "This instrument is made of my own free will as all my prosperity is owing to the kindness of Mr. John Valentine." [29]

Notwithstanding Valentine's sentiments and those of other women like her, it seems that slave women were more likely to be victimized than supported by their masters. One example of a woman who was sexually victimized by her master and subsequently physically punished by her mistress was the slave Pauline. Ebenezer Davis recounted the tale in a letter he wrote home while visiting New Orleans during 1845. Davis noted Pauline's sexual victimization by her master, then described how her mistress had turned on her and how Pauline had struck her mistress for her cruelty. In Davis's words, when Pauline tried to repay "in some degree the scorn and abuse with which her mistress had made her painfully familiar," she was arrested. At her trial, Pauline was found guilty of assaulting her mistress and sentenced to be hanged. Her tragedy did not end there, however. Before she could be hanged, it was discovered that Pauline was "in a condition to become a mother." Remanded to her cell, Pauline was forced to await the birth of her child before she was "hanged by her neck until she died." [30]

The household compound in New Orleans, as in other southern cities, might have led to intimacy, for good and for bad, but it was the most practical and secure place in which to house slaves. By the antebellum period, however, the city had become so congested that many slaveholders did not have the space in which to house their slaves. Instead, they and other slaveholders who found it more profitable to allow their slaves to hire themselves out also allowed them to "live out" or make their own living arrangements. A comprehensive law was passed in New Orleans in 1817 that attempted to control the city's errant slave population. The law required slaves to live on the premises of their owners, their owners' representatives, or their employers. It ordered that those who occupied, resided, or slept outside the purview of an owner, an owner's representative, or a lessor were to have a "ticket." And finally, to further discourage the practice of slaves living away from their owners, the law made it illegal for anyone to rent to slaves, even with the permission of the master. [31]

Despite the laws that attempted to limit the practice of "living out," many slaves did. Richard Wade argues, in fact, that "living out" and "hiring out" were integrally related. As soon as slaves began to earn their own wages, he noted, they were also able to pay rent. And furthermore, owners whose slaves worked out were usually more lenient when a slave asked permission to sleep out. Therefore, slave women who obtained their owners' permission, and some who did not, could be found all over the city. Many women lived with the people who hired them, either in their households or in their dependencies. More fortunate women rented small rooms or spaces in hallways, sheds, lean-tos, basements, and attics. Although most of the spaces were woefully inadequate, the women appear to have preferred their independence over the constant supervision and control of an owner or lessor.[32]

Slave women who could arrange to "live out" were better able to live with their families. But even then their living arrangements were tenuous, for slaveholders could relocate them back into their household or sell or rent them out to a distant location. A variety of sources suggest that urban slave women who lived within their owner's household and those who "lived out" had less opportunity to live with family members than did slaves on the plantation. Holdings were too small and housing too limited to allow slaves to live within more than just the simplest family form. The presumption that slave men and women were rarely able to cohabit is supported by the child-woman ratios of the population. Although child-woman ratios are not true measures of fertility, they are often used to demonstrate the gross fertility of the populations for which there is incomplete data. For New Orleans at this time, the data that allows for the best comparison of fertility rates are the census records and slave schedules that can be analyzed for child-woman ratios. Those records allow for the calculation of the percentage of children under the age of 15 years to women of childbearing age or, in this study, those between 15 and 49. According to comparative data, for every one thousand women between the ages of 15 and 45, slave women averaged less than one child per woman. Free women of color almost always had more than one child throughout the period of the study, and white women always had more than one child. Such information points to the destructive effects of urban slavery on the slave family with its concomitant effects on women.

The relative absence of slave children in the urban environment is so remarkable that it is more than likely explained by several factors. One reasonable explanation that actually has nothing to do with fertility is that many

*Table 2: Child/Woman Ratio for Children under 15
and Women between 15 and 49 in New Orleans*

|  | Ratio | | |
|---|---|---|---|
| Status | 1791 | 1830 | 1850 |
| Slave | 0.781 | 0.934 | 0.639 |
| FWC | 1.260 | 1.532 | 0.934 |
| White | 1.683 | 1.823 | 1.060 |

*Sources:* Census of New Orleans, 6 November 1791, Louisiana
Collection, New Orleans Public Library; *The Fifth Census or
Enumeration of the Inhabitants of the United States, 1830;
Statistical View of the United States, . . . Being a Compendium
of the Seventh Census, 1850.*

slave children, especially those over ten years of age, were sold away from
their mothers, probably out of the city, and these would not show up in the
data. This supposition is supported by Claudia Goldin's theory that urban
slaves were increasingly pulled out of southern cities in the final decades
before the war. Another explanation might well be that urban slave women
who spent most of their time in the shadows of their owners and who substantially outnumbered slave men would have had fewer chances to become
pregnant than plantation slave women, who usually lived on the plantation
with their husbands. And, too, urban slave women who would have had difficulty caring for their children might have practiced a crude form of birth
control, abortion, or even infanticide. Certainly the presence of children
would have vastly complicated the life of Fanny, who lived in a room behind
Louis Lamie's house and worked as a laundress in order to purchase her
own freedom.[33]

Yet, even though it appears that the urban environment constrained the
child-woman ratios of slave women and perhaps even their fertility, it is important to note that the same environment allowed urban slave women to
formulate a cohesive community away from the supervision of their masters and mistresses. Slaves in New Orleans formulated their own churches
and even their own neighborhoods. Indeed, an editor for the *New Orleans
Crescent* wrote that a traveler passing Baronne Street, between Perdido and
Poydras Streets, on any Sunday afternoon could easily imagine him or herself
in Africa. The area, he wrote, must have been some sort of slave exchange.
There were "coloured churches, coloured ice-cream parlours, coloured res-

taurants, coloured coffee-houses, and a coloured barber-shop, which we have heard has a back communication with one of the groggeries, for the benefit of slaves."[34]

Fearing a revolt by the slaves who were constantly congregating around town, New Orleans officials did attempt to more closely monitor the slave population by passing increasingly stringent laws. Laws to prohibit slaves from assembling were passed throughout the colonial period, revised in 1817, and reinforced in subsequent years. Slaves were also required to carry passes or wear badges. An editorial in the *New Orleans Crescent,* however, pointed out the inadequacies of the pass system. "Something must be done to regulate and prescribe the manner in which passes shall be given to slaves." The behavior of the slave population, the editor wrote, is deplorable because of the "indiscriminate license and indulgence extended them by masters, mistresses, and guardians, and to the practice of forging passes, which has now become a regular business in New Orleans." While the masters and mistresses of slaves were negligent in their policing, the editor noted, the greatest evil was a result of forged passes. "As things now stand, any negro can obtain a pass for four bits or a dollar, from miserable wretches who obtain a living by such infamous practices." The danger from the practice of forged passes, the editor pointed out, was that hundreds of slaves "spend their nights drinking, carousing, gambling, and contracting the worst of habits, which not only make them useless to their owners, but dangerous pests to society."[35]

However, such laws proved impossible to enforce, and society's fears grew, leading to the increasing arrest of slaves, including women. Records reveal that nearly all of the women who were arrested were those who were found out and about after the city's 8 P.M. curfew. A few, however, were runaways. Pierre Lemoine's slave, Louise, was arrested at the house of Caroline McGary, ten days after running away. Louise was punished for running away and Caroline McGary was punished for harboring a slave. In another example, the slave Hannah and her child, both of whom belonged to Monsieur Avet & Bros., were captured July 10, 1852. Yet, even though slave women ran away regularly, it appears that they were still far less likely to try to escape from their owners than were men, perhaps because at least some of the women would have had to take a child or children with them. In fact, a preliminary estimate suggests that less than 10 percent of New Orleans slaves who were official runaways were women. Yet the records also show that a few of these women were so desperate to escape their circumstances that they took their small children with them.[36]

Slave women who violated the city's restrictions were arrested and placed in the city's police jail, an institution that was created specifically to incarcerate and punish slaves. The disciplinary measures inflicted upon errant slave women depended upon the severity of their crimes and the reactions of their owners. Most women were arrested for breaking curfew. Others were taken to the police jail by their owners to be whipped. Still other women were taken to the jail by their owners for safekeeping. On February 16, 1853, Mary was brought to the guardhouse at 10:45 A.M. by her master for safekeeping. A few women even turned to the jail for help. For instance, Angel, the slave of Mrs. Louis Garcia, gave herself up to the jailer at 7 P.M. on January 24, 1853, at the Watch House. She told the guard that she was turning herself in because she was "ill-treated by her mistress."[37]

Most of the slaves incarcerated in the jail were men. Women rarely numbered more than 15 percent of the jail's population, and they infrequently remained for more than a few days. For instance, J. B. Petrand's slaves, Martha and Jenie, were jailed on November 1, 1838, and released on November 2. The slave of Monsieur Arceuil, Euphrasie, was also arrested on November 1 and released two days later. The overwhelming number of slaves who found themselves in the police jail were arrested for roaming about the city after curfew without a pass. That is more than likely why Jane, Nancy, Mary, Rosalie, Clementine, Margarethe, Betty, Nancy, Matilde, and Anna were arrested on December 31, 1838, and released January 3, 1839.[38]

Slave women who committed more serious crimes or who were remanded to the jail by their owners could be employed on the chain gang. Women who were picked up by the patrol and not claimed by their owners within five days were assigned to the chain gang. Evidently not many owners felt compelled to protect their slave women from the brutal conditions of the chain gang. In fact, since the jail paid a daily fee to the slave's owner for time spent on the chain gang, owners had little to lose when their slaves were "put to the chain." The *Rapport de la Geole de Police du 6 au 7 Janvier, 1830* reported 170 slaves in custody. Of those, 71 were men who were assigned to work on the chain gang, and 25 were women.

Certainly, slavery in New Orleans was not necessarily any less abusive nor exploitive than that on the plantation. The day-to-day lives of urban slave women, their routines of work, even the organization, or disorganization, of their families, were ordered by the exigencies of the city. Yet, even as the nature of housing in the city often isolated slave women from family and friends, the nature of their work could carry them away from their owners' constant supervision. The same women who were locked up at night with their owners could be seen rambling about the streets during the day. Thus, even as the conditions of urban bondage could take away, they could give back. It was within those contradictions, or tensions within the system, that slave women grasped as much power over their lives as possible.

## NOTES

1. Marietta Morrissey, *Women in New World Slavery* (Lawrence, Kans.: University of Topeka, 1989), 30–31. For a comprehensive examination of slaves on Louisiana sugar plantations, see Roderick McDonald, *The Economy and Material Culture of Slaves: Goods and Chattels on the Sugar Plantations of Jamaica and Louisiana* (Baton Rouge: Louisiana State University Press, 1993).

2. Frederick Law Olmsted, *The Cotton Kingdom,* ed. Arthur M. Schlesinger (New York: Modern Library, 1969), 407–8.

3. The sacramental records for whites, free people of color, and slaves with surnames are being published by the Archdiocese of New Orleans. At this time, eight volumes have been published under the direction of Dr. Charles Nolan. The Archives of the Archdiocese are housed in the Ursuline Convent on Chartres Street and are readily accessible to scholars.

4. The Notarial Archives, housed in the Civil Court Building, are well preserved and readily accessible to scholars.

5. The Historical Center of the Louisiana State Museum in New Orleans houses the judicial records of both the French and Spanish periods.

6. Dolores Labbé, "Women in Nineteenth Century Louisiana" (Ph.D. diss., University of Delaware, 1975); Gwendolyn Midlo Hall, *Africans in Colonial Louisiana* (Baton Rouge: Louisiana State University Press, 1992); Ann Patton Malone, *Sweet Chariot: Slave Family and Household Structure in Nineteenth-Century Louisiana* (Chapel Hill: University of North Carolina Press, 1992); John Blassingame, *Black New Orleans, 1860–1880* (Chicago: University of Chicago Press, 1973). For an excellent source that incidentally considers slave women in Spanish New Orleans, see Kimberly Hanger, "Personas de Varias Clases y Colores: Free People of Color in Spanish New Orleans, 1769–1803" (Ph.D. diss., University of Florida, 1991).

7. Mary Karasch, *Slave Life in Rio de Janeiro* (Princeton: Princeton University Press, 1986); Barbara Bush, *Slave Women in the Caribbean, 1650–1838* (Bloomington: Indi-

ana University Press, 1989); Morrissey, *Slave Women;* Barry Higman, *Slave Populations of the British Caribbean, 1807–1834* (Baltimore: Johns Hopkins University Press, 1984); Hilary Beckles, *Natural Rebels: A Social History of Enslaved Black Women in Barbados* (New Brunswick: Rutgers University Press, 1989).

8. Robert S. Starobin's *Industrial Slavery in the Old South* (New York: Oxford University Press, 1970) includes some information on the slaves who labored in the industries in the southern city; as Wade points out, however, most of the South's industries were located in the hinterland. Richard Wade's *Slavery in the Cities: The South, 1820–1860* (New York: Oxford University Press, 1964) is also an excellent source for anyone considering slavery as an urban institution. In *Urban Slavery in the American South, 1820–1860* (Chicago: University of Chicago Press, 1976) Claudia Dale Goldin revisits the issue of the compatibility of slavery with the urban environment raised by Richard Wade. Goldin's book, too, is invaluable for anyone attempting to recover the experiences of urban slaves, as is that of Howard N. Rabinowitz, *Race Relations in the Urban South, 1865–1890* (New York: Oxford University Press, 1978); Michael P. Johnson and James L. Roark, *Black Masters: A Free Family of Color in the Old South* (New York: W. W. Norton, 1984); Loren Schweninger, *Black Property Owners in the South, 1790–1915* (Urbana: University of Illinois Press, 1990); and Barbara J. Fields, *Slavery and Freedom on the Middle Ground: Maryland during the Nineteenth Century* (New Haven: Yale University Press, 1985).

9. *New Orleans in 1805: A Directory and a Census Together with Resolutions Authorizing Same Now Printed for the First Time from the Original Manuscript* (New Orleans: Pelican, 1936); *Statistical View of the United States* (Washington, D.C.: A. O. P. Nicholson, 1854). The 1830 Census is compiled and analyzed in *The Fifth Census or Enumeration of the Inhabitants of the United States, 1830* (Washington, D.C.: Duff Green, 1932). Statistics for the 1840 Census can be found in the *Compendium of the Sixth Census* (Washington, D.C.: Thomas Allen, 1841). Statistics for the 1850 Census can be found in *Statistical View of the United States* (Washington, D.C.: Beverly Tucker, 1854); Wade, *Slavery;* Goldin, *Urban Slavery;* Rabinowitz, *Race Relations;* Albert J. Pickett, *Eight Days in New Orleans* (n.p., 1847), 19.

10. *New Orleans in 1805; Statistical View of the United States.*

11. The 1837 Tax Assessor's records of the First Municipality of New Orleans are housed at the New Orleans Public Library, Louisiana Collection.

12. Starobin, *Industrial Slavery;* the 1837 Tax Assessor's records.

13. The 1771 Spanish Census of New Orleans, Lawrence Kinnaird, ed., "Spain in the Mississippi Valley, 1765–1794," *Annual Report of the American Historical Association for the Year 1945* (Washington, D.C.: Government Printing Office, 1946). *New Orleans in 1805; Statistical View of the United States.*

14. In *The Free Women of Petersburg* (New York: W. W. Norton, 1984) Suzanne Lebsock also states that slaveholding women in Petersburg preferred to own women.

15. Property records are found in the New Orleans Notarial Archives, Civil Court

Building. L. T. Caire, notary, February 1834, a deed of sale to Marianne for the purchase of her daughter Julie; L. T. Caire, notary, February 4, 1845, a deed of sale from Barron to Houlin; L. T. Caire, notary, a deed of sale from Mr. Alexander Periera to Mr. Jeremiah.

16. See *Juliette Moran v Euphemié Lemelle Moran,* Third District Court of New Orleans, January, 1859; *Tabé, FWC v Vidal,* First District Court of New Orleans, November, 1847; *Milky v Millaudon,* Third District Court of New Orleans, 1847.

17. Benjamin Henry Latrobe, *The Journal of Latrobe* (New York: D. Appleton, 1905), 182–83.

18. *New Orleans Bee,* 13 October 1835.

19. Latrobe, *Journal,* 203.

20. Ellen Call Long, *Florida Breezes, or Florida, New and Old* (1883; reprint, Gainesville: University of Florida Presses, 1962), 26–27.

21. Bush, *Slave Women,* 49. Bush explains that slave women were central to marketing in the Caribbean. Sidney Mintz and Douglas Hall suggest in "The Origins of the Internal Marketing Systems" in *Papers in Caribbean Anthropology,* ed. Sidney Mintz (New Haven: Human Relations Area Files Press, 1970) that it was through those activities that slave women contributed directly to the creolization of the population of the Islands. It appears that the same patterns of cultural transmission can be found on the Gulf Coast. Also see Sidney Mintz, "Caribbean Marketplaces and Caribbean History," *Radical History Review* 27 (1983): 110–20. Morrissey, *Slave Women,* 53–54.

22. Bush, *Slave Women,* 49; Arlette Gautier, *Les Soeurs de Solitude: La Condition Feminine dans L'eslavage aux Antilles du XVIIe du XIXe Siècle* (Paris: Editions Caribbiennes, 1985); David Barry Gaspar, *Bondmen and Rebels: A Case Study of Master-Slave Relations in Antigua, with Implications for Colonial British America* (Baltimore: Johns Hopkins University Press, 1985); Hall, *Africans;* Gwendolyn Midlo Hall, *Social Control in Slave Plantation Societies: A Comparison of St. Domingue and Cuba* (Baltimore: Johns Hopkins University Press, 1971), 80–92; Maria Rosa Cutrufelli, *Women of Africa: Roots of Oppression* (London: Zed Press, 1983).

23. Latrobe, *Journal,* 203.

24. Notarial records, L. T. Caire, 30 May 1827, 106.

25. *Fanny, FWC v Thomas McGovern,* Third District Court of New Orleans, 1851, 37–38.

26. Isidore Löwenstern, *Les États-Unis et La Havane: Souvenirs d'un Voyageur* (Paris: Leipsick Press, 1842), 277.

27. Wade, *Slavery in the Cities,* 61.

28. Latrobe, *Journal,* 204.

29. Succession of Sarah Valentine, Orleans Parish Succession Records, Court of Probates, Second District Court, No. 11, 194.

30. This account of the hanging of Pauline is recorded in Ebenezer Davis, *American*

*Scenes and Christian Slavery: A Recent Tour of Four Thousand Miles in the United States* (London: John Snow, 1849), 20–21.

31. Ordinances of the Municipality of New Orleans, 1817, New Orleans Public Library, Louisiana Collection.

32. Wade, *Slavery in the Cities,* 55–79.

33. *Fanny, FWC v Thomas McGovern.*

34. Olmsted, *Cotton Kingdom,* 234.

35. As quoted in Olmsted, *Cotton Kingdom,* 234–35.

36. *Rapport de la Geole de Police du Juillet 1845.*

37. *Rapport de la Geole de Police du Janvier et Fevrier, 1853.*

38. *Rapport de la Geole de Police du Novembre et Decembre, 1838 et Janvier 1839.*

CYNTHIA LYNN LYERLY

# Religion, Gender, and Identity

## BLACK METHODIST WOMEN IN A
## SLAVE SOCIETY, 1770-1810

At parting, my mother told me that I had "nobody in the wide
world to look to but God." These words fell upon my heart
with pondrous weight, and seemed to add to my grief. . . . After
this time, finding as my mother said, I had none in the world
to look to but God, I betook myself to prayer, and in every
lonely place I found an altar. — "Old Elizabeth"

OW ARE WE to interpret "Old Elizabeth's" testimony that God
alone comforted her in 1777 when she was separated from her
mother in slavery? The literature on slave religion is extensive, yet with the exception of Jean Friedman's study, slave
women are examined in these works only as part of the slave community.[1]
There is a growing body of work on women and gender in antebellum evangelical churches, but little attention has been paid to the slave woman's perspective.[2] Pioneering works on slave women call attention to the racial and
gender oppression of slavery, yet focus little on bondwomen's religiosity.[3]

"Old Elizabeth" was a woman, a slave, and a Christian, and her experience was followed by a long history of slave women's involvement in Protestant churches. By examining slave women of the Revolutionary and early
national era in one such body, the Methodist Church, we can arrive at a
deeper understanding of the historical legacy of religious slave women and
of what slave women found and made in the church. In many respects, the
religious experiences of slave women resembled those of other Methodists.
But the context in which slave women lived, loved, and labored was unique,
and it is in this context that we must interpret their religious experience.

Dually oppressed because of their race and gender, slave women were bombarded by whites' negative images of black womanhood. White stereotypes of enslaved women portrayed them not as persons but as "Jezebel" or, in later antebellum years, as "Mammy."[4] Both Jezebel and Mammy were images cast in religious terms. Jezebel, the stereotype, was the antipious woman, the devil's seductress, tempter of white men. Mammy, the stereotype, was Jezebel's antithesis. Unsexed, pious, and unopposed to slavery, the Mammy of white lore put the interests of her slave-owning "family" above those of other slaves. With their origins in white paranoia, fear, and guilt, these images were designed to obscure a reality of racial and gender oppression. They offered little to black women in the way of positive gender identity.

Although enslaved women were part of a larger world with bifurcated gender roles, they were offered none of the protections supposedly offered to white "ladies." They were not spared physically demanding labor, they were not protected from sexual aggression, and their roles as mothers were not respected.[5] Yet most historians agree that enslaved women did not accept the negative gender identity that slavery attempted to thrust upon them.[6]

The experience of early Methodist slave women suggests that many bondwomen found in religion a means to resist internalizing whites' negative images of black women. In Evangelical belief, slave women shaped a worldview within which they created positive self-images and gender identities. Through religion, slave women defined motherhood as a sacred relationship and not as an economic activity. They denied ownership of their souls and reclaimed some control over their bodies. Through churches, slave women expressed their sense of self-worth and personhood.

Slave women appear often in early Methodist sources, although they are usually seen through the filter of white clergymen. These men did hold some Anglo-American prejudices about blacks and women. Ministers used phrases like "he speaks well for a Negro."[7] A clergyman referred to a black congregation as "simple hearted."[8] Even ministers who deplored racial segregation of services rarely chose to speak out against such segregation.

White ministers also believed that a "godly" family was male-headed and that women were biologically the weaker sex. They did not question the legal, political, or economic subordination of women to men. They did not address some of the special concerns of slave women. There is no evidence that early Methodist preachers ever spoke publicly against sexual abuse and rape of slave women by white men, as later antislavery advocates would.

It should be noted, however, that some of the most destructive racist imagery and language common to this era are absent from clergymen's un-published journals. Black women were not referred to, in the sources con-sulted for this study, as "wenches," an odious term commonly employed by slave owners in runaway ads.[9] Slave women were not portrayed as sexu-ally promiscuous, as bad mothers, or as inefficient workers. When ministers commented on inadequate slave dress, they faulted slave owners for mal-treatment.

One particular difficulty encountered in these sources is their mode of referring to African Americans. Clergy often referred to black parishioners by their race and not their civil status, describing them as "black," "Afri-can," "colored," "Ethiopian," or "sable."[10] Sometimes ministers seem to have noticed *only* the race of their black congregants. One preacher reported that "9 men 10 women and 32 Blacks" were members of a congregation.[11] Clergy were acutely conscious of race, and they unproblematically (and erro-neously) accepted race as physically evident. They saw slave women first as blacks and only secondarily as women. As these views and statements show, the documents left by early Methodists are not transparent accounts of the past but products of people who were in turn products of an Anglo-American culture with racial and gender biases.

The experience of Methodist slave women cannot be understood as just the intersection of the experience of slave Methodists and the experience of Methodist women, yet it is nonetheless important to look at the values and positions of the church on both slavery and gender roles before turning to bondwomen as a distinct group. Slave women had reasons for becoming Methodists that were unrelated to their gender. First among these was the fact that many early Methodist clergymen were opposed to slavery.[12] Some preached openly against slaveholding, many proselytized privately against slavery, and all actively sought black converts.[13] Methodism was a major force in manumissions in the early national era, especially in the Upper South.[14] The church's antislavery views were undoubtedly one reason slave women became members. Although the official church position against slavery weakened over the years studied here, slaves must have preferred a church with some emancipation record to one with no such record.

If Methodist clergy made special appeals for the emancipation of slave women, the evidence has not survived. Suzanne Lebsock noted that three-fifths of slaves freed before 1806 in Petersburg, Virginia, were women, and she claims this might have resulted from the greater antislavery impact of freeing women, since children inherited slave status from their mothers.[15] It is possible that Methodist owners freed more women than men, but no quantitative study has been made. Some women were freed by Methodist owners outright, like Hannah, Jenny, Sarah, and Frances, who were manumitted on Christmas Day, 1788.[16] Others were freed after a period of service in which Methodist owners recouped their expenses. In Nags Head, North Carolina, the church required Brother McBried to free a slave woman after she served him twelve years. Any "ishue" (children) she had would be free at birth.[17]

There is evidence that bondwomen belonging to non-Methodists were aware of the church's emancipation efforts. A shrewd Maryland slave woman named Alley ran away from her owner in 1790. Alley eluded capture by telling suspicious whites that she had been freed by a Methodist minister who had married into a slave-owning family. Alley's religious beliefs were not recorded in the ad, yet it is clear she knew of Methodist emancipators.[18]

The church held other positions that contributed to its success among slaves of both genders. Methodist values were a direct inversion of slaveholding gentry values. Methodism prized humility, piety, charity, plain dress, sobriety, love, and simplicity. The church hierarchy, fundamentally patriarchal from "God the father" down through his earthly clerical representatives who disciplined and oversaw the church "family," was nonetheless a patriarchy substantially different from that of slaveholders in this period, for it was founded on piety not property, humility not status, poverty not wealth. By joining the church, slaves could demonstrate their rejection of their owners' value system.[19]

Clergymen spoke out against the values of gentry patriarchy, but they rarely did so against those of familial patriarchy. Yet a discussion of Methodists' position on gender roles cannot be contained within Methodism's acceptance—as an ideal—of female subordination to males. The church's practices and its parishioners' actions and beliefs subverted men's authority over women in important ways. Women were not expected to obey (nor excused if they did obey) impious men, whether their fathers, brothers, or husbands.[20] White women routinely disobeyed orders of their male family members not to attend Methodist services, even under threat of violence.[21]

Interestingly, in the sources used for this study there were no reports of black men removing female relatives from church or of black men barring women in their families from services, although there were many such cases with white men. Deborah Gray White argues that slave marriages were more egalitarian than those of whites, which may explain this dissimilarity in the sources.[22] Other explanations might be advanced, but whatever the cause, the experience of black women in the church appears to have been different from that of white women.

Before analyzing what enslaved women found and made in the church, it is necessary to examine what black women actually did in the church. African American Methodist women were free and enslaved, young and old, house servants and fieldhands, women who hired out their time and women who did not. Slave women were among the first Methodists in America. Betty, a slave owned by the woman often credited with founding Methodism in America, Barbara Heck, was a member of the first church group in New York City.[23] Slave women were at some of the first church services that John Wesley's missionaries attended in the New World.[24] From Methodism's beginnings in America, slave women were a visible part of the church community.

Black women attended services on Sabbaths and weeknights. A small number of slaves were forced by their owners to attend Methodist services, but, more often, non-Methodist owners prohibited their slaves from joining the church or worshiping with Methodists.[25] Even where attendance was mandated, membership was voluntary, and slave women joined and left the church of their own accord.[26]

Black women offered themselves and their children for baptism, and a few were married by the church.[27] They attended camp meetings, took communion, and sang hymns. Black women gave money to the church, even those who had so little to give. A free black Methodist woman of Charleston, South Carolina, sixty years old, supported herself by "picking oakum, and the charity of her friends." Once, she donated to Bishop Francis Asbury a "French crown" because, he said, "she had been distressed on my account."[28]

The church consoled black women in illness and suffering. A slave woman belonging to a "G. Connor" sent for a Methodist minister when she was "under bodily affliction." He found her "crying for mercy," and he "visited and prayed for her."[29] A black woman of New York City was attended by a preacher on her deathbed in 1771. He asked her if she was afraid of death: " 'Oh no,' said she, 'I have my beloved Saviour in my heart.' " She gave a moving testimony of her faith and "continued to declare the great things that God had done for her soul, to the astonishment of many, till the Lord took her to Himself."[30]

Slave and free black women prayed, shouted, and testified in love feasts, services, and classes. In 1771 a New York bondwoman in a biracial love feast "declared, her heart was so full of divine love that she could not express it."[31] Although the church provided such opportunities for public self-expression, women of color were not accorded the same chances as black men or white women for leadership. They, unlike black men, were not licensed as exhorters or preachers in this era. Slave and free black women rose to lay leadership positions such as that of class leader less often than did white women.[32]

Although black women frequently prayed in public, I have found no instances where they were asked to lead congregations in prayer. They gave testimony in public, but were very rarely described as exhorters. "Old Elizabeth," born a slave in 1766 and emancipated at age thirty, organized a black women's prayer meeting around 1808 in Baltimore where she acted as unofficial preacher, but the opposition of area whites, including Methodist elders, caused her to surrender control of the meeting to a man. Some years later she began preaching again, apparently unofficially, this time meeting with both support and opposition from clergymen. She even traveled into slave states and preached against slavery.[33] Women like "Old Elizabeth" were noteworthy exceptions. Most free black and slave women in the early church were denied positions of leadership. It might seem that the church had little to offer most slave and free black women—if, that is, we examine slave and free black women in the church from the outside in. If we work in the opposite direction, from the inside out, interpreting the experience of these women in light of the larger context of their experiences in slavery and freedom, we gain insight into what they found and made in the church. Although Methodist slave women shared many experiences and beliefs with other members, they lived, labored, and loved under unique conditions. Let us begin at the end, at death, to see how we might consider the experience of slave and free black women in the church from this larger context.

*Methodist descriptions of* sickbed and deathbed scenes show remarkable similarities regardless of the gender, race, or status of the sick and dying, but slave women had special reasons to find them comforting. While some slave owners might have considered their illness or death as solely a capital loss, Methodists valued the humanity of sick and dying believers. Slave women probably confronted the possibility of death more often than other members, because of the greater risks of dying in childbirth, coupled with the harsh working conditions, inadequate shelter and diet, and poor medical care that slaves generally faced.

Death for all Methodists was a victory, a passage to a more joyful life away from their "vale of tears" on earth. Slave women, subject to sexual abuse by white men, torn from their children and spouses, and valued by the slave system for their economic roles as both producers and reproducers, had compelling reasons to long for release from life in slavery. Heaven was also a place where slave women could reunite for all time with family and friends from whom they were rent asunder on earth. Last but not least, Heaven was a place of judgment, where slave owners would be punished for wrongs done to slaves and for slavery itself. Thus, even though the Methodist death-bed ritual was almost universal in appearance, the significance of dying (and going to Heaven) was different for slave women than for other members.

Even as slave and free black women began their affiliation with the church, their unique experiences in the larger world of racial and sexual oppression shaped their religious life and worldview. Though they were denied administrative power in the church, the supreme "power" for Methodists was that of God or the Holy Spirit. This power was open to all, and black women had special reasons for enjoying its fruits.

A believer's first intimacy with the Holy Spirit occurred during conversion. Central to Methodism, conversion was where a person acknowledged her prior sinful life, repented, and agreed to live a new, Christ-centered life. The relationship between African American women and God was personal, palpable, and vivid. In 1793 an African-born bondwoman experienced this immediacy during a Methodist service. She "seemed wonderfully transported Oh said she my blessed God I see you coming." [34]

Most Methodists converted in emotionally and physically demonstrative ways, and black women were no exception. In Granville County, North Carolina, "two Black wemen [*sic*] under powerful agonies" were "powerfuly [*sic*] delivered" during a 1798 service.[35] A Virginia woman was "struck down under the power of God" at a prayer meeting for slaves. Other blacks "got round her on their knees and cried out to the Lord for her, and in a few minutes he set her soul at liberty." [36]

That "power" and "liberty" should have been linked is important. In their daily lives, slave women had little of either. The ritual of conversion gave enslaved women control over their spiritual destiny. Describing a service for slaves in 1794, a different preacher used strikingly similar language: "The Lord broke in upon the people one Black woman came thro[ugh]: and was set at liberty to praise God."[37] Having a part of herself beyond her owner's control, a part she could freely infuse with meaning, was undoubtedly important to a slave woman.

Methodist belief and practice offered other social and psychological benefits to bondwomen. Methodists believed that all people, regardless of race, class, gender, color, or status, confronted God on equal terms. The conversion ritual reinforced this concept, for in conversion people became dead to their former lives and were "born again" to a new life. As Jean Friedman perceptively noted in *The Enclosed Garden,* bondwomen had special reasons to start their lives anew.[38] In conversion slave women could re-create themselves in their own image, and the spiritual foundation upon which this new self was built was one of equality and dignity. Slave owners often denied slave women's humanity and personhood, but in conversion rituals, slave women could reclaim and proclaim their humanity and personhood.

Methodist slave women not only felt the power of God but brought others to God while experiencing it. Such influence was important, for Methodists remembered the circumstances of their conversions for the rest of their lives in the church. In 1789 a slave woman's spiritual exercises initiated the conversion of fourteen others. A "young men's class" had met upstairs in an Annapolis, Maryland, home. When the meeting ended, the preacher heard "a poor soul groaning and praying." He and the other class members went downstairs to find "in the passage a black woman in great distress." They exhorted, sang, and prayed with her. Others heard them and came in, among them another black woman and the head of the household. In all, fourteen people besides the bondwoman converted. The preacher describing the events credited her for this "work of conversion."[39] This story, printed in a Methodist periodical in 1790, illustrates the religious influence of black women over both whites and blacks. When we consider that, in Methodist views, she had guided them to eternal joy and happiness, her influence was profound and something in which she could take pride.

As many historians of slavery have noted, slave women lived not only with slavery's routine restraints upon their will; they also had to fight for control over their bodies. Victims of sexual abuse by whites, slave women were often subject to the will of others in the most intimate ways. In this context, spiritual possession takes on added significance for two reasons. First, a bondwoman possessed by the Holy Spirit was asserting the spark of the divine and pure in herself. She was saying to others, in essence, that she was connected intimately to God. Second, possession was by nature beyond the control of slave owners, and in this subtle way, slave women could reclaim some control over their bodies. Under the power of the Holy Spirit, Methodist slave women cried out, fell as if dead, swooned, jumped, shouted, and trembled.

It is not coincidental that white onlookers, especially slave owners, took special offense at slave women's enthusiasm in services. A slave woman of Maryland "cry'd out for sanctification" during a biracial service at Gunpowder Chapel in 1791, and, according to the preacher, "the noice [sic] she made offended some of my delicate hearers."[40] An analysis of this incident reveals how race, gender, white opposition, and Methodist belief intertwined in slave women's religious experience.

This area of Maryland (Harford Circuit) had 131 black and 633 white members in 1791, and white membership declined as black membership rose over the next four years. (In 1795, 210 blacks and 433 whites were members here.)[41] Numerous "black classes" met in this region, and one of these classes met at Gunpowder Chapel. The minister assigned here spoke in public and private against slavery, including to whites at Gunpowder Chapel.[42] It is possible that the whites offended here were only concerned with the volume of this slave woman's religious expression, but the wider context of the minister's antislavery activity and the increase in black members—and decrease in white members—strongly suggests that, in this case, more was at issue than simply "noice."

This Maryland bondwoman cried out for sanctification, the highest spiritual state a Methodist could aspire to. Coming after conversion, sanctification was the attainment of perfect moral purity and absolute holiness. When considered in tandem with white eighteenth-century images of African women as "lascivious" and of black women as full of "lust," the contrast between white image and the sanctified bondwoman becomes more stark and the implications of her cry more significant.[43] By attaining sanctification, she denied her oppressors the opportunity to define her "nature." Though we cannot read this woman's mind, the context of white views about black women suggests that slave women's religiosity may have had a significant impact on their gender identity. Alternatives to the persona that would come to be called "Jezebel" existed and were embraced by slave women.

The church did not speak openly against sexual abuse of slave women by white men, and slave women apparently did not turn to clergymen to protest sexual victimization by whites. Slave women did, however, try to use the church disciplinary process to protect themselves from slave men, as did, for example, a Methodist slave woman who accused a Methodist bondman of "makeing [*sic*] to[o] free" with her.[44] The public nature of her complaint also suggests that she felt empowered to assert control over her own body in the church.

Another slave woman told her religious experience to minister Freeborn Garrettson in 1783. Like other Methodists, she was "almost ready to [despair] of mercy" until God "set her soul at liberty." She was faithful to the church, for Garrettson had "frequently seen her at five sermons running." Her attendance record was impressive, for she "hire[d] her time of her master" and thus could have made more money during the hours she spent at worship. She lived alone in a room of a boardinghouse, and regularly "[rose] several times in the night to pray." Unsatisfied with conversion, she sought sanctification "by day and night" until God spoke to her a second time and told her, she reported, "Be clean."[45] Her desire to be sanctified was in one sense merely typical of early Methodists. Yet her status as a female slave places her aspiration to "be clean" in a context that gives her quest special significance. Methodist slave women not only privately redefined themselves and their gender identity but also publicly told and showed others that they had done so.

In coming decades, proslavery whites would invent a pious, proslavery black female persona to defend the peculiar institution. The fact that she bears little resemblance to religious women in this earlier period, and likely to religious women of later antebellum years, should give us pause. If Jezebel was created to assuage white guilt, perhaps Mammy was created to ease white fears of religious black women. If religious slave women were also docile, loyal, and content as slaves, there would be no reason to fear the effects of religion on bondwomen. And there would be no need to feel discomfort about religious slave women if whites could calm their fears by recounting the fable of Mammy.

In reality, there was often an assertive quality to bondwomen's spirituality, one that militates against finding Methodist slave women as the prototype of the pious Mammy. A minister recorded an illuminating incident that took place in a white widow's house: "Here I had a very lively little company of both black and white . . . some prostrate on the floor and others wept out loud. But I saw a great deal of resentment in the old widow lady. . . . She said afterward she could not bear such hollering, and in the morning gave one of her servants a lecture for her conduct the night past."[46] Another "negro woman, armed with a hoe," bravely rescued a Methodist preacher from a mob that had seized him from the pulpit and threatened to "duck him" in a bayou.[47]

Sometimes the consequences of joining a church that many slaveholders rejected were fortuitous for slave women. Bishop Francis Asbury told of a strange case where a master emancipated a Methodist bondwoman "*because she had too much religion for him.*"[48] We can only guess at her behavior. Some slaves and free blacks reported on whites who had broken church rules.[49] Historian Mechal Sobel cites a case where Hannah, a slave woman belonging to Thomas Jefferson, lectured him in a letter about his lack of Christian faith.[50] Albert Raboteau describes an incident where a slave mother began praying aloud for God to hasten Judgment Day (when whites would be punished for wrongs committed against slaves) after her daughter was whipped by her owner.[51] Any one of these might have also been the case for this fortunate woman. What is important is that it was her *religion,* somehow demonstratively evident, that discomfited her owner.

These cases illustrate the tension between some owners and slave women over religion, although many slave women were not fortunate enough to be freed for having "too much religion." Some owners barred slaves from attending services, such as those in Prince George, Maryland, who ordered their slaves to attend no more night meetings at layman Luke Branson's house.[52] Other owners did not allow slaves to join the church, as was the case with over three hundred slaves converted in a 1787 revival in Virginia.[53] Black members of a Charleston, South Carolina, congregation were all arrested on a Sunday in 1807, and a "watchman" broke up the black women's prayer meeting begun by "Old Elizabeth" in Baltimore around 1808.[54] At least twice in this era, white opposers burst into Methodist services and beat slave worshipers.[55] Both violent incidents took place in front of white clergy. What slaves suffered in services they conducted for themselves must have been worse.

Despite such persecution, the psychological benefits of Methodism seem to have helped the inner slave woman, for she could, through oral testimony, hymns, shouts, and Holy Spirit possession, demonstrate to others her sense of self-worth, her own concept of gender identity, and her determination to worship God in the way she chose. Methodism also helped strengthen the sisterhood of slave women.

Part of the reason Methodism helped foster sisterhood among slave women was that its beliefs and practices fit well with those already a part of slave life. Slaves had a flexible definition of family. As scholars like Herbert Gutman have noted, the practice of including in the family people not biologically related, termed "fictive kin," helped slaves retain family life despite forced separations of blood relatives.[56] Methodism, too, fostered "fictive kinships," for every female member was a "Sister," and each male, a "Brother." Small groups that met weekly to give testimony and share experiences, called "classes," formed a Christian "family." The similarities of Methodist practices to those of the slave community probably attracted slaves to the church and helped reinforce the sisterhood of slave women.

Black Methodist women found other church values and practices useful in strengthening their sense of sisterhood with one another. Methodists believed all confronted God as equals. They were exhorted to stay united in heart and mind and urged to respect and love one another. Although work routines, owner treatment, and privileges in many ways separated domestic slaves from field slaves, Methodist beliefs might have helped militate against Methodist slave women adopting this separation in their religious lives.

Another way the church helped strengthen the sense of sisterhood of slave women was purely practical. The church, in its prayer meetings, classes, love feasts, and services, provided opportunities for slave women belonging to different owners to meet. Camp meetings were especially useful in this regard, for slaves could meet up with long-lost relatives and friends at these gatherings.

The inner workings of the Methodist black sisterhood are difficult to reconstruct. Methodist sources provide very few glimpses into the lives of black women when not at worship. These glimpses are, however, suggestive of a vibrant and supportive community. Black women, despite the opposition of male church leaders, helped "Old Elizabeth" establish women's prayer meetings and encouraged her to preach.[57] Mary Ann Berry, a Charleston woman freed because of her "faithfulness and virtue," was described as a "lady-like nurse" who selflessly served the "Church and poor."[58] That Berry was described in gender-specific language, as "lady-like" and as a "nurse," indicates that black Methodist women performed church work like nursing the ill and infirm, work that if done in slave quarters would have been less visible to white clergy than Berry's urban ministry.

In helping provide an ideological alternative to white visions of black womanhood, in using language that promoted sisterhood, in encouraging unity and harmony, and in offering to perform gendered church work, Methodist slave women supported the church community and carved out a niche in it for a sense of gender identity and pride.

It is possible that black women included some white women in their Methodist sisterhood, but there were factors that would have discouraged them from seeing all white women as sisters. In areas with small memberships, classes were often split by gender, so that free black, slave, and white women might all comprise the "women's class." When there were many members in an area, white women were placed into the "women's class" and black women into the "black class." Thus, the more Methodism prospered in a community, the less likely it was that black women would have had white women as class members.

Many white women did acquire a greater respect for the humanity and personhood of slaves in the church. Some at least partially included black women in their vision of Methodist sisterhood. A wealthy Delaware Methodist, Sister Bassett, filled with "the love of God" at turn-of-the-century camp meetings, "would as soon embrace a pious dusky daughter of Africa, in her rejoicing, as a white sister."[59] Yet even this story can be read as showing the limits of white women's sororial feelings, for it was used by John Lednum, the author of an 1859 church history, to indicate how far away Methodists of his day were from the halcyon earlier days of greater equality. A few white women of early Methodism spoke out against slavery in church services, and some freed their slaves.[60] These women might well have been considered sisters by slave and free black women. But evidence suggests that enslaved Methodist women would have been reluctant to embrace unrepentant slaveholding women as sisters.

Slave women had reason enough as slaves and as women to exclude slaveholding women from their sisterhood. Methodism merely reinforced these values. Many clergy believed, as one preacher wrote, that slaves would go to Heaven while "their cruel bloody oppressive Masters will sink and burn in Hell fire for ever and ever."[61] Another put the matter of judgment more directly upon slaves: "How many of these poor Slaves will rise up in judgment against their Masters, and porhaps [*sic*], enter into life, while they are shut out." [62] One preacher noted that slaves "held by professors of religion are hard to move." [63] Slave testimony from later antebellum years indicates that Christian slaves believed slaveholding was a sin — and for many, an unpardonable sin. [64] It is difficult to believe that Methodist slave women in the Revolutionary and early national period, the peak antislavery years of the church, would have been more forgiving.

The actions and statements of some slaveholding women illustrate in the extreme how hard it would be for slave women to include all white mistresses in their sisterhood. One woman was expelled from the church in 1790 for "puting so many irons on her negro woman." [65] Another, warned that if she persisted in beating her slaves she would be expelled, retorted that she could "serve the Lord out as well [as] in" the church. [66] Yet another, a Sister Bryan of North Carolina, told a preacher she would free her slaves by will only if she had no children to inherit them at her death. [67]

Though these white women were either punished by the church or counseled to emancipate and thus do not represent the entire female slave-owning membership, their existence cautions against assuming that religion promoted universal sisterhood. Even those slave women who worshiped with their mistresses and those who were comparatively well treated by their owners realized that if they were not emancipated, they and their families incurred the risk of being sold, beaten, and abused — if not by their present owners, then maybe by their future ones. The sole guarantee against being mistreated by an owner sometime in their lives as slaves was to be manumitted. It is unlikely that a common religion alone would have fostered a sisterhood of all Methodist women, especially since enslaved women saw religion as antithetical to slaveholding.

Slave women found in conversion an opportunity to re-create the self, to formulate a positive gender identity, and to further cement their bonds with other slave and free black women. In the church, they had a forum where they could express their new sense of self-worth and reject white views of black womanhood. In the church's rituals, slave and free black women found additional ways to express their values and hopes. One of the most important rituals for slave women appears to have been baptism.

A slave woman presenting herself for baptism at the Hopkins home in 1790 "wept and cryed out for mercy" during the ceremony. The minister exhorted her "while the water was pouring," that "Jesus might Baptize her with the Holy Ghost and with fire." [68] That this woman was baptized at the home of Brother and Sister Hopkins is significant. We discover nine months later that the Hopkinses had freed their slaves. This chain of events suggests that some whites were moved to manumit slaves in part because of witnessing slaves participating in Christian rituals that affirmed their humanity and piety. Slave women, by taking part in rituals like communion and baptism, pricked the consciences of some slaveholding whites.

Slave women who were mothers had special reasons for seeing baptism as a special event and as one that demonstrated to some whites their humanity. It is the wider context of slavery, here again, that forms the necessary backdrop. In a system that did not recognize their maternal rights or respect their maternal feelings, slave mothers had few opportunities to voice their dissent at the separation of slave families. Baptism offered a public forum in which slave women could demonstrate to whites their affection, love, and concern for their children. Baptism was seen by white Christian parents as a parental duty, whereby they showed their willingness to rear their children in the faith. It goes without saying that a mother separated from her child could not fulfill this Christian responsibility.

Methodist clergy took seriously the idea that parents would raise baptized children in Methodist doctrine and practice. Although the baptismal service included no wording by which the child's parents were identified, clergy commonly questioned the mother (white or black) of each child they baptized as to her own religious beliefs. One minister revealed his procedure by speaking of an incident in 1791 where, in his words, "I had my poor heart touched by asking where the Mother of one of the childrens [*sic*] was. The answer was she is sold away from the child." [69]

This same minister a year earlier asked a free black woman about her beliefs when she presented her child for baptism. She was not herself religious, yet she assured the minister she would "try and do all for its spiritual good that she could." The minister was satisfied with her promise, and although he disapproved of the fact that the child was not "legally begotten," he baptized it. [70] This episode shows how common the questioning of black mothers was. It also indicates that some black women regarded baptism as a ceremony with secular significance.

It is hard to draw a line between the sacred and secular meanings of baptism for mothers of slave children. Religiously, baptism was a ceremony where a child was dedicated to God. Yet for mothers of slave children, this dedication might have this-worldly significance not applicable to white parents. If the mother were separated from her slave children, God could watch over and protect them. Baptism was a child's initiation into the Christian community on earth and in Heaven. For a mother of a slave child, the importance of a family reunion in Heaven would have a specific meaning that whites could not share.

Mothers of slave children knew they might be unable to care for their little ones in the future, and this fact lends a poignancy to baptismal ceremonies for black children that was not evident in ceremonies for whites. A minister who baptized several black children in North Carolina reported that his audience "seemed a little diverted the first part of the dedication" but that "tears [were] shed before I was done telling the duties of parents."[71] This audience became serious as the ceremony progressed, specifically during the preacher's discourse about parental duties. The timing of their tears was not coincidental. A black woman of New Kent, Virginia, perhaps reflecting on her maternal duties and the precariousness of her family, was greatly affected during the baptism of her child in 1792, for "the power struck her as also many others then present."[72]

Baptism was a rite in which parental, and especially maternal, ties were recognized. For slave mothers and freedwomen with slave children, this public ceremony was one of the few opportunities to demonstrate their commitment to their children and, implicitly, to register their dissent at the separation of slave families. It was a ceremony where mothers could invoke God's promise to protect children if they became unable to. It began the process that assured their children a place in Heaven.

Black mothers with slave children used other church procedures to protect their offspring. A freedwoman of Virginia complained to a Methodist minister that her slave children were being harshly whipped by their owner, her former master. The owner claimed in his defense that all children needed strict discipline and that he beat his own white children more severely than he did slave children. The freedwoman, determined to have some justice served, retorted that this slave owner also whipped a grown black man (a bondman who was to be freed but whose time was not up yet). This the clergyman would not countenance, and he lectured the man until he expressed contrition. It might seem to a modern reader that the owner deserved expulsion from the church, but the preacher's course was practical—he would have no leverage over the man if he expelled him. And this freedwoman had no redress for wrongs committed against her children and other slaves outside the church.[73] Her complaint was lodged with a clergyman who that very day had encouraged slave owners to liberate their slaves on religious grounds. She knew that this minister might be sympathetic to her plight and would exhort her child's owner *as a Christian,* and perhaps she had cause to believe that such an approach would work.

Mothers of slave children had other reasons to become Methodists. A school for black children was opened by the church in Baltimore, Maryland, and ministers encouraged masters to teach slave children to read.[74] Most important for slave mothers was probably the church's rule against buying, selling, or trading slaves. This rule was enforced by zealous antislavery clergymen as well as by those more lukewarm about emancipation.[75] Members convicted of buying slaves were required to write deeds emancipating those slaves after a period of service in which they recouped their expenses; otherwise, they faced expulsion. Members like James Tooley, convicted of selling a slave, were expelled.[76] As Tooley's case makes clear, not all slave owners modified their behavior to avoid expulsion from the church. But this policy did give mothers of slave children some slender hope that if they belonged to other Methodists, their family might be kept together.

Slave mothers had allies in the clergy for keeping families together. To some ministers, the separation of slave mothers and children was the height of slavery's evil. Motherhood in general was viewed by Methodists as a sacred office, and the love of a mother for her child was the closest earthly analogue to the unconditional love of God for humanity. A poem published twice in early Methodist periodicals shows this sentiment:

> What is more tender than a mother's love
> To the sweet infant fondling in her arms?
>
> .  .  .  .  .  .  .  .  .  .  .  .  .  .
>
> Now if the tend'rest mother was possess'd
> Of all the love, within her single breast,
> Of all the mothers, since the world began,
> 'Tis nothing to the love of God to man.[77]

In this context, we can see why ministers would be most outraged at the separation of slave mothers and children. Yet Methodist rules did not address one common reason that slave families were separated: death of the slave owner.

Religion was important to slave mothers even when the church could not or would not intervene to stop owners from separating slave families. One Methodist preacher witnessed a heartrending scene where a mother was torn from her children in Virginia in 1789, and the words of this woman illuminate how her religious beliefs helped her at this critical moment. The owner of this Virginia slave family had died and had willed slave children, including a "sucking child," to someone in Virginia and their mother and father to a man in the Carolinas. Amid the minister's stream of consciousness description of the scene are the mother's final words to her children: "O the crys of the poor captive Woman is enough to move the heart of the most Obdurate, on her Taking leave of her Children, [']O my children, my children no more to see my children,['] with her little ones around her crying[, ']my Mamma my Mamma is agoing away.['] . . . Trembling in the Melting streams of Tears extorts the cry, [']I hope I shall see you again at Judgment Day, whether I am prepared or not I hope to see my children.[']"[78] It is important that she referred to "Judgment Day" and not to "Heaven." In her anger and grief, eternity became a place and time of reckoning. Yet intermingled with her tears and anger is her hope that she will be reunited with her children in a future world.

She stated this for all present to hear, a fact which strongly suggests that Heaven and Judgment were not just of otherworldly value to her. Her religion was a source of comfort in *this world,* a way she could reassure her children that they would meet again. It is also quite possible that she addressed the whites who were responsible for her grief, too, since she referred specifically to "Judgment."

Many bondwomen throughout the years of slavery would echo this mother's plaintive cry. Reverend Josiah Henson recalled that his mother also turned to God when her children were sold away from her.[79] Old Elizabeth's Methodist slave mother told her to look to God when they were parted as slaves. Kate Drumgoold's mother entrusted her children to God when she was sold apart from them during the Civil War.[80] This event, perhaps the most painful in the life of slave women, was one that united these women from different decades in common suffering. Their Christianity, providing comfort and, for many, retribution, united them across the years in common hope.

*In the church's* respect for their humanity and personhood, in striving for a new self after conversion and a new gender identity after sanctification, slave and free black Methodist women were able to redefine themselves and shape a gender identity of their own choosing. Through participation in church activities, these women could publicly demonstrate their self-esteem and their refusal to accept white visions of black womanhood. Through disciplinary channels and in rites like baptism, mothers of slave children could bear witness to their commitment to their children. And in their darkest hours, at death or upon being torn from their children, Methodist slave women found solace in their faith.

The experience of these women and their accessibility in the sources shows that other work remains to be done to fully appreciate the impact of religion on slave women's gender identity. Did Catholic slave women identify with female saints? What gender attitudes can be gleaned from slave spirituals? How did conjure women and male slave preachers interact in the slave community, and how did this interaction influence gender roles? How do attitudes about gender of Moslem and so-called unchurched slave women compare with those of Christian slave women? These are just a few of the possibilities for further research.

As the experience of Methodist slave women in the Revolutionary and early national period shows, enslaved women's religious history is more than just the intersection of the history of slave women, slave religion, or religious women. Armed with a new understanding of the complexity of slave women's religious experience, we can better appreciate the layers of meaning in even the most typical scene. On March 29, 1807, a bondwoman shouted joyfully during a Methodist service. The sermon that day spoke to her as a woman, a slave, and a Methodist, and in it we see echoes of the sanctified bondwoman to whom God said, "Be clean," of the righteous slave mother hoping to see her children on Judgment Day, and of the freedwoman demanding better treatment for her slave children. The text for the sermon was Isaiah 1:16–17, Isaiah's prophetic warning to Judah and Jerusalem: "Wash you, make you clean; put away the evil of your doings from before mine eyes; cease to do evil; Learn to do well; seek judgment, relieve the oppressed, judge the fatherless, plead for the widow." [81]

To explore the role of religion for women who lived under the shadow of slavery and racism is to illuminate both slavery's gendered history and the struggle of these women for hope and dignity within this brutal system. Although Methodist slave women shared many rituals and beliefs with other members, their double oppression as slaves and as women meant that they approached Methodism from a unique perspective. So, too, did free black women who endured the racism and sexism of a slave society. In the church, these women created positive gender identities and affirmed their worth and hope. In their faith, they could find meaning and value in their lives and, through their darkest hours, could even find "in every lonely place . . . an altar."

## *NOTES*

The majority of the evidence presented here comes from the southern colonies and states from Delaware to Georgia on the seaboard, Tennessee, and Kentucky, with occasional reference to evidence from the northern colonies and states in the years before slavery was gradually abolished there. I wish to thank Prof. Joan Cashin, Prof. Patricia Morton, Anya Jabour, and especially Prof. John Boles for their comments and advice on earlier drafts of this essay. This essay was completed with the assistance of a Doctoral Dissertation Fellowship from the National Endowment for the Humanities.

1. Eugene D. Genovese, *Roll, Jordan, Roll: The World the Slaves Made* (New York: Vintage Books, 1976); John B. Boles, ed., *Masters and Slaves in the House of the Lord: Race and Religion in the American South, 1740–1870* (Lexington: University Press of Kentucky, 1988); Albert J. Raboteau, *Slave Religion: The "Invisible Institution" in the Antebellum South* (New York: Oxford University Press, 1978); Lawrence W. Levine, *Black Culture and Black Consciousness: Afro-American Folk Thought from Slavery to Freedom* (New York: Oxford University Press, 1977), 3–80; Mechal Sobel, *Trabelin' On: The Slave Journey to an Afro-Baptist Faith* (Princeton: Princeton University Press, 1988); Jean Friedman, *The Enclosed Garden: Women and Community in the Evangelical South, 1830–1900* (Chapel Hill: University of North Carolina Press, 1985). A pioneering work that examines both slave religion and religious white women is Donald G. Mathews, *Religion in the Old South* (Chicago: University of Chicago Press, 1977).

2. Friedman, *Enclosed Garden;* Suzanne Lebsock, *The Free Women of Petersburg: Status and Culture in a Southern Town, 1784–1860* (New York: W. W. Norton, 1984), 142-43, 215-26. A. Gregory Schneider's book *The Way of the Cross Leads Home: The Domestication of American Methodism* (Bloomington: Indiana University Press, 1993) examines gender and gender roles among white Ohio Valley Methodists in the first half of the nineteenth century.

3. Deborah Gray White, *Ar'n't I a Woman? Female Slaves in the Plantation South* (New York: W. W. Norton, 1985), and Jacqueline Jones, *Labor of Love, Labor of Sorrow: Black Women, Work, and the Family, from Slavery to the Present* (New York: Vintage Books, 1985), chap. 1, deal little with religion. In *Within the Plantation Household: Black and White Women of the Old South* (Chapel Hill: University of North Carolina Press,

1988), chap. 6, Elizabeth Fox-Genovese acknowledges the centrality of religion for black women, yet does not explore bondwomen's religion in detail.

4. White, has an in-depth discussion of Mammy and Jezebel in chap. 1 of *Ar'n't I a Woman?* See also Patricia Morton, *Disfigured Images: The Historical Assault on Afro-American Women* (Westport, Conn.: Greenwood Press, 1991), especially chap. 1. I am not focusing here on the "real" Mammy as explored in Eugene Genovese's *Roll, Jordan, Roll,* 353–61, but on the slave-owning antebellum myth of Mammy as explored in White. For the New South, see Cheryl Thurber, "The Development of the Mammy Image and Mythology," in *Southern Women: Histories and Identities,* ed. Virginia Bernhard et al. (Columbia: University of Missouri Press, 1992), 87–108.

5. See, for example, Jones, *Labor of Love,* chap. 1; White, *Ar'n't I a Woman?;* Fox-Genovese, *Within the Plantation Household,* 290–98; Thelma Jennings, " 'Us Colored Women Had to Go Through a Plenty': Sexual Exploitation of African-American Slave Women," *Journal of Women's History* 1 (winter 1990): 45–74.

6. Fox-Genovese, *Within the Plantation Household,* chap. 6, and White, *Ar'n't I a Woman?* 22, 119–21.

7. Journals of Richard Whatcoat, 1 June 1799, original at Garrett-Evangelical Theological Seminary. Microfilm courtesy of University of Chicago Divinity School Library.

8. Diary of Jeremiah Norman, 13 April 1800, Stephen B. Weeks Papers, Southern Historical Collection, University of North Carolina at Chapel Hill.

9. See, for example, the ads in Lathan A. Windley, comp., *Runaway Slave Advertisements: A Documentary History from the 1730s to 1790, Vol. 2: Maryland* (Westport, Conn.: Greenwood Press, 1983).

10. See, for example, Elmer T. Clark et al., eds., *The Journal and Letters of Francis Asbury* (London: Epworth Press, 1958). Asbury used all of these terms to describe blacks.

11. Journals of Richard Whatcoat, 23 April 1795.

12. For the church's changing positions on slavery, see Donald G. Mathews, *Slavery and Methodism: A Chapter in American Morality, 1780–1845* (Princeton: Princeton University Press, 1965).

13. For antislavery sermons, see 26 February and 10 March 1797, James Meacham Papers, Special Collections Department, Duke University, Durham, N.C. See also "The Journal of Thomas Coke," in *Arminian Magazine,* July 1789, 344. For an example of private appeals for manumission, see 8 October 1795, William Ormond Papers, Special Collections Department, Duke University, Durham, N.C.

14. Ira Berlin, *Slaves without Masters: The Free Negro in the Antebellum South* (New York: Pantheon Books, 1974), 24–26.

15. Lebsock, *Free Women of Petersburg,* 95.

16. The emancipation deed for these women is reprinted in Elizabeth Connor, *Methodist Trail Blazer: Philip Gatch, 1751–1834* (Rutland, Vt.: Academy Books, 1970), 150.

17. Journals of Richard Whatcoat, 20 January 1798.

18. Windley, *Runaway Slave Advertisements, Vol. 2: Maryland,* 186–87.

19. Mathews, *Religion in the Old South,* 35–38; Schneider, *The Way of the Cross Leads Home,* 196–201. See also Rhys Isaac, *The Transformation of Virginia, 1740–1790* (New York: W. W. Norton, 1988).

20. Nor were children to obey a parent's order if it was contrary to God's will. See John Wesley's sermon on Colossians 3:20, *Methodist Magazine,* September 1797, 388.

21. There are many incidents of white men trying to keep female relatives from the Methodists or physically removing white women from church. For a small sample, see the story of Sarah Jones in William R. Phinney et al., eds., *Thomas Ware, a Spectator at Christmas Conference* (Rutland, Vt.: Academy Books, 1984), 167–69; 24 May 1790, 9 June 1792, Rev. John Kobler's Journal, Baltimore-Washington Conference United Methodist Historical Society, Lovely Lane Museum, Baltimore; 30 March 1792, 5 September 1792, 29 July 1794, Meacham Papers; 11 November 1792, George Wells's Journal, Baltimore-Washington Conference United Methodist Historical Society, Lovely Lane Museum, Baltimore; 19 May 1792 and 4 July 1792, Ormond Papers.

22. White, *Ar'n't I a Woman?* 158.

23. Clark et al., *Francis Asbury,* 1:9 n. 19.

24. Ibid., 1:9–10 and Frederick E. Maser and Howard T. Maag, eds., *The Journal of Joseph Pilmore, Methodist Itinerant* (Philadelphia: Message Publishing House for the Historical Society of the Philadelphia Annual Conference, 1969), 74.

25. Slaves were "called in" to hear a preacher in 1775 Maryland. John Lednum, *A History of the Rise of Methodism in America* (Philadelphia: Author, 1859), 154. Asbury twice used wording suggesting owner-mandated attendance. Clark et al., *Francis Asbury,* 1:57, 2:622. Charleston, in 1805, forbade Methodists from meeting slaves before sunrise or after nine at night. Ibid., 2:455. For slaves kept from services, see discussion below.

26. The best evidence that membership was voluntary is the fact that black women withdrew from the church of their own accord. See 19 January 1798, Diary of Jeremiah Norman.

27. For marriage, see 6 July 1793, Journals of Richard Whatcoat. Methodist clergy could not marry, baptize, nor administer communion until December 1784, when they split from the Anglicans.

28. Clark et al., *Francis Asbury,* 2:120.

29. Norman Diary, 18 January 1798.

30. Richard Boardman to John Wesley, 2 April 1771, in William B. Sprague, *Annals of the American Pulpit, Vol. 7: The Methodists* (New York: Robert Carter, 1865), 9.

31. Maser and Maag, *Journal of Joseph Pilmore,* 96.

32. Black women might have preached and exhorted in all-black services. Black women did preach in Methodist churches in later years. Free black women Jarina Lee, Zipha Elaw, and Julia Foote served as itinerant ministers—Lee from 1819, Elaw from

1828, and Foote in the 1830s. Their autobiographies are in William L. Andrews, ed., *Sisters of the Spirit: Three Black Women's Autobiographies of the Nineteenth Century* (Bloomington: Indiana University Press, 1986). Lydia Maria Child described an 1841 sermon by a black Methodist woman in *Letters from New York* (New York: Charles S. Francis, 1843), 61–68. Controversy ensued in the 1840s over a petition by the "Daughters of Zion" urging that African Methodist Episcopal church leaders allow women to preach in A.M.E. churches. Daniel A. Payne, *History of the African Methodist Episcopal Church* (1891; reprint, New York: Johnson, 1968), 300–301.

33. *Memoir of Old Elizabeth: A Coloured Woman,* (1863), reprint in *Six Women's Slave Narratives* (New York: Oxford University Press, 1988) 10–12, 17. The content of her sermons was not recorded.

34. Norman Diary, 6 August 1793.

35. Whatcoat Journals, 12 August 1798.

36. Kobler's Journal, 12 July 1791.

37. Meacham Papers, 27 July 1794.

38. Jean Friedman, *Enclosed Garden,* 69–73. Conversion as a remaking of the self is also discussed in Mathews, *Religion in the Old South,* 35, 67.

39. John Hagerty to Francis Asbury, extract printed in *Arminian Magazine,* July 1790, 355–56.

40. William Colbert Journal, 10 July 1791, original at Garrett-Evangelical Theological Seminary, photocopy courtesy of Baltimore-Washington United Methodist Historical Society.

41. Membership for Hartford Circuit can be found in *Minutes of the Annual Conferences of the Methodist Episcopal Church, for the Years 1773–1828* (New York: T. Mason and G. Lane, for the Methodist Episcopal Church, 1840).

42. Colbert Journal, 6 August 1791.

43. Winthrop Jordan, *White over Black: American Attitudes toward the Negro, 1550–1812* (New York: W. W. Norton, 1968), 35, 150–51.

44. Wells's Journal, 4 August 1792; see also the case detailed in Marjorie Moran Holmes, "The Life and Diary of John Jeremiah Jacob (1757–1839)" (master's thesis, Duke University, 1941), 153.

45. Robert Drew Simpson, ed., *American Methodist Pioneer: The Life and Journals of the Rev. Freeborn Garrettson, 1752–1827* (Rutland, Vt.: Academy Books, 1984), 227.

46. Kobler's Journal, 7 July 1791. Perhaps the mistress was upset that both black and white were participating, but why then did she host a biracial service? Perhaps she objected to enthusiasm generally, but if so, why did she open her home to a sect known for enthusiasm? Most plausibly, the mistress objected to her loss of control over her slave and to the power her slave found in religion.

47. M. H. Moore, *Sketches of the Pioneers of Methodism in North Carolina and Virginia* (Nashville: Southern Methodist, 1884), 288.

48. Clark et al., *Francis Asbury,* 1:656.

49. Thomas Mann Papers, 30 June 1805, Special Collections, Duke University, Durham, N.C.

50. Mechal Sobel, *The World They Made Together: Black and White Values in Eighteenth-Century Virginia* (Princeton: Princeton University Press, 1987), 215.

51. Raboteau, *Slave Religion,* 312–13.

52. Colbert Journal, 6 June 1794.

53. Philip Cox to Thomas Coke, July 1787, extract printed in *Arminian Magazine,* February 1790, 94.

54. Charles F. Deems, ed., *Annals of Southern Methodism for 1855* (New York: J. A. Gray, 1856), 253; *Memoir of Old Elizabeth,* 11.

55. Connor, *Methodist Trail Blazer,* 132; "A Journal and Travel of James Meacham," 30 August 1789, [Trinity College] *Historical Papers* 9 (1912): 94.

56. Herbert G. Gutman, *The Black Family in Slavery and Freedom, 1750–1925* (New York: Vintage Books, 1976), 216–27.

57. *Memoir of Old Elizabeth,* 10–14.

58. Charles F. Deems, ed., *Annals of Southern Methodism for 1856* (Nashville: Stevenson and Owens, 1857), 233.

59. Lednum, *Methodism in America,* 275.

60. Sister Whitehead condemned slavery at a heavily attended service in Virginia in 1791: "A Journal and Travel of James Meacham," [Trinity College] *Historical Papers* 10 (1914): 92–93. Mrs. Selby was one of the Methodist women who freed her slaves, in Clark et al., *Francis Asbury,* 2:153.

61. Meacham Papers, 21 August 1792.

62. Maser and Maag, eds., *Journal of Joseph Pilmore,* 137.

63. Clark et al., *Francis Asbury,* 2:46.

64. Eugene Genovese, *Roll, Jordan, Roll,* 250–51; Lawrence Levine, *Black Culture and Black Consciousness,* 34–35; Albert Raboteau, *Slave Religion,* 291–93.

65. Colbert Journal, 17 May 1790.

66. "A Journal and Travel of James Meacham," 3 October 1791, [Trinity College] *Historical Papers* 10 (1914): 90.

67. Ormond Papers, 26 August 1796.

68. Baptism, 9 September 1790, slaves free, 27 May 1791, Meacham papers.

69. Meacham Papers, 2 September 1790.

70. "A Journal and Travel of James Meacham," 10 September 1791, [Trinity College] *Historical Papers* 10 (1914): 89–90.

71. Norman Diary, 23 March 1800.

72. Meacham Papers, 23 February 1792.

73. Meacham Papers, 4 March 1790.

74. Clark et al., *Francis Asbury,* 2:46, 2:128, 2:380.

75. For a preacher lukewarm about antislavery enforcing this rule, see Norman Diary, 16 March 1799, 23 September 1799, 9 October 1799. For a preacher zealous about antislavery, see Whatcoat Journals, 20 January 1798, 25 August 1798, 26 January 1799, 2 March 1799, and 15 June 1799.

76. Ormond Papers, 19 August 1796.

77. *Arminian Magazine,* December 1789, 594–95 and *Methodist Magazine,* February 1797, 96.

78. Meacham Papers, 12 January 1789.

79. In Chester W. Gregory, "Black Women in Pre-Federal America," in *Clio Was a Woman: Studies in the History of American Women,* ed. Mabel E. Deutrich and Virginia C. Purdy (Washington: Howard University Press, 1980), 65.

80. Kate Drumgoold, *A Slave Girl's Story,* 7–8, in *Six Women's Slave Narratives.*

81. Mann Papers, 10 August 1807. A second sermon preached this day on "put on the whole armour of God" is also suggestive.

PATRICIA K. HUNT

# The Struggle to Achieve Individual Expression through Clothing and Adornment

## AFRICAN AMERICAN WOMEN UNDER AND AFTER SLAVERY

FADED HOMESPUN DRESS and apron and a grey woolen sacque an [sic] a blue and white check linen bonnet [sic]."[1] This short phrase in an Augusta, Georgia, newspaper during the nineteenth century describes the dress of Elsey, a fugitive slave woman. Another newspaper description indicates that a woman wears a "striped copperas homespun frock."[2] One woman runaway, according to a fugitive slave notice in a third Georgia newspaper, had on a "homespun habit and . . . a blue handkerchief tied around her head."[3] These brief descriptions actually give evidence of the individuality of slave women's dress and adornment and the value of it for identifying a particular slave woman. In fact, this study will argue that the clothing and adornment of African American women both under and after slavery reveals that African American women did find a way to express themselves as individuals through their dresses, skirts, bodices, headwear, hairstyles, jewelry, and other accessories.

Adorning the body is a universal concern, and African American women strove against the harshest conditions of slavery and the years following slavery to utilize clothing and adornment to express their individuality. As sociologists Mary Ellen Roach and Joanne B. Eicher have pointed out, the expressive functions of clothing and adornment are basically twofold: to "express individuality by stressing unique physical features or by using unique aesthetics" and to "express group affiliation or the values and standards of the group."[4] It is the first function in particular that this study examines.

Even though there have been a large number of books and articles published about slavery—with recent studies bringing a new attention to the experience and perspectives of slave women—social historians still usually devote only a small space (one paragraph to a few pages) to slave clothing, and they devote even less space to the discussion of slave women's clothing. Specifically, Robert W. Fogel, Stanley L. Engerman, and John W. Blassingame have remarked on the general allotment of clothing to all slaves and the issuance of finer clothing to house servants and favored slaves. Fogel and Engerman also have noted the ability of some slaves to supplement the typical issues of clothing through purchases of other clothing or fabric with their own money.[5] Eugene D. Genovese has interpreted the headcloths worn by African American women as "a mark of servility."[6] Deborah Gray White has remarked on slave women's dress and undress as significant in the expression of their status as slaves, stating that "some women had such tattered clothes that they were almost naked. Sometimes bondwomen were exposed because of the nature of their work."[7] In short, most of this scholarship has indicated the generalities of slave clothing, discussed slave men's dress rather than women's, or remarked on the white-authored stereotypes of slave dress—interpreting clothing as a "pillar of white supremacy" with little discussion of how the slave women themselves perceived dress and attempted to make it their own.

Several researchers have examined the clothing conventions of both African American slave women and men in specific states; several others have completed both general and specific studies of the dress of African American women after slavery. Patricia Campbell Warner and Debra Parker examined the fabric and clothing worn by slaves in North Carolina during the eighteenth and early nineteenth centuries. Linda Baumgarten studied the dress of slaves in Virginia during the eighteenth century; Margaret T. Ordonez concentrated her study on clothing availability and production for African American slaves in Leon County, Florida. Patricia K. Hunt and Barbara M. Starke both examined slave narratives for information on slave clothing and fabric production in slave communities in Georgia and other southern states. And Gerilyn Tandberg examined both written sources and clothing worn by slaves on plantations in Mississippi and Louisiana to gain an understanding of the design and construction of slave clothing. These are significant studies that shed light on the specific types of clothing worn by slave men and women.[8]

Equally important is the scholarship that focuses on clothing worn by African American women after slavery. For example, Lydia J. Wares has examined women's clothing from 1500 to 1935. Anna A. Simkins has analyzed the significance of hair and headwear, and Patricia Hunt has examined photographs of clothing worn in Georgia from 1870 to 1915. All three have not only documented the clothing worn after slavery but also interpreted its impact—whether stereotypical or individualized.[9] However, this study attempts to emphasize the positive role clothing played in the lives of women, under and after slavery.

Before we proceed, some discussion about sources is needed. In their continuing attempt to study clothing and textiles from the past, researchers have often been more frustrated than successful, especially when there is a lack of extant clothing and textiles to study. Over the years, however, determined and creative scholars of textiles and clothing have discovered methods of study that use written records, photographs, paintings, and other artwork as primary sources of data. For this study's examination of the clothing and personal adornment of African American women during and after slavery, a variety of sources were utilized. I have examined traditional sources such as slave narratives and other reminiscences of enslaved women, newspaper notices of fugitive slave women, published letters from planters to overseers, diaries, and other written accounts. I have also studied books written by men and women who lived or traveled throughout the South after the Civil War and letters from southern teachers and missionaries, as well as such underutilized sources as photographs and the descriptions of former slaves recorded by Federal Writers' Project (FWP) interviewers during the 1930s. Photographs constitute a particularly significant contribution to the study of African American women's dress in the years after slavery. Moreover, although this study is focused on women in Georgia, it has also utilized sources from other states. Thus, the findings and conclusions of this study may be more generally applicable.

Clothing for slave women was usually made on the plantation or handed down from the planter's family. Most dresses were shapeless, of poor construction, and of cheap fabric, coarse in texture and drab in color. Former slaves interviewed for the FWP in the 1930s recalled that dresses were made "right on de body so that none of the cloth was wasted"[10] or "made to slip over the head with straight seams up both sides."[11] Dresses were made quickly and cheaply to be worn until the planter distributed the next allotment of fabric. Slave owners as a general rule had little or no consideration for the appearance, let alone the tastes, of the wearers.[12]

However, some slave women were allowed to dress more elaborately. This was the case with house servants, since they were in close proximity to the planter's family and since outsiders might readily see a house servant upon visiting the planter's home. These women represented the planter and must therefore be dressed accordingly.[13] Former slave Victoria Adams recalled that she "had a heap of pretty clothes to wear 'cause my missus give me de old clothes and shoes dat Missy Sally throw 'way."[14] Fugitive slave notices in nineteenth-century Georgia newspapers also reveal such cases. For example, one fugitive slave woman wore "a blue silk frock flounced with flowered silk and blue ribbon."[15] Another notice indicated the following on two women runaways: "one wearing plain white homespun the other, more dressy than usually [sic] for a servant, having fine articles of clothing of almost every description."[16] The latter slave woman might have been a house servant, a favorite, or a runaway with clothing stolen from the planter's family. Whatever the case, the fugitive slave notices give evidence that some slave women wore fine clothing.

Yet slave women other than house servants and favored slaves were able to achieve distinctive styles of dress. Newspapers often gave specific information about the types of fabric and colors worn by slave fugitives (runaways). For example, the Macon *Weekly Telegraph* reported of one woman: "She usually wore on her head and her neck yellow cotton handkerchiefs."[17] Another notice mentioned a woman runaway's hairstyle rather than her clothing: her hair was "nearly straight, done up in a twist and fastened with a comb."[18] According to another Georgia newspaper, a woman "generally goes with her head tied up in a handkerchief."[19]

In letters and diaries, visitors to the South often commented upon individuality in slave women's dress. Basil Hall, who traveled to Georgia in 1828, remarked that the slaves were "generally dressed in what is called White Welsh plains for winter clothing. They prefer white cloth, and afterwards dye it of a purple colour to suit their own fancy."[20] Moreover, the FWP interviews provide information on dress. For example, Mary Childs,[21] a former slave, recalled that checked dresses were dyed purple. Another former slave recounted, "Everything was stripedy cause Mammy like to make it fancy.

She dye it with copperas and walnut and wild indigo . . . and make pretty cloth."[22] So it becomes clear that even though plain cloth tended to be a standard issue, if the cloth was produced on the plantation many slave women were able to counter this uniformity by dyeing the cloth a particular color or adding stripes of color in the weaving process. Thus, slave women could and did strive to achieve personal expression through fabric color and design.

In addition to making the cloth distinctive, the women used accessories to individualize their appearance. Head handkerchiefs or turbans were frequently mentioned. For example, during the Civil War Charlotte Forten, a teacher from New England, observed that the slave women "were neatly dressed in their Sunday attire, the women mostly wearing clean, dark frocks, with white aprons and bright-colored head handkerchiefs. Some had attained to the dignity of straw hats with gay feathers but these were not nearly as becoming nor as picturesque as the handkerchiefs."[23] Another visitor to the South, Laura Towne, commented in May 1862, "It was beautiful this morning at church. The crowd was greater, and the dresses cleaner and more picturesque too. . . . But the turbans were grand."[24] Many sources indicate that the headcloths varied in design and size. For instance, one teacher living in the Sea Islands of South Carolina in 1862 wrote a letter describing a slave woman as having her hair carefully concealed by an "enormous turban."[25] One contemporary viewer described a headcloth of "unusual" height,[26] while another indicated that a headcloth was constructed from small pieces of cloth.[27] Although many recent historians have interpreted the headcloth as a simplistic sign of slavery, one has only to read the descriptions of those who viewed them to recognize that the headcloths were much more. Yes, the headcloths did represent a connection to slavery. But, although this researcher has not completely researched the African traditions of slave women's dress, one could also see these headwraps as part of an African heritage preserved by these women.[28]

Most important, whether it is a former slave's memory of dress, a planter or overseer's description of a runaway's appearance, or a traveler's comments on slave clothing and adornment, a host of descriptions gives evidence that slave women expressed their individuality through dress. In particular, the fugitive slave notices document the uniqueness of the slaves' clothing choices. In many cases, it was a headkerchief that facilitated the personal expression in dress as is revealed in later photographs of African American women. Nevertheless, the sources clearly signify that clothing constituted more than mere body covering. For slave women, it became one important means of exhibiting the individuality that a racist, dehumanizing society denied.

After the Emancipation Proclamation, the passing of the Thirteenth Amendment, and the end of the Civil War in 1865, slave women were transformed into freedwomen.[29] Yet they found themselves with a new set of obstacles: fitting into a society that had previously excluded and stigmatized them as women. This "fitting in" also included clothing themselves appropriately. This change only intensified their struggle to express themselves through their wardrobes, whether this expression came from wearing fashionable styles (i.e., the norm in women's clothing at the time which was seen as ladylike and modest) or personalizing ordinary clothing.

Traditional thought indicates that African American women after the Civil War had little time, money, or interest in clothing. Yet photographs and writings indicate that there was a continued desire to express individuality in dress whenever economically or aesthetically possible. Many teachers and other women living and working in the South after the Civil War left diaries and other writings that recorded their daily lives among newly freed African American women and that reveal the type of clothing they wore. For example, even in an isolated place like St. Helena Island, South Carolina, at the turn of the century, such outsiders as teacher Rossa B. Cooley noticed the strong interest in dress of African American women. Cooley wrote, "With the hunger for books very naturally came the hunger for clothes, pretty clothes and more of them! And so with school and freedom best clothes came out and ragged clothes were kept for the fields."[30] Former slave Willis Williams observed, "Negro women . . . fell into imitating their former mistresses and many of them who were fortunate enough to get employment used part of their earnings for at least one good dress. It was usually made of woolen a yard wide, or silk."[31] Thus it is clear that some African American women after slavery did indeed dress in the norm of American society by adopting fashionable dress.

This interest in demonstrating newly found personal freedom through being stylish is also evident in the comments and articles published in African American newspapers and periodicals of the late nineteenth and early twentieth centuries. African American author and lecturer Fannie Barrier Williams, in her 1904 article "The Smaller Economies," indicated that dress was a concern of the day and argued that women should care not only about what they wore but also about how much money they spent on clothing: "The art of living well without spending all our income is one of the most important problems of our everyday [*sic*]." She argued that women needed to know how to obtain the most from their money and not be controlled by the grocer, milliner, or dressmaker. "In our wearing apparel, for example, we are more or less at the mercy of the modiste and the milliner. We go to them with all our vanities, our social ambitions and our envies, but seldom with any independent judgement or individuality of taste as to our pocket book limitations or to what becomes us." Williams also stipulated that a woman had a right to be "well gowned" but that she should learn how to manage her money in doing so.[32] Perhaps Williams saw the need for her essay based on her observations of women spending too much money on apparel. However, she also asserted that it was important for a woman to use her own judgment about the styles of clothing that looked good on her and that she liked to wear. Thus, Williams encouraged economic and creative independence in wearing apparel.

Indeed, becoming dress was a symbol of social and economic status in the late nineteenth and early twentieth centuries, and for African American women newly freed from slavery it was an important indicator of their new status. Throughout this period most women learned about current styles through women's magazines and fashion columns in local newspapers. African American newspapers like the *Atlanta Independent* and the *Afro-American* of Baltimore often published fashion columns. These gave women the latest information on dress silhouette, skirt length, hat style and trim, and hairstyles worn in the major cities of the United States. And this knowledge of fashion gave African American women a choice: to follow the current styles of dress, to individualize and personalize these styles, or to wear clothing that reflected their African heritage and/or slave heritage.

One specific example of clothing and adornment that expressed heritage is the headcloth. Julia Peterkin, writing about African Americans living on her family's plantation after slavery, observed, "Love of dress and adornment undoubtedly plays its part in the pleasure of going to church. The older women tie up their heads in headkerchiefs [and] wear Sunday hats perched up above them."[33] Former slave Ellen Thomas wore "the old fashioned bandana handkerchief bound about her head,"[34] according to one FWP interviewer. The headcloth was both worn and in the process of being given up. For instance, Frances Butler Leigh remarked, "The women showed a strong inclination to give up wearing their pretty, picturesque head hand-kerchiefs, 'because white people didn't' [wear them]." Yet she added, "Now that ladies everywhere have taken to wearing silk handkerchiefs made into turban-shaped caps, I suppose the negro women may become reconciled to their gay bandanas."[35] Indeed, the headcloth was an item of adornment frequently mentioned in the written documents and photographs of African American women after slavery.

Photographs of African American women living in Georgia after the Civil War richly illustrate clothing and adornment. Some women expressed them-selves through hairstyles: from braids (see fig. 1) to pompadours. In figure 2, no two hairstyles are alike; each makes its own statement. Other photo-graphs reveal how African American women utilized fabric to make personal statements in their headdresses, creating a brim effect over the forehead or a curtain at the back to shield the neck from the sun (figs. 3 and 4). And within these parameters of protection, the headdresses were unique. Photographs also illustrate that after slavery many of these women did continue to express their independence through their dress, and that no mere uniforms of fash-ion were worn. Those women who could not afford to buy fabrics to make

*FIGURE 1. Woman wearing a braided hairstyle. Courtesy, Georgia Department of Archives and History.*

FIGURE 2. *Members of the Mother's Club of Grady County, Georgia.*
*The women wear stylish fashions from the turn of the century and display*
*individualized versions of the fashionable pompadour hairstyle. Courtesy,*
*Georgia Department of Archives and History.*

the latest styles or could not afford to hire a seamstress had other methods by
which to express themselves: through the way they shaped and wore a particular garment, selected certain colors, or wrapped a piece of fabric around
the head.

The tradition of wearing distinctive clothing and accessories can also
be found in the descriptions of former slaves recorded by FWP interviewers. For example, Sally Banks Chambers, a former Louisiana slave, wore
"heavy gold earrings . . . and she dresses, even in midsummer, in a long-
sleeved calico shirt, heavy socks and shoes, and a sweeping skirt many
yards wide." [36] Another interviewer described a former Georgia slave woman
named Susannah, who "was dressed in a dress composed of strips of cham-
bray and calico sewed together. Her apron was soiled, but her head cloth was
clean." [37] Besides commenting on distinctive styles or combinations of clothing, many FWP interviewers commented on hairstyles. For example, Anne
Hawthorne wore her hair in "little pigtails and wrapped in beach string." [38]
Another interviewer described Ma Eppes: "Proudly the old woman un-
wrapped her 'headrag' to display a thick mop, wooly white but neatly parted

FIGURE 3. *This woman's headcloth wraps around to form a brim over her forehead and a curtain in back to shield her neck from the sun. Courtesy, Georgia Department of Archives and History.*

FIGURE 4. *Another example of a woman's headcloth. A curtain of fabric hangs down to protect her neck from the sun. Courtesy, Georgia Department of Archives and History.*

into squares." Her hair was arranged in "dozens of little plaits, wrapped with yards of twine."[39] Photographs reveal that not all African American women after the war wore their hair in braids or plaits and that probably as many did as did not. And, while many post–Civil War African American women wore fashionable hairstyles, some copied the exact modes and others created their own variations of popular styles.

*African American women* under and after slavery consistently, determinedly utilized clothing and adornment to express their individuality. In slavery they altered the clothing allotted to them, refashioning it to their personal tastes and preferences. When the standard issue of cloth for clothing was white, slave women either dyed it in various natural dyestuffs to obtain othe colors, or slave women in charge of weaving cloth created their own striped or "checkedy" variations to the cloth. Slave women also demonstrated their personal style through their creative headcloths, and this tradition continued after the war. Although some historians label the headcloth a symbol of servility (Quaker Oats removed the bandanna from its Aunt Jemima trademark in 1968 and replaced it with a headband),[40] the headcloth is more than a mark of servitude. Although these stereotypical interpretations may have some credence, it is very likely that headcloths represented something more positive to the slave women themselves, especially when the women fashioned it themselves from whatever size of cloth was available for their use. Thus, the headcloths gave them a chance to express their individuality.

After slavery African American women utilized headcloths, hairstyles, and types and styles of clothing to indicate personal expression. Many who could afford the newest, most fashionable styles of dress often did so—not necessarily to copy or mimic the white social norm in dress but rather to express their new freedom by wearing "new dress." It was not uncommon after slavery to see African American women in ragged, worn-out clothing— a picture of any woman who had little money and worked long hours every day to feed, house, and clothe her family. What is exciting is to find that even those women had the desire and will to dress distinctly or to dress in a way that pleased them.

In sum, African American women were able to endure and persevere through the oppression they experienced under and after slavery. This is evidenced by how they used clothing and adornment to express their creativity, femininity, and individuality. Perhaps clothing and adornment gave them the freedom they otherwise did not have. As long as they had a piece of cloth or natural dyestuffs to create something of their own, they could exhibit personal creativity. This situation was true for women after slavery as well, because clothing symbolized freedom and expressed their own tastes, choices, and self-worth. And, both under and after slavery, African American women have creatively and positively converted rags into "clothes that would outshine the sun."[41]

## NOTES

1. *Daily Chronicle and Sentinel,* 27 November 1864.
2. *Georgia Journal and Messenger* (Macon), 7 January 1841.
3. *Augusta Herald,* 15 December 1814.

4. Mary Ellen Roach and Joanne B. Eicher, "Origins and Functions of Dress and Adornment," in their *Dress, Adornment, and the Social Order* (New York: John Wiley, 1965), 6.

5. Robert W. Fogel and Stanley L. Engerman, *Time on the Cross: The Economics of American Negro Slavery* (Lanham, Md.: University Press of America, 1984), 116–17; John W. Blassingame, *The Slave Community: Plantation Life in the Ante-bellum South* (1972; reprint, New York: Oxford University Press, 1979), 292.

6. Eugene D. Genovese, *Roll, Jordan, Roll: The World the Slaves Made* (New York: Pantheon Books, 1972), 558–59.

7. Deborah Gray White, *Ar'n't I a Woman? Female Slaves in the Plantation South* (New York: W. W. Norton, 1985), 32.

8. Patricia Campbell Warner and Debra Parker, "Slave Clothing and Textiles in North Carolina, 1775–1835," in *African American Dress and Adornment: A Cultural Perspective,* ed. Barbara M. Starke, Lillian O. Holloman, and Barbara K. Nordquist (Dubuque, Ia: Kendall/Hunt, 1990), 82–91; Linda Baumgarten, " 'Clothes for the People': Slave Clothing in Early Virginia," *Journal of Early Southern Decorative Arts* 14 (November 1988): 26–70; Margaret T. Ordonez, "Plantation Self-Sufficiency in Leon County, Florida, 1824–1860," *Florida Historical Quarterly* 60 (April 1982), 428–39; Patricia K. Hunt, "Fabric Production in the Nineteenth-Century African American Slave Community," *Ars Textrina* 15 (1991): 83–92; Barbara M. Starke, "U.S. Slave Narratives: Accounts of What They Wore," in Starke et al., *African American Dress and Adornment,* 69–79; Gerilyn Tandberg, "Field Hand Clothing in Louisiana and Mississippi during the Antebellum Period," *Dress* 6 (1980): 89–103.

9. Lydia J. Wares, "Dress of the African American Woman in Slavery and Freedom, 1500 to 1935" (Ph.D. diss., Purdue University, 1981); Anna A. Simkins, "The Functional and Symbolic Roles of Hair and Headgear among Afro-American Women: A Cultural Perspective" (Ph.D. diss., University of North Carolina, 1982); Patricia K. Hunt, "The Influence of Fashion on the Dress of African American Women in Georgia: 1870–1915" (Ph.D. diss., Ohio State University, 1990).

10. George P. Rawick, ed., *Georgia Narratives,* vol. 12, pt. 2 of *The American Slave: A Composite Autobiography* (Westport, Conn.: Greenwood Press, 1977), 33. Alice Green was a former slave interviewed in Georgia at the age of 76.

11. Rawick, *Georgia Narratives,* suppl., ser. 1, vol. 4, pt. 2 of *American Slave,* 415. From Caroline Malloy, who was 96 years old when interviewed.

12. Robert M. Myers, ed., *The Children of Pride: A True Story of Georgia and the Civil War* (New Haven: Yale University Press, 1972), 264, 265, 809, 1004, 1123, 1126.

13. Leslie H. Owens, *This Species of Property* (New York: Oxford University Press, 1976), 23; Richard C. Wade, *Slavery in the Cities* (New York: Oxford University Press, 1964), 125; Myers, *Children of Pride,* 138.

14. Rawick, *South Carolina Narratives,* vol. 2, pt. 1 of *American Slave,* 11.

15. *Georgia Journal* (Milledgeville), 8 August 1826.

16. *News* (Washington, Ga.), 28 August 1834.

17. *Weekly Telegraph,* 3 March 1832.

18. *Daily Sun* (Columbus, Ga.), 29 May 1834.

19. *Columbus Enquirer,* 29 November 1834.

20. Basil Hall, *Travels in North America* (Edinburgh, 1829), quoted in *The Rambler in Georgia,* ed. Mills Lane (Savannah, Ga.: Beehive Press, 1973), 67.

21. Rawick, *Georgia Narratives,* suppl., ser. 1, vol. 3, pt. 1 of *American Slave,* 200. Mary Childs was a former slave born in 1846. She was interviewed in Georgia.

22. Norman R. Yetman, *Life under the 'Peculiar Institution': Selections from the Slave Narrative Collection* (New York: Holt, Rinehart and Winston, 1970), 271.

23. Charlotte Forten, "Life on the Sea Islands," *Atlantic* 13 (May 1864): 589.

24. Rupert Sargent Holland, ed., *Letters and Diary of Laura M. Towne: Written from the Sea Islands of South Carolina, 1862–1884* (1912; reprint, New York: Negro Universities Press, 1969), 32.

25. Elizabeth Pearson, ed., *Letters from Port Royal: Written at the Time of the Civil War* (Boston: W. B. Clarke, 1906), 192.

26. Leon Stone Bryan Jr., "Slavery on a PeeDee River Rice Plantation, 1825-1865" (master's thesis, John Hopkins University, 1963), 31.

27. Elizabeth H. Botume, *First Days amongst the Contrabands* (1893; reprint, New York: Arno Press, 1968), 32.

28. Blassingame, *Slave Community,* 20–22; Lawrence W. Levine, *Black Culture and Black Consciousness* (New York: Oxford University Press, 1977), 3–5, 138.

29. Peter M. Bergman, *The Chronological History of the Negro in America* (New York: Harper and Row, 1969); Lulamae Clemons, Erwin Hollitz, and Gordon Gardner, *The American Negro* (New York: McGraw-Hill, 1965); Michael Perman, *Emancipation and Reconstruction* (Arlington Heights, Ill.: Harlan Davidson, 1987).

30. Rossa B. Cooley, *Homes of the Freed* (1926; reprint, New York: Negro Universities Press, 1970), 169–70. Cooley came to St. Helena Island in 1904.

31. Rawick, *Florida Narratives,* vol. 17 of *American Slave,* 350.

32. Fannie Barrier Williams, "The Smaller Economies," *Voice of the Negro* 1 (May 1904): 184–85.

33. Julia Peterkin, *Roll, Jordan, Roll* (New York: Robert O. Ballou, 1933), 76. Peterkin was a Pulitzer Prize winner from South Carolina. She inherited her family's plantation, Lang Syne, and wrote stories and documentaries about the African Americans who lived and worked on the plantation.

34. Rawick, *Alabama and Indiana Narratives,* vol. 6 of *American Slave,* 376.

35. Frances Butler Leigh, *Ten Years on a Georgia Plantation since the War* (1883; reprint, New York: Negro Universities Press, 1969), 94.

36. Rawick, *Texas Narratives,* suppl., ser. 2, vol. 3, pt. 2 of *American Slave,* 681.

37. Rawick, *Georgia Narratives*, suppl., ser. 1, vol. 4, pt. 2 of *American Slave*, 660.

38. Rawick, *Texas Narratives*, vol. 4, pt. 2 of *American Slave*, 118.

39. Rawick, *Alabama and Indiana Narratives*, vol. 6 of *American Slave*, 119.

40. Cathy Campbell, "A Battered Woman Rises: Aunt Jemima's Corporate Makeover," *Voice*, 7 November 1989, 45–46.

41. Peterkin, *Roll, Jordan, Roll*, 125.

MARIE JENKINS SCHWARTZ

# "At Noon, Oh How I Run"

## BREASTFEEDING AND WEANING

## ON PLANTATION AND FARM IN

## ANTEBELLUM VIRGINIA

## AND ALABAMA

Dey hab a ho'n up in de house an' dey blow it . . .
for de mammies to come up an' nuss dey li'l babies.
—Betty Simmons

T NO TIME were the contradictions inherent in the southern slave system more exposed than at the moment of a slave's birth. Each time a child was born into bondage, slave owners and parents alike confronted the need to nurture and guide the child into adulthood. Each set of adults had its own expectations for the child's future. Owners hoped children would become productive and loyal members of the plantation household, capable not only of contributing to their economic interests but also of playing a role in the elaborate paternalistic drama that characterized southern slavery. Slaves also hoped their infants would survive childhood to become loyal and productive adults. They expected, however, that children would form loyalties to their families and to the larger slave community, and the productivity they envisioned was of youngsters contributing to the welfare of their families. Thus, slaveholders and slaves celebrated the births of slave children and joined together to nurture the newborn, each for different reasons.

Because slave owners valued slave infants, they readily agreed to work routines that allowed new mothers at least some time to breastfeed their children. The slaveholder's commitment to nurturing slave children was incomplete, however. Time and again owners found themselves torn between the desire to accommodate the nutritional needs of infants by releasing new mothers from fieldwork and the conflicting wish to use all resources at hand, including the labor of all adults, to produce the largest possible cash crop. Each strategy held out economic advantage, for allowing mothers to nurture their infants served to protect an owner's future crops and other economic interests as much as sending the women to the field. Providing time for mothers to care for their infants also benefited masters and mistresses in nonpecuniary ways. Fostering the maternal care of infants enabled owners to think of themselves as humane and enlightened managers, or even parental figures, rather than as the cruel and despotic creatures that inhabited the pages of abolitionist tracts.

Mothers turned their owners' desires for slave children to their own advantage, gaining time from the field or other chores to breastfeed their babies. Women resisted owner-mandated policies that interfered with breastfeeding and threatened their infants' health and safety. They instead followed advice on infant nurture handed down by generations of black women.

Slave parents of both sexes asserted their right to establish families and demonstrated love for their children by carrying out daily chores on their behalf. Primary responsibility for feeding and nurturing infants, however, fell primarily to mothers. Fathers contributed to the care of infants indirectly. Men, for example, supplemented the diets of breastfeeding wives, who required additional nourishment, by hunting, fishing, gardening, or appropriating food—with or without their owners' permission. Because fathers and mothers performed different functions within the slave family, two-parent families represented the ideal living arrangement among slaves. The slave family was neither "matriarchal in form" nor "matrifocal."[1]

This paper considers breastfeeding and weaning in two areas of the South —the Alabama black belt and the Virginia piedmont—localities that demonstrated dramatically different demographic and economic trends during the years 1820 to 1860. The black belt is a stretch of prairie and woodland that girds central Alabama. Beginning with Alabama's admission to statehood in 1819, this area experienced an influx of migrants, free and unfree, as planters flocked to the area seeking profits in the lucrative cotton market. Many entered the state with sizable slaveholdings, but others parlayed modest holdings into large estates in the period of rapid growth. In 1820, slaves in the region numbered only a little over 10,000; forty years later the slave population stood at more than 210,000, making the Alabama black belt one of the most densely populated areas of the South and home to some of the South's largest slaveholders.[2]

The piedmont region of Virginia extends from the fall line running through Richmond in the east to the Blue Ridge Mountains in the west. This rolling plateau, which covers nearly half of the present-day state, produced in the antebellum period wheat and tobacco for market. During these years, the Virginia piedmont experienced outward migration and other dislocations that had their origins in economic hard times lasting until the 1850s. Although the piedmont boasted some of Virginia's largest slaveholdings, smaller holdings were far more numerous. The number of slaves in the Virginia piedmont increased in the period of study as slave mothers gave birth to children, but not nearly as rapidly as that of the Alabama black belt because the interregional slave trade and migration of owners to the West and South diminished Virginia's slave population. In 1860, nearly 250,000 slaves lived in the Virginia piedmont, an increase from 200,000 in 1820.[3]

Slaves and owners in both of these areas preferred daytime arrangements for slave infant care that kept mothers and infants close to one another, because infants did not thrive when deprived of a mother's breast in the days before sterilization made bottle feeding practical. Keeping nursing mothers near their infants was often the most or only practical solution to the problem of maintaining the mother's productivity while meeting the nutritional needs of the infant. From the standpoint of the slaveholder, allowing mothers to work near their infants enabled infants to suckle, while mothers maintained an acceptable pace of work. Mothers who worked too far away from their babies lost time journeying to and from the field. Their Alabama owner assigned nursing mothers Rachael and Lucy to "chopping in Mill Field . . . as it is convenient for sucklers." Generally, efforts by owners to extract as much work as possible from nursing mothers concentrated on improving the efficiency with which mothers journeyed back and forth from infants to field, rather than on reducing the time mothers actually spent in breastfeeding. So great was concern over efficiency that even the location of slave cabins might be decided, in part, on their convenience for mothers coming from the field to breastfeed their babies.[4]

Mothers who worked at domestic chores, rather than field tasks, usually kept their children with them as they worked, in part so they could breastfeed them as the need arose. Ned Chaney recalled that his mother, an Alabama slave, kept each of her thirteen infants with her as she worked at the loom and performed other chores: "She nuss 'em, totin' 'em around if she was busy." Levi Pollard's mother, a seamstress on a large Virginia estate, also tended to the needs of her babies as she worked. The cook on the Meadows plantation in Alabama managed to fulfill her parenting and work obligations with the help of the young master who devised a swing for her baby. Apparently, the infant swayed in the wind nearby, while her mother cooked in the kitchen, no doubt stopping from time to time in response to the baby's cries.[5]

To facilitate breastfeeding, many slaves and slaveholders preferred that mothers keep their infants by their side wherever they worked. When mothers went to the field, infants often accompanied them. Owners liked the arrangement because it saved the mother "the time of going to the house to nurse."[6] For mothers, attending to infants at the side of the field broke up long and grueling work regimens with pleasurable recesses and offered reassurance that their children were safe and well. They could respond to their infants' needs at the first sign of distress.

Inclement weather sometimes prevented field slaves and other women who worked outdoors from keeping their babies with them as they worked. When winter temperatures fell below freezing, babies remained in the cabin alone or with slightly older children to care for them. Often their only supervision came from visitors, usually mothers who returned at appointed times to breastfeed their youngest babies, although owners occasionally sent other adults to check on the children or checked on the infants themselves. Infants left in the quarter on Sherman Varner's Alabama plantation had only older brothers or sisters to mind them, but the master visited the quarter regularly to bring them milk.[7]

When infants stayed in the cabin, owners and parents alike preferred that mother work nearby. Owners objected to leaving work undone, however, simply because it lay some distance from the slave quarter, so this arrangement did not always prevail. Advice on the "Management of Negroes" appearing in a popular agricultural journal circulated among southern planters reflected the dilemma created when the demands of crop and baby conflicted with one another: "A woman nursing is allowed ample time to attend to her child, and I avoid *as much as possible* sending them to a distance from the house to labor." Alabama slave owner Willis P. Bocock advised his plantation manager to work "suckling women" near the house, but only "if possible."[8]

Slaves objected to leaving children unsupervised. The designation of one

slave—often a young girl or an elderly woman—to care for infants of working mothers offered a solution to the problem of supervising infants when
mothers worked at some distance from their cabins. However, slaveholders
adopted this practice only when a slave marginal to the production process
was available to assume this chore, and slaves accepted the practice only if
they believed the health and safety of their infants required it. Consequently,
many plantation "nurseries" functioned only on the largest estates and only
when winter weather and heavy demands for labor made them necessary.

Adult supervision in the nurseries tended to be minimal, for owners expected slaves left in charge of infants to perform other chores, such as spinning, sewing, or cooking, while they minded their small charges. Former
Alabama slave Vicey Williams, for example, had to prepare food and spin
while she watched babies, but she could count on help from their mothers
when they arrived from the field to nurse at about ten o'clock. Children,
barely past infancy themselves, also helped care for babies in the nursery.[9]
Despite their shortcomings, owners and slaves alike preferred nurseries to
leaving infants home alone or with older brothers and sisters. Indeed, safety
was a primary argument for the creation of nurseries, which became more
common over the course of the antebellum period.

Mothers who left their children alone in the cabin or in a nursery returned periodically to breastfeed them. The *Southern Cultivator*'s "Rules
of the Plantation" recommended that nursing mothers "visit their children,
morning, noon and evening until they are eight months old, and twice a
day from thence until they are twelve months old." Slaveholders expressed
anxiety that overseers might neglect the needs of nursing infants in the interest of bringing in a crop, and rules for overseers reiterated the expectation
that mothers have time to breastfeed, even during harvest. "Sucklers must
be allowed time to suckle children," read one set of rules. Another directed
the overseer to allow nursing mothers an extra half-hour to get to the field in
the morning, so they could attend to their infants.[10]

In addition to specifying the number of times a mother could breastfeed
her children each day, some slaveholders attempted to impose other restrictions that reflected prevailing ideas about breastfeeding. One planter specified not only that women on his plantation could come in from the field to
nurse their babies four times each day, but also insisted that they wait "until
they become properly cool" before nursing their babies. Such warnings
against breastfeeding when "overheated" were common.[11] Hungry babies

surely wailed in protest, but mothers may have welcomed the respite from the field or other work offered by the requirement to cool down before feeding their children and insisted on prolonging their absence from the field accordingly. Generally, however, they resented interference with breastfeeding.

A few slaveholders held bizarre ideas about breastfeeding and tried to impose them on their slaves, but mothers resisted implementing them. One physician and planter recommended that owners withhold mother's milk for the first ten days of a slave baby's life, substituting as nourishment "sweet oil and molasses in such proportions as will keep the bowels loose." During this time the mother's milk was to be drawn off "by the nurse, the midwife, another and older child, or by a puppy." Touted as a preventative for lock-jaw, the scheme never gained popularity. In fact, slave mothers on the doctor's own plantation apparently refused to abide by his instructions, for he found it necessary to hold another slave woman responsible for the distribution of the oil and molasses and the "faithful execution" of the plan. Despite this effort, mothers did not carry out his instructions, and the woman charged with supervising the plan's implementation apparently appropriated much of the oil and molasses for her own use.[12] The advocacy of this plan by a major agricultural journal, however, illustrates the bewildering medley of advice that owners confronted when making decisions about nursing routines, as well as the difficulties they encountered in ensuring that the slaves complied with them. An owner's doubts about the best course of action enhanced the mother's ability to influence the development of policies relating to breastfeeding.

No matter what slaveholders or slaves desired, the nature of the work regime determined, in part, when mothers breastfed their children. Women working in the field on plantations employing a gang labor system — in which groups of slaves worked at a common task for a specified period of time — generally adhered to a fixed schedule for nursing their babies, at least during working hours. Betty Simmons described the practice of calling mothers from the field to nurse their children in Alabama. "Dey hab a ho'n up in de house an' dey blow it in de middle of de mawnin' an' afternoon for de mammies to come up an' nuss dey li'l babies." Former slave H. C. Bruce, recalling life on a large Virginia plantation, described a regimen for nursing infants similar to that ascribed to the Alabama black belt. "During the crop season . . . sucklings were allowed to come to [their infants] three times a day between sun rise and sun set, for the purpose of nursing their babes, who were left in the care of an old women." [13]

Slave women who worked under a task system—a work regimen in which individual slaves were expected to complete a given amount of work in a day—enjoyed more flexibility in deciding when to feed their infants. Rather than calling women in from the field at appointed times, owners who assigned slaves specific tasks provided time for women to breastfeed by reducing their work loads. The overseer on George Walker's Alabama estate apportioned work so that mothers of nursing infants hoed 55 rows, 70 yards long, while other women were held responsible for hoeing 60 rows of the same length.[14] One advantage of the task system was that fathers or other slaves could assist women in completing chores so they could spend more time with their infants. Of course, owners may have counted on this possibility and deliberately assigned tasks difficult for the women to complete.

Even when fixed schedules were the rule, however, mothers were sometimes summoned from the field to care for an infant in distress. On one Alabama plantation, mothers routinely came from the field to nurse their children at 9:00 A.M. and at noon, but mothers also returned at other times to quiet their fussy infants. "Mammy Larkin," who cooked for the hands and who also watched the babies while their mothers worked in the field, found it easier to care for them if their mothers returned to suckle any who wailed. She dispatched a young child, also left under her supervision, to the fields to fetch a mother when her infant cried, apparently assuming that the baby needed to suckle.[15]

Sometimes nursing mothers worked as a separate group or joined so-called trash gangs composed of workers who could not keep pace in the field with other hands. Early in December 1858, "sucklers" and women in an advanced stage of pregnancy shucked corn, while other slaves picked cotton and gathered corn on one black belt estate. Later that month, six breastfeeding mothers worked with a man to repair plantation fences, while other women were "pulling and trashing cotton stalks in the field over the road." Such assignments not only kept mothers working near their infants, but also prevented infants from disrupting the work of other hands, as would have occurred if they had been taken to the field. The assignment of different tasks to nursing mothers may have been the exception, rather than the rule, however, during the cotton-picking season in Alabama. Most breastfeeding mothers apparently went to the field each day to pick cotton in Alabama.[16]

Highly regimented feeding schedules were more typical of large plantations than smaller farms and thus more common in Alabama than in Virginia. They were also more prevalent in the late antebellum period than in

Alabama's early years when slaveholders and slaves first entered the area.[17] The handful of slaves living on small holdings would have prevented a slaveholder from establishing elaborate routines for nursing infants and forced owners and slaves alike to improvise as best they could to feed babies. Also, because women on small farms worked close to their infants, breastfeeding mothers lost little time traveling between field and infant.

Although the majority of mothers left their work to breastfeed their babies or kept their babies with them throughout the day, other arrangements were possible. An Alabama slave took babies to the field at times appropriate for nursing on one plantation. The routine was probably unique to this plantation and made possible by the availability of a slave man whose disability prevented his working in the field but did not interfere with his carting babies to their mothers working there. Some owners theorized that infants could nurse at an animal teat, but few tried to implement this practice.[18]

Slave infants who fed regularly at the breast of their white mistresses were uncommon but not unknown. When Mack Brantley's mother died in Alabama, his sister tended to his other needs, but his mistress suckled the infant along with her own daughter. Former Virginia slave George White reported that his mistress nursed him along with her own child whenever his mother had to be in the field.[19]

Although men — masters or overseers — usually made final decisions about where nursing mothers worked and when they might leave the field to feed their children, they designated women to oversee the process. One popular plantation manual recommended putting the overseer's wife in charge of seeing that the "children are well nursed and taken care of." [20] More often, however, another slave woman assumed this role. Mistresses involved themselves with nursing arrangements mainly on smaller farms or under unusual circumstances. When mothers died in childbirth or were unavailable for breastfeeding for other reasons, mistresses became involved in deciding the best solution to the problem of feeding infants.

Circumstances beyond the control of either slave or owner complicated efforts to devise arrangements for nursing infants. Even when plantation rules were conducive to breastfeeding, the poor health of the mother might undermine its success. "Rachel's child from sucking has become almost as sick as she is, and I fear will die," warned her overseer. Barbara, whose difficult pregnancy and labor threatened her life, was in such poor health that she could not lift her child to her breast for nursing. The need for a wet nurse by the white family put an additional strain on a breastfeeding mother, who might find herself nursing another child in addition to her own. According to one calculation, at least one-fifth of mistresses relied on a wet nurse at least part of the time. Also, slave mothers sometimes breastfed black babies in addition to their own. Henry Baker's mother died when he was only two weeks old, and the young Alabama slave was given to a wet nurse "til' I could eat an' git about." [21] Finally, a slave mother's death or absence endangered the lives of infants who might not have available alternate sources of safe and adequate nutrition.

Slave babies only rarely received nourishment from a bottle, a dangerous practice in the days before bottles were commonly sterilized. While the dangers of bacteria in milk were little understood, everyone knew the results of hand feeding infants: high rates of illness and mortality. The preference was to provide infants, both black and white, with wet nurses when the mother could not breastfeed the child. Giles Smith's experience in Alabama was exceptional. The slave infant became a wedding gift for the young mistress when only a few months old. Weaned precipitously from his mother's breast, the infant resisted the bottle so long that his mistress considered returning him to his mother. Smith explained years later that he would have been given to a wet nurse, but there "was no cullud women on de Missy's place dat could nurse me." Smith survived, but others did not. Despite the best efforts of another woman to feed Mary Montgomery's baby "by hand," the infant died shortly after her mother "took to the woods" when she fled her Virginia plantation for freedom. [22]

Weaning, just as nursing, was an activity subject to interference by owners. Most children appear to have been weaned gradually as mother's trips in from the field for this purpose grew less frequent as the infant aged. The *Farmer and Planter* called for mothers to feed their infants before leaving for the field in the morning and on arriving in the quarter at night. Infants were to be nursed three times during daylight hours until they were eight months old, when one of the feedings could be eliminated. Another set of rules for plantation management published in a different agricultural journal also recommended reduced feedings at eight months, and weaning at one year old, at least between dawn and dusk. Thus, weaning probably occurred gradually for slave infants, some of whom from a very early age received foods meant to supplement breastfeeding. The babies left under the care of former slave Vicey Williams suckled breast milk from their mothers at ten o'clock each morning, when the women came in from the field. In the afternoon, however, they had to make due with "potlicker" (the broth left in a pot after greens are cooked). Later in the day, babies joined slightly older children in downing a meal of "mush and skimmed milk." Other common foods included clabber and "cush" (bread mashed into gravy).[23]

Feeding babies old enough to receive supplemental foods in addition to mother's milk or old enough for weaning presented problems for women left in charge of groups of slave babies. Many, shorthanded, oversaw a system in which very young children fed at troughs like so many farm animals. In their later years, former slaves who recalled this practice expected listeners to express incredulity on learning of it. Former Virginia slave Nannie Williams, who as a girl helped "Aunt Hannah" feed fourteen black babies left in her charge, prefaced her explanation of the procedure with a declaration: "You ain't gonna believe dis, but it's de gospel truf." The young girl watched Aunt Hannah "po' dat trough full of milk an' drag dem chillun up to it. Chillun slop up dat milk jus' like pigs."[24]

Tensions between owners and slaves increased in periods of peak labor demands—especially during planting and harvesting—in part because owners pressured mothers to spend more time in the field and less time caring for their infants. Owners who otherwise granted women "ample time to attend" their children looked for ways of supplementing the diets of infants to stretch the time between feedings. Some slaveholders required mothers to carry their infants to the field, even in severe weather, if they needed the women's labor. One Virginia slave owner apparently provided brandy to infants to fortify them against extremely cold temperatures.[25]

However much an owner wished to minimize the time mothers spent away from field or other chores, the necessity of caring for an infant decreased a mother's productivity. The dramatic decrease in the amount of cotton picked by new mothers on the Mary Foreman Lewis plantation in the black belt suggests that mothers were allowed only one month from the field to care for their infants following their confinement. On this plantation, mothers of infants under six months old picked substantially less cotton than they did the year before, or even the year after when their children were older. Elizabeth, who managed to keep pace with some of the best hands, picked an average of 219 pounds each day in 1858. One year later, with a six-month-old child to tend, she averaged only 127 pounds, a decline of 42 percent. One black-belt planter complained he would be shorthanded during the 1835 cotton-picking season, in part, because one of his hands had "a young child to suckle." He must have had such declines in productivity in mind. Once their babies passed their first birthdays, the amount of cotton picked by mothers on the Lewis plantation increased, but not to levels achieved before the births of their children, indicating that even during the second year of life, babies placed demands on slave women that kept them from keeping pace in the field with childless women or women whose children were older.[26]

The falling productivity among new mothers in the Alabama cotton fields suggests that women withdrew from the fields for certain periods during the day to tend to their infants. Equally compelling evidence suggests, however, that the work routine experienced by new mothers remained rigorous enough to jeopardize the health of slave infants during the busiest times of year. Deaths of infants under one year of age peaked in September and October of 1850, the height of the cotton-picking season. As harvest drew to a close, the number of infant deaths fell to their lowest numbers in November and December. Infant deaths increased sharply in January, clearly the result of increased congestive ailments described in the records as whooping cough, pneumonia, and croup. A lull in the infant death rate followed in February that cannot be explained solely by the shortness of the month. As plowing began in March, infant deaths rose again to January levels. The mortality rate tapered off through spring as planting was completed, remained low as crops were laid by, and rose only slightly during the summer months before harvest began the cycle again.[27]

Whereas cotton production placed heavy demands on laborers for months at a time in the late summer and early fall, Virginia's mixed farming economy (tobacco, wheat and other cereal crops, and livestock) tended to spread the need for labor more evenly throughout the year. Intense periods of labor involving large numbers of slaves occurred during wheat harvests, but they were of short duration compared to cotton harvests. Thus, when mothers were forced to neglect infants during wheat harvests, the consequences were less catastrophic.

In both Alabama and Virginia, work routines that accommodated the needs of breastfeeding women and their infants succeeded in that enough infants survived to reproduce—even expand—the slave population. The heavy demands of the field, however, meant that infant care was sometimes neglected and the health of newborn babies taxed, particularly during the busy season.[28]

The need for infant care did not end at the completion of the work day. With nightfall, mothers assumed greater autonomy in caring for their infants. Plantation rules intended to ensure that fieldhands got a good night's rest so they could work at full capacity the following day were not applied to a mother who might be expected to be "up with her child" at night. Mothers willingly provided the care needed by their babies, but they often found it necessary to work while other slaves slept to ensure that their infants were fed, warm, clean, and dry.[29]

Nursing regulations applied only to daylight hours, and mothers apparently continued to breastfeed infants morning and night long after owners ceased allowing them to leave the field or interrupt other chores for this purpose. Many owners encouraged or acknowledged prolonged breastfeeding by denying infants under age two the weekly food rations they distributed to other members of slave families. Some of these children consumed meals prepared expressly for them by a caretaker or children's cook during the day, but the policy of withholding rations from infants under age two meant that many—probably most—mothers found it desirable to continue breastfeeding a baby through the infant's second year of life. The failure of owners to distribute rations to children under age two may have reflected a long-standing custom among African Americans of prolonged breastfeeding.[30]

*No one system* of child care predominated in either Virginia or Alabama, although nurseries—associated with larger plantations—were more prevalent in the Alabama black belt than in the Virginia piedmont.[31] Even on larger plantations, different methods of feeding and supervising infants were practiced, depending on such factors as the weather, seasonal demands for labor, the availability of older slave women or nearly grown girls to care for infants, and the type of work performed by mothers. Thus, different infants on the same plantation or farm experienced different arrangements for breastfeeding, and the same infant was cared for differently from time to time.

While slaves and owners shared an interest in the growth of the slave population and the development of slave children, they sometimes found themselves at odds with one another over the issue of infant nurture. The owners' overwhelming power gave them the ability to control by fiat, through direct intervention, and by subtle influences when mothers breastfed their children. Slave women countered this power, however, through direct confrontation, prolonged negotiations, and equally subtle influences. In the contest to determine how infants would be nurtured, mothers enjoyed particular advantages, including the common recognition that infants who were not breastfed might not survive.

The need to breastfeed infants encouraged slaves and slaveholders alike to believe that mothers should remain near their infants and assume primary responsibility for infant care. Slave parents and owners appreciated the dangers infants faced when left at the side of the field in inclement weather or alone in the cabins, however, and the trend in the antebellum period, at least on larger plantations, was toward the establishment of nurseries where infants could receive at least minimal supervision. Slave mothers accepted these arrangements when they believed their infants benefited from them, but in warmer weather, they insisted on keeping their babies with them at the side of the field. Owners agreed because the only alternatives were to release mothers from the field periodically to breastfeed their babies or to jeopardize the infants' health by offering them dietary supplements.

Owners relied on mothers to increase the size of their slaveholdings by bearing and nurturing children. Slave parents also counted on a mother's loving care to ensure the survival of infants, as well as to foster the loyalty of children to family and community. Fathers contributed indirectly to the task of infant nurture by supporting their wives with food, fuel, and other commodities as circumstances allowed, but they, too, considered mothers more suited by nature to caring for infants. The system of infant nurture that developed in the Alabama black belt and the Virginia piedmont reflected common notions held by owners and slaves about the importance of a mother's care for infant survival.

## NOTES

I gratefully acknowledge support for the research upon which this paper is based from the American Historical Association; Africa and Africa in the Americas Project; Virginia Historical Association; and Department of History, University of Maryland at College Park. I am also thankful for funding from the National Endowment for the Humanities, which provided financial support for writing the dissertation from which this paper is drawn. "At noon, oh how I ran" is taken from an 1847 untitled poem by William Wells Brown, reprinted in *Puttin' on Ole Massa,* ed. Gilbert Osofsky (New York: Harper and Row, 1969), 196. The epigram is quoted from the Texas Narratives, one of 41 volumes of Federal Writers' Project interviews, compiled by George P. Rawick four decades later as

*The American Slave: A Composite Autobiography* (Westport, Conn.: Greenwood Press, 1972–79). This collection is cited hereafter by series number and volume title.

1. One of the most distinguishing features of slavery in the American South was the ability of slaves to form families. A mere 4.5 percent of the more than ten million slaves delivered by traders to the New World between about 1550 and 1850 made their way to areas that now form part of the United States. Yet, on the eve of the Civil War, over four million slaves called the American South home. This slave population grew mainly because mothers bore children who survived infancy. In other New World slave societies, slaves usually died without progeny, and slaveholders relied on slave traders to reproduce their bonded populations.

The discovery in 1969 by Philip D. Curtin (*The Atlantic Slave Trade: A Census* [Madison: University of Wisconsin Press, 1969]) of the unique demographic pattern that characterized North American mainland slavery revised and invigorated the study of slavery. Numerous scholars considered the development of the slave family, debating its nature rather than its existence. Some—most notably Kenneth M. Stampp—labeled the slave family "matriarchal." See Stampp, *The Peculiar Institution: Slavery in the Ante-Bellum South* (New York: Vintage, 1956), 344. Other historians and social commentators substituted the term "matrifocal" to describe slave family life. See especially E. Franklin Frazier, *The Negro Family in the United States* (Chicago: University of Chicago Press, 1939), and Brenda Elaine Stevenson, "All My Cherished Ones" Ph.D. diss., Yale University, 1990, 415-16. Sen. Daniel Patrick Moynihan introduced the debate about the nature of the slave family (and more modern black families) into the American political agenda with the publication of *The Negro Family: The Case for National Action* (Washington, D.C.: U.S. Government Printing Office, 1965). Herbert G. Gutman rejected the concept of matrifocality as applied to slave families in his study, *The Black Family in Slavery and Freedom, 1750–1925* (New York: Pantheon, 1976), by arguing that most slave children lived in two-parent households. Other works that discuss the importance of two parents to slave households include Ann Patton Malone, *Sweet Chariot: Slave Family and Household Structure in Nineteenth-Century Louisiana* (Chapel Hill: University of North Carolina Press, 1992); Robert William Fogel and Stanley L. Engerman, *Time on the Cross: The Economics of American Negro Slavery* (New York: W. W. Norton, 1974). The notion that most slave children grew up in two-parent households has begun to figure in textbook descriptions of slave life. See, for example, Steven Mintz and Susan Kellogg, *Domestic Revolutions: A Social History of American Family Life* (New York: Free Press, 1988). Historians who emphasize the shared and complementary roles played by slave husbands and wives include Deborah Gray White, *Ar'n't I a Woman? Female Slaves in the Plantation South* (New York: W. W. Norton, 1985), especially 158–59, and Jacqueline Jones, *Labor of Love, Labor of Sorrow: Black Women, Work and the Family, from Slavery to the Present* (New York: Vintage, 1986), 32, 36–37. Orville Vernon Burton called the slave family "male dominated" and "patriarchal" in *In My Father's House Are Many Mansions: Family and Community in Edgefield, South Carolina* (Chapel Hill: University of North Carolina Press, 1985), 148, 164.

2. Information on the size and value of farmlands in Alabama and Virginia, as well as the sizes of slaveholdings, is drawn from U.S. Bureau of the Census, *Agriculture of the United States in 1860; Compiled from the Original Returns of the Eighth Census* (Washington, D.C.: Government Printing Office, 1864), 2, 154, 158, 162, 193, 218, 223, 243–45. James F. Woodruff describes black-belt estates in 1850. See Woodruff, "Some Characteristics of the Alabama Slave Population of 1850," *Geographic Review* 52 (July 1862). For a discussion of Dallas County, Alabama, in 1850, see James Oakes, *The Ruling Race: A History of American Slaveholders* (New York: Vintage, 1983), 249. For demographic and economic data on the Alabama black belt, the Virginia piedmont, and the rest of the South in the antebellum period, see Sam Bowers Hilliard, *Atlas of Antebellum Southern Agriculture* (Baton Rouge: Louisiana State University Press, 1984).

3. For a description of a typical Bedford County, Virginia, estate in 1850, see Cynthia A. Kierner, "Women's Piety within Patriarchy: The Religious Life of Martha Hancock Wheat of Bedford County," *Virginia Magazine of History and Biography* 100 (January 1992): 84. Lynda J. Morgan discusses size of worth of slaveholdings in Virginia in *Emancipation in Virginia's Tobacco Belt, 1850–1870* (Athens: University of Georgia Press, 1992), especially 19–22. For a discussion of the changing demography and economy of two northern piedmont counties in the antebellum period, see John Thomas Schlotterbeck, "Plantation and Farm: Social and Economic Change in Orange and Greene Counties, Virginia, 1716 to 1860" (Ph.D. diss., Johns Hopkins University, 1980), chaps. 3–8.

4. "Management of Cotton Estates," *DeBow's Review* 26 (May 1859), quoted in James O. Breeden, ed., *Advice among Masters: The Ideal in Slave Management in the Old South* (Westport, Conn.: Greenwood Press, 1980), 287; entries for 13, 14, 15, 22, 23 May 1846, Plantation Diary, vol. 2, Sturdivant Collection, Sturdivant Museum, Selma, Ala. (microfilm, Southern Historical Collection, University of North Carolina, Chapel Hill); Franklin, "Overseers," *Southern Cultivator* 2 (10 July 1844): 107; R.W.N.N., "Negro Cabins," *Southern Planter* 16 (March 1856): 121.

5. Rawick, *Mississippi Narratives,* suppl., ser. 1, vol. 7, 371 and *Alabama Narratives,* vol. 1, 256 of *American Slave*; Charles L. Perdue Jr., Thomas E. Barden, and Robert K. Phillips, eds., *Weevils in the Wheat: Interviews with Virginia Ex-Slaves* (Charlottesville: University Press of Virginia, 1992), 226–27.

6. Responses of James M. Davison and O. T. McCann, Nixon Questionnaire on Slavery, 1912–1913, Alabama Department of Archives and History, Montgomery; "Oliver Bell: That Tree Was My Nurse," in Virginia Pounds Brown and Laurella Owens, *Toting*

*the Lead Row: Ruby Pickens Tartt, Alabama Folklorist* (University: University of Alabama Press, 1981), 135; Rawick, *Alabama Narratives,* suppl., ser. 1, vol. 1 of *American Slave,* 99; R. W. Gibbes, "Southern Slave Life," *DeBow's Review* 24 (April 1858), in Breeden, *Advice among Masters,* 207–8.

Southern Renaissance writer and educator H. C. Nixon, best known as a contributor to *I'll Take My Stand, by Twelve Southerners* (New York: Harper and Brothers, 1930), distributed a questionnaire on Alabama slavery in 1912–1913. The survey, hereafter referred to as the "Nixon Questionnaire on Slavery," addressed such topics as slave housing, clothing, food, work, and child care. The majority of respondents were former slaveholders or members of their families, but informants included at least one and possibly two former slaves. The respondents' assessments of slaves and slavery reflected the racial prejudices of the time, but details on slave life and work did not differ in substance from those found in other sources, including planters' papers and interviews with former slaves conducted by government agents in the 1930s under the auspices of the Works Progress Administration and published by Greenwood Press as *The American Slave: A Composite Autobiography,* ed. George P. Rawick.

7. Rawick, *Alabama Narratives,* suppl., ser. 1, vol. 1 of *American Slave,* 426.

8. [Emphasis added.] *Southern Cultivator* 9 (June 1851): 88; Agreement with Overseer, Willis P. Bocock Papers, Southern Historical Collection, University of North Carolina, Chapel Hill. See also Mississippi Planter, "Plantation Management," *Southern Cultivator* 17 (June 1859): 169.

9. See "On the Management of Slaves," *Southern Agriculturist* 6 (June 1833), in Breeden, *Advice among Masters,* 51. Also see response of P. F. Mitchell, Nixon Questionnaire on Slavery. Rawick, *Alabama Narratives,* suppl., ser. 1, vol. 1 of *American Slave,* 449; Perdue, Barden, and Phillips, *Weevils,* 185, 323; Rawick, *Alabama Narratives,* suppl., ser. 1, vol. 1 of *American Slave,* 28.

10. (June 1849), quoted in Breeden, *Advice among Masters,* 168; Franklin, "Overseers," *Southern Cultivator* 2 (10 July 1844): 107; T. E. Blunt, "Rules for the Government of Overseers," *Southern Cultivator* 5 (April 1847): 61; "Rules for the Government and Management of ——— Plantation to Be Observed by the Overseer," in John Spencer Bassett, ed., *The Southern Plantation Overseer, as Revealed in His Letters* (Westport, Conn.: Negro Universities Press, 1972), 28.

11. A Mississippi Planter, "Management of Negroes upon Southern Estates," *DeBow's Review* 10 (June 1851); "The Duties of an Overseer," *Farmer and Planter* 8 (June 1857); and "Management of Cotton Estates," *DeBow's Review* 26 (May 1859), quoted in Breeden, *Advice among Masters,* 283, 205, 287. See also Mississippi Planter, "Plantation Management," *Southern Cultivator* 17 (June 1859): 169.

12. "Health of Young Negroes," *DeBow's Review* 20 (June 1856), quoted in Breeden, *Advice among Masters,* 284–85.

13. Rawick, *Texas Narratives,* suppl., ser. 2, vol. 9, 3541 and *Texas Narratives,* vol. 5,

1523 of *American Slave;* H. C. Bruce, *The New Man: Twenty-Nine Years a Slave, Twenty-Nine Years a Free Man* (1895; reprint, Miami: Mnemosyne, 1969), 14.

14. Entry for 8 May 1835, George Augustus Beverly Walker diary, Alabama Department of Archives and History.

15. "Ank Bishop: Gabriel Blow Soft! Gabriel Blow Loud!" in Brown and Owens, *Toting the Lead Row,* 126–27.

16. Entries for 6 and 29 December 1858, "Market Book," Mrs. W. G. Jones Papers, Alabama Department of Archives and History.

17. Rawick, *Alabama and Indiana Narratives,* ser. 1, vol. 6 of *American Slave,* 87–88.

18. Rawick, *Arkansas,* ser. 2, vol. 11, pt. 7 of *American Slave,* 42. Cheney Cross cared for a white baby who suckled the milk teat of a goat. See Rawick, *Alabama and Indiana Narratives,* ser. 1, vol. 6 of *American Slave,* 98.

19. Rawick, *Arkansas Narratives,* ser. 2, vol. 8, pt. 1 of *American Slave,* 241; Perdue, Barden, and Phillips, *Weevils,* 309. Cases of white women nursing black babies were uncommon in the South, as Sally G. McMillen maintains in *Motherhood in the Old South: Pregnancy, Childbirth, and Infant Rearing* (Baton Rouge: Louisiana State University Press, 1990), 129. This is because most slave women could and did nurse their own children, just as most planter women did. Owner and slave women surely nursed each other's children out of convenience on occasion, but such incidents are difficult to document.

20. *Plantation and Farm Instruction, Regulation, Record, Inventory and Account Book,* by a Southern Planter (Richmond, Va.: J. W. Randolph, 1852), 5, Philip St. George Cocke Papers, Virginia Historical Society, Richmond.

21. Robert Byrd Beverley to William Bradshaw Beverley, 20 June 1839, and Robert Byrd Beverley to Robert Beverley, 23 July 1841, Beverley Family Papers, Virginia Historical Society; B. M. Pearson to Samuel Pickens, 13 June 1842, Pickens Family Papers, Alabama Department of Archives and History. See also "Sarah Fitzpatrick," in *Slave Testimony: Two Centuries of Letters, Speeches, Interviews, and Autobiographies,* ed. John W. Blassingame (Baton Rouge: Louisiana State University Press, 1977), 641. McMillen, *Motherhood in the Old South,* 118, also Table 6, 193. McMillen estimates that the majority of white southern mothers (85 percent) breastfed their babies, while 20 percent relied on a wet nurse, and 10 percent fed their babies by hand, some employing more than one method. While McMillen's research did not focus on the two regions of the South studied here, there is no reason to believe that customs relating to infant feeding among the planter class varied significantly throughout the South. While some of the wet nurses employed by planter families were no doubt white, a significant number of slave mothers must have been recruited for this purpose from time to time. While many full-time wet nurses probably had babies who were weaned or who had died, occasional wet nurses must have come from the ranks of women who were nursing their own children simultaneously. Rawick, *Alabama Narratives,* suppl., ser. 1, vol. 1 of *American Slave,* 32.

22. Rawick, *Texas Narratives,* suppl., ser. 2, vol. 9, pt. 8 of *American Slave,* 3602. For an example of another slave raised on a bottle, see *Texas Narratives,* vol. 6, pt. 5 of *American Slave,* 2077. Benjamin Drew, *A North-Side View of Slavery. The Refugee; or, the Narratives of Fugitive Slaves in Canada* (1856; reprint, New York: Johnson, 1968), 71.

23. "The Duties of an Overseer," *Farmer and Planter* 8 (June 1857), quoted in Breeden, *Advice among Masters,* 205; "Rules of the Plantation," *Southern Cultivator* 7 (June 1849), quoted in Breeden, *Advice among Masters,* 168. McMillen states that physicians recommended weaning children between the ages of six and twelve months, although many women chose to breastfeed longer. See *Motherhood in the Old South,* 120–21. In her examination of childbearing and infant rearing in the nineteenth-century urban North, Sylvia D. Hoffert found physicians recommending gradual weaning to begin between the ages of nine and twelve months. Like McMillen, however, Hoffert found that mothers did not abide by any "hard-and-fast rules." See Hoffert, *Private Matters: American Attitudes toward Childbearing and Infant Nurture in the Urban North, 1800–1860* (Urbana: University of Illinois Press, 1989), 155–56. Rawick, *Alabama Narratives,* suppl., ser. 1, vol. 1 of *American Slave,* 449; Virginia Clay-Clopton, *A Belle of the Fifties: Memoirs of Mrs. Clay, of Alabama,* ed. Ada Sterling (1905; reprint, New York: Da Capo Press, 1969), 7.

Studies of childbearing among slave women support the pattern reported here, in which women breastfed babies for at least a year. See Robert William Fogel and Stanley L. Engerman, *Time on the Cross: The Economics of American Negro Slavery* (New York: W. W. Norton, 1989), 136–37. Cheryll Ann Cody found that on the Ball family plantation in South Carolina, mothers extended breastfeeding beyond eighteen months. See Cody, "Slave Demography and Family Formation: A Community Study of the Ball Family Plantations, 1720–1896" (Ph.D. diss., University of Minnesota, 1982), 173. See also Herbert S. Klein and Stanley L. Engerman, "Fertility Differentials between Slaves in the United States and the British West Indies: A Note on Lactation Practices and Their Possible Implications," *William and Mary Quarterly* 35 (April 1978): 369–70.

24. Perdue, Barden, and Phillips, *Weevils,* 323.

25. James M. Towns, "Management of Negroes," *Southern Cultivator* 9 (June 1851): 88; Rawick, *Alabama and Indiana Narratives,* ser. 1, vol. 6 of *American Slave,* 198.

26. Plantation Book of Mary Foreman Lewis, vol. 1, 1857–74, Lewis Plantation Records, Southern Historical Collection; John S. Haywood to George W. Haywood, September 1835, Ernest Haywood Papers, Southern Historical Collection. For references to the period of confinement, see *Plantation and Farm Instruction, Regulation, Record, Inventory, and Account Book,* 5, 29; Response of O. T. Mann, Nixon Questionnaire on Slavery; Plantation Record of James H. Ruffin, Ruffin, Roulhac, and Hamilton Family Papers, Southern Historical Collection.

27. Evidence from seven Alabama black-belt counties suggest that the work routines associated with cotton cultivation contributed to infant neglect and consequent infant mortality at certain times of year. Data from Marilyn Davis Hahn, comp., *Alabama Mor-*

*tality Schedule, 1850: Seventh Census of the United States* (Easley, S.C.: n.p.), 61–70, 80–91, 122–27, 141–49, 183–97, 203–7, 230–36. Counties analyzed were Dallas, Greene, Lowndes, Marengo, Montgomery, Perry, and Sumter.

28. The death rate among slave infants and children for the South as a whole rose in the period 1820 to 1850, leveling off or declining only in the decade before the Civil War, suggesting that infant and child neglect increased in these years. See Robert William Fogel, *Without Consent or Contract: The Rise and Fall of American Slavery* (New York: W. W. Norton, 1991), 128. Fogel discusses infant mortality among slaves in more detail, 142–47.

29. Rawick, *Mississippi Narratives,* suppl., ser. 1, vol. 8 of *American Slave,* 1062; Tattler, "Management of Negroes," *Southern Planter* 11 (February 1851): 41; Rawick, *Missouri Narratives,* ser. 2, vol. 11 of *American Slave,* 306.

30. *Plantation and Farm Instruction, Regulation, Record, Inventory, and Account Book,* 6. A study by Herbert S. Klein and Stanley L. Engerman of intervals between births among nineteenth-century slave women in the United States suggested that these women breastfed their children for a period of about one year. Their conclusion rested on the belief that breastfeeding retarded conception and accounted, at least in part, for differences in intervals of births between slave women in the United States and the British West Indies, who were believed to breastfeed infants for about two years. As Klein and Engerman acknowledge, however, the link between breastfeeding and contraceptive protection is far from clear. The connection between breastfeeding and lactation is complicated for slaves in the Alabama black belt and the Virginia piedmont, for many slave infants in these areas received supplemental foods from a very young age, particularly during the busy season. Slave women in these regions may have continued to breastfeed their infants at night for periods well beyond a year without repressing ovulation. If so, the breastfeeding experiences of these slave women paralleled those of British West Indies slave women and African women more closely than the study by Klein and Engerman suggests. See Klein and Engerman, "Fertility Differentials," esp. 358, 368–71, n. 35.

31. Rawick, *Alabama and Indiana Narratives,* ser. 1, vol. 6 of *American Slave,* 87–88.

*HÉLÈNE LECAUDEY*

# Behind the Mask

## EX-SLAVE WOMEN AND INTERRACIAL

## SEXUAL RELATIONS

 OD IS WONDERFUL to some us to spare us dis long, honey, to tell de tale." When Patience M. Avery was interviewed in 1937 by Susie R. C. Byrd, a Federal Writers' Project worker, she expressed to her interviewer her satisfaction and relief that her recollections of slavery, as well as those of other former slaves, should not be lost. Indeed, Mrs. Brown, another informant interviewed in Virginia, told Byrd that old friends had been meeting for years, taking pleasure and comfort in sharing their memories about "dem ole slave days."[1] These women were anxious to transmit their lived experiences, memories, and culture. The New Deal's Federal Writers' Project set out to provide employment to persons on relief and to give a voice to nearly 3,500 ex-slaves—men and women—throughout the South.[2] The Slave Narrative Collection is thus one of the few sources available for examining slave women's testimony on the institution of slavery and their own experiences, inclusive of their sexual experience.

In the past twenty years a major focus of slavery studies has been the slave family, community, and culture, and scholars have drawn heavily on the oral slave narratives, in concert with their search for evidence on the slaves' own perceptions of slavery. Revisionist historians have accentuated the strength of the slave family and the slaves' ability to create a culture of their own, one shaped by their African origins and their adaptive faculties in dealing with new surroundings. However, it may well be that this emphasis on the agency over their lives that slaves were able to maintain has led to an underplaying of the harshness of the institution. "Slavery was not only a brutal, but also a brutalizing experience," as Peter Kolchin put it, especially in the case of slave women who were specific targets of sexual exploitation.[3] And yet, ironically enough, the reality of this experience for the slave women as well as their perceptions have been largely ignored.

Traditional studies mentioning the sexual exploitation of slave women have emphasized its economic aspects (breeding) and its social aspects (forced mating and marriages), with its impact on the slave family as a whole and on the slave male psyche in particular. Several studies have dealt either with the white male perspective or the black male perspective. For example, in his *Roll, Jordan, Roll: The World the Slaves Made,* Eugene D. Genovese took into consideration the complexity of interracial liaisons and recognized their impact on southern life. And yet, his treatment of miscegenation (a term that emphasizes affectionate forms of interracial sexual relations according to Angela Y. Davis)[4] focused on the planter's perception of black-white liaisons. According to Genovese, testimonies from the slave narratives underlined both sexual abuse and genuine bonds of affection between slave women and their masters, but he dealt largely with the positive bonds.[5] In contrast, in his study of *The Slave Community: Plantation Life in the Antebellum South,* John W. Blassingame underlined the psychological devastation suffered by slave men as a result of the sexual abuse experienced by slave women. However, he also ignored its impact on the women.[6]

On the other hand, as early as 1937, at least one scholar had completed a comprehensive study of black-white sexual liaisons that devoted large sections to the slave woman's perceptions of this experience. James Hugo Johnston's *Race Relations in Virginia and Miscegenation in the South* showed that interracial liaisons had multiple facets and that it is extremely difficult to distinguish between sexual abuse and consent under a system that did not permit the individual much latitude. Yet this black historian noted that black-white sexual relations often took the form of sexual abuse — a specific extension to black women of the more general oppression of slavery.[7] As Joel Williamson has noted, while white women were sometimes involved in interracial liaisons, the most frequent patterns of interracial sexual relations involved white men (in particular upper-class slaveholders) and slave women (especially mulattos).[8]

Recently many studies have been devoted specifically to slave women and their experiences. But although sexual abuse is often mentioned to illustrate the workings of the institution as in some aspects of the slave woman's experience (for example, resistance, slave family, marriage, chil-

dren, or the effects on white female-male relationships), the perspective of
the slave women themselves in this regard has not been sufficiently taken
into consideration. And while slavery studies have stressed the agency slaves
retained over their lives, a particular example of this theme is to be found
in today's tales of slave women resisting sexual oppression.[9] It is clear, however, that acts of resistance were on an individual rather than collective level,
as Deborah Gray White, Elizabeth Fox-Genovese, and Melton A. McLaurin
have noted.[10] These historians have also argued that resistance was not a
"viable option," foremost because some form of retribution would follow,
either through physical violence (such as whippings, more abuse, or threats)
or through moral anguish (separation from their family or surroundings
when sold away). The impact that interracial sexual relations bore on the
slave family has been emphasized in most major studies. The intervention
of the master or of the white overseer in the sexual life of the slave woman
has been seen as an intrusion in the sexual life of the slave family, and served
as a reminder of the master's absolute power over the most intimate aspects
of their lives. It was a factor of disruption that often bore on the marriages
(though these had no legal recognition) and relationships between female
and male slaves. Moreover, the impact on children could be devastating:
they were made aware at an early age of the rules of the institution and of the
hopelessness and utterly dependent status of slaves. Deborah Gray White
and Paula Giddings have also underlined the anxiety of slave women who
feared rape of their daughters by black or white men.[11]

Clearly some historians are redefining traditional approaches and emphasizing sexuality as an operative tool to further our understanding of the
institution. Melton McLaurin calls for "a comprehensive theory with which
to evaluate the manner and degree to which the sexual exploitation of female
slaves influenced the routine operations of the institution of slavery."[12]
Catherine Clinton states that "sexuality is a central and significant element"
in the system of power devised by the slave society.[13] Victoria E. Bynum notes
that the sexual abuse of slave women by white men "marked the distinct
convergence of racial, sexual, and economic systems."[14] Nell Irvin Painter
emphasizes how sexual competition between white and black women (competition from the white women's perspective) affected antebellum families
and society.[15] Darlene Clark Hine shows how a "culture [of dissemblance]
born of rape and fears of rape shaped the course of black women's history."[16] And recently historians have sought to discover sources illuminating
the sexual experience and perspectives of slave women themselves.

Melton McLaurin has illustrated this approach in *Celia, a Slave,* a case study of a slave woman's sexual exploitation. Celia was a nineteen-year-old slave who, in 1855 in Missouri, was tried for the murder of her master; he had raped her when she was fifteen and had fathered her two children. Although Melton McLaurin did not have access to Celia's own testimony to tell her story, he was able to reconstruct her experience by weaving together pieces of evidence originating from sources such as court and census records, local histories, and newspapers. Thelma Jennings has based a study of the sexual exploitation of slave women on the oral slave narratives. She addressed the main issues underlined by Melton McLaurin and Catherine Clinton: the institution of slavery as a system of economic "reproduction" using the bodies of slave women, a system of social and sexual control through forced marriages and mating, and a system that established its oppression by the constant threat of sexual abuse and physical violence.[17] And that Jennings was able to give a voice to the slave women themselves on the different aspects of the institution after examining the oral slave narratives suggests the narratives' potential richness as sources revealing the sexual experience of these women. On the other hand, these narratives undoubtedly pose special interpretative challenges that must be addressed.

Some scholars have expressed concern with the nature of the interviews and the role played by the informants and the interviewers themselves. They have charged that the interviewers were amateurs, with unscientific techniques, and that few were aware of the biases inherent in the interviewing situation, especially the racial bias. Moreover, the informants were often destitute blacks striving under the Great Depression, who hoped to get relief through the white interviewers (and these did not always state the purpose of their visits). The age of the informants in particular has led to debates: most of the ex-slaves were over eighty years old. On the one hand, some historians have argued that the ex-slaves could not be representative of the slave population because their very age testified to a favored treatment under slavery and also because, as children, they had not fully experienced slavery.[18] Moreover, some have found older people's memory to be unreliable.[19] On the other hand, Norman R. Yetman has found that the narratives by the oldest slaves were the most descriptive, while Paul D. Escott, relying on psychological studies, has argued that age did not impair memory.[20] But other historians, such as Jerrold Hirsch, have sought to clarify the value of the ex-slaves' testimony by evaluating the interactive process between the two persons taking part in a "conversational narrative" set against a specific cultural background.[21] George P. Rawick and John W. Blassingame have also called attention to the comparative study of individual narratives as well as sets of narratives compiled by the same interviewer.[22] Further, the narratives abound with stories told to the former slaves by their parents or relatives. They must thus be seen as the repository of an oral tradition, which transmitted the lived experiences and culture of the slaves and which shaped the knowledge and the vision of themselves that the ex-slaves interviewed were able to partake with their interviewer.[23]

This author's own research in interracial sexual relations shows the possibility and potential rewards of developing a theoretical framework that, through recognition and analysis of the biases inherent to the oral slave narratives, can illuminate to what extent and how these narratives can validly be interpreted as expressive of the actual experience and perspectives of former slaves, particularly of women. This framework has been developed on the basis of my own research comparing sets of interviews by fieldworkers, black and white, in two states: Virginia, where most of the interviewers were black, and South Carolina, where most of the interviewers were white. Only the conversations conducted by interviewers whose race was ascertained were retained for the purpose of this study. In South Carolina, ten out of ninety-seven female informants (10.3 percent) mentioned black-white liaisons to seven interviewers. In Virginia, fifteen out of sixty-one female informants (25 percent) described interracial sexual relations to five interviewers. Within the states, this researcher's choice of interviewers was based on their gender, race, and the number of interviews they recorded, as well as on the number of informants who referred to black-white sexual relations. Susie R. C. Byrd, a black fieldworker in Virginia, interviewed twenty-one former slave women, six of whom mentioned black-white liaisons. In South Carolina, W. W. Dixon was a white fieldworker who conducted interviews with twenty-one female informants, four of whom told him about this topic.

In order to evaluate the bearing and influence of the interviewers and their possible biases on the interviewing situation, it was useful to know their position and role in their community (fieldworkers often lived in the area where they conducted the interviews). Such information could sometimes be gathered from the narratives themselves through a textual analysis that provided some insights into the general perceptions and attitudes of the interviewers. Certainly it is clear that a significant element in the interviewing process was the web of relationship between black/former slave and white/dominant white in the 1930s segregationist era. For example, two studies published around that time were intended to assess the role and influence of these unequal race relations on the interviewer. Robert Russa Moton, a black writer, analyzed the discriminations to which blacks were subjected at the time and their reactions. And Bertram Wilbur Doyle, a white sociologist, presented a scholarly study of what he and others have termed the "etiquette of race relations."[24]

Doyle's research demonstrated that distinct rituals still controlled the social relationships of the two races in the 1930s, which reflected the continuing reality that the status of blacks had not changed dramatically since the days of slavery. Contemporary forms of address were especially revealing in this respect. Blacks were expected to use a reverent "Sir" or "Mrs./Ma'am" with whites, while blacks would be commonly referred to by their Christian names or appellations such as "Uncle" or "Aunt." Similarly Robert Moton exposed various forms of derogatory appellations reminiscent of the status of slaves, and also clarified the consequent feelings of humiliation and inferiority experienced by blacks. The word "nigger" was the most resented, followed by terms such as "negress," "darky," and "coon." The word "Negro" he deemed acceptable depending on the spelling. As for terms of direct address, Robert Moton stressed that appellations such as "Aunt" and "Uncle" were resented by blacks because they connoted a disrespectful familiarity from whites. He also found blacks resentful at whites' unwillingness to use formal forms of address such as "Mr." or "Mrs." Throughout the Slave Narrative Collection, elderly persons were generally referred to or called by their Christian names (preceded sometimes by "Aunt" or "Uncle") by white interviewers. In short, it is clear that the etiquette used under slavery still prevailed in the 1930s. These studies also clarify that the race of the interviewers was a major factor in the interviewing process and that its final product, the narrative, needs to be analyzed in terms of forms of address and tone to reveal the interaction between interviewer and interviewee. For these reasons, the sets of interviews underpinning this author's essay have been carefully analyzed in terms of the form of each text.

It is obvious that W. W. Dixon, the white male fieldworker in South Carolina, addressed his informants or referred to them according to the prevalent etiquette analyzed by Moton and Doyle. And with regard to black women, his forms of address denoted a condescending attitude toward a person seen primarily as inferior on the social scale—as a black woman as well as an ex-slave — thus creating a very hierarchical relationship between them. In this context the former slave women's responses to questions showed restraint and an awareness of the social distance and the racial etiquette separating them from their white interviewer. On the other hand, although Susie R. C. Byrd, the black female interviewer in Virginia, did not record the forms of address she used, we have another source of information on which to rely, namely, her own notes, which clarify her use of courteous appellations for ex-slaves (i.e., "Rev. Brown," "Mr. Brown," or "Sir" and "Mr. and Mrs. Brown"). Moreover, the narratives themselves show that, in response to their interviewer, familiar and affectionate terms predominated when informants addressed Susie Byrd, and thus, in all likelihood, more honest responses were expressed in this context, rather than what was in accordance with racial etiquette.[25]

Certainly informants addressed black and white interviewers in very different ways. While the former slave women demonstrated a deferential attitude toward W. W. Dixon, they clearly felt much more comfortable with Susie Byrd and did not hesitate to use familiar expressions with her. And it is precisely these findings that can be brought to bear upon analysis of what these interviews can tell us about the experience and perceptions of these former slave women.

A comparison between the narratives compiled by Byrd and by Dixon does show significant differences in the way former slave women talked about their experience of slavery and about the slaveholders. Byrd had organized several meetings with a large group of former slaves in Petersburg, Virginia, and she noted the keen interest in "Negro history" that she and the former slaves shared.[26] As a result, her informants dwelt significantly more on their own perspectives and achievements and less on their owners' families than the white interviewer's informants in South Carolina. Indeed, several interviews conducted by Dixon make it clear that he was well known among the former slaves and the former planters' families in the Winnsboro community (his mother was a member of a slaveholding family). The interviewees gave many details on the slaveholding families and connections, sometimes at Dixon's own stated request, but only sparse information on the slave families themselves. For example, one ex-slave woman kept asking Dixon whether he was acquainted with her former "young mistresses," while another reminded him of her own father, who used to be the interviewer's "Uncle Remus" and would tell some Bible tales to black children only, thus implicitly suggesting that the white interviewer would also get a bowdlerized version of her own recollections.[27] Indeed, a textual analysis reveals the major impact that the race and gender as well as the expectations of the interviewers bore on the reported recollections of the former slave women.

Certainly it becomes clear that the question of interracial sexual relations deserves much more specific scholarly attention as a major aspect of the slave women's experience, and that the study of the ex-slave women's oral narratives in the light of black-white sexual relations can richly enlighten this particular aspect of the institution of slavery from the black woman's perspective.

For example, the interviews clarify that, among the four informants who mentioned interracial sexual relations to their white interviewer, W. W. Dixon, in South Carolina, three had had a mulatto or white father or grandfather. Delia Thompson's grandfather was white, "and no poor white trash neither," and she referred to her descendants as belonging to the "colored aristocracy" of the town.[28] Although Thompson seemed proud of her white connections, she did not disclose her grandfather's name, nor did she give any details concerning her paternal grandmother or the circumstances under which sexual intimacy had occurred between her grandparents. Similarly, Rosa Starke remained evasive on the relationship between her grandparents and their races; she only mentioned that her father was "a half white man." Dixon merely asked if she had anything more to tell him about slavery in general.[29] Obviously, Dixon did not wish to hear more on this highly sensitive subject in the 1930s. Similarly, Sena Moore stated that her grandfather was a free "blue-eyed nigger," but again, this informant did not give any details either on her grandfather's parents or on the way her grandfather had become free—whether he had been manumitted or had been born free.[30] Again, the white interviewer lost a chance to learn more, for his next question pertained to money.

These three narratives by Delia Thompson, Rosa Starke, and Sena Moore present striking resemblances, not only in the type of information given to the white interviewer, but also in the form this information was given. They consist of mere statements without any details as to the circumstances and meaning of the interracial liaisons that occurred, the impact on the actors and their reactions, or the reactions of the informants themselves. No one mentioned the grandmother or great-grandmother who had been involved in these sexual relations. The white interviewer, on the other hand, never followed up on cryptic statements, and he even changed the subject of the conversation in two cases. The informants did not voice any opinion or perspective on the situation. One of them, though, seemed to express pride at her white ancestry. An important point here that also links these testimonies is that these women apparently volunteered their information; an obvious reason for this would be that one paternal ascendant having been white or mulatto, the fact could not escape the attention of the interviewer (Delia Thompson referred early in her interview to her light complexion), who could also have been cognizant of the situation since he was well acquainted with the community — black and white — in Winnsboro, as several narratives clarify.[31]

Another aspect of interracial sexual relations revealed in these oral narratives involves the offspring of the informant's own mother or female relatives with the white master. In South Carolina, Savilla Burrell talked about her firsthand memory in this respect during slavery, but her testimony must be analyzed step by step to reveal what really happened. Burrell gave a sarcastic description of her master's second wife who, as a widow, had managed to "captivate" Tom Still, a wealthy planter, but whose marriage did not prove a happy one. As Burrell stated, "Her had her troubles with Marse Tom after her git him, I tell you, but maybe best not to tell dat right now anyways." Later on, Savilla Burrell mentioned her mother's grief when one of her children was sold away, and she told how the slave owner scolded her mother for crying and threatened to whip her if she did not stop. Dixon interrupted her at this point and asked her about clothing. Clearly, as the slaveholder had refused to hear the slave woman's utterance of pain, the white interviewer did not want to hear more about this topic. Subsequently, Burrell shifted from the recollection of her mother's grief, which she was not allowed to express, to that of the slaveholding woman, and she revealed what type of trouble the latter had had with her husband: "Old Marse was de daddy of some mulatto chillun. De 'lations wid de mothers of dese chillun is what give so much grief to Mistress." This tense aspect of the slave-owner couple's relationship must have been important to Savilla Burrell for her to come back to it, and it might also have been a way for this informant to testify to the general tension that prevailed on that plantation. She added: "He [Tom Still] would sell all dem chillun away from dey mothers to a trader. My Mistress would cry 'bout dat." Burrell gave pieces of information here and there, and we need to fit them together, as in a puzzle, thus recognizing the significance of the interviewer's race and potential bias, to understand the relationships involved: master-mistress and master/mistress-slave woman.[32]

Savilla Burrell's phrasing concerning the sale of "one of [her] mother's chillun" (she did not refer to that child as one of her siblings) takes another dimension when we learn that the slaveholder had mulatto children whom he would sell. It seems fair to assume that the child of Burrell's mother whom the informant mentioned was a mulatto daughter or son fathered by the slave owner. The two women, mistress and slave woman, black and white, shared grief and helplessness, but the slave woman was powerless to prevent being separated from her child, and she was not even allowed to express her grief. Savilla Burrell's mother was apparently not the only slave woman with whom Tom Still had sexual relationships. Burrell referred to the mothers (in the plural form) of his mulatto children. Tom Still entertained sexual relationships with several slave women, had no qualms about selling his offspring away, and threatened Burrell's mother with a whipping to stop her from expressing her grief. In this case, interracial liaisons evidently took the form of recurrent sexual abuse. The evidence further suggests that the slave owner did not experience positive feelings toward his slave mistresses or his mulatto children. And it is clear that even if these slave women had been consenting partners, these sexual relations did not improve their lot in life or that of their children.

It is also significant that Burrell did not explain to Dixon the slave women's point of view on this very intimate part of their lives. This ex-slave woman did mention her mother's grief at the sale of her child, but she dwelt much more on the grief of her mistress over her husband's sexual relationships with slave women. Nowhere did she give any hint as to the slave woman's feelings—or hers, for that matter. She was as noncommittal on the impact sexual abuse had on slave women's personal experiences and their family life. On the contrary, she presented a white perspective on the issue. And yet, we can still get some insight into her own feelings at the end of her interview when she recalled Exodus 15 at Tom Still's deathbed. "I went to see him in his last days and I set by him and kept de flies off while dere. I see the lines of sorrow had plowed on dat old face and I 'membered he'd been a captain on hoss back in dat war [the Civil War]. It come into my 'membrance de song of Moses: 'de Lord had triumphed glorily and de hoss and his rider have been throwed into de sea.' " Thus, despite the biases present in the interviewing situation, and despite the white interviewer's obviously negative attitude, this testimony does shed some light on the workings of that plantation. Slave women were used as breeders by the slaveholder, who added to his wealth by selling his mulatto children. Clearly, tension ran high on the plantation, between the slave women and the slaveholder, between the slave women and the mistress, and also between the slaveholder and his wife. Moreover, tension was not restricted to the plantation itself; it permeated the local community: Burrell mentioned that the white neighbors "talked" about these black-white liaisons, and clearly unanimity did not prevail in matters of morality and roles within the white class. On the other hand, as already mentioned, this ex-slave woman could not express the slave community's point of view to her white interviewer.[33]

However, in Virginia, an ex-slave woman's testimony made it clear that some members of the black community experienced a deep resentment toward the white slaveholders who thus intruded into the most intimate aspects of their lives and that this resentment could be transferred onto the very symbol of these interracial sexual relations, the mulatto offspring. Patience M. Avery told her black interviewer, Susie Byrd, about her white father, the son of her mother's owner. This informant had a vivid memory of her first encounter with her father when he came to visit her mother and meet his daughter after the Civil War. Avery had not been told about him, and her emotion was still perceptible when she shifted from the past tense to the present tense in her narration. Certainly, her disbelief ("He no father o' mine! He white!") reflected the ambivalence that interracial liaisons carried in the black community. Moreover, the cruel treatment the orphaned Avery experienced later at the hands of her own kinfolk, because she was mulatto, testifies to the continuing anger and bitterness that ran in the black community.[34]

Another informant, Octavia Featherstone, was also fathered by a white man in Virginia, but she said she did not know her father's name, and she did not give many details about him to Susie Byrd. Her mother was free, as the informant insisted, and this interview was included in this research because the few elements the informant disclosed seemed to hint at an unusual pattern, namely, intermarriage between a white man and a black/mulatto woman. In antebellum Virginia, intermarriages were not strictly prohibited as they would be after the Civil War (and would still be in the 1930s, at the time of the interviews), but they were heavily sanctioned by fines and banishment, as well as years of servitude for the mulatto children of such liaisons.[35] Featherstone's grandmother had mixed ancestry—Indian, Irish, and presumably black as well. Featherstone stated she had never seen her father, but she was aware that he was white. Her mother had married twice and had borne children to both her husbands. She added: "I don' know de name of de first husban'. I've never seen my daddy to know him, but he was a white man." However, she knew the name of her mother's second husband. Apparently, her father had been white and had been killed in the Civil War.[36] Featherstone's reluctance to provide specific details to Susie Byrd might have been due simply to the fact that she had not been enslaved, and thus she considered that her experience was not relevant for the interviewer's purposes. On the other hand, it might also reflect the continuing stigma attached to black-white liaisons in the 1930s and the reluctance to speak of them as a personal experience, even to a black interviewer. The fact that Octavia Featherstone was probably a well-known member of the community—she was one of the organizers of the Zion Baptist Church—might also account for this reluctance.[37]

However, without ambiguity, Liza McCoy and Mary Wood told Susie Byrd, their black interviewer, about relatives who bore their master's children and were ultimately sold away. Liza McCoy's narration was short, yet she mentioned right away that her aunt had been sold away from her infant child, a "white baby by her young master. Dats why de sold her south." This informant also mentioned, without details, that her mother was used as a breeder by the slaveholder.[38] Mary Wood's Great-aunt Fannie was also sold down South. She had had three children by her owner who, according to Wood, "thought . . . much of her." When Betty Snead, the slaveholder's wife, surprised both of them in a barn, she "rared and charged so the next week they sold Fannie."[39] Apparently it took Betty Snead a long time to realize that Fannie's "three white chillun" were fathered by her husband. On the other hand, one must bear in mind the often cited remark by Mary Boykin Chestnut: "Every lady tells you who is the father of all the mulatto children in everybody's household, but those in her own she seems to think drop from the clouds, or pretends so to think."[40] Betty Snead had preferred to ignore some disturbing facts until she could not keep pretending. In this case, the angry and jealous wife succeeded in having Fannie sold away (Mary Wood did not mention the fate of the children; apparently they were not sold together). There might have been some affectionate bond between the slave woman and her married master since their relationship had been continuous for several years. Fannie had had some advantages from her position: she would not be whipped, would refuse to obey orders ("She would get stubborn sometimes. Her ole mistress would tell her to do something and if she didn't feel like hit, didn't do hit."), and may have hoped for a betterment of her children's status. But clearly such a position was very insecure. The relationship between the slaveholding couple prevailed, and Fannie's fate did worsen since she was sold away and separated from her family.[41]

Similarly, two other informants in Virginia volunteered information on obvious cases of sexual abuse. Fannie Berry told her black female interviewer the illuminating story of Sukie, a strong-headed slave woman whom her owner kept trying to seduce. Exasperated, he ordered her one day to take off her dress so that he could whip her. "She tole him no." A short fight ensued: "Den dat black gal got mad. She took an' punch ole Marsa an' made him break loose an' den she gave him a shove an' push his hindparts down in de hot pot o' soap. . . . It burnt him near to death. . . . Marsa never did bother slave gals no mo'."[42]

There are several telling details in this story. It is striking to find such concrete evidence that some slave women expressed their refusal to play an active role in their own physical oppression. Sukie refused to become a participant and humiliate herself by stripping in front of her tormentor, which would have provided him with sexual and sadistic satisfaction. Fannie Berry's crisp and short expression, "She tole him no," embodies all the flat determination—and courage—of the slave woman. Moreover, as such testimony reflects, in some instances slave women defended themselves against physical abuse. Sukie not only resisted her owner victoriously, she also humiliated him in her turn through the rather melodramatic episode of the boiling soap. Such narratives confirm that, on an individual level, slave women could react to threats of sexual abuse and avoid it, thereby also providing a striking example of resistance to the slave community. In Sukie's case, the lesson was also carried home to the slaveholder, who never approached slave women again. But it should be noted that the consequences were also disastrous for Sukie, since she was sold to a trader a few days afterwards.

Minnie Folkes was one of those informants to whom recollections of slavery brought intense pain. She did not "like to talk 'bout dem times 'cause [her] mother did suffer misery." Asked by Susie Byrd to recall slavery times, the images that came to her mind were the "whelps an' scars" on her mother's body that she had seen "fer [her] own self wid dese heah two eyes." Recalling the beatings her mother suffered, she became suffused with pain and anger, and interrupted the flow of her memories to express her hatred: "Lord, Lord, I hate white people and de flood waters gwine drown some mo'."[43] Certainly this informant's testimony in Virginia shows that her mother refused to enter into a sexual relation with the white overseer and was repeatedly and viciously beaten. It also speaks volumes about the continuing anger of a daughter and about the tragic experience imposed on the children of such abused mothers.

Certainly Fannie Berry's and Minnie Folkes's narratives do illuminate the perspectives of both ex-slave and slave women. They testify to the courage, will, and strength of slave women who refused to comply with the demands of their owners whatever the consequences and who forced the admiration of their relatives and friends in such a way that their story was fixed in the memory of these women more than seventy years later. They are also striking examples of the endurance and attempt of slave women to make choices, even under a system that did not permit them much latitude, and to try to play an active role, even though limited. In fact, these informants' testimony in Virginia demonstrates the dual experience that these slave women lived. Clearly the ex-slave women's testimonies in Virginia and to some extent also in South Carolina suggest that the violation by the dominant whites of their sexual integrity was deeply resented by slave women. It is significant that with respect to this particularly intimate aspect of master-slave relations, ex-slave women depicted an experience fraught with tension, violence, and abuse that left little room for any feeling of mutual obligations and certainly did not provide slave women with the security and moral guidance that a paternalistic master was supposed to offer.

It is clear that the narratives of ex-slave women are not equally revealing in South Carolina and Virginia. In South Carolina the race and biases of the white male interviewer evidently shaped and repressed the expression of ex-slave women's own feelings and memories. And in this context, any and all references by these women to interracial sexual relations deserve careful and respectful attention, as well as recognition that even under such circumstances they could reveal something of their own perspectives. Indeed, Savilla Burrell managed to convey her perceptions and recollections of what the sexual exploitation of slave women had represented to her and the women she knew, in spite of her white male interviewer's clear wish to delete her feelings and memories in this respect from the record.

In comparison, the black female interviewer in Virginia clearly provided much more freedom for these women to express their own perspectives, and thus she was able to collect substantial accounts of the ex-slave women's perceptions of the impact and various forms of interracial sexual relations. Indeed, these Virginia narratives provide especially telling testimonials of slave women's own perceptions of "miscegenation."

However, analysis of the ex-slave women's oral narratives in the light of the framework used as above suggests that these narratives can in sum and in total, richly be used to uncover the sexual experience of slave women and to illuminate the perspectives of these women, when careful attention is brought to the context—and in particular, to the role of race and gender— in shaping the extent to and ways in which ex-slave women could and did voice their own perceptions.

Certainly, attention to the ex-slave women's oral testimonials may counter-balance sources that either ignore or romanticize the realities of interracial sexual relations under slavery or else devote very little attention to the per-spectives of slave women. Indeed, although "miscegenation" remains a par-ticularly sensitive topic in slavery studies, the testimonials of the ex-slave women who dared and wished—like Patience Avery—"to tell de tale" are clearly deserving of attention.

## NOTES

1. Patience M. Avery, in Charles L. Perdue Jr., Thomas E. Barden, and Robert K. Phillips, eds., *Weevils in the Wheat: Interviews with Virginia Ex-Slaves* (Charlottes-ville: University Press of Virginia, 1976; Bloomington: Indiana University Press, 1980), 15, 386.

2. Norman R. Yetman, "Ex-Slave Interviews and the Historiography of Slavery," *American Quarterly* 36 (summer 1984): 202. George P. Rawick has published most of the interviews in *The American Slave: A Composite Autobiography*, 41 vols., series 1 and 2, supplement series 1, and supplement series 2 (Westport, Conn.: Greenwood Press, 1972, 1977, 1979). Perdue, Barden, and Phillips have recovered all the interviews collected in Virginia by the FWP fieldworkers.

3. Peter Kolchin, "American Historians and Antebellum Southern Slavery, 1959-1984," in *A Master's Due: Essays in Honor of David Herbert Donald*, ed. William J. Cooper Jr., Michael F. Holt, and John McCardell (Baton Rouge: Louisiana State Univer-sity Press, 1985), 94. See also Peter Kolchin's *American Slavery, 1619-1877* (New York: Hill and Wang, 1993), 148-51.

4. Angela Y. Davis, *Women, Race, and Class* (New York: Random House Vintage Books, 1983), 25.

5. Eugene D. Genovese, *Roll, Jordan, Roll: The World the Slaves Made* (New York: Random House Vintage Books, 1976), 415-19.

6. John W. Blassingame, *The Slave Community: Plantation Life in the Antebellum South,* rev. ed. (New York: Oxford University Press, 1979), 164-65, 172-73.

7. James Hugo Johnston, *Race Relations in Virginia and Miscegenation in the South, 1776-1860* (Ph.D. diss., University of Chicago, 1937; Amherst: University of Massachusetts Press, 1970).

8. Joel Williamson, *New People: Miscegenation and Mulattoes in the United States* (New York: Free Press, 1980), 42-53. On interracial sexual relations, see also Martha Hodes, "Wartime Dialogues on Illicit Sex: White Women and Black Men," in *Divided Houses: Gender and the Civil War,* ed. Catherine Clinton and Nina Silber (New York: Oxford University Press, 1992), 230-42.

9. See Deborah Gray White, *Ar'n't I a Woman? Female Slaves in the Plantation South* (New York: W. W. Norton, 1985), 76-88; Harriet A. Jacobs, *Incidents in the Life of a Slave Girl, Written by Herself,* ed. Jean Fagan Yellin (Cambridge: Harvard University Press, 1987).

10. White, *Ar'n't I a Woman?* 76, 78; Elizabeth Fox-Genovese, *Within the Plantation Household: Black and White Women of the Old South* (Chapel Hill: University of North Carolina Press, 1988), 308, 325-26; Melton A. McLaurin, *Celia, a Slave* (Athens: University of Georgia Press, 1991), 116-17.

11. White, *Ar'n't I a Woman?* 95-96, 152-53; Paula Giddings, *When and Where I Enter: The Impact of Black Women on Race and Sex in America* (New York: William Morrow Bantam Books, 1988), 43-45.

12. McLaurin, *Celia,* 116.

13. Catherine Clinton, " 'Southern Dishonor': Flesh, Blood, Race, and Bondage," in *In Joy and in Sorrow: Women, Family, and Marriage in the Victorian South, 1830-1900,* ed. Carol Bleser (New York: Oxford University Press, 1991), 52.

14. Victoria E. Bynum, *Unruly Women: The Politics of Social and Sexual Control in the Old South* (Chapel Hill: University of North Carolina Press, 1992), 5.

15. Nell Irvin Painter, "Of *Lily,* Linda Brent, and Freud: A Nonexceptionalist Approach to Race, Class, and Gender in the Slave South," *Georgia Historical Quarterly* 76 (summer 1992): 241-59.

16. Darlene Clark Hine, "Rape and the Inner Lives of Southern Black Women: Thoughts on the Culture of Dissemblance," in *Southern Women: Histories and Identities,* ed. Virginia Bernhard, Betty Brandon, Elizabeth Fox-Genovese, and Theda Perdue (Columbia: University of Missouri Press, 1992), 177-89.

17. Thelma Jennings, " 'Us Colored Women Had to Go Through a Plenty': Sexual Exploitation of African-American Slave Women," *Journal of Women's History* 1 (winter 1990): 45-74.

18. See David Thomas Bailey, "A Divided Prism: Two Sources of Black Testimony on Slavery," *Journal of Southern History* 46 (August 1980): 385-86, 403.

19. David P. Henige, *Oral Historiography* (New York: Longman, 1982), 117.

20. Norman R. Yetman, ed., *Life under the "Peculiar Institution": Selections from the Slave Narrative Collection* (New York: Holt, Rinehart and Winston, 1970), 5; Paul D. Escott, *Slavery Remembered: A Record of Twentieth-Century Slave Narratives* (Chapel Hill: University of North Carolina Press, 1979), 6–7.

21. Jerrold Hirsch, "Reading and Counting," *Reviews in American History* 8 (September 1980): 312–15.

22. Rawick, *American Slave*, Suppl., ser. 1, vol. 11, John W. Blassingame, ed., *Slave Testimony: Two Centuries of Letters, Speeches, Interviews, and Autobiographies* (Baton Rouge: Louisiana State University Press, 1977), liv–lv.

23. Benjamin A. Botkin, ed., *As I Lay My Burden Down: A Folk History of Slavery* (Chicago: University of Chicago Press, 1945), 14.

24. Robert Russa Moton, *What the Negro Thinks* (New York: Doubleday, Doran, 1929); Bertram Wilbur Doyle, *The Etiquette of Race Relations in the South: A Study in Social Control* (1937; reprint, Port Washington, N.Y.: Kennikat Press, 1968).

25. Perdue, Barden, and Phillips have published Susie R. C. Byrd's "Notes on Interviewing Ex-Slaves" in *Weevils*, appendix 8, 383–88.

26. Ibid., 384–86.

27. Violet Guntharpe, in Rawick, *American Slave*, ser. 1, vol. 2, pt. 2, *South Carolina Narratives*, 216; hereafter, all references to the South Carolina Narratives, will be cited only by volume, part number, and page. Charity Moore, ibid., vol. 3, pt. 3, 205.

28. Ibid., vol. 3, pt. 4, 161–62.

29. Ibid., 150.

30. Ibid., vol. 3, pt. 3, 210.

31. Rosa Starke's statement to Dixon (at the end of her interview) reads like this: "My pappy, you know, was a half white man." This expression could be a mere figure of speech, but it might as well remind the interviewer of a fact he was aware of: ibid., vol. 3, pt. 4, 150.

32. Ibid., vol. 2, pt. 1, 149–50.

33. Ibid., 150–51.

34. Perdue, Barden, and Phillips, *Weevils*, 15–16. See also Jacqueline Jones, *Labor of Love, Labor of Sorrow: Black Women, Work, and the Family from Slavery to the Present* (New York: Basic Books, 1985), 38; Brenda Stevenson, "Distress and Discord in Virginia Slave Families, 1830–1860," in *In Joy and in Sorrow*, ed. Bleser, 103–24.

35. Johnston, *Race Relations*, 172–74; Williamson, *New People*, 8.

36. Perdue, Barden, and Phillips, *Weevils*, 90.

37. Virginia Hayes Shepherd acknowledged her high sensitivity about being the daughter of a slave woman and a white man to her black female and male interviewers in Virginia: ibid., 255. Allen Wilson, also interviewed by Susie Byrd in Virginia, mentioned Octavia Featherstone's role in the organization of the church: ibid., 329.

38. Ibid., 199–201.

39. Ibid., 332.

40. C. Vann Woodward, ed., *Mary Chestnut's Civil War* (New Haven: Yale University Press, 1981), 29.

41. Perdue, Barden, and Phillips, *Weevils,* 332.

42. Ibid., 48–49.

43. Ibid., 92–93.

MARLI F. WEINER

# Mistresses, Morality, and the Dilemmas of Slaveholding

## THE IDEOLOGY AND BEHAVIOR OF

## ELITE ANTEBELLUM WOMEN

IN AUGUST 1856, Ella Gertrude Clanton Thomas, daughter of one wealthy Georgia planter, wife of another, and the mother of one small child, wrote in her diary: "Judy and Maria Jones are expecting to be confined in a month or two and in that condition I think all women ought to [be] favoured. I know that had I the sole management of a plantation, pregnant women should be highly favored. A woman myself, I can sympathise with my sex, wether [*sic*] white or black."[1] Judy and Maria Jones were, of course, slaves, and one reason Thomas may have felt sympathy for them was that they were probably part of the generous marriage settlement provided by her father and so well known to her. Another reason Gertrude Thomas was sympathetic was that she had suffered both a premature birth and a miscarriage, shortly after the birth of her son. Even so, for Thomas to identify with these slave women on the basis of their common experiences with pregnancy and childbirth and to question both the conventional morality and customary practices of her society on that basis suggests the importance of examining plantation dynamics through a gendered lens. Thomas clearly believed that being female led her to view slave women with a degree of sympathy not possible for men and in spite of the vast race and class differences that separated her from these women. Her comment, presumably written quickly and unselfconsciously during a pause in a busy day, raises fundamental questions about the nature of elite white women's power, morality, authority, and oppression in the antebellum South.

*Nineteenth-century American* society defined the ideal woman (who was assumed to be white and at least middle class) as the moral superior of man.[2] Her piety and purity, virtue and benevolence placed her far above men, whose days were spent in the rough-and-tumble world of competitive business and politics. The only power men willingly granted to women through this ideology of female domesticity was the power of moral authority, a position accepted by southern social critic, political economist, and essayist Louisa McCord. Well connected among South Carolina's elite families and owner of a plantation near Columbia, McCord published in the antebellum South's most important journals aimed at men. She claimed:

> Woman's duty, woman's nature, is to love, to sway by love, to govern by love, to teach by love, to civilize by love! . . . Pure and holy, self-devoted and suffering, woman's love is the breath of that God of love, who, loving and pitying, has bid *her* learn to love and to suffer, implanting in her bosom the one single comfort that she is the watching spirit, the guardian angel of those she loves. . . . Each can labour, each can strive, lovingly and earnestly, in her own sphere.[3]

Women's moral authority was indeed powerful—within her home.

The ideology of domesticity, which delineated spheres of appropriate activity for men and women in all parts of the nation, took a peculiar form in the slaveholding South, where the presence of slaves and cavalier traditions of paternalism and chivalry combined to create a wrinkle on conventional wisdom elsewhere.[4] For example, southern poet Mrs. S. A. Dinkins offered women a set of directions for conventional behavior:

> Minister to those whom God has plac'd within your reach,
> And lessons of philanthropy and charity thus teach!
> I've read your heart, I knew it well, its latent powers, too.
> Oh! do not let them dormant lie, while there's so much to do!
> Brood not in idleness, but let your sympathies extend,
> To those who need a kindly voice, a sister or a friend.[5]

In the slaveholding South, elite white women were expected to extend the net of their moral benevolence widely, encompassing not only their own family, sisters, and friends, but also their slaves. Indeed, white women's moral universe was supposed to include all needy recipients of care. One father publicly advised his newly married daughter how to arrange domestic concerns effectively: "Unite liberality with a just frugality; always reserve something for the hand of charity; and never let your door be closed to the voice of suffering humanity. Your servants, in particular, will have the strongest claim upon your charity;—let them be well fed, well clothed, nursed in sickness, and never let them be unjustly treated." [6]

Another contemporary writer urged southern womanhood to follow a less direct approach to the same end. "Under the elevating and benign influences of christianity [*sic*], she proceeds to subdue, to reform, to elevate, to ennoble, and to perfect every thing around her; and by this supernatural power, she so softens the affections and refines the feelings of the lords of creation, as to dispose them to ameliorate the condition of classes of his fellow beings still more abject." [7]

Southern women writers were especially likely to encourage women to behave charitably toward slaves. Maria McIntosh made the connection between domesticity and benevolence toward slaves quite explicit in her directions to southern women. "Especially should the gentle care of woman not be withdrawn from the home of the slave. She should be there to interpose the shield of her charity between the weak and the strong, to watch beside the sick, to soothe the sorrowing, to teach the ignorant, to soften by her influence the haughty master, and to elevate the debased slave." [8] McIntosh refused to comment on the morality of slavery, considering that to be the responsibility of men because only they make the law. Even so, she believed women's "benevolence and charity should be a law unto themselves, softening the pressure of the fetters which they cannot break, and lightening the darkness which they may not wholly dispel." [9]

Writers of didactic fiction also urged white southern women to think of the needs of slaves, as did the mother in a story called "The Selfish Girl" published in a magazine for southern girls. "Do you think servants are so destitute of feeling, that you have so little consideration for them? Remember that although they belong to you, and you can do as you please with them, you will hereafter have to give an account of your conduct to them. . . . Believe me, my child, if we do not think of the comforts of others, we shall neither be respected nor valued ourselves, and shall find few friends."[10]

A character in Mary Eastman's 1852 novel, *Aunt Phillis's Cabin,* made the connection directly: "[A planter's wife] must care for the health and comfort of her family, and of her servants. After all, a hundred servants are like so many children to look after."[11] Slaveholding women, whether they wanted moral responsibility for slaves or not, were clearly charged by their society to behave in ways that recognized their fundamental humanity.

The parameters of white women's expected moral behavior were clear, but the distance could be great between what women were told to do and what they actually could do and were willing to do. Gertrude Thomas, after all, truly wanted to be able to allow pregnant women time off from field labor, but could not: her husband, like all planters, set the rules for work on their plantation. Why, if southern society defined white women as moral caretakers of slaves, did Thomas and women like her feel unable to act on the responsibilities their society defined for them? The answers are complex. Some elite white women did make efforts to mediate some of the harshest aspects of slavery, to the best of their abilities given the circumstances of their lives, their relations with their husbands and individual slaves, and the limits to their ability to perceive what slaves wanted and needed.[12]

*Many elite women* clearly believed that the moral injunctions defining the ways they should treat slaves required them to ameliorate the worst conditions of slaves' lives. Thus, they provided several types of direct and indirect assistance to their slaves, particularly to the women. Some provided material goods. For example, when Sophia Watson's slave Patience was ill, her mistress feared for her ability to survive but comforted herself by telling her husband, "Whatever she fancies to eat I get for her if I can—Eveline attends to her room—keeps things clean and nice about her."[13] Eugenia Woodberry's mistress "carr[ied] em nice basket uv t'ing eve'y time dey wuz sick," in addition to the medicine she mixed herself from ingredients gathered in the woods.[14] Some mistresses tried to prevent slaves from being punished, as Ben Horry informed an interviewer for the Federal Writers' Project. "Anybody steal rice and they beat them, Miss Bessie cry and say, 'Let 'em have rice! My rice—my nigger!' "[15] Nelson Cameron remembered his mistress also protected slaves from punishment. "Her mighty good to de slaves. Take deir part 'ginst de marster sometime, when him want to whup them."[16]

Other mistresses ameliorated the harshness of slavery in other ways. For example, on two separate occasions, the DeRosset sisters of North Carolina persuaded their father to purchase the husband of a female slave to avoid breaking up the marriage.[17] Gus Feaster recalled the time his mother and another slave woman were sexually accosted by the overseer and threatened with whipping when they refused his advances. The slaves pushed him into some blackberry bushes and "put out fer de 'big house' fas' as our legs could carry us." Once there, the mistress was called. "She come and ax what ailing us and why we is so ashy looking. Well, my Mammy and old lady Lucy tell de whole story of dey humiliations down on de creek." Feaster's mistress dismissed the overseer on the spot, even though her husband was away and the overseer questioned her authority to do so.[18]

Women's efforts to mediate the worst aspects of slavery stemmed from genuine feelings of concern and not simply from pecuniary considerations. Slave mistress Ada Bacot spent at least one afternoon reading to a dying slave woman, and Mary Ross Banks's mother read to a paralyzed woman unable to do more than knit.[19] On the other hand, there were important limits to what white women did or thought they could do, as Thomas's complaint about her inability to help the pregnant women suggested. The location of those limits, the line between cultural prescriptions of white women's moral responsibility and the reality of wealthy mistresses' behavior, offers clear insight into the dynamics of daily life and gendered realities on the plantation.

Mistresses recognized the extent of their moral responsibility for slaves and often struggled with their inability to conform to the behavior expected of them. Lucilla McCorkle was typical. From 1846 to 1858 she filled a combined diary and commonplace book with material quoted and clipped from newspapers and periodicals that defined the virtues to which women should aspire. She also wrote frequent assessments of her progress in living up to her ideals. Usually she found herself falling far short of her goal. In 1852 she berated herself: "I have to confess a want of patience & forbearance towards forward & slothful servants." On another occasion she complained, "Our servants are a source of discomfort. There is a lack of confidence so necessary to the comfort of that relation. O for more forbearance. . . . I pray to be divinely directed."[20] Catherine Edmondston also struggled to live up to expectations in her dealings with slaves:

> This teaching of negroes is a sore problem to me. It ought to be done
> & I ought to do it. I am afraid I magnify the Lions in the Path because it

is disagreeable. . . . My difficulties I am convinced beset many a well intentioned mistress who like me because she cannot do what she feels she *ought* does *nothing.* It is not right. I ought to do something, but I do not know what. . . . We are put here with a heavy responsibility on our shoulders which we do not discharge aright.[21]

One of the most ferocious lions in the path of mistresses was the daily struggle to compel the labor of slave women. Encouraged to do so in the spirit of nurturing benevolence, the realities of slavery made violence or the threat of violence far more common mechanisms for accomplishing the multitude of tasks necessary for domestic survival than mistresses liked to admit. Slave women could—and did—behave in ways mistresses found exasperating, and mistresses whose self-esteem as wives, mothers, hostesses, and neighbors depended on slaves' work were often frustrated.

Slaves offered testimony about the results. Susan Merritt's mistress was brutal: "Lots of times she tie me to a stob in the yard and cowhide me till she give out, then she go and rest and come back and beat me some more. . . . She stomp and beat me nearly to death and they have to grease my back where she cowhide me and I'se sick with fever for a week. If I could have a dollar for every cowhidin' I get, I'se never have to work no more."[22] Dinah Cunningham's mistress only beat her once: "I had de baby on de floor on a pallet and rolled over on it. Her make a squeal like she was much hurt and mistress come in a hurry." After comforting the baby, the mistress cut a switch from a tree and beat the mother.[23] Yet mistresses who resorted to violent punishments usually found it a difficult experience, as Ada Bacot noted when several of her slaves behaved unacceptably: "I had a most unpleasant duty to perform. . . . I had to go this morning & see them punished. My very soul revolted at the very idea, but I knew if I let it pass I would have more trouble so I thought the best way was to have a stop put to it at once. I hope I shall have nothing more of it." On another occasion, Bacot found one of her slave women idle with nothing but a sullen look for an explanation. "I could have had her well wiped [*sic*] . . . but I commanded my self, so far as [possible] to order her to get to work instantly."[24]

Keziah Brevard was also frustrated by what she saw as impudent and lazy slaves and her own uncertainty about the best remedy. Sometimes she found herself "compelled to speak harshly to them." Although she claimed she was never "cross to my servants without cause," she believed she had taken "gross impudence hundreds of times & let it pass unpunished." However, Brevard believed that punishment was sometimes necessary, and she apparently did not hesitate to use it. "I have slaves under my care—some are very good—never give the least trouble—but I have a few terrible spirits to keep in order. Some we manage by kindness, some nothing but the fear of punishment will restrain in the least." Her slave Sylvia was one of those she thought needed frequent punishment. Brevard complained often about Sylvia's impudence, her slow and careless work, and her own inability to make Sylvia change: "Nothing on this earth can change her heart—it is a bad one." Sylvia and her three sisters were "just as impudent as they desire to be, whipping did very little good and good treatment made them think themselves better than white people." [25] Like most mistresses, Brevard thought of herself as kind to her slaves, although her catalog of laziness and impudence scolded and punished lasted as long as she kept her diary. And like other mistresses, she agonized over each decision to use the whip and claimed her slaves' failings as her own. Whether mistresses applied the whip themselves or caused a surrogate to do so for them, it was for many women an immediate solution to a distressing problem, used in anger and often accompanied—or followed—by uncertainty. Even premeditated violence intended to correct what mistresses perceived as chronic problems caused some women to feel guilty and inadequate even as they were determined to make slaves' behavior conform to their wishes. Moral expectations of white womanhood were indeed difficult to sustain in the face of recalcitrant slaves and the pressures of daily life.

Mistresses who simultaneously beat their slaves and bemoaned their inability to behave as their society taught them they should behave typically chastised themselves for failure without crediting their accomplishments—or acknowledging the difficulties they faced. In fact, their moral behavior required the cooperation of husbands who were often unwilling to share their wives' points of view. White men may have defined women as guardians of morality, but they did not necessarily behave according to women's notions of what was proper. In spite of such obstacles, some mistresses persisted in their efforts. When one slaveholder became so angry he vowed to kill a slave named Leonard, Miss Sally ran to Leonard's aid. A former slave described what happened next:

> She run up to Marse Jordan an' caught his arm. Old Marse flung her off an' took de gun from Pappy. He leveled it on Leonard an' tole him

to pull his shirt open. Leonard opened his shirt and stood dare big as er black giant sneerin' at Ole Marse.

Den Mis' Sally run up again an' stood 'tween dat gun an' Leonard.

Ole Marse yell to Pappy an' tole him to take dat woman out of de way, but nobody ain't moved to touch Mis' Sally, an' she didn' move neither; she jus stood there facin Ole Marse. Den Ole Marse let down the gun. He reached over an' slapped Mis' Sally down, den picked up de gun an' shot er hole in Leonard's ches' big as yo' fis'. Den he took up Mis' Sally an' toted her in de house.[26]

Violence always threatened when white women used their moral authority to try to help slaves, and clearly most women considered Miss Sally's example too dangerous to follow. Former slave Hayes Shepherd reported the results when a slave named Diana asked her mistress to protect her from being raped by her master: "The mistress sympathized with the girl, but couldn't help her, because she was afraid of her own husband. He would beat her if she tried to meddle. Indeed he would pull her hair out."[27] White men held the ultimate authority in the South, and that authority extended over their wives as well as over the slaves their wives tried to help.

Certainly, white women who considered risking their husbands' wrath too dangerous to their own personal or emotional safety were directly confronted with the moral dilemmas of slaveholding. The contradiction between their views of how they thought women should behave, which reflected their understanding of the ideology of domesticity, and what was actually possible in their daily lives could be great. Mistresses knew how much self-discipline was required to treat slaves in light of the way they thought they should behave, and they struggled to attain the qualities of character and temperament they considered necessary. But maintaining their own self-control could be a simple task compared with the additional frustrations these white women confronted from external sources: husbands, as well as other agents of slaveholding society who limited their freedom of action such as overseers, creditors, ministers, and other community authorities. The slaves themselves resisted. In actuality, mistresses simply did not have free reign in determining how slaves should be treated.

The moral authority white women were granted by their society could really only be expressed through influence—a weapon singularly lacking in effectiveness. Charged with the responsibility for upholding moral standards and the fair treatment of slaves, mistresses had few tools with which to accomplish their mission. The personal dilemmas they encountered as a result of their own relative ineffectiveness in shaping slavery reinforced their frustration with their ultimate powerlessness to live up to their own expectations. Mistresses could never forget the moral dilemmas imposed by slaveholding; they lived with them on a daily basis. The moral choices they made directly influenced their perceptions of both themselves and their society. Thus, in a significant sense, elite white women's moral dilemmas helped challenge the efficacy of the slaveholding regime, making their failure to resolve those dilemmas all the more tragic and historically meaningful.

Mistresses' moral dilemmas were compounded by the actions of slaves themselves, particularly the behavior of the slave women with whom they worked most closely. Not only were slave women reluctant to follow the rules of labor imposed by mistresses; they also clearly resented white women's power over their lives. While slaves were usually pleased by whatever assistance white women provided, their acceptance of care rarely took the form of the grateful loyalty mistresses considered their due. Instead, slave women knew in complete detail the discrepancies between the behaviors expected of white women and their actual activities; their presence and behavior could and often did serve as a persistent reminder of mistresses' failings. Slaves' behavior was seldom unproblematic, and their independence sometimes forced mistresses to unpleasant conclusions about the consequences of their ministrations. White women who struggled to behave the way their society told them they should and to resolve the moral dilemmas posed by slaveholding did so in a context in which slaves both actively resisted their influence and tried to live autonomous lives. At the same time they took advantage of their assistance. Although few mistresses recognized slaves' resistance as anything other than recalcitrance, slaves' activities nevertheless made the moral difficulties these mistresses faced even more troubling.

*Perhaps the most* difficult moral dilemma southern white women faced resulted when their beliefs about the way they should behave toward slaves conflicted with their beliefs about sexual morality. In this context, white men's behavior was a source of profound frustration and moral anxiety for white women. Taught that sexual purity was an essential component of their own identity and moral power, white women naturally expected no less of their husbands. The men, of course, had other ideas, and southern society offered few censures for men who slept with—raped—slave women. Wives were dismayed by white men's behavior but were often unable to do anything about it, because criticizing men was dangerous in every sense of the word: it could provoke violence, cause rejection, and generally make life miserable. Instead, these wives generally directed their anger toward black women, transforming them from targets of white men's sexual aggression into shameless seducers. White women reacted this way primarily to the slave women who were the objects of their *husband's* attentions. Slave women who were the sexual targets of overseers or other low-status white men could be viewed with a good deal of sympathy by mistresses, as was Gus Feaster's mother, whose complaints caused the overseer's dismissal.[28] The moral confusion facing mistresses whose husbands were sexually active with slave women was potentially much more intense as they tried to reconcile views of slave women as needy, defenseless, and childlike recipients of their care with images of these women as tempters and seducers of white men.

Harriet Jacobs, author of a narrative detailing the sexual abuses she had experienced and observed as a slave in North Carolina, was sharp in her criticism of the way her mistress resolved this contradiction.

> Mrs. Flint possessed the key to her husband's character before I was
> born. She might have used this knowledge to counsel and to screen
> the young and the innocent among her slaves; but for them she had no
> sympathy. They were the objects of her constant suspicion and ma-
> levolence. . . . I was an object of her jealousy, and, consequently, of her
> hatred; and I knew I could not expect kindness or confidence from her
> under the circumstances in which I was placed.

But even Jacobs admitted that not all mistresses made the same moral choice that Mrs. Flint did.

> I have myself known two southern wives who exhorted their husbands to
> free those slaves towards whom they stood in a "parental relation"; and
> their request was granted. These husbands blushed before the superior
> nobleness of their wives' natures. Though they had only counselled them
> to do that which it was their duty to do, it commanded their respect, and
> rendered their conduct more exemplary. Concealment was at an end,
> and confidence took the place of distrust.[29]

Jacobs did not indicate the impact of such events on these white women's marriages or their relations with slaves.

The moral dilemmas posed by the tension between sexual jealousy and elite women's beliefs about how they should behave toward slaves could be resolved in varying ways. Most, like Mrs. Flint, placed a higher priority on white sexual "virtue" than on the circumstances of slave women. In spite of Mary Chesnut's comment that "every lady tells you who is the father of all the mulatto children in everybody's household, but those in her own she seems to think drop from the clouds, or pretends so to think," white women thought often about the connections between sexuality and slavery. Chesnut, writing in her diary about the sexual politics of slavery from her vantage point among the Confederate elite, certainly knew the two were linked.

> I wonder if it be a sin to think slavery a curse to any land. . . . Men &
> women are punished when their masters & mistresses are brutes &
> not when they do wrong — & then we live surrounded by prostitutes.
> An abandoned woman is sent out of any decent house elsewhere. Who
> thinks any worse of a Negro or Mulatto woman for being a thing we can't
> name? God forgive *us,* but ours is a *monstrous* system & wrong & iniq-
> uity. . . . [L]ike the patriarchs of old our men live all in one house with
> their wives & their concubines.

When Chesnut saw a woman sold in Montgomery, Alabama, she reported feeling faint and tried hard to explain the situation to herself. "I sat down on a stool in a shop. I disciplined my wild thoughts. . . . You know how women sell themselves and are sold in marriage, from queens downward, eh? You know what the Bible says about slavery — and marriage. Poor women. Poor slaves."[30] Chesnut's willingness to link marriage and slavery and her sympathy for all the female victims of white men suggests that she understood morality and oppression in rather different terms than those favored by most defenders of slavery. Chesnut knew that efforts at moral behavior and belief in slavery as a beneficial system had no meaning in the face of white men's superior power.

Chesnut was not the only white woman who linked sexuality and slavery and came to conclusions at odds with the predominant way of thinking in the South. Gertrude Thomas, who had been so sympathetic with her preg-nant slaves, also concluded that slavery degraded women of both races. She was angered by the plight of light-skinned slave women and by the implications of their treatment for southern morality. Light-skinned slave women, she felt, were

> subject to be bought by men, with natures but one degree removed from the brute creation and with no more control over their passions — subjected to such a lot are they not to be pitied. I know that this is a view of the subject that it is thought best for women to ignore but when we see so many cases of mulattoes commanding higher prices, advertised as "Fancy girls," oh is it not enough to make us shudder for the standard of morality in our Southern homes?

Miscegenation destroyed family life, but Thomas despaired of finding a solution. She believed that she, like other white women, was powerless to solve a problem she did not create.

> There is an inborn earnestness in woman's nature to teach her to do right, but this is a mystery I find I cannot solve — Southern women are I believe all at heart abolitionists but then I expect I have made a very broad assertion but I will stand to the opinion that the institution of slavery degrades the white man more than the Negro and oh exerts a most deleterious effect upon our children.[31]

Thomas also criticized the sexual double standard prevalent in the South that condemned white women for transgressions that not only did not bring any criticism to white men but could elevate them in the eyes of other men. Thomas's concern with the morality of slavery may have been a result of her discomfort with the behavior of the men in her own family. Her father, Turner Clanton, was also the father of several children by a slave woman named Lurania Clanton; Nell Irvin Painter suggests Thomas's husband may have fathered a slave child at about the same time her own first child was born.[32] Moral issues were never far from daily life in the plantation South.

As Chesnut's and Thomas's comments suggest, elite women's moral dilemmas could lead them to rather heretical views regarding slavery. Such views are not uncommon in the papers of plantation mistresses. Many mistresses grounded their doubts about slavery on the threat it presented to the bonds of marriage and family among slaves and whites. Their regrets regarding the necessity of separating slave families and their complex reactions to interracial sex were for some a short step away from discontent with the institution that caused these things. Eliza Ann DeRosset explicitly connected her reluctance to separate slave husbands and wives with doubts about the morality of slavery. She confided her concerns to her sister Mary Curtis: "Poor Fanny is in trouble—her husband's master sent for him to Fayetteville about a fortnight ago and intends carrying him to the West. . . . It is really a sin to separate them they are so affectionate—is not it the most deplorable thing connected with slavery—I wish it were possible to prevent it." [33]

Kate Stone Holmes also struggled with the moral implications of slavery:

> As far as Mamma could, the Negroes on our place were protected from cruelty and were well cared for; they were generally given Saturday evening and had plenty to eat and comfortable clothes. Still there were abuses impossible to prevent. And constantly there were tales circulated of cruelties on neighboring plantations, tales that would make one's blood run cold. And yet we were powerless to help. Always I felt the moral guilt of it, felt how impossible it must be for an owner of slaves to win his way into Heaven. Born and raised as we were, what would be our measure of responsibility? [34]

While Holmes's comments clearly bear the stamp of hindsight, sympathy for slaves and the impulse to aid them were genuinely felt even at the time. Slaveholding presented a responsibility and a moral dilemma these women could not ignore.

Those wealthy white women who sympathized with slaves and who were sensitive to the practical and moral responsibilities they represented did not want to abandon the institution of slavery. Most kept their discomfort to themselves or articulated it in contradictory and ambivalent terms to female correspondents; they did not develop a program to end slavery nor could they imagine a world without it. Relatively few turned their sense of sympathy with the plight of slaves and discomfort with the moral responsibilities of slaveholding into questions about the institution itself. Although they were critical of slavery, they acknowledged its legitimacy. Rather than confront the consequences of their moral dilemmas, these white women chose only to hedge, perhaps because they knew the risks were high. For example, shortly before the outbreak of war, Keziah Brevard expressed her doubts about slavery, or at least about fighting to defend it, in her diary. "I think we all have some, the fewest in number, who would not butcher us—but I am sure the most of them aim at freedom—tis natural they should and they will try for it. O that God would take them out of bondage in a peaceable way. Let no blood flow. We are attached to our slaves." [35]

Other white women responded to the moral dilemmas posed by slavery by defending it while at the same time urging it be practiced in a more humane manner. Late in the war, Mary Jones, widow of Presbyterian minister and slave missionary Charles Colcock Jones, promised, "If we ever gain our independence there will be radical reforms in the system of slavery as it now exists. . . . [W]e shall be free to make and enforce such rules and reformations as are just and right." [36] Others did not wait so long to urge reforms. Letitia Burwell insisted that her "mother would as soon think of selling her children as her servants." [37] Susannah Sutton, like many other women, imposed financial sacrifice on her heirs when she stipulated in her will that her slaves should not be separated but "kept as much together as possible or conveniently can." [38] Former slave Houston Holloway reported in his autobiography that his aunt Suasan's [*sic*] master bought her back from the slave trader to whom she had been sold. According to Holloway's autobiography, the master suffered several sleepless nights during which he could not erase the images of Suasan leaving her husband and of his own wife's broken heart. [39] Even Louisa McCord, an ardent defender of slavery, claimed that the institution was not only established by God but in the South was "beautifully developing to perfection, daily improving the condition of the slave, daily waking more and more the master to his high and responsible position." [40]

Still other white women reacted to the moral dilemmas posed by slavery by arguing that there were no dilemmas at all. These women were convinced that white women lived up to the moral demands made of them without frustration or contradiction; consequently, they contributed to elevating slaves from savagery. The daily difficulties of living with slaves, from sexual jealousy to compelling them to work, were incidental to the greater good that white women accomplished as mistresses. For example, southern novelist and essayist Mary Howard Schoolcraft was, she said,

> so satisfied that slavery is the school God has established for the conversion of barbarous nations, that were I an absolute Queen of these United States, my first missionary enterprise would be to send to Africa, to bring its heathen as *slaves* to this Christian land, and keep them in bondage until *compulsory* labor had tamed their beastliness, and civilization and

Christianity had prepared them to return as missionaries of progress to their benighted black brethren.

The teachers in God's school for slaves, according to Schoolcraft, were mistresses.

> [S]he has not only every principle of self-interest to urge her to be up and doing at sunrise; but from her very nursery she is taught that the meanest creature on God's earth is a master or mistress who neglects those that Providence has made utterly dependent on them. Her conscience, educated to this self-denying nobility of action, would feel as wounded by the neglect of her helpless children as by disregard for her hard working slaves.

Schoolcraft believed that rather than feeling frustrated by their inability to reconcile moral requirements with daily realities, mistresses should congratulate themselves for their accomplishments as married women.

> But the moment she becomes a planter's wife, her domestic talents grow by the square-yard every year; for by a quick transformation, she is changed from a laughing, thoughtless flirt, seeking only to make herself beautiful and admired, into a responsible, conscientious "sister of charity" to her husband's numerous dependents.

Rather than berate themselves for their moral failing to reconcile the dilemmas of slaveholding, mistresses should recognize the extent of their sacrifices:

> I am certain that wives have suffered more intense, more hopeless anguish, from brutal, non-appreciative husbands, than any slave has ever experienced, since God first gave the command to his people to bring heathen nations into bondage to his Christian nations; for the slave being made, by the mercy of his Creator, property, secures a more undying interest, in a selfish master's heart, than a wife, who can be so easily replaced, particularly when her husband begins to get tired of her; which is so often the case.[41]

In this view, women suffered because of Eve's transgressions. Schoolcraft thought the surest way for them to improve their situation was to defer to men, even if specific men were not worthy of deference. No matter how inferior men were or how imperfect a society they had created, they were still superior to women, who had little choice but obedient acceptance of their destiny. To admit a moral dilemma about slavery was, for Schoolcraft, to question God's will; acceptance of male authority was the only path to follow to a moral life.

Mary Howard Schoolcraft was not the only white woman to accept slavery as a moral institution without acknowledging contradiction. Louisa McCord was convinced that human society was "improving, improvable, ceaselessly and boundlessly" and that slavery was inherent in human progress.[42] Women were the agents of progress; as such, they could have no doubts about their goals:

> Her mission is one of love and charity to all. It is the very essence of her
> being to raise and to purify wherever she touches. Where man's harder
> nature crushes, her's exaults [*sic*]. Where he wounds, she heals. . . . God,
> man and nature alike call upon her to subdue her passions, to suffer, to
> bear, to be meek and lowly of heart; while man, summoned by nature,
> and often by duty, to the whirl of strife, blinded in the struggle, forgets
> too often where wrath should cease and mercy rule. What, then, more
> beautiful than woman's task to arrest the up-lifted arm, and, in the name
> of an all-pardoning Heaven, to whisper to his angry passions—"Peace,
> be still!"[43]

Here we have come full circle: McCord enjoined women to behave according to a moral code that defined them as protectors of slaves, but rather than acknowledging that that code contained inherent contradictions or that men's behavior made it impossible to follow, she insisted that women bear their suffering meekly and fulfill their tasks.

*White women's idealized* moral authority, and the demands and dilemmas it imposed upon them, provoked responses ranging from preliminary and apolitical rejections of slavery itself to ever more insistent demands that women do what their society expected of them. Given most elite white women's genuine efforts to conform to those expectations, antebellum society imposed an impossible position on them. Still the question remains: If the pressures of daily life with slaves were so difficult and witnessing the transgressions of white men with slave women so painful, why were so few white women able or willing to question out loud the institution that caused their difficulties? Why did women like McCord and Schoolcraft—the most intellectually prominent white women of the South—turn their attention to enforcing moral injunctions rather than challenging the institutions of their society? Perhaps the best answer suggests that white women who struggled to behave according to moral precepts thought they were in fact challenging slavery as it was commonly practiced. They genuinely believed in women's moral superiority and assumed that their efforts on behalf of slaves would be truly beneficial for all. Wealthy women saw themselves as mediators of slavery, a role that gave purpose to their daily struggles to compel slave labor and meaning to their efforts to subdue their own tempers and transgressions and those of their husbands. In their view, the difficulties they faced were not the result of anything fundamentally wrong with the institution of slavery itself. Challenging slavery overtly was simply too dangerous a position for them to take: it smacked of the heresies of women's rights and abolitionism. Instead, while women acknowledged the difficulties of their situation, they often blamed themselves for their failings as individuals. Some were able to recognize themselves as oppressed and regretted their lack of power; some even made reference to themselves as slaves. Caroline Rush claimed, "As a general thing, the greatest slave on a plantation is the mistress. She is like the mother of an immense family, of some fifty up to five or six hundred children." [44] Caroline Howard Gilman was even more direct. "However well educated and disciplined in domestic duties housekeepers may be, they are still slaves to the ignorance and caprice of others." [45] But even such personal identification with the plight of slaves was an unsatisfactory method of resolving white women's moral dilemmas. That resolution would eventually be made for them, when northern guns and the demands of slaves combined to make the moral question moot.

As long as slavery lasted, even when white women acknowledged the limits slavery imposed on their autonomy and the difficulties of their roles as mediators, the moral dilemmas remained. Plantation mistresses, facing the difficult realities of daily life on the plantation, were left with no room to maneuver. Taught that as women they were more moral than men and charged with upholding the morality of their society, they took seriously the requirement that they ameliorate the suffering of slaves. Taught that they were inferior to men and punished for even the slightest challenges to male authority, they found ameliorating suffering an almost impossible undertaking. And yet the concern they showed for the lives of slaves and the efforts they made to improve the quality of their lives in whatever fashion they could were dramatic given the circumstances. When Gertrude Thomas said she sympathized with pregnant slaves and regretted her inability to relieve them of field labor, she offered eloquent testimony indeed to the difficulties not only of slave women but of white women as well.

## NOTES

Abbreviations used in notes:

Duke: Manuscript Department, William R. Perkins Library, Duke University, Durham

LC: Manuscript Division, Library of Congress, Washington, D.C.

S.C. Archives: South Carolina Department of Archives and History, Columbia

UNC: Southern Historical Collection, Louis Round Wilson Library, University of North Carolina at Chapel Hill

USCar: South Caroliniana Library, University of South Carolina, Columbia

AS: *The American Slave: A Composite Autobiography,* ed. George P. Rawick, 41 vols. (series 1 and 2, supplement series 1 and 2) (Westport, Conn.: Greenwood Press, 1972–79).

1. Ella Gertrude Clanton diary, 18 August 1856, Duke.

2. Many historians have written about the "cult of true womanhood" or ideology of domesticity. See for example Barbara Welter, "The Cult of True Womanhood, 1820–1920," *American Quarterly* 18 (summer 1966): 151–74; Nancy F. Cott, *The Bonds of Womanhood: "Woman's Sphere" in New England, 1780–1835* (New Haven: Yale University Press, 1977).

3. L[ouisa] S[usannah] M[cCord], "Enfranchisement of Women," *Southern Quarterly Review* n.s. 5 (April 1852): 325.

4. See for example Anne Firor Scott, *The Southern Lady: From Pedestal to Politics, 1830–1930* (Chicago: University of Chicago Press, 1970); Catherine Clinton, *The Plantation Mistress: Woman's World in the Old South* (New York: Pantheon, 1982); Jane Turner Censer, *North Carolina Planters and Their Children, 1800–1860* (Baton Rouge: Louisiana State University Press, 1984); Steven M. Stowe, *Intimacy and Power in the Old South: Ritual in the Lives of the Planters* (Baltimore: Johns Hopkins University Press, 1987); Elizabeth Fox-Genovese, *Within the Plantation Household: Black and White Women of the Old South* (Chapel Hill: University of North Carolina Press, 1988); Marli F. Weiner, *Plantation Women: South Carolina Mistresses and Slaves, 1830–1880* (Urbana: University of Illinois Press, forthcoming).

5. Mrs. S. A. Dinkins, "A Letter from a Village Bride to a Friend in the City, and the Reply Thereto," *Southern Literary Messenger* 33 (December 1861): 453.

6. "Advice from a Father to His Only Daughter, Written Immediately after Her Marriage," *Southern Literary Messenger* 1 (December 1834): 188.

7. "Thoughts on Slavery, by a Southron," *Southern Literary Messenger* 4 (December 1838): 745.

8. Maria J. McIntosh, *Woman in America: Her Work and Her Reward* (New York: D. Appleton, 1850), 118. See also W., "The Lyceum, No. II: Old Maids," *Southern Literary Messenger* 3 (August 1837): 474; and "A Few Thoughts on Slavery," *Southern Literary Messenger* 20 (April 1854): 199.

9. McIntosh, *Woman in America,* 117.

10. M, "The Selfish Girl," *The Rose Bud, or Youth's Gazette* 1 (13 April 1833): 129–30. See also William H. Holcombe, "Little Kindnesses," *Southern Literary Messenger* 34 (April 1862): 256; Mary Howard Schoolcraft, *The Black Gauntlet: A Tale of Plantation Life in South Carolina* (1860; reprint, Freeport, N.Y.: Books for Libraries Press, 1971), 113–15.

11. Mary Henderson Eastman, *Aunt Phillis's Cabin; or, Southern Life as It Is* (1852; reprint, New York: Negro Universities Press, 1968), 256.

12. The messages about moral behavior aimed at white women were remarkably similar throughout the South. However, the ways in which women understood and acted upon those messages varied according to region, economic status, religion, and individual circumstances and personality. In general, elite women of the plantation South were among those most likely to respond to social injunctions regarding their behavior, in part because they were more likely than less privileged women to read the literature containing them. Their affluence also provided sufficient leisure for them to behave in prescribed ways. Elite women were those whose husbands or fathers owned twenty or more slaves; most of the women discussed here were affiliated with men whose personal wealth was even greater. While such affluent women were a tiny minority even among slaveholders, their disproportionate wealth meant that they owned a significant percentage of the slave population. Plantation South refers to those long-settled areas of the South dominated by a staple-crop plantation economy. Both the slave and white women discussed here lived in Virginia, North Carolina, South Carolina, Georgia, or Alabama.

13. Sophia Watson to Henry Watson, 15 July 1848, Henry Watson Jr. Papers, Duke.

14. Eugenia Woodbery, *AS,* Vol. 3, pt. 4, 221.

15. Ben Horry, *AS,* Vol. 2, pt. 2, 317.

16. Nelson Cameron, *AS,* Vol. 2, pt. 1, 172.

17. Eliza Ann DeRosset to Mary Curtis, 18 September 1838; Armand John DeRosset to Mary Curtis, 23 December 1841; Eliza Ann DeRosset to Mary Curtis, 30 December 1841, Moses Ashley Curtis Family papers, UNC.

18. Gus Feaster, *AS,* Vol. 2, pt. 2, 65.

19. Ada Bacot diary, 1 April 1861, USCar; Mary Ross Banks, *Bright Days in the Old Plantation Time* (Boston: Lee and Shephard, 1882), 19–20.

20. Lucilla Gamble McCorkle diary, "Fifth Sabbath of May 1852," 14 June 1846, William Parsons McCorkle Papers, UNC.

21. Catherine Ann Devereux Edmonston, *"Journal of a Secesh Lady": The Diary of Catherine Ann Devereux Edmondston, 1860–1866,* ed. Beth G. Crabtree and James W. Patton (Raleigh, N.C.: [North Carolina] Division of Archives and History, Department of Cultural Resources, 1979), 21–22.

22. Norman R. Yetman, *Life under the "Peculiar Institution": Selections from the Slave Narrative Collection* (New York: Holt, Rinehart and Winston, 1970), 225.

23. Dinah Cunningham, *AS,* II, 1:234. Whipping could be done with any of a variety of instruments, including switches, ropes, leather straps, hairbrushes, or whatever else came to hand. Mistresses also sometimes slapped, punched, kicked, bit, or pinched slaves in response to the provocations of the moment.

24. Ada Bacot diary, 16 April 1861, 1 July 1861, USCar. Mistresses varied in their decision to apply the whip themselves or direct someone else to do it for them. Some inflicted all whippings themselves; others, like Bacot, rarely if ever did so. Perhaps most common were mistresses who whipped some slaves on some occasions themselves, while directing someone else (husband, overseer, driver) to do the actual whipping in other circumstances.

25. Keziah Brevard diary, 19 September 1860, 9 November 1860, 14 November 1860, 16 January 1861, 30 January 1861; also 5–9 February 1861 and passim, USCar.

26. Fanny Cannady, *AS,* Vol. 14, pt. 1, 162. See also Frances Ann Kemble, *Journal of a Residence on a Georgian Plantation in 1838–1839* (New York: Harper and Brothers, 1864), 210–11.

27. Charles L. Perdue Jr., Thomas E. Barden, and Robert K. Phillips, eds., *Weevils in the Wheat: Interviews with Virginia Ex-Slaves* (Charlottesville: University Press of Virginia, 1976), 257.

28. Gus Feaster, *AS,* Vol. 2, pt. 2, 65.

29. Linda Brent [Harriet Jacobs], *Incidents in the Life of a Slave Girl,* ed. Lydia Maria Child (Boston: Author, 1861), 49, 53, 57.

30. Mary Boykin Chesnut, *The Private Mary Chesnut: The Unpublished Civil War Diaries,* ed. C. Vann Woodward and Elisabeth Muhlenfeld (New York: Oxford University Press, 1984), 42; Mary Boykin Chesnut, *Mary Chesnut's Civil War,* ed. C. Vann Woodward (New Haven: Yale University Press, 1981), 15, see also *Private Mary Chesnut,* 21. Fox-Genovese interprets these passages rather differently. See *Within the Plantation Household,* chap. 7. See also C. Vann Woodward, "Slaves and Mistresses," *New York Review of Books* 35 (8 December 1988): 3–6 and Drew Gilpin Faust, "In Search of the Real Mary Chesnut," *Reviews in American History* 10 (March 1986): 54–59.

31. Ella Thomas journal, 9 February 1858, Duke.

32. Herbert G. Gutman, *The Black Family in Slavery and Freedom, 1750–1925* (New York: Pantheon, 1976), 389; Nell Irvin Painter, "Introduction: The Journal of Ella

Gertrude Clanton Thomas: An Educated White Woman in the Eras of Slavery, War, and Reconstruction," in Ella Gertrude Clanton Thomas, *The Secret Eye: The Journal of Ella Gertrude Clanton Thomas, 1848–1889,* ed. Virginia Ingraham Burr (Chapel Hill: University of North Carolina Press, 1990), 55–66.

33. Eliza Ann DeRosset to Mary Curtis, 18 September 1838, Moses Ashley Curtis Family Papers, UNC.

34. Sarah Katherine Stone Holmes, *Brokenburn: The Journal of Kate Stone, 1861–1868,* ed. John Q. Anderson (Baton Rouge: Louisiana State University Press, 1955), 8, see also 84, 86.

35. Keziah Brevard diary, 8 January 1861, USCar.

36. Robert Manson Myers, ed., *The Children of Pride: A True Story of Georgia and the Civil War* (New Haven: Yale University Press, 1972), 1244.

37. Letitia M. Burwell, *A Girl's Life in Virginia before the War* (New York: Frederick A. Stokes, 1895), 64.

38. Will of Susannah Sutton, Wills of Barnwell County, vol. 2, 1826–1856, Book C:70, South Carolina Archives.

39. Houston H. Holloway autobiography, p. 19, LC.

40. [Louisa Susannah McCord,] *"Uncle Tom's Cabin:* A Book Review," *Southern Quarterly Review,* n.s. 7 (January 1853): 109.

41. Schoolcraft, *Black Gauntlet,* vii, 114–15, viii.

42. L[ouisa] S[ussannah] M[cCord], "Justice and Fraternity," *Southern Quarterly Review* 15 (July 1849): 357.

43. L[ouisa] S[usannah] M[cCord], "Woman and Her Needs," *DeBow's Review* 1 (September 1852): 285–86.

44. Caroline E. Rush, *The North and South; or, Slavery and Its Contrasts* (1852; reprint, Freeport, N.Y.: Books for Libraries Press, 1971), 226.

45. [Caroline Howard Gilman,] "Recollections of a Housekeeper, chap. 14," *Southern Rose Bud* 3 (15 November 1834): 41.

LAUREN ANN KATTNER

# The Diversity of Old South White Women

## THE PECULIAR WORLDS OF

## GERMAN AMERICAN WOMEN

*C*ONFLICTING SPHERES: two words that produce images of Anglo and African American women at odds with each other within a male-dominated plantation system. Catherine Clinton and Elizabeth Fox-Genovese, among others, have provided insight into the nature of such a conflict as it pertains to native-born plantation women of British heritage (Anglo-Americans); Fox-Genovese also refers to Franco American women. Both historians demonstrate that plantation women viewed African American women through the warped lens of racism: a racism inflamed by white male philandering that, in effect, forced them to compete with African American women for sexual attention. Thus, Anglo and Franco American plantation mistresses came into conflict with their female slaves, especially when they tried to control not only the work regimen but also the personal relations of enslaved women. Fox-Genovese adds information about class-based aspects of the conflict. Plantation women were, in her words, "elitist and racist." That is, they understood their privileged position in terms of wealth and social propriety while also upholding slavery on the basis of race.[1]

By discussing the German rather than the Anglo or Franco American women of slave-owning households who lived in both urban and rural settings, I hope to expand our present knowledge of the diversity of Old South white women who lived amid slavery. Thus, this essay focuses on a range of social interactions and attitudes that prevailed among women of German ancestry who lived within urban and rural areas of the South (chiefly, Louisiana and Texas). This discussion is necessarily based on various types of sources because few German American women living in the households having female slaves left conventional records (e.g., letters or diaries). Therefore, the sources include not only letters and diaries but also travelogs, oral histories, and works of art. In addition, since social behavior is reflective of attitudes and demonstrative of actions, this essay incorporates descriptive statistics that I have calculated largely from census records.[2] Providing important details about a set of origins and settlement patterns that differed from that of Anglo American plantation mistresses, such records reveal the influences of diverse German ancestries and cultures that emerge as factors shaping American-born and German immigrant women's attitudes toward slavery.

Despite the "German" label, no monolithic "German" of "German American" population existed in the Old South. Rather, German American women actually had a variety of regional origins with which they identified. In this way, they appeared similar to Anglo women who also identified with various regions of the United States and who likely reflected British regional heritages as well. Before the antebellum era, Germans had primarily emigrated to the American South from south-central Europe, that is, from today's Alsace in France, from the southern third of today's united Germany, from northern Switzerland. The antebellum era saw the arrival of German-speaking immigrants from what is now known as northern Poland, northwestern Russia, and Lithuania as well as Germany, France, and Switzerland. By 1860, German-born people, American-born persons having a known German-born parent or ancestor, and other Americans who retained unaltered or little altered German surnames made up 15 to 95 percent of the white populations within specific counties and parishes of the West Gulf South (Louisiana, Texas, and western Mississippi). Among the antebellum Germans overall, women with roots in German-speaking areas of south-central Europe (immigrants and descendants) more likely had both female and male slaves in their households than did other German-American women, and urban more likely than rural dwellers owned more female than male slaves.[3]

Although we do not yet have concrete evidence as to why nineteenth-century women with a south-central European heritage jointly owned slaves with their husbands or owned slaves as widows more often than did other women, we may make inferences based on what we know about intergenerational ownership. The proclivity of these select German American women to have slaves of either sex during the antebellum era in Louisiana most likely derived from the initial eighteenth-century ownership of female slaves by men from the south German region of Europe. In Louisiana, the colonial French government had offered short-term loans (mainly, to German rice growers) so that these German-born men could own enslaved African-born women to do domestic chores while the German men and their wives worked in the fields. Thus, a little over half of the 78 household heads in the German Coast of Louisiana had owned slaves by 1731 irregardless of the extent of their acreage or livestock holdings.[4] Eventually, female slaves had received African-born husbands and had given birth to male and female children to be passed on to the native-born descendants of the original South German settlers. South German women of the lower-middle class of artisans, craftworkers, and small-scale farmers who came to late eighteenth-century Spanish Louisiana (many who were still alive during the early antebellum era) also had female slaves in their homes. In fact, by that time, German- and American-born women had secured joint slave ownership with their husbands. Among the American-born, many women of German heritage possessed separate as well as joint claims to a number of household slaves.[5]

Going beyond the mere ownership of slaves, Spanish law reinforced a European-based social hierarchy that stressed class differences. It did so by legally separating elites and middle classes from the "servant" and "peasant" classes. Consisting of native-born as well as immigrant women, the new German group, for the most part, accepted the social and legal order of late eighteenth-century Louisiana not only due to their remembrance of European tradition but also because they had lived in German-populated American states where a combination of class and race may have separated free from enslaved women.[6]

During the early to mid-nineteenth century, one possible regional influence on even newer immigrant women involved enslaved women's potential usefulness as wetnurses. Of all the German regions, the southern area had the highest fertility index among women who married between 1820 and 1849 (.85 in the German South as compared with .69 in far northern East Frisia). To sustain high birthrates, women of this region seldom breastfed their children and may have attempted to continue such a practice in the American South.[7] When they came to Louisiana or Texas towns, however, they confronted the stiff opposition of such physicians as Bavarian-born Dr. Lutzenburg of New Orleans, who worried about infants getting enough nutrition to sustain them through yellow fever epidemics and who thus encouraged breastfeeding. In response to such an attack on their cultural background, these women likely welcomed the opportunity to use enslaved wetnurses to continue their cultural practice while ensuring the improved nutrition for their infants.[8] Within this context, women from south-central Europe would have expected their enslaved women, like female servants in Europe, to perform the role of wetnurses.

By 1850, within urban areas of the West Gulf South, German-owned slaves generally included African American wetnurses and domestics with young children, but such was not the case in Richmond. Whereas German elite and middle-class men in Richmond desired greater control over male labor and found more uses for them than for enslaved women of any familial situation, West Gulf Coast German men and women, especially those of the mid-income merchant class, wanted more control over their domestic servants and had a greater desire to own female workers. In the West Gulf South, German American women expected submissiveness from their servants; if they could not achieve this end with German-born women, they sought enslaved substitutes.[9]

Such a situation disrupted lower-middle-class European traditions within the Old South context. In Europe, German Catholic and Lutheran women of the lower-middle class generally expected to spend their years between confirmation and marriage as servants; in the Old South, such women sought temporary domestic work with people of their own language between their landing and a likely marriage. Within the American South, they sometimes competed with Irish Americans for jobs, but more often, they vied with enslaved African Americans for domestic positions.[10] For the most part, moderately well-to-do merchants used enslaved in lieu of free-born female workers.

The patterns of slave ownership among second and later generations of rural German slave owners were generally similar to those of Anglo slave owners in the sense that both groups depended on slave labor for both field and domestic work and, within this context, owned more slave men than slave women (commonly, with a ratio of 2:1), but contrasting patterns in this regard did emerge within the urban context. Indeed, by 1860, urban, slave-owning German immigrants tended to own one enslaved mother in her early twenties with an infant or toddler. In contrast, urban, slave-owning, native-born Anglos more likely owned a woman and her husband in their thirties and their two or three children. An overabundance of German-born artisans and craftworkers, the shortened time between arrival and marriage among German-born women, and most important, the Germans' perception that enslaved women with young children were more controllable than free, unmarried, German-born women without children: these factors likely contributed to urban Germans' decisions to obtain single mothers rather than couples with children by 1860 in the West Gulf South.

In sum, diversity existed within the German American community; this cultural heritage manifested a significant influence. As seen herein, cultural heritage shaped German American women's perceptions of slavery and marked differences in slave ownership as manifested by these women and their families over time and place. Moreover, the information above has shown that patterns in contrast with those of Anglo slaveholders surface when the urban context is unveiled. In short, attention to cultural heritage emerges as a meaningful element in an understanding of the peculiar worlds of Old South German American women.

To understand more fully their distinctive attitudes toward slavery and slaves, it is equally important to examine the actual behavior of German American slave-owning women, especially with regard to their female slaves. Did German American women fundamentally share Anglo American mistresses' feelings of racial superiority to the enslaved? And did their relationships with enslaved women likewise conflict?

Relationships between German American mistresses and their enslaved African American women were actually apt to be less conflictuous than those involving Anglo plantation women and their female slaves. Such a situation existed because, due to their cultural heritage, German American women brought distinctive attitudes to slavery that reflected a particular emphasis on socioeconomic standing as the basis of legitimate power relationships and thus as fundamental to slavery. Under these circumstances, women of German heritage basically treated their female slaves as "servants"—in such ways that their social interaction seems more European than Southern, that is, more in harmony with a traditional, European-based concept of appropriate class behavior than in accordance with social relations based on a racial caste system.

The cultural backgrounds discussed above related to but did not evenly go hand in hand with attitudes and expectations regarding enslaved women as "servants." German women of the West Gulf South, for example, did not conveniently divide their attitudes and actions along the lines of native vs. foreign birth any more than they did in accordance with town or countryside habitation; yet, although many rural slave-owning native-born and immigrant women of German heritage in the West Gulf South lived within a context similar to that of Anglo plantation women, the bases for the elitist attitudes among slaveholding German American women and the resultant social interactions differed. In large part due to their overall backgrounds as women of German ancestry, many German American female slave owners— in the countryside as well as in cities—above all valued and expected submissiveness from both servants and slaves, and in so far as female slaves seemed to act "cooperatively" rather than combatively, their German mistresses viewed and treated their enslaved, African American women as "servants." In contrast, those select rural immigrant women who had participated in one of the German revolutions of 1830 and/or 1848 displayed notions and ideals of egalitarianism. Among those women, egalitarian attitudes and actions likely prevented conflicts between free-born German American and enslaved African American women. Taking the cultural backgrounds of both types of women into consideration, we now follow the stories of three sets of rural women and the life experiences of others.

Marie Kuechler probably preferred milking cows to spinning or doing laundry any day. At least, those were the activities that her brother Richard Petri selected when he sketched and painted Marie, his other sister, and Marie's enslaved women at work on their west-central Texas farms.[11] The three siblings came to Texas during the early 1850s from the eastern German city of Dresden. Because well-to-do German women most often preferred spinners from a lower class, it would not have been so surprising to watch Marie's slave spinning each evening while Marie busied herself with finer embroidery after her chores.[12]

Hundreds of miles away, in east-central Texas, German-born Elise Willrich worked alongside her female slave on a small farm. Together, they meticulously cleaned the house and hoed among the lush kitchen garden growth. Elise was typical of upper-middle-class women who had lived in northern Germany during the 1830s and/or 1840s revolutions, not in the fact that she co-owned an enslaved woman but in her egalitarian attitude. A revolutionary and the daughter of a German army officer, Elise set up her work routine on the basis of equality. Within a few months of her arrival in Texas during the summer of 1847, she and her husband obtained an enslaved couple to help them on their tobacco farm. The word *help* is underscored here: Elise did not expect her female slave to do all of the housework for her while she simply supervised.[13]

Still farther away, on a sugar plantation in southern Louisiana, widowed Thonie Wichner, like many native-born plantation women of German ancestry, hardly ever saw any of her female slaves except the house servants. Whatever troubles she had with either female field or house slaves were more apt to involve conflicts among themselves than with her. In fact, enslaved Peggy had walked around for three years with a ball and chain for contributing to the death of another slave woman.[14] By sustaining a personal aloofness from her female field slaves, Thonie accented a class as well as a racial separation of herself from the plantation's "peasantry," although her actions could have been interpreted by non-Germans as purely racist.

Three rural women; three different work environments. Though living within contrasting environments, their behavior as slave owners suggests that Old South German women (whether native-born or immigrants) did not generally relate to their female slaves as much on the basis of a strictly racial caste system as on the foundation of a more complex social hierarchy. Marie Kuechler expressed her perception of an acceptable and natural social hierarchy by assigning the same work to her female slave that most women of her station assigned to their servants in German-speaking areas of Europe. Elise Willrich showed her desire to break down the social barriers caused by the unequal distribution of wealth (and not simply resulting from the racial caste system) by working alongside her female slave. Thonie Wichner demonstrated the continuation of an eighteenth-century, European-styled social hierarchy by essentially distancing herself from her female slaves.

Certainly, more than the rural American-born women of German ancestry, German-born farmwomen contrasted with the Anglo plantation women who adhered to a racial caste system. Displaying their social values and ideals through work patterns and the distribution of labor, these German-born women showed a relationship with their female slaves that paralleled the mistress/servant relations of nineteenth-century Germany. Well-to-do women in German-speaking areas of Europe at that time chose one of two ways to manage their households: elitist women gave their female servants the most difficult or unpleasant tasks (usually, the spinning and laundry) as did Marie Kuechler; within the homes of wealthier people, wives expected their maids to keep their houses spotless while they reserved the cooking, milking, fine handwork, and similarly pleasant tasks for themselves and, if they had any, their eldest teenaged daughters.[15] Thus, some German immigrant women expected their female slaves to know their social place as had servants in the Germany. In contrast, immigrant revolutionaries expected and wanted to work alongside their female slaves just as they had worked with their servants in the Germany. Thus, German-born revolutionary women, like Elise Willrich, divided the work fairly equally between themselves and their female slaves. Among these women, gender-specific work routines translated into ideals of republicanism, a republicanism that assigned jobs on the basis of gender with all work aiming toward the common social and economic good of their community.[16]

When German American women worked side by side with their female slaves, they at least faced a shared inequality with men on the basis of gender. Many German American men on small and medium-sized farms made gender-specific assignments: they assigned fieldwork to female slaves as well as to their own wives on a seasonal basis. On cotton farms in Texas, for example, work assignments involved these men leading their free and enslaved women and children into the fields to do the planting and picking. They left the heavier tasks such as plowing and setting fence posts for themselves, their teenaged sons, and male slaves.[17] Working under such arrangements, slave and free-born rural women toiled together without the work of one being defined as any more or less important than the other.

Like work routines, the notion of freedom itself faced gender barriers among German-American advocates of republicanism. Although well-to-do German-American men opposed monarchies, they restricted republicanism to a love of freedom where boys should not be forced to take orders. Republican mothers were expected to instill such a love in their sons while teaching daughters to obey their fathers; after marriage, wives were expected to obey their husbands. These expectations centered around an assumption that men knew what was best for their families.[18] The behavior of republican German American women seemed designed to promote both a love of freedom in this sense and obedience to gender prescriptions of male dominance. Of course, indoctrinating slaves with republican virtues increased the risk of having runaways. When female slaves ran away, German American women naturally reacted as did Elise Willrich, who commented: "I was rather sorry, for the negress was a fit and able woman, but of course was forced to follow her husband."[19]

Rural immigrant mistresses who stressed social more than racial inequality expected nothing more, nothing less of slaves than what they required of free-born servants. As Baroness von Roeder and others like her itemized the duties of a meticulous housekeeper or a gourmet cook, they illuminated the importance that they attached to submission to authority and their views of female slaves within such a context. As this baroness reported to her sister, "They are big-hearted, humble creatures, and learn our way of life readily. They are learning German faster then we learn English." [20] If she had employed a Lithuanian servant in Europe, this baroness would have expected a similar adaptation. In short, German cultural attitudes to servitude and servants as well as congeniality on the part of German American slave mistresses and actions that they interpreted as willing submissiveness on the side of female slaves worked together to prevent conflict.

Nevertheless, within cities of the West Gulf South, German perceptions of obedient, enslaved African American town women worked with the codes that oppressed enslaved women. Slave codes controlled the movement of urban as well as rural slaves but did not involve free-born servants in the way that parallel codes did in Germany. Within such a contrasting setting, German American women soon discovered that they could not control immigrant servants as well as they could slaves. [21]

Transient, city-based immigrant women sometimes carried with them the perception of obedient African Americans as ideal servants when they left the South. Such was the case of German-born Clara von Gerstner, who ultimately settled in the United States North. There, she transferred a preference for enslaved to free African American servants: not due to racism but rather due to her observation that enslaved African American women acted more like the German servants she had known in Europe than did immigrant white domestics in America. Clara did not state that she personally had owned slaves when she lived in several Old South states, yet when she finally settled in Philadelphia, she selected free African American servants over German or Irish immigrant cooks, maids, and nannies. Contrasting the different servants, she described Irish women as "indolent and arrogant" and "Negro" women as the opposite, showing "more obedience and submissiveness." [22]

This woman's concluding perception thus leads us back to the contrasts that separated Old South German American women from Anglo plantation women. German American women of the Old South contrasted, in some ways markedly, with the portraits of plantation mistresses presented by historians such as Catherine Clinton and Elizabeth Fox-Genovese. Viewing this study's findings, the historian, therefore, should begin to recognize that the experiences and perspectives of Anglo-American slaveholding women should become the basis for generalizations neither with reference to Old South white womanhood in general nor with regard to the racial attitudes and relationships of these women. Certainly, because of their cultural heritage, German American women brought distinctive perspectives to the institution of slavery and to their relations with enslaved women while simultaneously constituting a diverse group of Old South women.

*By examining both* native-born and immigrant, elitist and republican German American women, this essay has presented diverse sets of attitudes toward slavery and enslaved women. I have found that native-born German American women who owned or co-owned female slaves undoubtedly reflected and reinforced both social and racial elitism within the context of having been born and raised in the slave South. Shaped more by nineteenth-century German hierarchical class relationships and the accompanying social expectations regarding servitude and servants, many German-born women, as immigrants, brought to slavery and slaves yet another elitist view: when slave owners, these Old South women transferred traditional German society from Europe to America (including fundamentally elitist notions regarding socioeconomic standing, status, and servitude). In sum, many slaveholding German American women of the Old South likely combined both social and racial notions about the proper place of "Negro" women as perpetual servants, and in this sense they resembled Anglo-American plantation women. Notwithstanding, it is important to recognize that their attitudes and behavior were greatly influenced by their own cultural heritage and that, in contrast, other German American women brought with them from Europe the preemigration ideals of social equality: ideals that had led up to and underpinned the German revolutions of 1830 and 1848; ideals that had shaped their own egalitarian and republican values. It is important to recognize that many slaveholding immigrant, republican German American women felt and attempted to express a spirit of sisterhood with their enslaved women, a sisterhood that crossed both social and racial boundaries. Such women do contrast most strikingly with typical Anglo plantation women. In short, conflict less likely occurred in German than Anglo American households having female slaves; contrasting ideas and expectations contributed in large part to such differences. Attempting to demean and in significant ways to dehumanize African American women, Anglo plantation women strove to control both the public and private lives of their female slaves. In contrast, while German American women pushed toward controlling the work environment, even the most elitist, native-born women of German heritage separated themselves from their female slaves' private lives for the most part and for social more than racial reasons. In so doing, they revealed and stressed their ideal of a congenial working relationship; when their female slaves acted according to their mistresses' expectations, German American women interpreted the results favorably and rewarded their female slaves accordingly.

Whether regarding the interaction of German American slaveholding mistresses and their female slaves or slave ownership among women, diversity in attitudes and actions among slave-owning women both existed and persisted despite the extent to which the institution of slavery shaped the Old South's models and expectations of white womanhood. The argument has been that this diversity was largely rooted in the ethnic and cultural heritages that shaped the distinctive attitudes which these women brought to the institution of slavery. Certainly, a non-Anglo point of view helps to reveal that neither American-born nor immigrant German women simply accepted the views or lifestyles of Anglo women intact; rather, they incorporated some ideas and models of behavior and rejected others. To bring particular attention to their diverse and distinctive perceptions of and interactions with enslaved women helps to illuminate the significance of their own peculiar worlds and of their attempts to define and shape their present situations in light of their past experiences and culturally rooted expectations. Thus, it is hoped that the findings of a study such as this may encourage historians to bring more attention to the peculiar worlds of "other" slave-owning women from various ethnic groups so that we may better recognize and understand the real diversity of the Old South women who lived with as well as under slavery.

*NOTES*

The author thanks Shearer Davis Bowman, Orville Vernon Burton, Ray Arsenault, Patricia Morton, and the two anonymous readers of this anthology for their comments on earlier versions of this essay. She also appreciates the following for funding to complete research for this article: the University of Texas at Austin, the University of Texas at Dallas, the American Association of University Women, the Kempner and Leila P. Williams Foundation of the Historic New Orleans Collection, and the Daughters of the Republic of Texas.

1. Catherine Clinton, *The Plantation Mistress: Woman's World in the Old South* (New York: Pantheon Books, 1982), 91, 182–98, 202, 208–9, 215; Elizabeth Fox-Genovese, *Within the Plantation Household: Black and White Women of the Old South* (Chapel Hill: University of North Carolina Press, 1988), 29, 35.

2. For a list of the specific censuses, civil registers, tax lists, church records, and other sources used for the quantification and household composition analyses as reported in this essay, see Lauren Ann Kattner, "German-Americans and the Ownership of Female Slaves in Antebellum Louisiana and Texas" (Ph.D. diss., University of Texas at Austin, 1995). At present, this author has not yet found manuscript letters or diaries written by German women who lived in slaveholding households; thus, she has of necessity relied on published accounts.

3. Lauren Ann Kattner, "Growing up Female in New Braunfels: Social and Cultural Adaptation in a German-Texan Town," *Journal of American Ethnic History* 9 (spring 1990): 52–54; David Hackett Fischer, *Albion's Seed: Four British Folkways in America* (New York: Oxford University Press, 1989), 212, 388, 411.

4. Minutes of the Council of Louisiana, 17 January 1723, Correspondance à l'arrivée en provenance de la Louisiane, 1678–1819, series C$^{13A}$, VII: 902–94, Centre des Archives d'Outre-Mer, Archives Nationales de France, Versailles, France (Washington, D.C.: Library of Congress, Manuscript Division, Foreign Copying Service, 1970); Council of Louisiana to Directors of the Company of the Indies, 28 August 1725, in series C$^{13A}$ above, IX: 239–52; Charles d'Arensbourg, Notes to Census of 1726 for German Coast, La., Recensements et Correspondance General, Series G1 464, Centre des Archives d'Outre-Mer, Archives Nationeles de France, Versailles, France (microfilm, Salt Lake City: Genealogical Society of Salt Lake City, 1974).

5. For the legal aspect of women's ability to own slaves at this time, see *Las Siete Partidas del Rey* (1767), 1, pt. 5, title 2, pt. 49, titles 5 and 6, pt. 7, title 18. For information on the nature and extent of slave ownership among late eighteenth-century German and French women in eastern Louisiana, see Kattner, "German-Americans and Female Slaves."

6. For a description of women and slavery in such states, see Allan Kulikoff, *Tobacco and Slaves: The Development of Southern Cultures in the Chesapeake, 1680–1800* (Chapel Hill: University of North Carolina Press, 1986). See also Kattner, "German-Americans and Female Slaves."

7. John Knodel, "Demographic Transitions in German Villages," in *The Decline of Fertility in Europe: The Revised Proceedings of a Conference on the Princeton European Fertility Project,* ed. Ansley J. Coale and Susan Cotts Watkins (Princeton: Princeton University Press, 1986), 355–62.

8. Dr. Lutzenburg, interview by Friederich von Wrede, between July and December 1839, New Orleans, La., in *Letters of Life in the United States of North America and Texas,* by Friederich von Wrede, comp. Emil Drescher, trans. Chester W. Geue (1844; reprint, Waco, Tex.: Texian Press, 1970), 104.

9. Lauren Ann Kattner, "Shaping German-American Womanhood: The *Wartezeit,*" paper presented at the annual meeting of the Social Science History Association, Chicago, 3–6 November 1988. For a specific example of one German woman's complaint concerning her free-born female servants and her subsequent change to enslaved

labor, see "Lady of Galveston," interview by unidentified Antwerp emigration organizer, ca. 1845, Galveston, Tex., in *The Emigrant to Texas: A Handbook and Guide . . .*, trans. Otto W. Tetzlaff (1846; reprint, Burnet, Tex.: Eakin, 1979), 37.

10. Kattner, "Growing up Female," 49–60; Die Deutsche Gesellschaft von New Orleans, yearly reports, 1849–1860.

11. Schmitz Hotel records, Sophienburg Archives, New Braunfels, Tex.; Richard Petri, sketchbooks, ca. 1853–57, and watercolor, "Hauling Water," ca. 1856, Texas Memorial Museum, Austin; Richard Petri, "The Pioneer Cowpen," ca. 1853, watercolor, in possession of Russell Fish III as of 1978; Richard Petri, "Bertha Quiessar's Parlor," ca. 1850, watercolor, in possession of Alice Wupperman Lundy as of 1978.

12. "Spinnen am Morgen," folk poem, recited by unidentified docent, in interview with author, 26 April 1992, Muehlenhof Freilichtmuseum, Muenster, Germany.

13. Elise Willrich to Georg Ludwig Kuckuck, 18 and 21 April 1848, trans. Minnie Groos Wilkins, in *The Golden Free Land: The Reminiscences and Letters of Women on an American Frontier,* ed. Crystal Sasse Ragsdale (1952; Austin: Landmark Press, 1976), 54–60.

14. [Louisiana] *State v Peggy* Papers, Historic New Orleans Collection, New Orleans.

15. For differentiation of German women's work, see labelled artifacts at the Muehlenhof Freilichtmuseum, Muenster, Germany; George Klein, *Das Elsaessische Museum in Strassburg* (Strasbourg, France: Musées de la Ville de Strasbourg, 1992); Michael Mitterauer, "Gesindedienst und Jugendphase im europaeische Vergleich," *Geschichte und Gesellschaft: Zeitschrift für Historische Sozialwissenschaft* 11 (1985): 185–86; Kattner, "Growing Up Female," 49–63.

16. Willrich to Kuckuck, in Ragsdale, *Golden Free Land,* 54–60.

17. See for example Charles W. von Rosenberg, ed., *Ancestral Voices: The Letters of the Von Rosenberg and Meerscheidt Families, 1844–1897,* trans. Laura Miller Wingo and Ernest A. and Irma Goeth Guenther (Round Top, Tex.: Von Rosenberg Family Association, 1978).

18. Georg Carl Willrich, letter, 1850, trans. Anna Willrich Groos, in Ragsdale, *Golden Free Land,* 59; Auguste Wiegreffe, interview by Sarah S. McKellar, *San Antonio [Texas] Express,* 8 September 1935.

19. Willrich to Kuckuck, in Ragsdale, *Golden Free Land,* 55.

20. Caroline Luise von Roeder to her sister, 24 March 1835, trans. Sigismund Engelking, *Comfort [Texas] News,* 2 March 1944.

21. "Lady of Galveston," interview, in Tetzlaff, *Emigrant to Texas,* 37.

22. Clara von Gerstner, *Beschreibung einer Reise durch die Vereinigten Staaten von Nordamerica in den Jahren 1838 bis 1840* (Leipzig, Germany: J. C. Hinrichs'chen Buchhandlung, 1842), 254–360, 443–48, 450–54. Clara von Gerstner's travelog has been the only one found by this researcher which was written by a German woman who discusses slavery.

# SELECTED BIBLIOGRAPHY

The following is intended to provide a selected list of the monographs and collections published during and since the 1980s that bring attention to women's experiences of slavery in the American context. While this selected bibliography is by no means comprehensive, its emphasis on recent scholarship is chosen to point to today's expanding attention to including and placing women in the history of slavery. It is hoped that this listing, together with the bibliographical direction provided by the essays presented herein, may provide a starting place for the reader's own exploration.

## SOURCES

Alexander, Adele Logan. *Ambiguous Lives: Free Women of Color in Rural Georgia, 1789–1879.* Fayetteville: University of Arkansas Press, 1991.

Aptheker, Bettina. *Woman's Legacy: Essays on Race, Sex, and Class in American History.* Amherst: University of Massachusetts Press, 1982.

Barker-Benfield, G. J., and Catherine Clinton, eds. *Portraits of American Women: From Settlement to the Present.* New York: St. Martin's Press, 1991.

Bernard, Jacqueline. *Journey toward Freedom: The Story of Sojourner Truth.* 1967; reprint, New York: Feminist Press, 1990.

Bernhard, Virginia, Elizabeth Fox-Genovese, Betty Brandon, and Theda Perdue, eds. *Southern Women: Histories and Identities.* Knoxville: University of Tennessee Press, 1991.

Bleser, Carol, ed., *In Joy and in Sorrow: Women, Family, and Marriage in the Victorian South, 1830–1900.* New York: Oxford University Press, 1991.

Bynum, Victoria E. *Unruly Women: The Politics of Social and Sexual Control in the Old South.* Chapel Hill: University of North Carolina Press, 1992.

Campbell, Edward D. C. Jr., and Kym S. Rice, eds. *Before Freedom Came: African-American Life in the Antebellum South.* Charlottesville: University Press of Virginia, 1991.

Cashin, Joan E. *A Family Venture: Men and Women on the Southern Frontier.* New York: Oxford University Press, 1991.

Censer, Jane Turner. *North Carolina Planters and Their Children, 1800–1860.* Baton Rouge: Louisiana State University Press, 1984.

Christian, Barbara. *Black Women Novelists: The Development of a Tradition, 1892–1976.* Westport, Conn.: Greenwood Press, 1980.

Clark Hine, Darlene, and David Barry Gaspar, eds. *Black Women and Slavery in the Americas.* Bloomington: Indiana University Press, forthcoming.

Clifford, Deborah Pickman. *Crusader for Freedom: A Life of Lydia Maria Child.* Boston: Beacon Press, 1992.

Clinton, Catherine. *The Other Civil War: American Women in the Nineteenth Century.* New York: Hill and Wang, 1984.

———. *The Plantation Mistress: Woman's World in the Old South.* New York: Pantheon Books, 1982.

———, ed. *Half Sisters of History: Southern Women and the American Past.* Durham: Duke University Press, 1994.

Clinton, Catherine, and Nina Silber, eds. *Divided Houses: Gender and the Civil War.* New York: Oxford University Press, 1992.

Cornelius, Janet Duitsman. *"When I Can Read My Title Clear": Literacy, Slavery, and Religion in the Antebellum South.* Columbia: University of South Carolina Press, 1991.

Davis, Angela Y. *Women, Race, and Class.* New York: Random House, 1981.

Dillman, Caroline Matheny, ed. *Southern Women.* New York: Hemisphere, 1988.

Evans, Sara M. *Born for Liberty: A History of Women in America.* New York: Free Press, 1989.

Faust, Drew Gilpin. *Southern Stories: Slaveholders in Peace and War.* Columbia: University of Missouri Press, 1994.

Finkelman, Paul, ed. *Women and the Family in a Slave Society.* New York: Garland, 1989.

Fox-Genovese, Elizabeth. *Within the Plantation Household: Black and White Women of the Old South.* Chapel Hill: University of North Carolina Press, 1988.

Fraser, Walter J. Jr., R. Frank Saunders Jr., and Jon L. Wakelyn, eds. *The Web of Southern Social Relations: Women, Family, and Education.* Athens: University of Georgia Press, 1985.

Friedman, Jean E. *The Enclosed Garden: Women and Community in the Evangelical South, 1830–1900.* Chapel Hill: University of North Carolina Press, 1985.

Giddings, Paula. *When and Where I Enter: The Impact of Black Women on Race and Sex in America.* New York: William Morrow, 1984.

Goodfriend, Joyce D., and Claudia M. Christie. *Lives of American Women: A History with Documents.* Boston: Little, Brown, 1981.

Gwin, Minrose C. *Black and White Women of the Old South: The Peculiar Sisterhood in American Literature.* Knoxville: University of Tennessee Press, 1985.

Harris, J. William, ed. *Society and Culture in the Slave South.* New York: Routledge, Chapman, and Hall, 1992.

Hawks, Joanne V., and Sheila L. Skemp, eds. *Sex, Race, and the Role of Women in the South.* Jackson: University Press of Mississippi, 1983.

Hull, Gloria T., Patricia Bell Scott, and Barbara Smith, eds. *All the Women Are White, All the Blacks are Men, But Some of Us Are Brave: Black Women's Studies.* Old Westbury, N.Y.: Feminist Press, 1982.

Inscoe, John C. *Mountain Masters, Slavery, and the Sectional Crisis in Western North Carolina.* Knoxville: University of Tennessee Press, 1989.

Jensen, Joan M. *Promise to the Land: Essays on Rural Women.* Albuquerque: University of New Mexico Press, 1991.

Jones, Anne Goodwyn. *Tomorrow Is Another Day: The Woman Writer in the South, 1859–1936.* Baton Rouge: Louisiana State University Press, 1981.

Jones, Jacqueline. *Labor of Love, Labor of Sorrow: Black Women, Work, and the Family from Slavery to the Present.* New York: Basic Books, 1985.

Jordan, Winthrop D., and Sheila L. Skemp, eds. *Race and Family in the Colonial South.* Jackson: University Press of Mississippi, 1987.

King, Wilma, ed. *A Northern Woman in the Plantation South: Letters of Tryphena Blanche Holder Fox, 1856–1876.* Columbia: University of South Carolina Press, 1993.

Kubitschek, Missy Dehn. *Claiming the Heritage: African-American Women's Novels and History.* Jackson: University Press of Mississippi, 1991.

Lebsock, Suzanne D. *The Free Women of Petersburg: Status and Culture in a Southern Town, 1784–1860.* New York: W. W. Norton, 1984.

Mabee, Carleton. *Sojourner Truth: Slave, Prophet, Legend.* New York: New York University Press, 1993.

Malone, Ann Patton. *Sweet Chariot: Slave Family and Household Structure in Nineteenth-Century Louisiana.* Chapel Hill: University of North Carolina Press, 1992.

McLaurin, Melton A. *Celia, a Slave.* Athens: University of Georgia Press, 1991.

McMillen, Sally G. *Motherhood in the Old South: Pregnancy, Childbirth, and Infant Rearing.* Baton Rouge: Louisiana State University Press, 1990.

———. *Southern Women: Black and White in the Old South.* Arlington Heights, Ill.: Harlan Davidson, 1992.

Midlo Hall, Gwendolyn. *Africans in Colonial Louisiana.* Baton Rouge: Louisiana State University Press, 1992.

Morton, Patricia. *Disfigured Images: The Historical Assault on Afro-American Women.* Westport, Conn.: Greenwood Press, 1991.

Moss, Elizabeth. *Domestic Novelists in the Old South: Defenders of Southern Culture.* Baton Rouge: Louisiana State University Press, 1992.

Muhlenfeld, Elisabeth. *Mary Boykin Chesnut: A Biography.* Baton Rouge: Louisiana State University Press, 1992.

Pease, Jane H., and William H. Pease. *Ladies, Women, and Wenches: Choice and Constraint in Antebellum Charleston and Boston.* Chapel Hill: University of North Carolina Press, 1990.

Rable, George C. *Civil Wars: Women and the Crisis of Southern Nationalism.* Urbana: University of Illinois Press, 1989.

Rodgers-Rose, La Frances, ed. *The Black Woman.* Beverly Hills, Calif.: Sage, 1980.

Samuels, Shirley, ed. *The Culture of Sentiment: Race, Gender, and Sentimentality in Nineteenth-Century America.* New York: Oxford University Press, 1992.

Schweninger, Loren. *Black Property Owners in the South, 1790–1915.* Urbana: University of Illinois Press, 1990.

Scott, Anne Firor. *Natural Allies: Women's Associations in American History.* Urbana: University of Illinois Press, 1991.

———. ed. *Unheard Voices: The First Historians of Southern Women.* Charlottesville: University Press of Virginia, 1993.

Smith-Rosenberg, Carroll. *Disorderly Conduct: Visions of Gender in Victorian America.* New York: Oxford University Press, 1986.

Sterling, Dorothy, ed. *We Are Your Sisters: Black Women in the Nineteenth Century.* New York: W. W. Norton, 1984.

Venet, Wendy Hamand. *Neither Ballots nor Bullets: Women Abolitionists and the Civil War.* Charlottesville: University Press of Virginia, 1991.

Wallace, Michele. *Black Macho and the Myth of the Superwoman.* New York: Warner Books, 1980.

Weiner, Marli F. *Plantation Women: South Carolina Mistresses and Slaves, 1830–1880.* Urbana: University of Illinois Press, forthcoming.

White, Deborah Gray. *Ar'n't I a Woman? Female Slaves in the Plantation South.* New York: W. W. Norton, 1985.

Winter, Kari J. *Subjects of Slavery, Agents of Change: Women and Power in Gothic Novels and Slave Narratives, 1790–1865.* Athens: University of Georgia Press, 1992.

Woodward, C. Vann, and Elisabeth Muhlenfeld, eds. *The Private Mary Chesnut: The Unpublished Civil War Diaries.* New York: Oxford University Press, 1984.

Wyatt-Brown, Bertram. *Southern Honor: Ethics and Behavior in the Old South.* New York: Oxford University Press, 1982.

Yee, Shirley J. *Black Women Abolitionists: A Study in Activism, 1828–1860.* Knoxville: University of Tennessee Press, 1992.

Yellin, Jean Fagan. *Women and Sisters: The Antislavery Feminists in American Culture.* New Haven: Yale University Press, 1989.

## FURTHER READING

While article publications are not listed here, many are included in the collections noted above, as well as in the very useful sixteen-volume series *Black Women in United States History: From Colonial Times to the Present,* edited by Darlene Clark Hine, Elsa Barkley Brown, Tiffany R. L. Patterson, and Lillian S. Williams (New York: Carlson, 1990). See also Darlene Clark Hine, Elsa Barkley Brown, and Rosalyn Terborg-Penn, eds., *Black Women in America: An Historical Encyclopedia,* 2 vols. (New York: Carlson, 1993). Also providing useful direction to article publications are the continuously updated bibliographies of "Southern History in Periodicals," in the *Journal of Southern History,* and of "Guide to Periodical Literature," in the *Journal of Women's History.*

# CONTRIBUTORS

VICTORIA E. BYNUM is a professor of history at Southwest Texas State University. She is the author of *Unruly Women: The Politics of Social and Sexual Control in the Old South*, which won the 1993 Phi Alpha Theta Award for the best first book by a historian, and many articles, including her essay on divorce in Reconstruction North Carolina in *Divided Houses: Gender and the Civil War*.

VIRGINIA MEACHAM GOULD is a professor at DeKalb College. Her recent publications include contributions to *Black Women in United States History* and *Black Women in America: An Historical Encyclopedia*. She recently finished a manuscript entitled "Chained to the Rock of Adversity: The Johnson Women of Natchez." Her forthcoming publications include an essay on free creoles of color in *Creoles of the Gulf South*.

KIMBERLY S. HANGER is a professor of history at the University of Tulsa. Her articles on free people of color have appeared in *Louisiana History, Revista/Review Interamericana,* and *Military History of the Southwest*. Her forthcoming publications include *Free People of Color in Spanish New Orleans, 1769–1803*.

PATRICIA K. HUNT is a professor of textiles, merchandising, and interiors at the University of Georgia. Her articles on clothing as an expression of history and on the dress of African American women have appeared in the *Georgia Historical Quarterly* and *Clothing and Textiles Research Journal*.

JOHN C. INSCOE is a professor of history at the University of Georgia and the editor of the *Georgia Historical Quarterly*. He is the author of *Mountain Masters, Slavery, and the Sectional Crisis in Western North Carolina*, coeditor with John David Smith of *Ulrich Bonnell Phillips: A Southern Historian and His Critics*, and editor of *Georgia in Black and White: Explorations in the Race Relations of a Southern State, 1865–1950* (Georgia, 1994). His forthcoming publications include *Highland Homefronts: The Civil War in Western North Carolina*.

LAUREN ANN KATTNER is a doctoral candidate at the University of Texas, examining German Americans and female slaves in antebellum Louisiana and Texas. Her articles have appeared in *Amerikastudien/American Studies* and the *Journal of American Ethnic History*. She has contributed an essay to *Emigration and Settlement Patterns of German Communities in North America*.

MARGARET M. R. KELLOW is a professor of history at the University of Western Ontario. She has published in the *Journal of Women's History*, and is currently writing a biography of Lydia Maria Child.

WILMA KING is a professor of history at Michigan State University. Together with articles on slave children and parents, her publications include *A Northern Woman in the Plantation South: Letters of Tryphena Blanche Holder Fox, 1856–1876*. Her forthcoming publications include *Africa's Progeny—America's Slaves: Children and Youth in Bondage in the Nineteenth-Century American South*.

HÉLÈNE LECAUDEY, an independent scholar, is researching slave women, sexuality, and oral slave narratives, while working as a linguistic revisor.

CYNTHIA LYNN LYERLY is a doctoral candidate at Rice University. She is a National Endowment for the Humanities doctoral dissertation fellow and a contributor to *Methodist History*.

PATRICIA MORTON is a professor of history at Trent University, Ontario. Her publications include *Disfigured Images: The Historical Assault on Afro-American Women*.

CAROLYN J. POWELL is a high school teacher as well as a doctoral candidate at the City University of New York, examining sexuality and slavery. Her essay "In Remembrance of Mira" was presented under a different title at the Association for the Study of Afro-American Life and History.

MARIE JENKINS SCHWARTZ is an instructor at Anne Arundel Community College. She recently received her doctoral degree from the University of Maryland, where she completed her dissertation on slave childhood in the Virginia Piedmont and the Alabama black belt.

DAVID M. K. SHEININ received his doctoral degree from the University of Connecticut and is a professor of history at Trent University, Ontario. His publications on North American and Latin American history have appeared in the *International Journal*, the *Hispanic Journal*, and *NS: Canadian Journal of Latin American and Caribbean Studies*.

MARLI F. WEINER is a professor of history at the University of Maine. She recently finished two manuscripts entitled "Plantation Women: South Carolina Mistresses and Slaves, 1830–1880" and "A Heritage of Woe: The Diary of Grace Brown Elmore, 1864–1868."